£73·71

# SHAKESPEARE AND HISTORY

**EDITORIAL ADDRESSES:**
The Edwin Mellen Press
PO Box 450
Lewiston, NY 14092, USA

**General Editor**
Holger Klein
Institut für Anglistik
und Amerikanistik
Universität Salzburg
A-5020 Salzburg
Austria
Fax: 0043-662-8044-613

**Reviews Editor**
C. N. Smith
School of Modern Lang. and
European Studies
University of East Anglia
Norwich NR4 7TJ
England, UK
Fax: 01603-250599

The *Shakespeare Yearbook* is an annual dealing with all aspects of Shakespeare and his period, with particular emphases on theater-oriented, comparative, and interdisciplinary studies. From Volume IV (1993) onwards each volume has a main theme, but there will always be space for some independent contributions on other issues. As a rule, articles are double-read before acceptance.

**Members of the Editorial Board**
Dimiter Daphinoff (Fribourg)
Péter Dávidházi (Budapest)
James Harner (Texas A&M)
Joan Hartwig (Lexington)
André Lorant (Paris)
Peter Milward, S.J. (Tokyo)
Rowland Wymer (Hull)
Simon Williams (Santa Barbara)

**Contributions:** Please type 60 digits per line, use line-spacing 1.5, employ MLA style and send in hard copy plus a disk (MS DOS, Word 6 for Windows, or WordPerfect. *both geared to IBM*; please note: IBM *cannot read* Apple, which is, therefore, not suitable for our purposes). Reviews (not usually longer than 1000 words; one hard copy plus disk): **send to** Dr. C.N. **Smith,** University of East Anglia, School of Modern Languages and European Studies, Norwich NR4 7TJ England, Fax: 01603-250599, Tel. 01603-56161. Articles (below 30 pages including notes; two hard copies needed plus disk): **send to** Professor H.M. **Klein,** Institut für Anglistik und Amerikanistik, Universität Salzburg, Akademiestraße 24, A-5020 Salzburg, Austria. Fax: +43-662-8044-613: The General Editor also welcomes **announcements, ideas** and **suggestions.**

Published annually. Subscription price $ 49,95 (hardcover). To order please contact the Order Fulfillment; The Edwin Mellen Press; P.O. Box 450; Lewiston, NY 14092-0450; (716)754-2788; FAX: (716)754-4056.

# SHAKESPEARE AND HISTORY

Edited by
Holger Klein
and
Rowland Wymer

A Publication of the Shakespeare Yearbook
Volume 6

The Edwin Mellen Press
Lewiston/Queenston/Lampeter

Library of Congress Cataloging-in-Publication Data

This volume has been registered with the Library of Congress.

ISBN 0-7734-8837-5

This is volume 6 in the continuing series
Shakespeare Yearbook
Volume 6   ISBN 0-7734-8837-5
SY ISSN 1045-9456

A CIP catalog record for this book is available from the British Library.

Copyright © 1996 The Edwin Mellen Press

All rights reserved. For information contact

The Edwin Mellen Press
Box 450
Lewiston, New York
USA 14092-0450

The Edwin Mellen Press
Box 67
Queenston, Ontario
CANADA L0S 1L0

The Edwin Mellen Press, Ltd.
Lampeter, Dyfed, Wales
UNITED KINGDOM SA48 7DY

Printed in the United States of America

# CONTENTS

## SHAKESPEARE AND HISTORY

ROWLAND WYMER (Hull)
Introduction                                                                 1

GLENN BURGESS (Hull)
Revisionist History and Shakespeare's Political Context                      5

JEAN-CHRISTOPHE MAYER (Montpellier III)
Power of Myths and Myths of Power: Shakespeare's
History Plays and Modern Historiography                                     37

LISA HOPKINS (Sheffield)
New Historicism and History Plays                                           53

MICHAEL SCOTT (De Montfort)
Truth, History and Stage Representation:
The *Henry VI* Plays at Stratford upon Avon                                 75

STEVE LONGSTAFFE (Lancaster)
The Limits of Modernity in Shakespeare's *King John*                        91

ROBIN HEADLAM WELLS (Hull)
*Henry V* and the Chivalric Revival                                        119

CHRISTOPHER SMITH (Norwich)
History's Sir Thomas and Shakespeare's Erpingham                           151

DERMOT CAVANAGH (Northumbria)
"Possessed With Rumours": Popular Speech and *King John*                   171

DAVID FARLEY-HILLS (Swansea)
*Coriolanus* and The Tragic Use of History                                 195

ZARA BRUZZI (Brunel)
Instruments of Darkness: *Macbeth*, Ovid, and Jacobean
Political Mythologies                                                      215

B.J. SOKOL (London)
*Macbeth* and the Social History of Witchcraft — 245

RACHANA SACHDEV (Susquehanna)
Changing Histories and Ideologies of "Colonialist" English
Drama: Shakespeare's *The Tempest* and Fletcher and Massinger's
*The Sea-Voyage* — 275

MARGARITA STOCKER (Oxford)
Shakespeare's Secrets: Family, Politics, Religion,
and a Source for *Love's Labours Lost* — 301

## OTHER CONTRIBUTIONS

ANN CHRISTENSEN (Houston)
'Playing the Cook': Nurturing Men in *Titus Andronicus* — 327

CINDY CARLSON (Denver)
Trials of Marriage in *Measure for Measure* — 355

SABINE COELSCH-FOISNER (Salzburg)
A Note on Shakespeare's *Tempest* and Iris Murdoch's
*The Sea, The Sea* — 375

ROBERT F. FLEISSNER (Central State, Wilberforce)
*M. Arden of Feversham* as a Mystery Play — 383

## REVIEWS

Roy Battenhouse, ed. *Shakespeare's Christian Dimension:
An Anthology of Commentary*
(Peter Milward) — 395

Deborah Kuller Shuger. *The Renaissance Bible: Scholarship,
Sacrifice, and Subjectivity.*
(Elizabeth Hodgson) — 398

Jonathan Goldberg, ed. *Queering the Renaissance.*
(Gregory W. Bredbeck) — 402

Carole Levin. *The Heart and Stomach of a King: Elizabeth I
and the Politics of Sex and Power.*
(Christy Desmet) — 406

Nigel Smith. *Literature & Revolution in England, 1640-1660.*
(Clark M. Brittain) 413

Ilana Krausman Ben-Amos. *Adolescence & Youth in Early Modern England.*
(James H. Smart) 417

Charles Mathews. *Othello, the Moor of Fleet Street.*
(Simon Williams) 420

Christa Jansohn, ed. *William Shakespeare, 'A Lover's Complaint': Deutsche Übersetzungen von 1787-1894. Festgabe für Dieter Mehl.*
(Wolfgang G. Müller) 423

José Manuel González Fernández de Sevilla. *El Teatro de William Shakespeare Hoy - una interpretación radical actualizada.*
(Elizabeth MacDonald) 425

# EDITORIAL

The *Shakespeare Yearbook* was founded in 1990. I agreed, in autumn of 1992, to take over responsibility from Volume IV (1993) *The Opera and Shakespeare* (co-editor: C. N. Smith) onwards. Some delay was inevitable, but we have tried hard to minimize it. From Volume VII (1996) onwards, the usual publication time will be the autumn of the current year.

In the process of transition, the concept of the journal was redefined. It seemed particularly apposite to try and put the *Shakespeare Yearbook* on a broader international basis, and to place particular emphasis on the studies dealing with aspects of the theatre, with comparative literary issues and interdisciplinary question, as well as with Shakespeare reception in specific countries and regions, thus in some ways narrowing down the original conception, in others enlarging it.

It also seemed useful to focus on particular themes for each issue, while reserving some space for free contributions on any subject within the journal's scope. For most volumes co-editors have been won, as in the example of the present Vol. VI, Rowland Wymer (University of Hull), to whom I express my particular gratitude for all the work he has done.

Future volumes planned are:

No. VII (1996) *Shakespeare and Hungary* (co-editor: Péter Dávidházi)

*The Law and Shakespeare* (co-editor: J. B. Sokol)

No. VIII (1997) *Hamlet' on Screen* (co-editor: Dimiter Daphinoff)

No. IX (1998) *Shakespeare and Japan* (co-editor: Peter Milward)

No. X (1999) *Shakespeare and Italy* (co-editor: Michele Marrapodi)

No. XI (2000) *Shakespeare in the Visual Arts*


I will gladly consider suggestions for later volumes, and also invite items of News and Announcements to be inserted.


Salzburg, Autumn 1995                                     Holger Klein

*Ei, qui semel sua prodegerit, aliena credi non oportere.* 33

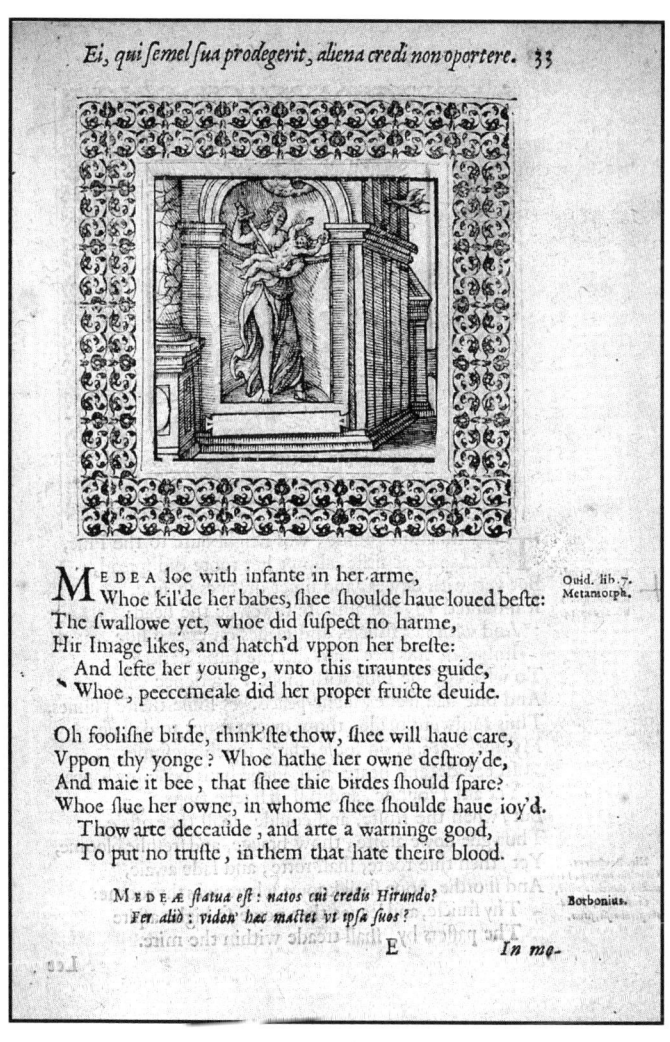

M EDEA loe with infante in her arme,
Whoe kil'de her babes, shee shoulde haue loued beste:
The swallowe yet, whoe did suspect no harme,
Hir Image likes, and hatch'd vppon her breste:
  And lefte her younge, vnto this tirauntes guide,
  Whoe, peecemeale did her proper fruicte deuide.

Oh foolishe birde, think'ste thow, shee will haue care,
Vppon thy yonge? Whoe hathe her owne destroy'de,
And maie it bee, that shee thie birdes should spare?
Whoe slue her owne, in whome shee shoulde haue ioy'd.
  Thow arte deceaude, and arte a warninge good,
  To put no truste, in them that hate theire blood.

Ouid. lib. 7.
Metamorph.

  MEDEÆ statua est: natos cui credis Hirundo?
  Fer alio: viden' hæc maćtet vt ipsa suos?

Borbonius.

E                    *In me-*

Illustration to the article by Zara Bruzzi, pp. 214-244. "Medea".
(BL C.57.L.2. By permission of the British Library.)

# INTRODUCTION: SHAKESPEARE AND HISTORY

## Rowland Wymer
## (University of Hull)

The essays gathered together in this volume exemplify a variety of critical positions and no attempt has been made to impose ideological or methodological uniformity. Nevertheless, in a number of them can be detected rumblings of discontent with much of the 'historical' criticism of Shakespeare, whether cultural materialist or new historicist, which has been produced in the last fifteen years. This discontent is articulated most forcefully in Glenn Burgess's excellent opening essay, written from the standpoint of a historian, which makes clear how out of touch many literary critics seem to be with what recent historians have actually been saying about Shakespeare's era. Whatever else it might represent, the 'return to history' in Renaissance literary criticism has not been a return to the main currents of contemporary historical debate about the Tudor and Stuart periods. It is not my intention here to summarise Burgess's arguments or to indicate precisely where all the subsequent essays might be situated in relation to the questions he raises. I should like simply to make a few brief points about desirable future developments in historical approaches to Shakespeare.

The minimum requirement of critics, surely, is that they should be aware of recent important historical work. If they wish to continue relying on a Marxist paradigm for their historical understanding of the period, then they should be aware that it is no longer good enough to assume that a couple of references to Christopher Hill will "prove" their case. The challenge posed by 'revisionist' historians will have to be confronted openly rather than evaded or ignored. As for those new historicists who, whilst being deeply indebted to such Marxist concepts as 'repressive tolerance', consider that they have avoided the totalising and teleological defects of Marxist thinking about history, they might look more closely at the detailed processes and contingencies of such things as patronage and censorship rather than continue to make easy and problematic generalisations about 'power' and 'absolutist ideology'. Both cultural materialists and new historicists might show a greater sensitivity to the fact that a play put on at a commercial theatre and capable of engaging later generations of readers and theatre-goers is a quite different kind of 'text', a quite different kind of speech act, from a report of Parliamentary proceedings or a piece of religious polemic.

Beyond this, there are larger questions about the nature of historical understanding and the uses we make of historical texts which need to be addressed. The development of a strong historical sense in nineteenth-century European thought at first produced arguments that the otherness of the past could be bridged through a self-consciously historical mode of interpretation. Later, of course, a more radical historicism was to insist on the historical situatedness of the interpreter and hence on the impossibility of ever achieving objective knowledge of the past. It should be possible to acknowledge the force of that later insight without being committed to complete epistemological relativism. There are many different stories we can tell about the past depending on the kind of questions to which we want answers; but conceding the narrative and 'constructed' element in all historical writing does not compel the conclusion that history is simply another form of fiction. Nor does a recognition of the strangeness and otherness of a text from the past preclude the possibility of an understanding as real as that resulting from those daily acts of interpretation which make social existence possible.

The problem of historical understanding is only a special version of a more general problem about how any understanding of another person or text is ever achieved, given that we are each situated uniquely in the world, each possessing a unique 'perspective'. The cognitive pessimism which denies any ability to 'transcend' our perspective and sees our relationship with past texts as limited to the alternatives of appropriation or incomprehension is invalidated by the everyday experience of understanding other human beings who are as radically 'other' as any historical text. The ability to enter into and imaginatively grasp an alien point of view is, in fact, a distinctive feature of human intelligence, most noticeable by its absence in cases of severe autism. The 'antihumanist' legacy of poststructuralist thinking has blocked off a generation of literary critics from some of the theoretical resources best equipped to deal with the problem of how understanding actually takes place - phenomenological hermeneutics and some aspects of speech act theory. It is not a question of abandoning all forms of theory in favour of a 'naive' empiricism but of looking again at some important theoretical positions which have been relatively ignored by recent critics.

In all this there is also a significant ethical dimension. To return, in however theoretically nuanced a manner, to questions of consciousness, intentionality, and sharable perspectives is simply to grant the writers of the past the same rights that we automatically extend to those irreducibly strange 'others' we encounter daily in the street, in the home, at work. That is to say, the right to have their voices heard, the right not to be silenced or misrepresented, the right to be treated as ends in themselves and not merely as the means by which we achieve our own, quite different, ends. The overtly political forms of historical literary criticism which have predominated in recent years are themselves forms of ethical criticism, deeply concerned with the injustices of the past and anxious to rectify them in the future. When, in the Epilogue to *The Tempest*, the actor playing Prospero comes forward to solicit our applause, Shakespeare appears to plead for our 'indulgence'. He has received more than enough applause in the four centuries since then not to need further 'indulgence' but the least we can do, as ethical interpreters, is to try to give him justice.

# REVISIONIST HISTORY AND SHAKESPEARE'S POLITICAL CONTEXT

### Glenn Burgess
### (University of Hull)

Early modern historians and Renaissance literary scholars are talking to one another as never before. Much optimism has been engendered by the dialogue, optimism about the possiblity of genuine 'interdisciplinary' studies, and about the advances in understanding that can come from cross-disciplinary fertilization. There can be little doubt that such activity may well enrich our approaches to sixteenth- and seventeenth-century English culture,[1] yet there is more than a little doubt about how far it has as yet done so. How much recent work in Shakespeare studies is *genuinely* interdisciplinary, engaging simultaneously with the most recent historical research and with the most recent literary theory and scholarship? How far, indeed, do many of the dominant theoretical and methodological predilections of literary scholars actually *permit*, in the end, an open engagement with revisionist historical research? Lurking beneath those questions there is another: should we not query the common assumption that interdisciplinary study is inevitably a good thing? After all, intellectual disciplines exist for a reason; and mixing them up can create little more than a babel of confused objectives, uncertain procedures, and comic misunderstandings.

There are too many questions here to tackle in a single essay, and I shall concentrate my attention on answering the first of them. How far have those literary scholars most associated with the return of history - the 'new historicists', 'cultural materialists', and others blessedly unlabelled[2] - confronted recent revisionist (and post-revisionist) historiography? Following from that, I hope to raise questions about what students of Renaissance literature might gain from a more intimate liaison with their colleagues, the historians.

I

Since the mid-1970s revisionist historians and their successors have transformed our understanding of early modern English political history. Very little of that transformation seems visible in the writings either of American new historicists or of British cultural materialists, both of which groups seem to remain firmly wedded to outdated (sometimes ludicrously outdated) perspectives on the history of Shakespeare's world.[3] It may be that the ingenuity of these scholars is more than equal to the task of producing theoretical defences of this situation. When there is no such thing as 'objective' history, then are we not free to work with whatever narratives we like?[4] If so, then clearly we are not confronted by a new interdisciplinary scholarship, but by a refusal to listen to what historians are saying. If we really do want to bring history and literature closer together, then that partnership needs to be a rather more equal one. The crude caricatures of historical thought and practice that are used to make so-called 'positivistic' empirical history look self-evidently absurd - arguments are so seldom provided that one must assume that the absurdity is supposed to be self-evident - can hardly serve as the basis for an interdisciplinary approach.[5] It is more a form of disciplinary imperialism. Even less charitably, much of the critical manoeuvring could perhaps be interpreted as an attempt to escape the demand, which historians so routinely accept, for adequate evidence in support of all claims.

The first task must be to decide what the historiography of the last two decades has taught us about early modern England.[6] At the most general level, we find ourselves today in a position in which socio-economic history and political history have been severed from one another. Such a situation may be neither healthy nor inescapable; but it cannot be ignored. That means that all attempts to explain politics, political 'ideologies' and political culture in social or economic terms have been rendered deeply problematic. It is not quite fair to say that such meta-narratives as "the rise of capitalism" or "the development of bourgeois culture and society" have been completely discredited as explanatory devices for the understanding of early modern history. It is certain, though, that they can no longer be taken for granted in the way that they are taken for granted by, for example, cultural materialist critics. As David Cressy has pointed out, the historians still most used by literary critics include Lawrence Stone and Christopher Hill, whose work has remained wedded to pre-revisionist patterns. Yet whereas the actual writings of Hill and Stone are more than redeemed by the detail, the evidence and the argument that they can produce in their own defence, literary critics rely on their highly contestable generalizations more than on the rich source material that they uncover. And their reliance betrays far too infrequently any awareness that many - perhaps most - historians would dissent vigorously from the claims being made.[7]

It would be interesting to see an attempt to examine gender issues in Shakespeare that took, say, Ralph Houlbrooke as a guide rather than Lawrence Stone.[8] It would be even more interesting to see what might happen if literary scholars were to take more seriously the scrupulously politically incorrect perspectives of Alan Macfarlane or Jonathan Clark.[9] Both of those historians argue that the early modern period was not one of transition, and was not characterised by significant (structural) socio-economic change. Macfarlane believes that modernity had already arrived in medieval England; Clark that it was not to arrive until after 1832; yet together they conspire to undermine accounts of sixteenth- and seventeenth-century England that give prominence to class conflict, dramatic change, modernisation or revolution.[10] It is no longer enough to rely on a history conceived in such terms: if you want to convince anyone that such old-fashioned history is still viable, then you must prove it. The most recent surveys of early modern social and economic history, thought they are not as iconoclastic in their dismissal of older accounts as some political historians tend to be, nevertheless provide little support for the largely Marxist-derived historical framework still employed by many critics. Above all, class and class-conflict have been undermined as central explanatory concepts.[11] Furthermore, for some time the cutting edge in the examination of early modern society has been wielded by the historians of the Cambridge Group. Its approaches and findings have barely been reflected in the historical understanding of literary critics.[12] Yet, as Kussmaul's work above all suggests, they pose the greatest challenge to historians, for their whole way of understanding is "systemic" rather than "intentional".[13] Explanation in such history is usually achieved by modelling the interaction of the impersonal components of a system, whereas explantion in political and cultural history is typically (though not always) achieved by examining the motives, intentions, goals, and so on, of human actors. In such fields, even those suspicious of a focus on intentional human action usually realise that they are at least required to *argue* for its unimportance. Wrigley and Schofield work on an altogether different plane. A social history thus centred on demography risks making the findings of social history increasingly redundant for political and intellectual historians. It is certainly true, that a demographically-based social history tells us much about the parameters of what early modern people could conceive of as social reality; but this does not in itself provide explanation or understanding at the level of detail usually required by political, cultural and intellectual historians.

There seem to be, then, at least three obstacles to producing a socio-economic history of Renaissance literature. They may not prove to be insuperable obstacles, but it seems nowadays quite unacceptable to write as if they do not exist. The obstacles are: (1) the difficulty of defending the sort of Marxist social history that most easily unites with political and cutural history;[14] (2) the difficulty of finding any plausible links at all between the demographically-based social history of the last decade and political, intellectual or cultural history; and (3), which is really perhaps an instance of (2), the difficulty of finding ways of mediating between 'systemic' and 'intentional' history. If Jonathan Clark is right - and in broad terms I think that he is - to suggest that *ancien régime* societies were held together primarily by law and religion,[15] then it may follow that the underlying problem with traditional *marxisant* social change explanations for the political and cultural events of the sixteenth and seventeenth centuries is one of sheer anachronism. Are social and economic change as devastating as we like to pretend to a society that, unlike ours, was not inclined to interpret the phenomena of the human world primarily in economic terms? Shakespeare's England undoubtedly was experiencing population growth, increasing agricultural output (if not an "agricultural revolution"), growing problems of poverty and vagabondage, trading and industrial diversification, urbanisation (especially the growth of London), and a numerical increase in the number of gentry families. But it is much too easy to assume that people responded to those phenomena in ways that would seem natural to us. Many of these phenomena are visible only in hindsight and with the employment of a way of seeing the world meaningful to us and us alone. That does not undermine the value of socio-economic history; but it does create serious problems for the attempt to mediate between such a history, and the history of the past in its own terms. Social and economic history - or some of it at least - is proof of the enlightenment that can be derived from categorial anachronism; but there are areas of history where categorial anachronism is the kiss of death. Arguably, it is one of those areas that Shakespeare inhabits.

If a way around these problems is to be found, then it seems most likely to come from the attempt to reflect more fully on what a non-anachronisitc social history might look like. How did people in the early modern period conceptualise their own social worlds? What sorts of social change could they recognise? How did they react to it? This kind of a social history will need to be built upon such concepts as the Fall, human sinfulness, corruption, the fragility of order, the millennium and its potential. It will need to look closely at early modern views of the role of law in keeping the effects of sin at bay. Historians will not cease wanting to look beneath this, and to apply to the past an understanding based on very different tools. Yet, for those of us who are interested more in how people in the past experienced their own world, the possibility of constructing a social history less dependent on categorial anachronism and more sensitive to the language and culture of the past is an exciting one. Already, there are signs that some of this is happening.[16]

It is not, however, here that I wish to concentrate my attention. Very often, Marxist-sociological frameworks are employed by new historicists to ground a theory of *political-ideological* conflict. A focus on this area will have the advantage of narrowing the body of evidence that we need to discuss, thus making possible a more precise diagnosis of some problems in their approaches to the politics of Shakespeare. David Cressy has put the essential question from the historians' side: "If the Jacobean age was not a time of pre-revolutionary tension, on the high road to civil war, where does that leave arguments about contested ideology and power in Jacobean literature?"[17] From the critics' side, Richard Dutton has pointed out how reliant so much of the historicist discussion of Renaissance literature is on a picture of Elizabethan and Jacobean government increasingly unacceptable to historians.[18]

Before the mid-1970s, historians usually portrayed the period c.1530-1640 as one of increasing conflict and polarisation. That 'conflict model' has since then been attacked on several fronts. The attack, though often misunderstood, has not denied the fact of conflict. (Name a period without it!) Instead it has tried to emphasise that conflict must be put in its place, that its very normality makes it wrong to place conflict at the centre of early modern history.[19] The goal for Elizabethan and Stuart people was always 'consensus politics'. Conflict was avoided rather than sought, something of which to be ashamed rather than proud.[20] Futhermore, what conflict there was seldom proves to have been ideologically generated. It reflected the normal and stable operation of the institutions of politics and not an attempt to alter or destroy those institutions. For that reason, amongst others, one must doubt the usefulness of a concept of *opposition* for the period.[21] We now know, for example, that much conflict in parliament was fomented by privy councillors and others, men who were of the government and using the Commons as an amplifier for their own voices. Court faction was another potent source of disruption, though it is true that factional conflict also involved disputes over matters of government policy.[22] There is little sign of a group of men consistently opposed to government policies, for the simple fact that much 'opposition' came from those who aspired to hold office themselves. What is lacking above all is any ideological division that separates people into groups with a (semi-)permanent tendency to disagree with one another. There were shifting alliances of men, all happy to work within the terms of the existing political system, in order to gain what they wanted (and that included satisfying their principles as well as their greed). And one of the chief rules of the game, of course, was that success most readily came when the monarch could be persuaded to agree with you. That more than anything else is why the patterns of conflict found in late-Tudor and early-Stuart England reinforced stability and order rather than undermining them.

Opposition was once also thought to have a natural affinity with puritanism. That subject too has been much revised (and, arguably, more securely revised than many other subjects). New historicists have been aware of some of this,[23] but not of how this revision fits into a pattern. It is not just that the existence of Neale's "puritan choir", the supposed Elizabethan parliamentary opposition, has been thoroughly discredited.[24] Beyond that, puritanism has come increasingly to seem an unradical thing, integrated into a broad religious consensus, loyal to the godly prince and (with one or two reservations) loyal also to his or her church.[25] Such a situation persisted until the rise to power of Laud and other "Arminians" drove many into a reluctant defence of the church against its supreme governor and his bishops.

Puritans, then, were neither an 'opposition' nor a fifth column of 'radicals'. Thus, if *opposition* is a problematic term, so too is *radicalism*. Historians and critics alike have been inclined to privilege 'radical' subversive voices (while making an extraordinary and misleading fuss about the supposed tendency of 'conventional' or 'orthodox' history to do the opposite). But is the term 'radical' even appropriate to the seventeenth century? At the very least, radicalism was a phenomenon rare and difficult to find in a "traditional" society like that of Stuart England.[26] Others have even suggested that the term is inherently anachronistic. In labelling thinkers (or anyone else) 'radical' we signal only our approval of them. In doing that we use a term that leads us to misdescribe what they were doing. In the sixteenth or seventeenth century people rushed like lemmings over the cliff to avoid being seen as *innovators*. Those who failed end up being called by us 'radicals'. At that point we tend to forget that they would have done just about anything to eschew giving us grounds for applying such a term to them.[27] Perhaps that puts the point a little too strongly. Yet it certainly remains true that the label 'radical' continues to be thrown about without precision or care, and used in such a way as to obscure the realities of seventeeth-century thought. There is no evidence for the existence of radicals in England before the 1640s.[28]

Whatever one might say about the nature of conflict, its social roots, and the labelling of those involved in it, an even greater significance attaches to exploding the 'myth of absolutism'.[29] Routinely, new historicist critics call the rule of Elizabeth I and James VI & I 'absolutist' (or worse); routinely, they refer to an 'absolutist ideology'.[30] But again, the historical underpinnings for such labelling have in recent years been substantially cut away.[31] Many historians would deny that the defences of monarchical rule written in the period constitute an absolutist ideology.[32] Tudor and Stuart monarchs ruled within and through the law. Even that thoroughly unpolitical king Charles I can be shown to have been a conscientious ruler with thoroughly conventional and unabsolutist ideas about his own authority (though that may not be the whole story).[33]

No doubt I have given a breathless and tendentious sketch of some themes in the recent historiography of early modern England. Even so, it will suffice to suggest that the history of the new historicism, far from being new, seems to have become fossilised in about 1970. Whatever verdict we might reach on revisionism, it has at least made it *essential* that attempts to utilise the approaches of Hill, Stone, and so on, are explicitly justified. What irritates are not so much the particular points being made, but the seemingly blithe disregard of the fact that there are alternatives to them. You cannot write history as if two decades of historical debate had not occurred. Would new historicists think someone who seems never to have heard of Barthes, Derrida, Foucault or Althusser well-equipped to write about literary theory? So why is it that they write history as if Morrill, Russell, Sharpe, Fletcher and the rest had never lived?[34]

## II

Critics of the new historicists have accused them of a variety of crimes, including "arbitrary connectedness" in their linking of *outré* anecdotal material to literature, and straight misreading of much of the material they write about.[35] From a variety of perspectives, critics have also assailed their theoretical presuppositions, and especially their reliance either on Foucault's analysis of power or on Althusser's analysis of ideology (or both).[36] I have much sympathy with all of these criticisms, but will myself bypass most of them in order to focus more closely upon an examination of the history employed and purveyed by new historicists.

Nonetheless one theoretical matter does deserve some preliminary comment. The characteristic new historicist framework of subversion and containment developed in Greenblatt's "Invisible Bullets",[37] whatever else it may do, serves to protect all argument from falsification. Other theoretical and methodological failings the new historicists may well possess; but none is more serious than this. In two crucial ways avenues for *testing* the claims advanced against *evidence* are blocked. Firstly, Greenblatt's Foucauldian assumptions lead him to write in ways that suggest that repression, subversion and containment are not the actions of any person. It is power, or perhaps the text itself, not Shakespeare, that provokes subversion the better to contain it. Unfortunately, while one can sensibly argue about what Shakespeare - or for that matter Elizabeth I or James VI & I, or anyone else - might have been trying to do, it would seem that the only limit on what power can be said to be attempting is constituted by the ingenuity of the critic.[38] Evidence is by-passed. Or, to put it another way, conclusions are generated theoretically and not empirically. It is difficult to call such a procedure history. A good case can be made for arguing that to do history *means* to follow certain rules for generating conclusions from evidence - above all, it means following procedures that allow for the testing of theories and concepts.[39] New historicism systematically evades such procedures.

Secondly, that same by-passing of evidence occurs on a grander scale. One could respond to the historical argument that I am about to construct - which will suggest that the new historicists' sense of what is 'subversive' relies on a vastly simplistic reading of what they might call (though I would not) the dominant ideology - by retorting that the various subtleties to which I shall draw attention are themselves simply examples of the way in which power provokes subversion, and then achieves victory over it. There is no real answer to that, other than to point out that by such means any wayward evidence at all can be side-stepped. It is hard to imagine a pattern of political ideas that could not be made to conform to a triadic model of dominant ideology, subversion and containment. (It is hard to imagine, for that matter, a model that better illustrates what Popperians would call a meaningless theory.) A theory compatible with any evidence tells us precisely nothing.

Let us, then, turn to some claims that can be examined against evidence. One of the central features of the context[40] constructed by new historicists is that there existed an 'absolutist ideology' in late-sixteenth and early-seventeenth century England. This absolutism is drawn in the crudest possible terms. Most extreme of all, perhaps, are the statements in one of the foundation works of new historicism, Stephen Orgel's *The Illusion of Power*. Orgel talks of "the developing movement towards autocracy" in early Stuart England, of "the absolute authority increasingly asserted by the Stuart monarchy"; and produces an extraordinarily inaccurate account of Charles I's "autocracy" (which must have been indefensible even when the book first appeared in 1975).[41] More recent new historicists share the same view of early Stuart government, it would seem.[42] Alan Sinfield's is the most developed account of the absolutist ideology underlying early modern monarchy. Attempts are made to guard against the knock-down reply by suggesting that England was only an "incomplete instance" of the absolutist state, and making a number of points about the dispersion of authority in absolute monarchies (seeming even to accept at one point that Louis XIV was *not* an absolute king!) and the role of ideologies in *masking* the realities of power.[43]

This becomes important for criticism when plays or poems - 'texts', I mean - are construed against the background of a dominant ideology. Regardless of whether their function is taken to be (in a classical Marxist sense) to mystify by veiling the darker truths on which absolutism relies, to challenge surreptitiously (now that Shakespeare has joined the ranks of 'the people'), or (in a more Foucauldian style) to reinforce power by allowing a controlled subversion of it, works of literature seem to address themselves to an absolutist orthodoxy. Naturally, the plausibility of that claim is closely linked to the plausibility of the claim that there was an orthodox dominant ideology to which we can give the label 'absolutist'.

By its enemies shall we know it. What, then, counts as a challenge to, or subversion of, absolutism? Greenblatt finds one form of challenge in "the Machiavellian hypothesis of the origin of princely power in force and fraud".[44] Sinfield, in effect, elaborates on this, using James VI & I's *Basilicon Doron* to suggest that the king wished to convey the idea that a legitimate ruler could never degenerate into a tyrant. Anything he did was legitimate, and hence "any violence in the interest of the status quo is acceptable".[45] Indeed, "his commitment to the State leads him [James] to justify even tyrannical behaviour in established monarchs". Thus it must be that the dominant ideology (or whatever we call it) denies that monarchical rule often originates in force, and obscures the fact that legitimate kings are capable of tyranny.

Does it? The answer is clearly no. The misapprehension into which these critics have fallen arises ironically from the fact that they repeat much the same errors as the much-reviled Tillyard.[46] Their dominant culture is monochromatic and inflexible. In fact, the political culture of early modern England seems much more sensitively characterised as pluralistic and ambiguous. And, as Debora Shuger has put it, "such pluralism is therefore not best understood in terms of orthodoxy and subversion, since these tend to reify a cultural centre (orthodoxy) which is, in fact, both Janus-like and protean".[47] The political culture of Shakespeare and his contemporaries was an array of concepts, assumptions and arguments - a set of languages - that could be used for a (limited) variety of purposes and assembled into a variety of patterns. That fact is, of course, inevitably invisible to those who are busy in gruesome celebration of the death of the author. Without the flexibility that comes from having cultural elements mediated through individual minds one can scarcely avoid producing anything but a ludicrously rigid and simplistic understanding of that culture. (Poor Marx! If only he had thought of the death of the author, he wouldn't have had to bother with a theory as implausible and patronising as that of "false consciousness".) The only odd thing about Shuger's remark that "it is more helpful to view Hooker as a fairly independent thinker rather than as simply a mouthpiece for a pre-existent World Picture" is that anyone should need to say it.[48] One is entitled to study the language rather than the speech-act, *langue* rather than *parole*; but it is no more than an arbitrary universalisation of one's own preferences to claim that the study of languages renders the study of speech-acts redundant.

Tillyard, again ironically, not only made the mistake of being a little too ready to assume the existence of a single monolithic world view. Like the new historicists, he assumed also the background reality of "the new despotism of Tudors and Stuarts".[49] The political implications of the World Picture were the condemnation of rebellion and the support of that new despotism; similarly, the dominant culture portrayed by new historicists supports absolutism.[50] The difference between the two comes with the question of where to locate Shakespeare: was he the gung-ho spokesman for orthodoxy or was he (I mean, were his plays) more ambivalent towards, even critical of, orthodoxy? Thus Tillyard seems never to have entertained the possibility that the greatest expression of the world view in Shakespeare, Ulysses' speech on degree, can be read as an indictment of Agamemnon as well as an indictment of Achilles.[51] There is ambiguity in the statement that "[t]he speciality of rule hath been neglected".[52] Disorder was the product of weak rule (or of tyrannical rule) as much as it was the product of disobedience. In their hurry to condemn Tillyard and find subversive challenges to a dominant culture (which they construct much too conventionally on Tillyardian lines[53]), new historicists seem mostly to have missed that historical work revealing the inherent ambiguity of, and diverse range of uses for, the order theory. It could be used to support, to justify, to criticise and to condemn kings. (The key concept here is *use*, and it is one that plays very little part in new historicist analyses.) To reduce such a "protean" thing to an ideology with a simple message is to ignore all the evidence.[54]

It is time to look a little more closely at some of the evidence. If King James can be accepted as a spokesman for the dominant culture, then it is obvious that both Greenblatt's and Sinfield's claims about its content are false. From Sinfield's portrait of the "State Ideology" of absolutism, as purveyed by James, one could gain no understanding of the intricacies involved in what the king actually said about tyranny. Sinfield completely obscures the fact that, far from justifying tyranny (however indirectly), James recognised that the tyrant would often be punished *in this life*. In *Basilicon Doron* he did indeed construct his image of the tyrant with special reference to "an usurping Tyran".[55] Yet, James's account makes it quite clear that he was warning his son Henry against the dangers of ruling tyrannically: "be ye contrare". He can scarcely, then, have been trying to say that a legitimate ruler could not act tyranically. The usurper was used as the touchstone because, almost universally, it was agreed that the usurper was the worst sort of tyrant. When James came to contrast the tyrant and the good king, it was clear that his remarks extended beyond the usurper. There was no point in warning Henry of the dangers of becoming a tyrant if he had no chance of ever being one. And warn James did. It is crucial to realise that, though no friend to resistance theory, the king accepted realistically that the tyrant "armeth in end his owne subjects to become his burreaux"[56] It seems odd, given the caricature of James usually presented (and caricatured itself to the second degree by Sinfield) that he was willing to see (and state) that subjects overthrew tyrants. He was perfectly clear about the fact that "although that rebellion be ever unlawfull on their part, yet is the world so wearied of him, that his fall is little meaned by the rest of his Subjects, and but smiled at by his neighbours".[57] The world was not a safe place for tyrants.

James was not alone in accepting that. Even someone to whom the "absolutist" label can be applied, Thomas Hobbes, recognised that, while resistance was never legitimate, nonetheless the "natural punishment" for the "Negligent government of Princes [...was] Rebellion".[58] By contrast, of course, the "good King [...] dieth in peace, lamented by his subjects".[59]

What has gone wrong here, I suggest, is that the very attempt to read the essentially *moral* discourse of seventeenth-century political thought as a dominant ideology, supporting power structures and blinding opposition, results in its systematic misdescription. There is an obliviousness both to the *realism* of thinkers like James I and Hobbes, whose efforts to argue for the illegitimacy of rebellion never blinded them or those whom they addressed to its possibility; and to their moral seriousness. They were thinkers trying to persuade and demonstrate, not to obscure and hide; and they confronted their worlds as honestly and openly as we try to confront ours. To treat them otherwise is an act of massive and unpalatable condescension. We do not have to agree with supposed 'absolutists'; we don't have to be blind to the self-serving nature of some of their arguments; we don't have to forget that the range of mental and linguistic tools available to them (as to us) was limited; but we have no right to assume that in defending the legitimacy of established authority they had such a bad case that only fraud could save the day.

Thus, when James argued for the illegality of resisting tyrants in the *Trew Law of Free Monarchies*,[60] we should read that discussion in the light of what he had said about tyranny in *Basilicon Doron*. Nor should we be surprised to discover that the king who supposedly wished to give the impression that only usurpers could be tyrants was elsewhere willing openly to declare that there were *two* types of tyrant, the usurper and the misgoverning legitimate king.[61] The distinction was a platitude of early modern political thought. Indeed, so much of a platitude was it that it is difficult to comprehend how Sinfield might have supposed that James was either able or willing to hide the possibility of royal misgovernment from the people's gaze.

What, then, of the proposition that government originates in force? Is that horrifying thought one that dominant ideologies obscured? Again, the answer is no. From the great classical scholar Sir Henry Savile to the *de facto* thinkers of the Engagement Controversy, the point was widely accepted. Savile, writing on Anglo-Scottish Union in 1604, remarked that of the kingdoms now possessed by princes "all of them and perhaps all that ever were [...were] first purchased by conquest".[62] Chapter two of Nedham's *The Case of the Commonwealth of England, Stated* (1650) was a demonstration "that the power of the Sword is, and ever hath been, the foundation of all titles to government".[63] Nedham is important, for the question that he faced after 1649 - how a regime founded on violence could gain, if not immediate legitimacy, then at least acceptance - was but a more pointed version of the question that ran through much political thinking before 1640. How, in a world essentially sinful and violent, could legitimacy be acquired for order and the institutions necessary to sustain it? We can evade that question no more than Shakespeare's contemporaries could. Early modern thinkers were every bit as aware of the miseries of their world as their new historicist critics who now think they know better. But those in the seventeeth century were not permitted the luxury of thinking that the struggle for legitimate rule could be denigrated or neglected. James VI & I fits exactly into that pattern. He, too, accepted that monarchy often originated in violent conquest.[64] But the whole point of divine-right theory was to provide a stable source of legitimacy (and morality) beyond the vicissitudes of this world. Which is to say that thinkers like King James recognised both the unpleasant realities of the world and the need to struggle against them.

One final point might be made about the new historicist accounts of dominant ideologies. They are quick to condemn poor Tillyard, yet show little awareness of work done on the idea of "cosmic harmony" since he wrote.[65] What has emerged so clearly from that work is that the "Elizabethan World Picture" can be used to criticise as well as to support established authority. God gave rulers *duties* as well as *rights* - and God demanded performance of those duties with a thoroughness and rigour that no merely human taskmaster could equal. (Another problem with much recent discussion is that it seems to find it very difficult to accept that fear of God was a very real and a very *effective* limitation on early modern people.) All of this suggests to me that the whole concept of a dominant or ruling ideology is deeply flawed. Oddly, the American new historicist language of ideology and containment suggests why that is so, for it captures in a very constrained manner the fact that ideas can be used in an enormous variety of ways. The concept of ideology is an insult to the mental ingenuity of human beings who - if the seventeenth century is anything to judge by - have no trouble whatsoever in using the same ideas for diametrically opposite purposes. We do much better to think of a political culture as a collection of shared tools used by a variety of workmen and -women, all keeping an eye on what everyone else was doing. There was a time when it was 'the people' whose mental life was condescended to by historians. Nowadays it is the intellectual elites of the past, rigorously brought to book in an effort to disclose the manipulative effects of power, whose moral integrity and intellectual independence needs defence. Judged by the evidence, many ideological readings of early modern culture have been based on an extremely over-simpified and uncharitably unsympathetic understanding of early modern writers and thinkers (and especially of those most easily implicated in the supposed processes of oppression).

There is something wrong, then, with both of the terms in the concept "absolutist ideology". It is interesting to note that the closest thing we see to an aspiring absolute (arbitrary, in this case) ruler in Shakespeare is ... Jack Cade: "Away, burn all the records of the realm, my mouth shall be the parliament of England".[66] The same Jack Cade, of course, gave voice also to the dream of an absurdist anarchical commonwealth. "There shall be in England seven halfpenny loaves sold for a penny; the thre hoop'd pot shall have ten hoops, and I will make it felony to drink small beer."[67] This close association between arbitrary rule and anarchy is a common pattern in Jacobean (and later) thought. So much so, that, far from being smothered in an absolutist ideology, the political culture of Jacobean England found one of its most-widely shared themes in the *hostility* to much of what we label 'absolutism'. King and subjects alike declared their horror of a misgovernent that might disorder the world. Such an attitude later in the seventeenth century helped to shape the widespread feeling that Hobbes's absolutism would be a source of anarchy, a "rebel's catechism".[68] If there was a dominant ideology in seventeenth-century England - and how one might demonstrate the fact is anybody's guess - then it might more plausibly be called an *anti*-absolutist one.[69] That is why Shakespeare could ridicule his peasant rebel by making him an aspirant to naked absolutism.

### III

I want, finally and very briefly, to suggest that a reliance on older 'Whiggish' accounts of history has palpably hindered the historical interpretation of

Shakespeare, and that an examination of Shakespeare's political languages may well provide evidence that helps to support and extend revisionist accounts of the period. My argument will concentrate on the example of *Coriolanus*. It is intended to suggest, in part, that there are ways of contextualising Shakespeare not dependent on such concepts as 'absolutism' and 'radicalism'. But it will also, I hope, do a little to redress an obvious imbalance in this essay. I have been concerned to give here an historian's account of new historicism; yet I should not wish to lose sight of the fact that there is much that historians have to learn from literary scholars about the reading of past texts. Historians can still too often turn to literature for simple "documentation". Attention to literary scholarship can help us to avoid such an approach. Thus my discussion of *Coriolanus* builds upon a range of critical work whose value should not be forgotten even though it often employs extremely doubtful historical contexts.

Given the common opinion that *Coriolanus* is Shakespeare's most political play, it might seem odd that there are relatively few readings of the play that place it into a fully-drawn historical context. Even more remarkable is the fact that few such readings of the play have obtained any significant degree of interpretative purchase over it. Anne Barton, for example, has said of one of the fullest contextual readings that it makes *Coriolanus* into "Shakespeare's apology for Jacobean absolutism".[70] That seems rather too generous. What *is* striking about Huffman's work is that its interpretation of *Coriolanus* makes, in the end, so *little* use of the rich contextual material that is assembled. Even then, he is compelled to force the evidence uncomfortably,[71] and blithely admits that after 3.1. "the play ceases to reflect contemporary politics"![72]

The inability of so many historical accounts of *Coriolanus* to bear much relationship to the play stems from the fact that they all tend to force it into a concern with 'absolutism' and constitutional issues that it does not possess.[73] Goldberg refers, for example, to "the absolutist strategies of Caesarism" revealed in *Coriolanus*;[74] while Thomas Sorge tells us that the play "presents three models

Shakespeare's Political Context 23

of government - the rule of one, the rule of the few, the rule of the many - to be evaluated by the audience, and by offering a choice of models, it potentially challenges authority's representation of monarchy as the only form of rule beneficial for England".[75] None of this seems at all justified. The play raises constitutional questions only obliquely, and it certainly has nothing whatsoever to do with the questioning of monarchy as an institution. Coriolanus's disputed consulship is treated as a matter of reward for public service and military virtue, and not at all constitutionally. There is not a hint in the play that Coriolanus is the archetype for absolute monarchy.[76] The problem, it seems to me, is that the obsession with absolutism leads to an obsession with political and constitutional conflict in the narrow sense. As these are marginal to the play, it is hardly surprising that the resulting interpretations are often forced, tendentious or unpersuasive. In addition to all that, the most recent work (which does not so much reject as absorb and extend the older political readings, much as new historicists treat Tillyard) adds another layer of improbability by attempting to find an authentic popular voice in *Coriolanus*.[77] The result can be extraordinary, as we witness Michael Bristol's resort to cycles and epicycles of Ptolemaic complexity in order to rescue the play from the charge that it portrays the *plebs* "unsympathetically";[78] or Sorge's account of the peoples hostility to Coriolanus and the things for which he stands, an account which seems oblivious to the fact that Coriolanus *does* manage - albeit awkwardly and uncomfortably - to win over the people (2.3), but is undone by the two tribunes, who build upon his very real failings of character to mount accusations against Coriolanus that *we know to be false*, and who deliberately provoke him into anger, thus turning the people against him.[79] If that's not unsympathetic, what is?

In spite of all of this, it is possible to place the concerns of *Coriolanus* into a (broadly) political-cultural context. Indeed, as we would expect, the traffic is two-way, for Shakespeare's dramatic employment of a number of stock themes can tell us much about a political culture that has been obscured by a concern with 'absolutism' and constitutional conflict. One revisionist historian has, indeed, used *Coriolanus* as evidence about parliamentary "elections" and the norms that governed them.[80] It is a most revealing account, but comes to a slightly uncomfortable end as Kishlansky gets close to crediting Shakespeare with a sort of Whiggish insight into the later development of seventeenth-century political history,[81] thus revealing (I think) his slight discomfort with the degree of social conflict evident in the play.[82]

Yet there remains in Kishlansky's reading of *Coriolanus* against the background of the 'consensus (-seeking) culture' of early Stuart England something of great value. At least one context which the play does seem to inhabit is a context of concern for what we might call 'social consensus'. Many existing interpretations do go some way to showing this (at least until distracted by other concerns).[83] Kenneth Muir calls this context a "literary tradition",[84] though it is perhaps more than that, being also a tradition of (in the broadest sense) political discussion. Shakespeare's participation in it tends to give *Coriolanus* something of the character of a drama of ideas. The social conflict evident in the play is not so much a representation of 'real' class conflict in Shakespeare's England as a dramatic vehicle for presenting two opposed visions of 'commonwealth'.[85] Does the term 'common weal' refer to the (economic) good of every individual person, or does it refer more to a good achieved in the political realm through the actions of particular citizens (though ultimately giving to all such political benefits as national independence)?

The drama of *Coriolanus* takes place in the space created by Menenius's fable of the belly.[86] He explains the point of the fable thus:

> The senators of Rome are this good belly,
> And you the mutinous members: for examine
> Their counsels and their cares; digest things rightly
> Touching the weal a' th' common, you shall find
> No public benefit which you receive
> But it proceeds or comes from them to you,
> And no way from yourselves. (1.1. ll. 148-54).

Faced with a populace for whom 'commonwealth' means economic equality, free grain (at least in times of scarcity and high prices), Menenius defines it as involving public services by which the few bring benefits to the many. Men contribute unequally to the common good; therefore, those who do most should receive the highest rewards. (This clash between a 'political' and an 'economic' reading of 'commonwealth' runs through the Tudor-Stuart discussion of the subject, and underlay the disquiet felt by some about the term 'commonwealth' itself.[87]) I should add that this clash is almost univerally misconstrued by interpreters as a clash between 'orthodoxy' or absolutism and its subversion. But from Thomas Cromwell in the 1530s to Charles I in the 1630s, Tudor and Stuart governments were themselves quite capable of acting on an economic understanding of 'commonwealth'.[88] We should rather see a much more open-ended dialogue between the two visions (which are, in any case, arguably much over-polarised in Shakespeare, where dramatic considerations take priority). What needs stressing, though, is that the view of 'commonwealth' expressed by Shakespeare's *plebs* was not a peasant voice in Shakespeare's England. It was a learned, élite political doctrine (most famously expressed in More's *Utopia*). The conflict of opinion dramatised in *Coriolanus* was not the clash of an élite with a peasant ideology: it was a debate amongst the learned.[89]

I have not the space here fully to develop the reading of *Coriolanus* that I am suggesting. Nevertheless, one can easily see the ways in which the theme raised by Menenius's fable runs through the action of the play. Coriolanus defends his refusal to support giving the people grain "gratis" on the grounds that "They ne'er did service for't" (3.1.122). They defended their country in war only unwillingly. When the tribunes then turn on Coriolanus, Sicinius charges him with being "A foe to th' public weal" (3.1.175), a charge that the play does everything to undermine. Coriolanus has not only saved the state and its citizenry once, but (more ambiguously) his act will again save them at the end of the play. The actions of one individual do more to maintain the public weal than the equal distribution of corn. Coriolanus warns the people that they:

> Have the power still
> To banish your defenders, till at length
> Your ignorance [...]
> deliver you as most
> Abated captives to some nation
> That won you without blows! (3.3.127-33)

Sicinius, after the banishment of Coriolanus, scornfully remarks "the commonwealth doth stand" (4.6.14). Almost immediately, the lie is given with the arrival of the news that Coriolanus has defected and he and the Volscians are invading Rome. Cominius draws the lesson:

> You have holp to ravish your own daughters, and
> To melt the city leads upon your pates,
> To see your wives dishonor'd to your noses (4.6.80-2)

The people's welfare does indeed depend upon the public actions of honourable and virtuous individuals, and they will pay a price for having denied that fact when they denied the consulship to Coriolanus. Even at this point the tribunes have not learnt the priority of politics over economics (i.e., so far as the play is concerned, self-interest). Brutus declares, "Would *half* my wealth / Would buy this for a lie" (4.6.159-60 - emphasis added). Only half? Not surprisingly in 5.4. the people turn against the tribunes, and the play closes when the people have once again been saved by the actions of Coriolanus, whose virtues his murderer Aufidius seems more generous in recognising than were the citizens of Rome.

Of course, a play is not a political or social treatise (though often enough treated as if it were). I have tried here to bring out the *action* of *Coriolanus* (and the structural implication in that action of 'commonwealth' themes), not state its *argument*, or uncover ideological mystification and manipulation. Yet, even though it seems to me a category error to attribute to the play an argument or a philosophical complexity that it does not seek to attain, it remains true that it both participates in a surrounding political culture, and helps to constitute that culture. Above all, it helps us to see the real concerns of a culture that has too often been seen through the monochromatic lens of 'absolutism'. Through *Coriolanus* we can listen to the real debates that moved and divided people in Shakespeare's England. We need not forget that some social groups were (to say the least) more advantaged than others by the sorts of attitudes revealed in the play. Nevertheless, if it says nothing else, *Coriolanus* tries to tell us that in the dominance of certain types of people lay benefits for all. Above all, it shows us the realism and scepticism of early modern political culture. This was not a world in which people were blind to the social inequality, the hardship, the brutality and bloodshed, that underlay political stability. Shakespeare and many others were prepared to confront - not to mystify, still less to manipulate - these realities; and so far as the evidence enables us to judge most of them concluded that maintaining authority and order was the least unpleasant of the choices before them. Who are we to judge them? Of course, we can choose differently; but surely we can also try to listen. We can attend seriously to their moral seriousness. If we don't listen, then the only voice we hear in the encounter with the past is our own. In that lies injustice to the past and a failure to enlighten the present.

*Notes*

1. Some of the results of this cross-disciplinary activity can be seen in such collective volumes as *The Historical Renaissance: New Essays in Tudor and Stuart Literature and Culture*, ed. Heather Dubrow & Richard Strier (Chicago: Chicago UP, 1988); *Politics of Discourse: The Literature and History of Seventeenth Century England*, ed. Kevin Sharpe & Steven N. Zwicker (Berkeley, CA: California UP, 1987); and *Culture and Politics in Early Stuart England*, ed. Kevin Sharpe & Peter Lake (Basingstoke: Macmillan, 1994).

2. In the remainder of this essay I shall usually employ "new historicism" as an umbrella term for all of these groups and individuals (unless there seems a need to be more precise). Cf. Howard Felperin, *The Uses of the Canon: Elizabethan Literature and Contemporary Theory* (Oxford: Oxford UP, 1990), pp. v-vi. "Historicism", because of the enormous variety of meanings that it possesses, is not a very happy choice of term. For a recent survey see Georg G. Iggers,

"Historicism: The History and Meaning of the Term", *Journal of the History of Ideas*, 56 (1995), pp. 129-52.

3. The problem extends more widely. One moderate critic of the new historicism, e.g, seems to have no better informed an understanding of history - see Brook Thomas, *The New Historicism and Other Old-Fashioned Topics* (Princeton, NJ: Princeton UP, 1991), p. 48; also Felperin, *Uses of the Canon*, pp. 145-6. There have been a few very good attempts to bring together revisionist historiography and literature (whether positively or negatively) - see e.g. Martin Butler, "Reform or Reverence? The Politics of the Caroline Masque", in *Theatre and Government under the Early Stuarts*, ed. J.R. Mulryne & Margaret Shewring (Cambridge: Cambridge UP, 1993). All of Butler's works, of which the most important is *Theatre and Crisis 1632-1642* (Cambridge: Cambridge UP, 1984) show an exemplary capacity to work in both history and literature. Kevin Sharpe, especially in *Criticism and Compliment: The Politics of Literature in the England of Charles I* (Cambridge: Cambridge UP, 1987) has made reinterpretation of Caroline literature central to his brand of historical revisionism. One might also point out the example of Leeds Barroll, cited below; and many of the contributions to Sharpe & Lake, *Culture and Politics*.

4. Attacks on historical objectivity are not uncommon, at least from outside the historical profession. A *locus classicus* might be Roland Barthes, "The Discourse of History", in Barthes, *The Rustle of Language* (New York: Hill & Wang, 1986), pp. 127-40. More guarded, perhaps, is the position of Hayden White, especially in the essays collected as *The Content of the Form: Narrative Discourse and Historical Representation* (Baltimore: Johns Hopkins UP, 1987); but the problems in his position have been well exposed in Wulf Kansteiner, "Hayden White's Critique of the Writing of History", *History & Theory*, 32 (1993), pp. 273-95; and *Probing the Limits of Representation: Nazism and the "Final Solution"*, ed. Saul Friedlander (Cambridge, MA: Harvard UP, 1992). More representative of working historians might be Lawrence Stone, "History and Post-Modernism", *Past & Present*, 131 (1991), pp. 217-18, and the subsequent debate in nos 133 & 135; and Perez Zagorin, "Historiography and Post-Modernism", *History & Theory*, 29 (1990), pp. 263-96. Revealing also is the discussion of Peter Novick's *That Noble Dream: The "Objectivity Question" and the American Historical Profession* (Cambridge: Cambridge UP, 1988) in *American Historical Review*, 96: 3 (June 1991). Also useful for defences of practising historians' assumptions are Thomas L. Haskell, "Objectivity is not Neutrality: Rhetoric vs. Practice in Peter Novick's *That Noble Dream*", *History & Theory*, 29 (1990), pp. 129-57; and Joseph M. Levine, "Objectivity in History: Peter Novick and R.G. Collingwood", *Clio*, 21 (1991), pp. 109-27. For an attempt to synthesise a post-modern history see Keith Jenkins, *Re-Thinking History* (London: Routledge, 1991), which manages to fulfil all those fears that we have repeatedly been assured are based on naive misunderstandings of post-modern culture or post-structuralist philosophy. There has been a recent attempt by three distinguished historians to confront the post-modern intellectual world: Joyce Appleby, Lynn Hunt & Margaret Jacob, *Telling the Truth about History* (New York: Norton, 1994), esp. ch. 7.

5. Such approaches to history, derived from post-structuralist thought, are not just out of touch with what historians actually do, but also with many recent developments in the philosophy of history. For such developments see, C. Behan McCullagh, "Can Our Understanding of Old Texts Be Objective?", *History & Theory*, 30 (1991), pp. 302-23; Raymond Martin, "Objectivity and Meaning in Historical Studies", *History & Theory*, 32 (1993), pp. 25-50; Chris Lorenz, "Historical Knowledge and Historical Reality: A Plea for 'Internal Realism'", *History & Theory*, 33 (1994), pp. 297-327; Mark Bevir, "Objectivity in History", *History & Theory*, 33 (1994), pp. 328-44; William Dray, *On History and Philosophers of History* (Leiden: Brill, 1989); and *Objectivity, Method, and Point of View: Essays in the Philosophy of History*, ed. W.J. van der Dusen & Lionel Rubinoff (Leiden: Brill, 1991). There is a useful canvassing of the issues in John H. Zammito, "Are We Being Theoretical Yet? The New Historicism, the New Philosophy of History, and 'Practising Historians'", *Journal of Modern History*, 65 (1993), pp. 783-814.

6. Other summaries of revisionism include Glenn Burgess, "On Revisionism: An Analysis of Early Stuart Historiography in the 1970s and 1980s", *Historical Journal*, 33 (1990), pp. 609-27; Simon Adams, "Early Stuart Politics: Revisionism and After", in *Theatre and Government*, ed. Mulryne & Shewring, ch. 2; Richard Cust & Ann Hughes, introduction to *Conflict in Early Stuart England: Studies in Religion and Politics, 1603-1642* (London: Longman, 1989); Ann Hughes, *The Causes of the English Civil War* (Basingstoke: Macmillan, 1991); and Thomas Cogswell, "Coping with Revisionism in Early Stuart History", *Journal of Modern History*, 62 (1990), pp. 538-51.

7. David Cressy, "Foucault, Stone, Shakespeare and Social History", *English Literary Renaissance*, 21 (1991), pp. 121-33.

8. Ralph Houlbrooke, *The English Family, 1450-1700* (London: Longman, 1984); Lawrence Stone, *The Family, Sex, and Marriage in England 1500-1800* (London: Weidenfeld & Nicolson, 1977). But cf. Theodore B. Leinwand, "Negotiation and New Historicism", *PMLA*, 105 (1990), pp. 477-90, esp. p. 481 for hints of a more historically respectable use of social history.

9. Especially Alan Macfarlane, *The Origins of English Individualism: The Family, Property and Social Transition* (Oxford: Blackwell, 1978); Macfarlane, *The Culture of Capitalism* (Oxford: Blackwell, 1987); J.C.D. Clark, *English Society 1688-1832: Ideology, Social Structure and Political Practice during the Ancien Regime* (Cambridge: Cambridge UP, 1985); and Clark, *Revolution and Rebellion: State and Society in England in the Seventeenth and Eighteenth Centuries* (Cambridge: Cambridge UP, 1986).

10. Historians have not, I think, done much to meet, either in breadth or in depth, the challenge posed by Macfarlane and Clark. Many of the broadest discussions are (unfortunately, at least for those of us who are not) from a Marxist or similar perspective, e.g. K.D.M. Snell, "English Historical Continuity and the Culture of Capitalism: The Work of Alan Macfarlane", *History Workshop*, 27 (1989), pp. 154-63; and Ellen Meiksins Wood, *The Pristine Culture of Capitalism: An Historical Essay on Old Regimes and Modern States* (London: Verso, 1992). Both historians were much discussed when their ideas were first published, but after the initial furore much has gone on as before. Among the initial responses see especially Joanna Innes, "Jonathan Clark, Social History, and England's 'Ancien Regime'", *Past & Present*, 115 (1987), pp. 165-200. Patrick Curry has recently tried to fashion a post-Marxist social history around the concept of hegemony, in the course of which he finds interesting (i.e. alarming) convergences between E.P. Thompson and Jonathan Clark; see his "Towards a Post-Marxist Social History", in *Rethinking Social History: English Society 1570-1920 and its Interpretation*, ed. Adrian Wilson (Manchester: Manchester UP, 1993), ch. 6. Perhaps we might conclude that - rather like H.R. Trevor-Roper in the famous gentry controversy - Clark has retained too much of the conceptual framework of those whom he has tried to stand on their heads (or, should that be put back on their feet?). His use of concepts like "ideology" and "hegemony" does indeed seem to mean that his attempt to create an early modern social history that mirrors the mentalities of those who lived in the period is vitiated from the start by being contaminated with the sociological history that he so deplores. In other words, he hasn't gone far enough in developing a clear account of what a non-anachronistic social history should be.

11. The fullest recent summary, C.G.A Clay, *Economic Expansion and Social Change: England 1500-1700* 2 vols (Cambridge: Cambridge UP, 1984), seems not to use the term. More specifically see Keith Wrightson, *English Society 1580-1680* (London: Hutchinson, 1982), chs 1 & 2, e.g. pp. 64-5; Wrightson, "The Social Order of Early Modern England: Three Approaches", in *The World We Have Gained: Histories of Population and Social Structure*, ed. L. Banfield, R. Smith & K. Wrightson (Oxford: Blackwell, 1986), pp. 177-202; J.A. Sharpe, *Early Modern England: A Social History 1550-1760* (London: Arnold, 1987), pp. 120-3; D.M. Palliser, *The Age of Elizabeth: England under the Later Tudors, 1547-1603* (London: Longman, 2nd ed.

1992), pp. 91 ff. See also Peter Laslett's (anti-Marxist) conception of a one-class society in *The World We Have Lost - Further Explored* (London: Methuen, 1983). Cf. Christopher Hill's review of the first version of Laslett's argument in Hill, *Change and Continuity in Seventeenth-Century England* (London: Weidenfeld & Nicolson, 1974), ch. 9; and E.P. Thompson, *Customs in Common* (Harmondsworth: Penguin, 1993), esp. chs 1 & 2.

12. Two of the key challenges are provided in Laslett, *The World We Have Lost*; and E.A Wrigley & R.S. Schofield, *The Population History of England 1541-1871: A Reconstruction* (Cambridge: Cambridge UP, rev. ed. 1989). Political and cultural historians who want a quick insight into the sorts of problems to which I allude should look at the discussion in the introduction to this 1989 edn of the controversy raised by Wrigley and Schofield's findings about the lag between changes in real income and changes in fertility. See also discussion in R.A. Houston, *The Population History of Britain and Ireland 1500-1750* (Basingstoke: Macmillan, 1992), esp. pp. 76 ff. No political historian, essentially concerned with individual human actions, could conceivably have been content to leave the matter at the point that Wrigley and Schofield originally did. Demographic-centred social history, however, does not primarily work at the level of human intention; and arguably provides, therefore, a poor context for those forms of history that are required to do so. Cultural and other histories that centre on the concept of ideology also often work with scant regard to human intention, but suffer in consequence from the inability to relate structural ideologies to individual speech acts (a problem usually resolved by the employment of a variety of specious arguments designed to denigrate the importance of willed individual actions).

13. Ann Kussmaul, *A General View of the Rural Economy of England 1538-1840* (Cambridge: Cambridge UP, 1990). Kussmaul convincingly determines the chronology of change in the English agricultural economy - finding the key period of transition in the late seventeenth century - by examining patterns of marriage seasonality. It is an approach, of course, that is inevitably collective, and works on a quite different level from that history concerned with individuals and their motives and intentions. Is there any way of bridging the gap?

14. For some insight into the scale of the difficulty see Robert Brenner, *Merchants and Revolution: Commercial Change, Political Conflict and London's Overseas Traders, 1550-1653* (Cambridge: Cambridge UP, 1993), and the symposium on the book by Ian Gentles, John Morrill and Alex Callinicos, *New Left Review*, 207 (September-October 1994), pp. 103-33.

15. Clark, *The Language of Liberty 1660-1832: Political Discourse and Social Dynamics in the Anglo-American World* (Cambridge: Cambridge UP, 1994), introduction.

16. For some important hints see Keith Wrightson, "The Enclosure of English Social History", in Wilson's *Rethinking Social History*, ch. 2; and for some examples *The Middling Sort of People: Culture, Society and Politics in England 1550-1800*, ed. Jonathan Barry & Christopher W. Brooks (Basingstoke: Macmillan, 1994), esp. Wrightson's essay. Brooks' work is useful for bringing social history into contact with the law: see in addition Christopher W. Brooks, *Pettyfoggers and Vipers of the Commonwealth: The "Lower Branch" of the Legal Profession in Early Modern England* (Cambridge: Cambridge UP, 1986).

17. Cressy, "Foucault, Stone, Shakespeare...", p. 128.

18. Dutton in *Shakespeare Survey*, 44 (1991), p. 226. Also Richard Dutton, Postscript to *New Historicism and Renaissance Drama*, ed. Richard Wilson & Richard Dutton (London: Longman, 1992), at pp. 221-3.

19. Paradigmatic might be G.R. Elton, *The Parliament of England, 1559-1581* (Cambridge: Cambridge UP, 1986), esp. ch. 14, which attempts to place the high political drama on which

historians have hitherto concentrated into a full account of the normal workings of parliament, with the result that conflict ceases to be a major theme of the subject.

20. See esp. Mark Kishlansky, *Parliamentary Selection: Social and Political Choice in Early Modern England* (Cambridge: Cambridge UP, 1986); and Kishlansky, "The Emergence of Adversary Politics in the Long Parliament", *Journal of Modern History*, 49 (1977), pp. 617-40.

21. Conrad Russell, "Parliamentary History in Perspective, 1604-1629", in Russell, *Unrevolutionary England, 1603-1642* (London: Hambledon, 1990). Cf. Robert Zaller, "The Concept of Opposition in Early Stuart England", *Albion*, 12 (1980), pp. 211-34.

22. This was the case especially in the 1620s, and with regard to foreign policy - one of the few areas in which early Stuart governments actually had policies in the modern sense.

23. Of, e.g., Patrick Collinson's seminal *Elizabethan Puritan Movement* (London: Cape, 1967).

24. See Elton, *Parliament of England*, ch. 14; Michael Graves, *Elizabethan Parliaments 1559-1601* (London: Longman, 1987), pp. 35-9. Cf. Jennifer Loach, *Parliament under the Tudors* (Oxford: Oxford UP, 1991), pp. 101-8; and Patrick Collinson, "Puritans, Men of Business and Elizabethan Parliaments", *Parliamentary History*, 7 (1988), pp. 187-211.

25. Nicholas Tyacke, *Anti-Calvinists: The Rise of English Arminianism c.1590-1640* (Oxford: Oxford UP, 1987); Patrick Collinson, *The Religion of Protestants: The Church in English Society 1559-1625* (Oxford: Oxford UP, 1982); Conrad Russell, *The Causes of the English Civil War* (Oxford: Oxford UP, 1990). It is important not to forget the earlier work of William Lamont, *Godly Rule: Politics and Religion 1603-1660* (London: Macmillan, 1969), unmatched in its demonstration of the ways in which puritan political thought was part of a broad protestant consensus. This is not to deny certain divisions within English protestantism - see especially Peter Lake, "Calvinism and the English Church 1570-1635", *Past & Present*, 114 (1987), pp. 32-76. Contrast Peter White, *Predestination, Policy and Polemic: Conflict and Consensus in the English Church from the Reformation to the Civil War* (Cambridge: Cambridge UP, 1992).

26. J.C. Davis, "Radicalism in a Traditional Society: The Evaluation of Radical Thought in the English Commonwealth, 1649-1660", *History of Political Thought*, 3 (1982), pp. 193-213.

27. See Conal Condren, "Radicals, Conservatives and Moderates in Early Modern Political Thought: A Case of Sandwich Islands Syndrome", *History of Political Thought*, 10 (1989), pp. 525-42; Condren, *The Language of Politics in Seventeenth-Century England* (Basingstoke: Macmillan, 1994), ch. 5; also Lotte Mulligan & Judith Richards, "A 'Radical' Problem: The Poor and the English Reformers in the Mid-Seventeenth Century", *Journal of British Studies*, 29 (1990), pp. 118-46.

28. Cf. J.C. Davis, "Radical Lives", *Political Science*, 37 (1985), pp. 166-72. Of course, one can argue that the lack of evidence is a product of the suppression of radicalism, which surfaced in the 1640s simply because the mechanisms of suppression broke down: see esp. Christopher Hill, "From Lollards to Levellers", in Hill, *Religion and Politics In Seventeenth Century England (Collected Essays, Volume II)* (Brighton: Harvester, 1986), ch. 7. But see the effective comments in Clark, *Revolution and Rebellion*, pp. 97-103.

29. Cf. Nicholas Henshall, *The Myth of Absolutism: Change and Continuity in Early Modern European Monarchy* (London: Longman, 1992). My remarks apply only to England.

30. Sometimes, especially with cultural materialists, there is a reliance on a Marxist concept of absolutism, and especially on Perry Anderson, *Lineages of the Absolutist State* (London: Verso, 1974). For the concept see *Marxism, Communism and Western Society: A Comparative Encyclopedia* 8 vols (New York, Herder & Herder, 1972), s.v. "Absolutism" (I, pp. 1-12). It should be noted that Anderson's book, even if one accepts its theoretical presuppositions, remains

unsatisfactory because it is itself based on pre-revisionist historiography, making it quite unacceptable to cite it without further ado as an authoritatative guide to the period.

31. For an early general account to reach such conclusions see Howard Nenner, *By Colour of Law: Legal Culture and Constitutional Politics in England 1660-1689* (Chicago: Chicago UP, 1977), which makes the general claim that the Stuart monarchs always ruled within the law, based partly on an extension of Elton's now generally accepted denial of Tudor despotism to the Stuart period.

32. Glenn Burgess, *The Politics of the Ancient Constitution: An Introduction to English Political Thought 1603-1642* (Basingstoke: Macmillan, 1992); Burgess, *Absolute Monarchy and the Stuart Constitution* (printing: Yale UP); Russell, *Causes of the English Civil War*, ch. 6. Contrast J.P. Sommerville, *Politics and Ideology in England, 1603-1640* (London: Longman, 1986).

33. Kevin Sharpe, *The Personal Rule of Charles I* (New Haven: Yale UP, 1992), esp. pp. 179-208.

34. This often remains true even when, occasionally, one of these historians' work is cited.

35. Walter Cohen, "Political Criticism of Shakespeare", in Jean E. Howard & Marion F. O'Connor, *Shakespeare Reproduced: The Text in History and Ideology* (London: Methuen, 1987), pp. 18-46. One supporter of the new historicism has made a similar point: Jean E. Howard, "The New Historicism in Renaissance Studies", in *Renaissance Historicism*, ed. A.F. Kinney & D.S. Collins (Amherst, MA: Massachusetts UP, 1987), pp. 3-33, esp. pp. 28-9. Of most relevance in the present context are those criticisms which examine the way in which new historicists construct historical contexts: see, e.g., Michael Neill, "Putting History to the Question: An Episode at Bantam in Java, 1604", *English Literary Renaissance*, 25 (1995), pp. 45-75; and Richard Levin, "Unthinkable Thoughts in the New Historicizing of English Renaissance Drama", *New Literary History*, 21 (1989-90), pp. 433-47.

36. For some of these influences see Catherine Gallagher, "Marxism and the New Historicism", and Frank Lentricchia, "Foucault's Legacy: A New Historicism?", both in *The New Historicism*, ed. H. Aram Veeser (New York: Routledge, 1989), chs 3 & 16. Foucault is undoubtedly the most pervasive influence on the American new historicists. For an introduction to his analysis of power see Michel Foucault, *Power/Knowledge: Selected Interviews and Other Writings 1972-79*, ed. Colin Gordon (New York: Pantheon, 1980). For an insight into the problems raised by Foucault and an account of how we may think ourselves through them, most valuable in the present context is Conal Condren, "Foucault's Cave: The Reification of Power and the Metaphorical Legacy of Early Modern Political Thought", *Common Knowledge* (1995), pp. 20-38.

37. Steven Greenblatt, "Invisible Bullets", in Greenblatt, *Shakespearean Negotiations: The Circulation of Social Energy in Renaissance England* (Oxford: Oxford UP, 1988), ch. 2; also Dollimore's introduction to *Political Shakespeare: Essays in Cultural Materialism*, ed. Jonathan Dollimore & Alan Sinfield (Manchester: Manchester UP, 2nd ed. 1994), ch. 1, at pp. 10-15. Note also Greenblatt's reservations in *Learning to Curse: Essays in Early Modern Culture* (New York: Routledge, 1990), pp. 165-6; and Jonathan Goldberg, "The Politics of Renaissance Literature: A Review Essay", *English Literary History*, 49 (1982), pp. 514-42, at p. 529. Sinfield calls the approach the "entrapment model" - see "Cultural Materialism, *Othello*, and the Politics of Plausibility", in Sinfield, *Faultlines: Cultural Materialism and the Politics of Dissident Reading* (Oxford: Oxford UP, 1992), pp. 38-42.

38. Cf. the similar criticisms made in Richard Levin, "The Poetics and Politics of Bardicide", *PMLA*, 105 (1990), pp. 491-504.

39. Cf. Adrian Wilson, "A Critical Portrait of Social History", in Wilson's *Rethinking Social History*, ch. 1, at pp. 40-5. See also ch. 9, also by Wilson, "Foundations of an Integrated Historiography".

40. I continue to use the language of text and context, while recognizing that many new historicists (though they can hardly avoid using it altogether) are critical of it. For a discussion with which I find myself in agreement see Brian Vickers, *Appropriating Shakespeare: Contemporary Critical Quarrels* (New Haven: Yale UP, 1993), pp. 225-31. I am also indebted to *Meaning and Context: Quentin Skinner and his Critics*, ed. James Tully (Cambridge: Polity, 1988). Contrast Dominick LaCapra, "Rethinking Intellectual History and Reading Texts", in *Modern European Intellectual History: Reappraisals and New Perspectives*, ed. Steven L. Kaplan & Dominick LaCapra (Ithaca, NY: Cornell UP, 1982), ch. 2.

41. Stephen Orgel, *The Illusion of Power: Political Theater in the English Renaissance* (Berkeley, CA: California UP, 1975, 1991), pp. 51, 57, 77-9. Pace Orgel, Charles in the 1630s did not claim "the rights of direct taxation", nor did he claim to make laws by "royal fiat", or to have an unfettered capacity for granting monopolies (a power which had been partially regulated by statute). For a useful corrective, see Sharpe, The *Personal Rule of Charles I*.

42. A particularly good example is Jonathan Goldberg, *James I and the Politics of Literature: Jonson, Shakespeare, Donne, and their Contemporaries* (Stanford: Stanford UP, 1989).

43. Sinfield, "Power and Ideology: An Outline Theory and Sidney's *Arcadia*", in *Faultlines*, ch. 4, at pp. 82-3. Sinfield's historical background is heavily reliant on Perry Anderson, *Lineages of the Absolutist State* (see above).

44. Wilson & Dutton, *New Historicism and Renaissance Drama* p. 85. The statement does not occur in this place in the version in Greenblatt, *Shakespearean Negotiations*, but has been moved to the end of the essay (pp. 23, 65). Greenblatt rather confuses, in the course of argument, two quite distinct propositions, one about the origins of princely power, the other about the origins of religion. For some devastating commentary on the latter, see Vickers, *Appropriating Shakespeare*, pp. 249-57.

45. Alan Sinfield, "*Macbeth*: History, Ideology and Intellectuals", *Critical Quarterly*, 28 (1986), pp. 65-6. Also in Sinfield, *Faultlines*, ch. 5, pp. 97-9.

46. Cultural materialists, in particular, do often recognize in themselves some affinity with Tillyard in the course of their attacks on him. See Dollimore, in Dollimore & Sinfield, *Political Shakespeare*, p. 5; Dollimore & Sinfield, "History and Ideology: The Instance of *Henry V*" in *Alternative Shakespeares*, ed. John Drakakis (London: Methuen, 1985), ch. 10, at pp. 206-7; also in Sinfield, *Faultlines*, pp. 109-10. Edward Pechter famously pointed out the similarities between Greenblatt and Tillyard, "The New Historicism and its Discontents: Politicizing Renaissance Drama", *PMLA*, 102 (1987), pp. 292-303, at p. 294; also Helperin, *Uses of the Canon*, pp. 149-50.

47. Debora Shuger, *Habits of Thought in the English Renaissance: Religion, Politics and the Dominant Culture* (Berkeley. California UP, 1990), p. 23.

48. Ibid, p. 18, n. 4.

49. Tillyard, *The Elizabethan World Picture* (1943; repr. Harmondsworth: Penguin, 1972) p. 97.

50. See also Tillyard, *Shakespeare's History Plays* (1944; repr. Harmondsworth: Penguin, 1991), pp. 70-6.

51. Tillyard, *Elizabethan World Picture*, pp. 17-18; Tillyard, *Shakespeare's History Plays*, pp. 18-25.

52. *Troilus and Cressida*, 1.3.75-137. All Shakespeare references are based on *The Riverside Shakespeare*, ed. G. Blakemore Evans *et al.* (Boston: Houghton Mifflin, 1974).

53. For a fascinating discussion of the ways in which new historicists rely on old history, see Leeds Barroll, "A New History for Shakespeare and his Time", *Shakespeare Quarterly*, 39 (1988), pp. 441-64. Also, Barroll, *Politics, Plague and Shakespeare's Theater: The Stuart Years* (Ithaca, NY: Cornell UP, 1991).

54. See references and further discussion at n. 65 below.

55. King James VI & I, *Political Writings*, ed. Johann P. Sommerville (Cambridge: Cambridge UP, 1994), pp. 20-2.

56. Ibid, p. 21.

57. Ibid, p. 21.

58. Thomas Hobbes, *Leviathan* ed. Richard Tuck (Cambridge: Cambridge UP, 1991), ch. xxxi, pp. 253-4. See the fuller discussion in Glenn Burgess, "On Hobbesian Resistance Theory", *Political Studies*, 42 (1994), pp. 62-83.

59. James VI & I, *Political Writings*, p. 21.

60. Ibid, pp. 70-2.

61. James VI & I, "A Meditation upon the 27.28.29 Verses of the XXVII Chapter of Saint Matthew", in *Political Writings*, p. 231.

62. *The Jacobean Union: Six Tracts of 1604*, ed. Bruce R. Galloway & Brian P. Levack (Scottish History Society: Edinburgh, 1985), p. 196. Savile was knighted by James I in 1604, and the recipient of royal favour on several other occasions.

63. Marchamont Nedham, *The Case of the Commonwealth of England, Stated*, ed. P.A. Knachel (Charlottesville: Virginia UP, 1969), pp. 15-29.

64. E.g. in the *Trew Law*: see *Political Writings*, p. 73; also his 1610 Speech, ibid, p. 183.

65. See W.H. Greenleaf, *Order, Empiricism and Politics: Two Traditions of English Political Thought 1500-1700* (Greenwood: Westport CT, 1980; orig. ed. 1964); James Daly, *Cosmic Harmony and Political Thinking in Early Stuart England* (*Transactions of the American Philosophical Society*, v. 69, part 7, 1979); Francis Oakley, *Omnipotence, Covenant and Order: An Excursion in the History of Ideas from Abelard to Leibniz* (Ithaca, NY: Cornell UP, 1984), esp. ch. 4. These works are built on by Glenn Burgess, "The Divine Right of Kings Reconsidered", *English Historical Review*, 107 (1992), pp. 837-61. The subverion and containment model might be said to capture some of this ambiguity, but at the price of imposing without warrant an assumption about what usage is "orthodox" (whatever that might mean).

66. *2 Henry VI*, 4.3.13-15.

67. Ibid, 4.2.65-8. The absurdist comedy in Shakespeare's treatment of Jack Cade is well brought out in Richard Helgerson, *Forms of Nationhood: The Elizabethan Writing of England* (Chicago: Chicago UP, 1992), pp. 204-15, a powerful antidote to attempts to find a subversive peasant ideology in Shakespeare. Helgerson's work is perhaps the finest thing to emerge so far out of new historicist criticism, but even it is remarkably Whiggish in its overall conception. See the revealing review by Mervyn James, in *English Historical Review*, 110 (1995), p. 734.

68. Glenn Burgess, "Contexts for the Writing and Publication of Hobbes's *Leviathan*", *History of Political Thought*, 11 (1990), pp. 675-702; Jean Hampton, *Hobbes and the Social Contract Tradition* (Cambridge: Cambridge UP, 1986), pp. 197-207.

69. See further Glenn Burgess, *Absolute Monarchy and the Stuart Constitution*.

70. Anne Barton, "Livy, Machiavelli, and Shakespeare's 'Coriolanus'", *Shakespeare Survey*, 38 (1985), pp. 115-29; also Bruce King, *Coriolanus* (Basingstoke: Macmillan, 1989), pp. 15-16. Both discuss Clifford Chalmers Huffman, *Coriolanus in Context* (Bucknell UP: Lewisburg PA, 1971), esp. ch. 6.

71. For example, the use of *Basilicon Doron* in Huffman, *Coriolanus in Context*, p. 189, utterly misrepresents James's argument by ruthlessly truncated quotation. Cf. James VI & I, *Political Writings*, ed. Sommerville, p. 21.

72. Huffman, *Coriolanus in Context*, p. 199.

73. The clearest example, perhaps, is W. Gordon Zeeveld, "'Coriolanus' and Jacobean Politics", *Modern Language Review*, 57 (1962), pp. 321-34. After a most promising beginning, in which Zeeveld examines the "commonwealth" themes in the play, he becomes sidetracked by Parliamentary politics. One extraordinary essay manages to produce a political reading only by using an utterly anachronisitc language that has minimal connection with the play: see Michael D. Bristol, "Lenten Butchery: Legitimation Crisis in *Coriolanus*", in Howard & O'Connor's *Shakespeare Reproduced*, ch. 9. Bristol has the nerve to accuse others of removing Shakespeare from history (esp. p. 218), but his own account has no history other than theoretical abstractions and Bakhtin's carnivals.

74. Goldberg, *The Politics of Jacobean Literature*, p. 189; cf. pp. 192-3.

75. Thomas Sorge, "The Failure of Orthodoxy in *Coriolanus*", in Howard & O'Connor's *Shakespeare Reproduced*, ch. 10, at p. 232.

76. Cf. Blair Worden, "Shakespeare's Politics", *Shakespeare Survey*, 44 (1991), pp. 1-15, at p. 8. Worden's is a salutary attempt by an historian to examine Shakespeare's historically contingent politics. For yet another example of the distraction caused by looking for a non-existent constitutional conflict, see King, *Coriolanus*, pp. 98-104.

77. The best such attempt is Annabel Patterson, *Shakespeare and the Popular Voice* (Oxford: Blackwell, 1989), ch. 6. Like all of Patterson's work, it is historically sophisticated. Yet, like much work of this sort, it seems to me to fall into the trap of assuming too simple a relationship between the *plebs* of Shakespeare's play and the multitude of early modern England.

78. Bristol, "Lenten Butchery", p. 212.

79. Especially *Coriolanus*, 3.3.1-5. On the falsity of these charges see the comment on this passage in the New Arden edition, ed. Philip Brockbank (Methuen: London, 1976); also Sorge, "Failure of Orthodoxy", *passim*.

80. Kishlansky, *Parliamentary Selection*, pp. 3-9.

81. Ibid, p. 8.

82. Cf. David Harris Sacks, "Searching for 'Culture' in the English Renaissance", *Shakespeare Quarterly*, 39 (1988), pp. 465-88, at p. 486-8; and Patterson, *Shakespeare and the Popular Voice*, pp. 128-9.

83. Of discussions already mentioned, those by Zeeveld and Sorge are relevant here. Also David G. Hale, "Intestine Sedition: The Fable of the Belly", *Comparative Literature Studies*, 5 (1968),

pp. 377-87; Hale, "*Coriolanus*: The Death of a Political Metaphor", *Shakespeare Quarterly*, 23 (1971), pp. 197-202; and David Margolies, *Monsters of the Deep: Social Dissolution in Shakespeare's Tragedies* (Manchester: Manchester UP, 1992), ch. 7.

84. Kenneth Muir, "The Background of *Coriolanus*", *Shakespeare Quarterly*, 10 (1959), pp. 137-45, at p. 145. Muir is also useful for his well-placed scepticism regarding the evidentially-thin claims put forward in the famous article by E.C. Pettet, "*Coriolanus* and the Midlands Insurrection of 1607", *Shakespeare Survey*, 3 (1950), pp. 34-40. Pettet's case is improved by Patterson, *Shakespeare and the Popular Voice*, pp. 135-46, though I remain unpersuaded. Witness, for example, the use of Robert Wilkinson's sermon (at pp. 140-1) to show that it is untrue to suggest that "protesters 'never challenged the social order' as such", an argument that uses the evidence of the protesters' enemies at face value. It is just this sort of employment of evidence that has bedevilled the understanding of mid-seventeenth-century radicalism: see J.C. Davis, *Fear, Myth and History: The Ranters and the Historians* (Cambridge: Cambridge UP, 1986). Richard Wilson rightly points out that there is no popular revolt in *Coriolanus*; see "Against the Grain: Representing the Market in *Coriolanus*", in Wilson, *Will Power: Essays on Shakespearean Authority* (Hemel Hempstead: Harvester, 1993), ch. 4, at p. 117. However, Wilson's own attempt to locate the play within "the epochal shift from collective values based on shared consumption to exchange values and private enterprise" (p. 84) seems to convert too much of the play's political language into economic terms.

85. One of the most puzzling features of much recent historical-political criticism of Renaissance literature is that, for all of its knowing scorn towards those who have *naive* beliefs about the representational character of language or literature, it still manages itself to find the most simple forms of representation present in literature (e.g. a real peasant voice in Shakespeare's many-headed multitude), and to take no account of the formal demands of literature that do indeed militate against simple representation.

86. As will be seen, my reading does not quite accept either Zeeveld's view that *Coriolanus* was an *anti*-commonwealth play ("'Coriolanus' and Jacobean Politics", p. 323), or Margolies's that it reveals irreconcilable splits between the interests of patricians and people (*Monsters of the Deep*, ch. 7).

87. E.g. Sir Thomas Elyot, *The Book named The Governor*, ed. S.E. Lehmberg (London: Dent, 1962), pp. 1-2; Edward Forsett, *A Comparative Discourse of the Bodies Natural and Politique* (London, 1606); Sir Robert Filmer (on Hobbes), in Filmer, *Patriarcha and Other Political Works*, ed. Peter Laslett (Oxford: Blackwell, 1949). Standard introductions to the 'commonwealth' concerns of the period include W. Gordon Zeeveld, *The Foundations of Tudor Policy* (Cambridge, MA: Harvard UP, 1948); Arthur B. Ferguson, *The Articulate Citizen and the English Renaissance* (Durham, NC: Duke UP, 1965); and W.R.D. Jones, *The Tudor Commonwealth, 1529-1559* (London: Athlone Press, 1970).

88. G.R. Elton, *Reform and Renewal: Thomas Cromwell and the Common Weal* (Cambridge: Cambridge UP, 1973); Sharpe, *Personal Rule of Charles I*, ch. 7.

89. Hence, in the end, my doubts about Patterson's account of the play which too easily finds a peasant voice (not only in Shakespeare, but - as noted above - in Wilkinson's sermon). One might add that her approach also tends, though never explicitly, to elide the differences between republicanism and democracy. The former, too, was an élite doctrine in the early modern period. It is possible to forget just how many ways early modern Englishmen had of domesticating republican politics.

# POWER OF MYTHS AND MYTHS OF POWER: SHAKESPEARE'S HISTORY PLAYS AND MODERN HISTORIOGRAPHY

Jean-Christophe Mayer
(Université Montpellier III)

> I am a scribbled form, drawn with a pen
> Upon a parchment, and against this fire
> Do I shrink up.
> *King John*, 5.7.32-4

In an article published in 1976 Pierre Sahel remarked that although the Tudor Myth had been seriously qualified – and to an extent "de-mythified" – it still remained for the scholar to "demystify" the interest and fascination it engendered in the field of literary studies.[1] Almost twenty years on, the Tudor myth remains a source of debate. It is also half a century since the publication of two of E.M.W. Tillyard's most influential books: *The Elizabethan World Picture* (1943) and *Shakespeare's History Plays* (1944). These have been construed by some as the constituents of an all-encompassing system. At once a well-wrought and awe-inspiring body of work, Dr Tillyard's "Cosmology" was followed by Dr Tillyard's "Politics", the whole being worthy of Aristotle.[2]

Many students and academics will confess to this day that these books formed the very first basis of their knowledge of Shakespeare. Yet, concurrently, criticism of Tillyard's so-called Tudor myth theory centred upon the rejection of what may be called a providentialist reading of history.[3] Traces of an ideology of power informed by the current political climate were also found. 1944 was indeed the year of publication of George Wilson Knight's patriotic essay *The Olive and the Sword*. Laurence Olivier's film of *Henry V* was released and *Shakespeare's History Plays* was published – a book whose influence clearly outlasted that of the two others. Interestingly, when reading Tillyard one is struck by the almost total absence of topical allusions. The timeless quality of his writing is intriguing. What is it that still makes such a text speak to us? Undeniably the author's apparently scrupulous setting aside of contemporary history (that of a world at war with Nazi Germany) is conducive to an impression of trust, scholarly impartiality, and concern for the text only. This partly accounts for the lasting effect of the Tudor myth theory. One must nonetheless be wary of the subtleties and deceptions of the Tillyard text. As Graham Holderness points out:

> Where Wilson Knight and Olivier declared, in their different ways, that Britain in her hour of need could turn to Shakespeare, Tillyard quietly affirmed that Shakespeare has always been, is, and always will be "England." The effectiveness of the enterprise can be measured by the fact that assent to that proposition can seem like recognition of the long familiar. [...] The scholarly imagination, revisiting a vanished past, severs the history it addresses from the exigencies of the present; and thus insidiously operates on the reader who, aware only of the attention he focusses on Shakespeare, is quite unaware of how an image of his own society is being implicitly celebrated and affirmed.[4]

These remarks bring to light the ambivalent mechanisms which are at work behind the Tudor myth theory. If *Henry V* has been the source of many a piece of providentialist criticism it is certainly because the play often wrestles with issues such as myth-making. Henry in 1.2. is concerned with the legitimization of his "claim" to France (1.2.12), which can only be established on the grounds of what has preceded. Thus, at the very outset of the play, the problem of the historical reconstruction of a lost past is posed. The King explicitly insists that there be no distortion of history:

> And God forbid, my dear and faithful lord,
> That you should fashion, wrest, or bow your reading,
> Or nicely charge your understanding soul
> With opening titles miscreate, whose right
> Suits not in native colours with the truth;  (1.2.13-17)[5]

## History Plays and Modern Historiography 39

The warning recalls Polydore Vergil's dedication to Henry VIII in his *Anglica Historia* in which he cautioned his reader against a certain type of historiography: "An Historie is a full rehearsall and declaration of things don, not a gesse or a divination."[6] What ensues after Henry's word of caution is the chronicle-like Salic law speech consisting of no fewer than sixty-two lines spoken by an Archbishop of Canterbury turned historian or genealogist. The 1994 R.S.C. uncut production of *Henry V* boldly underlines the fastidious length of Canterbury's demonstration.[7] The speech reveals itself as a highly interpretative construct that becomes part and parcel of Henrician mythology. Not only is the sovereign's claim legitimized but also his existence is validated through the Archbishop's probing into the origins. His somewhat fanciful story is one of creation, it tells how the present reality has been created in primordial times, how it has come into existence. This is in total agreement with the general definition of myth as expounded for example by Mircea Eliade.[8]

It is manifest that history, or rather the Henrician version of the Tudor myth, is in the making as the play opens. Henry's proleptic hope in posterity betrays it: "Either our history shall with full mouth / Speak freely of our acts, or else our grave, / Like Turkish mute, shall have a tongueless mouth, / Not worshipped with a waxen epitaph." (1.2.230-3). To conclude that Shakespeare chose to make himself the mouthpiece of this official view of history is evidently a little simplistic. What is blatant here is that the King seems deeply preoccupied by the establishment of *his* truth, whatever that may be. To an extent, kingship in the play can be viewed as "myth in action", to quote part of René Girard's definition of monarchy.[9] Even Henry's Saint Crispian's day speech in 4.3 belongs more to the mythology of the nascent modern state than to that of the monarchy. Henry indeed contends that value will be based on merit, on blood shed for the state rather than on hereditary blood, "For he today that sheds his blood with me / Shall be my brother . . . " (4.3.61-2). Again the tension between the story told on stage and the one recorded in the chronicles resurfaces. The King is now more assertive about posterity: "This story shall the good man teach his son" (4.3.56) It is worth remembering at this point the radical ambiguity of the word "story" for the Elizabethans. "Story", like the modern French word *histoire,* could mean either "story" or "history". Conversely, "history" often referred to a story told in the past tense that relied on what Aristotle called "mythos", that is to say, a plot.[10] The border between historical truth and a story verging on pure invention or the mythical was not yet clearly drawn, despite the many claims on the part of authors to be possessing the "truth."

The Prologue of *Henry V*, however, affects a belief in the reality of this opposition. The Chorus repeatedly alludes to the limits of the representation of historical reality in the theatre: ". . . Can this cock-pit hold / The vasty fields of France? Or may we cram / Within this wooden O the very casques / That did affright the air at Agincourt?" (Prologue, 11-14). These of course are false questionings – merely rhetorical questions. The Prologue plays on the (spurious) illusion that theatre should be a representation of the real and furthermore that this real exists as such *outside* the performance text.

Yet, what is this extra-textual reality? A partial answer could be that the 'real' in a history play is what is related to fact. Such an affirmation would rely on the assumption that facts have an independent existence. This is far from being the case. As Nietzsche has shown: "There are no facts in themselves. It is always necessary to begin by introducing a meaning in order that there can be a fact."[11] The Prologue addresses misconceptions of the sort. Any type of discourse on history is to an extent untrue to the life it claims to express. It follows that it can only belong to the realm of interpretation. In his valuable work on the historical narrative Roland Barthes has pointed to "History's refusal to assume the real as signified."[12] Any discourse, whether theatrical or historical, will necessarily fall short of representing the vast historical continuum. No stage or page can hold "The vasty fields of France" for the reason that "there is no such thing as isochrony."[13] Linearity of discourse is a fallacy.

Similarly, Hayden White's well-known analyses of the rhetoric of history expose the so-called "myth of literalness" of history that stems from "the dream of a nonfigurative language" which would be "purely denotative."[14] As a consequence, White further undermines the concept of historical truth or objectivity. He concludes that: "If rhetoric is the politics of discourse, as discourse itself is the politics of language, then there is no such thing as politically innocent historiography."[15]

Historical discourse is a sort of self-contained narrative which – ultimately – refers back to itself. In this respect it is not far removed from the language of fiction and particularly of storytelling. Because it creates, as it were, its own reality it also possesses the same performative quality as theatrical language, which brings to life what it names or describes. It is with these (illusory) dichotomies between two traditionally opposed genres that the Prologue of *Henry V* plays, in so doing using a particularly well-suited self-reflexive language, that of meta-theatricality.

A self-reflexive language can be one imbued with narcissism, that is to say words which are constantly checked in the mirror of grandeur until the delusive object is cracked. The tension between history and theatre reaches its height in *Richard II* when the King becomes openly engaged in the making of his own chronicle. Resemblances with *Henry V* come to mind at once, and yet Richard's speeches are pieces of lyrical but egotistical rhetoric which betray themselves likewise:

> For God's sake, let us sit upon the ground,
> And tell sad stories of the death of kings –
> How some have been deposed, some slain in war,
> Some haunted by the ghosts they have deposed,
> Some poisoned by their wives, some sleeping killed,
> All murdered.... (3.2.151-6)

These "sad stories" are such stuff as tales and myths are made on. History and legend are blended through storytelling. Richard, in his proleptic concern for the posterity of his name, views himself as one part of an overall narrative, which his wife – among others – has to contribute to: "Tell thou the lamentable fall of me, / And send the hearers weeping to their beds" (5.1.44-5). Meta-theatricality unites with meta-historicity as Richard II, the player/theatrical character/historical personage, discloses unawares the mechanisms of historical mythmaking and manipulation of history. History has been made by men whose *story* has been *told*; in a play this story is at each performance being made and told again by other men who speak in their name.[16] In both cases, it is a matter of storytelling. What, then, is the difference between the historical construct and the literary construct?

Very little at all, according to some critics. By legitimately denouncing the belief in history as a reality outside the text (or performance) they seem to toll the knell of history altogether. These views constitute mainly a reaction to former beliefs which used history as a reference point:

> History, in each of its manifestations, was the single, unified, unproblematic, extra-textual, extra-discursive real that guaranteed our readings of the texts which constituted its cultural *expression*. If it was never fully mastered, never absolutely known, if the matter of history was never settled, that meant only that there was more work to be done.[17]

No other play sums up quite so well as *Henry VIII* all the irony of the problem of pretended historical truth and reality. The play, whose performance title is the significant "All is True", has long been famous for passages such as Archbishop Cranmer's prophecy in 5.4. His eulogy of Elizabeth I and James I could content providentialist critics if its beginning was not so easy to construe as irony on the part of the playwright: "Let me speak, sir, / For heaven now bids me, and the words I utter / Let none think flattery, for they'll find 'em truth." (5.4.14-16). The irony is total when one tries to imagine the reaction of contemporary audiences to the ensuing unreal descriptions of the reigns of Elizabeth I and James I. The humour is that this prophecy about their present still remains in the distant future of political hopes for Jacobean audiences, who can measure the gap between the myth and their everyday reality.[18]

Yet, the play's Prologue dismisses such irony or mirth. The tone is set from the very first line: "I come no more to make you laugh." The Prologue, furthermore, professes verisimilitude: "Such as give / Their money out of hope they may believe, / May here find truth, too. ... " (Prologue, 7-9). As in the Prologue to *Henry V*, historical truth is grounded in the spectators' imagination: "*Think* ye see / The very persons of our noble story / As they were living . . ." (25-7; my italics). But if one pays closer attention to this piece of writing it appears that it could be read in a totally opposite way. Its suspiciously overemphasized claim to saying and possessing the truth exposes the speech as a brazen manipulation of facts and fiction to create an artifact. The Prologue only conveys truths that are fit to be heard. He deals in official truths and necessarily silences more discordant, subdued voices. *All is True* thus points to the coexistence of different interpretations within one seemingly unified work grounded in history:

> ... Shakespeare constructs a dramatic universe dominated by "deceptive appearances" and the "relativity of truth", in which, in Pirandellian fashion, "all is true" means precisely that *any* interpretation of the past may be true if one thinks it so, and no point of view is allowed to contain or control all others.[19]

The consequences of such an assertion are in turn multiple. One of them might be found in the dangers for literary exegesis of what could be named critical relativism. This point will be the source of some comment later in this paper. For the while, without endorsing the concept of critical relativism, one may safely say with Leontes that: "All's true that is mistrusted." (*The Winter's Tale*, 2.1.50)

Evidence to support the Tudor myth theory is scarce, and what is more, it never forms a structured whole that is not self-conflicting in one way or another. *Henry VIII*, in spite of its relative closeness to Shakespeare's time and of its sensitive historical material, is a case in point. The tension between providential views of history and the dismantling of such beliefs was very much alive. It is no doubt in its manner of dealing with these oppositions that the Renaissance as a whole reveals itself in all its subtlety:

> Despite the far-reaching implications of the conflict between the two views of historical causation, Renaissance historians often resolved it by the simple expedient of explaining the same course of events on both levels, often without even going so far as Hall does to acknowledge that they conflicted.[20]

*2 Henry IV* fully illustrates this point. Two radically opposite ways of explaining historical causation are juxtaposed by Shakespeare in a dialogue between the Earl of Warwick and a sick and sleepless King. Henry voices his fear that Richard II's ill-fated prophecy is about to prove true:

KING HENRY
O God, that one might read the book of fate,
And see the revolution of the times
Make mountains level, and the continent,
Weary of solid firmness, melt itself
Into the sea; [...]
[...]
... But which of you was by –
(*To Warwick*) You, cousin Neville, as I may remember –
When Richard, with his eye brimful of tears,
Then checked and rated by Northumberland,
Did speak these words, now proved a prophecy? –    (3.1.44-8; 60-4)

Warwick's answer comes from a man who has a more rational view of history. He dispels suggestions that the deposed king had any *divine* gift for telling the future. History for Warwick – and this is a common view in the Renaissance – is a book of examples. If well observed by the statesman it can be a source of learning about the workings of necessity, provided that the statesman is so gifted:

WARWICK
There is a history in all men's lives
Figuring the natures of the times deceased;
The which observed, a man may prophesy,
With a near aim, of the main chance of things

As yet not come to life, who in their seeds
And weak beginnings lie intreasurèd. (75-80)

History is slowly severing the links with legend to become an autonomous science. But the Renaissance historical perspective is often an inverted one: the past is seldom explored for other purposes than its bearings on the present or the future. The distinction is that the new science tends to deal in prediction – not prophecy. It is no surprise if Niccolo Machiavelli himself highlighted its pragmatic function and made its study one of the duties of his Prince:

> As for exercising the mind, a prince should read history and reflect on the actions of great men. He can see how they carried themselves during their wars, and study what made them win, what made them lose, so that he can imitate their successes and avoid their defeats. [...] Such are the rules that a wise prince should observe. He must never idle away his days of peace, but vigorously make capital that will pay off in times of adversity; thus, when fortune changes, it will find him in a position to resist.[21]

If Machiavelli insists upon the pragmatic uses of history he does not for all that believe in the sanctity of historiographical truth. The past is not a domain which inevitably engenders truth. On the contrary, his writings testify that he is conscious of the processes which history undergoes in its fabrication by unscrupulous historiographers: "The whole truth about olden times is not grasped, since what redounds to their discredit is often passed over in silence, whereas what is likely to make them appear glorious is pompously recounted in all its details."[22]

The same controversy revolving around the notions of truth and evidence lies at the heart of the modern historiographical debate. The Tudor myth theory appears as an expression – by no means the only one – of the critical urge to interpret and impose a meaning. What is most ironical, however, is that the so-called deconstruction of this theory has often led to a new construct in which, for example, a religious providentialism has been replaced by a providentialism of a materialistic nature, as in the case of some neo-Marxist interpretations. Marxism is but one instance of the tendency to keep interpretation within the confines of a unified perspective. As William M. Hawley puts it:

> ... we generally view history from a single, fundamental basis in truth. One must, at heart, hold either a Marxist, new historicist, or metadramatic view of history, or some other, because to adopt multiple perspectives is to risk the appearance of confusion in one's historical self-identity. Thus, we have been trained to validate monistic historical perspectives as being academically correct without realizing that historiography is an impure art.[23]

There is little doubt that Tillyard's own monistic interpretation has had some influence on even his most fierce opponents. Hawley goes so far as to claim that we still have to deal with what he calls "Tillyard's legacy."[24] It is a rather disheartening thought to reflect that criticism might have come full circle again – away from Tillyard and then back to him. The problem is very much, but not solely, that of Shakespeare criticism in general. The text ("which text?" some would argue. But this is a different matter) is a palimpsest covered by multiple layers of exegesis. So much so that it could be argued: "Immediately we begin to look back at Shakespeare in a historical perspective, it becomes evident that what we see is not Shakespeare in history, but the history of 'Shakespeare'."[25]

For a long time indeed history itself has been sacralized and respected by writers and researchers alike as the last refuge of political ideology. Michel Foucault has amusingly remarked that "Under the sign of the cross of history, every discourse became a prayer to the God of just causes."[26] After regarding the notion of historical truth in turn as external then as internal to the text, it is now time to define a third stage in criticism which would entail the abandonment of what Foucault calls "the great myth [yet another!] of interiority":

> Thus the contemporary critic is abandoning the great myth of interiority: *intimior intimio ejus*. He finds himself totally displaced from the old themes of locked enclosures, of the treasure in the box that he habitually sought in the depth of the work's container. Placing himself at the exterior

of the text, he constitutes a new exterior for it, writing texts out of texts.[27]

Much of the work carried out recently by the New Historicists and the Cultural Materialists has been influenced by the writings of Foucault. His theories have led the former to call for the breakdown of distinctions between literary texts and others of a social, political, or cultural nature. After decades of New Criticism, structuralism, and deconstruction there was undoubtedly cause to reintroduce history into literary studies. As Christopher Pye explains: "Literature is *part* of history, the literary text as much a context for other aspects of cultural and material life as they are for it."[28]

Be that as it may, criticism of this approach has been expressed very recently. The validity of Stephen Greenblatt's rhetorical appoach to history has been severely qualified. History is reduced to a narrative, which leaves very little space for well-documented evidence of a scientific nature. Jonathan Hart has even denounced this work as a reconstruction of another (Tudor) myth:

> His [Greenblatt's] intricate use of analogy, metaphor, and narrative often relies on the ability to persuade and to forge a new myth about Shakespeare and the Renaissance rather than appeal to a systematic presentation of evidence. Greenblatt's Renaissance is fragmentary, recalcitrant, and pluralistic: it is another displacement of E.M.W. Tillyard's more unified, normative and monolithic Elizabethan world picture. Whereas Tillyard observes the rule, Greenblatt seeks the exception.[29]

The problem with the rhetorical approach is that it can become an art of persuasion and nothing else. The importance given to form — which leads to the hegemony of the signifier — bears witness to the complete loss of faith in the notions of fact and evidence. The signifier *is* the signified, form *is* meaning. This is the point when the crisis affecting knowledge can become an obsession and when the consequent illusiveness of truth, the triumph of illusion, the hollowness and at the same time the mystery of representation is sought for everywhere and relished.

Interestingly, myth reappears in such a propitious context: "If there can be no truth, or if that truth remains so refractory as to seem darkness invisible, then the delight of the myth seduces the reader into further delights."[30]

We are, therefore, confronted with a type of historiographical discourse which proclaims itself as a sort of fiction and thus casts serious doubts on its own validity. Its solipsist philosophy denies it access to any kind of valid ethical judgement and runs the risk of making its critical standpoint appear like an abdication of social responsibility.

The partial "re-mythication" of criticism in Shakespeare studies today calls perhaps for a renewal of Pierre Sahel's 1976 plea for a "demystification" of the Tudor myth. These issues also draw our attention to the fact that an element of myth, of sacredness, still seems to be indispensable in our effort to recover meaning. We are faced with the daunting task of rebuilding on the ruins of deconstruction. After years of a philosophy of doubt we have to find a *cogito* that would enable us not only to establish the unquestioned and rational existence of a *res cogitans* – the critical mind – but also of a *res extensa* – the object of criticism – to use a Cartesian metaphor. Our difficulty is that we are no doubt still wrestling with the manifold implications of the fall of western metaphysics and the end of transcendence. Paradoxically, the death of a myth of divine power reveals the lasting hold of myths precisely when they have ceased to exist: "What surety of the world, what hope, what stay, / When this was now a king and now is clay?" (*King John*, 5.7.68-9).

*Notes*

1. "Il était donc essentiel, après avoir démythifié le "mythe Tudor", de le démystifier." Pierre Sahel, "Les fondements historiques d'une littérature politique au XVIe siècle, La démythification du 'mythe Tudor' ", *Études Anglaises* 66 (1976), 59.

2. Some critics have even severely criticized those books by calling their ideology totalitarian: "un système qui se veut totalisant, pour ne pas dire totalitaire." Henri Suhamy, "Shakespeare

historien: propagateur de mythes, ou recenseur sceptique?", M.-T. Jones-Davies, éd., *Mythe et Histoire*, Société Française Shakespeare, Actes du Congrès 1983 (Paris: Touzot, 1984), 13.

3. Henry Ansgar Kelly argues for instance that "... it is unlikely that Shakespeare meant his audience to pick up the implicit moral that the divine punishment originating with the overthrow of Richard II was brought to an end with the advent of Henry VII, since this point is not to be found explicitly stated elsewhere either by Shakespeare or by anyone else until it was formulated by Tillyard. The historiographers of Shakespeare's time and earlier never resort to the notion of collective divine punishment falling on guilty and innocent alike, except occasionally with reference to the lineal descendents of wrongdoers; and even then it is usually a matter of the descendents enjoying ill-gotten gains." Henry Ansgar Kelly and Paul N. Siegel, "Tillyard and History: Comment and Response", *CLIO: A Journal of Literature, History and the Philosophy of History* 10:1 (1980), 87.

4. Graham Holderness, "Agincourt 1944: Readings in the Shakespeare Myth," *Literature and History* 10:1 (1984), 44.

5. All references to Shakespeare's plays are taken from: William Shakespeare, *The Complete Works*, eds. Stanley Wells and Gary Taylor (Oxford: Clarendon Press, 1986, repr. 1988).

6. Quoted in: Geoffrey Bullough, ed., *Narrative and Dramatic Sources of Shakespeare*, vol. 3 (London: Routledge and Kegan Paul; New York: Columbia UP, 1960), 8.

7. William Shakespeare, *Henry V*, dir. Matthew Warchus, with Iain Glen, Monica Dolan, Royal Shakespeare Theatre, Stratford-upon-Avon, 1994.

8. I have here paraphrased Eliade's definition: "... le mythe raconte une histoire sacrée; il relate un événement qui a eu lieu dans le temps primordial, le temps fabuleux des 'commencements'. Autrement dit, le mythe raconte comment, grâce aux exploits des Etres Surnaturels, une réalité est venue à l'existence, que ce soit la réalité totale, le Cosmos, ou seulement un fragment [...] C'est donc toujours le récit d'une 'création': on rapporte comment quelque chose a été produit, a commencé à *être*." Mircea Eliade, *Aspects du mythe*, Folio Essais (Paris: Gallimard, 1963) 16-17.

9. La royauté est mythologie en action." René Girard, *Des choses cachées depuis la fondation du monde, Recherches avec Jean-Michel Oughourlian et Guy Lefort* (Paris: Grasset, 1978), 64.

10. David Scott Kastan remarks that " 'History play' is an odd term, virtually an oxymoron, for a radical tension exists between the two words. 'History' proclaims a commitment to fact, to events as they happened. [...] 'Play', on the other hand, declares a commitment to fiction, to an artificial verbal structure whose 'subject,' as Chapman writes, 'is not truth, but things like truth.'" Kastan, "'To Set a Form upon that Indigest': Shakespeare's Fictions of History", *Comparative Drama* 17:1 (1983), 1.

11. Quoted in: Roland Barthes, "The Discourse of History", *Comparative Criticism: A Yearbook* 3 (1978), 16.

12. Barthes, 18.

13. Barthes, 9.

14. Hayden White, "Rhetoric and History", *Theories of History: Papers Read at a Clark Library Seminar* (Los Angeles: William Clark Memorial Library, University of California, 1978), 7.

15. White 24.

16. "Increasingly opposing historical fact to literary artifact, Shakespeare exposes the processes of historical mythmaking even as he engages in them. [...] From the beginning, the plays [in the second tetralogy] seem guided by this double agenda: the historical story they tell is also a story of historiographic production." Phillis Rackin, *Stages of History: Shakespeare's English Chronicles* (London: Routledge, 1991), 61.

17. Catherine Belsey, "Making Histories Then and Now: Shakespeare from *Richard II* to *Henry V*", Francis Barker, Peter Hume, Margaret Iversen, eds. *Uses of History: Marxism, Postmodernism and the Renaissance* (Manchester and New York: Manchester UP, 1991), 26.

18. Lee Bliss convincingly argues against providentialist interpretations: "To accept Cranmer's vision of an earthly paradise as Shakespeare's praise of Elizabeth and James is also to accept its implicit progressive view of history, where a benevolent god provides the instrument (Elizabeth) for accomplishing the perfection of human existence. Yet even within the dramatic fiction of the play, the prophecy appears disjunctive rather than as the climactic revelation of a providential pattern in the events we have witnessed." Bliss concludes on this point that: "The 'wonders' in *Henry VIII* are limited to a glimpse of what a transformed England, under an inspired monarch, might be." Bliss, "The Wheel of Fortune and the Maiden Phoenix of Shakespeare's *King Henry The Eighth*", *ELH*. 42:1 (1975), 16, 23.

19. Peter L. Rudnytsky, "*Henry VIII* and the Deconstruction of History", *Shakespeare Survey* 43 (1991), 46.

20. Rackin, 8.

21. Niccolo Machiavelli, *The Prince*, trans. and ed. Robert M. Adams, Norton Critical Edition (New York and London: Norton, 1977), 41-2.

22. W. Stark, ed., *The Discourses of Niccolo Machiavelli*, trans. Leslie J. Walker, Rare Masterpieces of Philosophy and Science, Vol.1 (London: Routledge and Kegan Paul, 1950), 353.

23. William M. Hawley, *Critical Hermeneutics and Shakespeare's History Plays*, American University Studies (New York: Lang, 1992), 13.

24. Hawley, 12.

25. Holderness, 26.

26. Sylvère Lotringer, ed., *Foucault Live (Interviews, 1966-84)*, transl. John Johnston, Foreign Agents Series (New York: Semiotext(e), Columbia University, 1989), 12.

27. Lotringer, 21.

28. Christopher Pye, *The Regal Phantasm: Shakespeare and the Politics of Spectacle* (London and New York: Routledge, 1990), 7.

29. Jonathan Hart, *Theatre and World: The Problematics of Shakespeare's History* (Boston: Northeastern UP, 1992), 257.

30. Hart, 257.

# NEW HISTORICISM AND HISTORY PLAYS

### Lisa Hopkins
### (Sheffield Hallam University)

Of all the features of New Historicist practice, one of the most strikingly distinctive is its now characteristic habit of inaugurating discussion through anecdote, often one characterised both by lack of immediately obvious relevance to the topic ostensibly addressed by the title, and by the copious detail which results from its mimicking of Geertzian 'thick description' - a technique which has led Frank Lentricchia to comment that 'Greenblatt's beginnings seem to promise what, in theory, new historicism, so hermeneutically savvy, isn't supposed to promise - direct access to history's gritty, ground-level texture'.[1] My own beginning, overtly situating me in relation to a number of names and concepts which should immediately serve both to contextualise my argument and to suggest that I have a passable acquaintance with the topic I wish to discuss, obviously aims at a very different effect, more impersonal, more objective, and, in academic terms, less eccentric; nevertheless, my very use of the first person - so unthinkable, until recently, in British academic circles - demonstrates that I am myself indebted to many of the practices of New Historicism, and it is certainly not a blanket denunciation of it that I wish to attempt. What I aim to focus on is rather a specific critique of what seems to me to be the paradoxical ahistoricism of the New Historicist aproach to the Elizabethan history play, and I offer these remarks, as all critics do, from my own particular standpoint, of which the most relevant features for this purpose seem to me to be that I am British, and teaching in England.

I have, therefore, confined myself very narrowly to three particular examples of New Historicist writing, Stephen Greenblatt's "Invisible bullets: Renaissance authority and its subversion, *Henry IV* and *Henry V*", Leonard Tennenhouse's

"Strategies of State and political plays: *A Midsummer Night's Dream, Henry IV, Henry V, Henry VIII*", and Emily C. Bartels' discussion of *Edward II* in her book *Spectacles of Strangeness: Imperialism, Alienation, and Marlowe*. I have made these choices for the simple reason that these represent New Historicist readings which are widely available in England, and widely used by students. Both the Greenblatt and the Tennenhouse pieces are anthologised in Jonathan Dollimore and Alan Sinfield's seminal collection *Political Shakespeare: New essays in cultural materialism*, which has so far sold 7,000 copies in Britain alone; it continues to sell at the rate of 800 a year, and has achieved such status as a classic that it has recently gone into a second edition, with two new essays by Dollimore and Sinfield.[2] These two essays may thus, for most British students of the Renaissance, represent the only encounter with New Historicism they are ever likely to have; the influence of Greenblatt's essay, too, is further increased by the fact that it is reproduced in Richard Wilson and Richard Dutton's Longman Critical Reader *New Historicism and Renaissance Drama*. The phenomenal success of Dollimore and Sinfield's collection means that these two essays have, in effect, become canonical criticism - though it is, of course, ironic that this has been performed in a way which, through the operation of the book's title, tends to elide the very real differences between (American) New Historicism and (British) Cultural Materialism.[3] As for Bartels' book, monographs on Marlowe are much fewer and farther between than works on Shakespeare, and so any one work is correspondingly more likely to be influential; in Bartels' case, the book was referred to by all but one of the students who recently chose to write on Marlowe on my Renaissance drama option at Sheffield Hallam University, "Tragedy of Blood". These three examinations of Elizabethan history plays have, then, been wide-ranging in their effects.

I choose New Historicism's representations of history plays in particular because this, it seems to me, is where a tendency in New Historicism to deal with generalities rather than specifics is both most marked and most pernicious. Many critics have noticed that New Historicist practice tends often to blur the recorded events of history.[4] In his recent book *Will Power: Essays on Shakspearean Authority*, which itself engages very closely with the specifics of historical change, Richard Wilson remarks witheringly that "in its modish refusal to distinguish fact from fantasy, New Historicism reverts to the metaphysics of *The Name of the Rose*".[5] Wilson calls for "a *newer* historicism [which] will respond to Foucault's partition of universal history into local *histories*, without being seduced by the post-modern fashion of ultra-relativism; and it will do so by heeding his injunction to 'conduct the first-hand historical analysis' necessary to explode every 'sacred, intangible, all-explanatory' narrative".[6] New Historicism, by contrast, for all its apparent emphasis on '*la petite histoire*',[7] subscribes fundamentally to a *grand recit* of Geertzian truth, universally applicable despite the particularity of its grounding in the fractured world of the post-Second-World-War period;[8] and in doing so, it paradoxically sacrifices the very quality which its founding father Greenblatt so eloquently lauds,[9] the ability to marvel; for in its failure to perceive the difference of the past, it strips it of the wonder which ought to make us cautious how we phrase our assertions about it.

New Historicist practice is rarely cautious in its statements. Tennenhouse declares of *A Midsummer Night's Dream* that "the entire last act of the play [...] theorises the process of inversion whereby art and politics end up in [a] mutually authorising relationship",[10] which surely accords with no known audience reaction – and it is particularly in the area of the Elizabethan history play that the sense of wonder tends to be lost, for in two of the cases which I want to examine here New Historicist practice locates these plays so insistently within the past in which they were written that it fails to perceive the yet further pastness of the events they represent. (In the third case, I am, with apparent perversity, going to argue exactly the opposite; but I hope to make it apparent that both tendencies are, in fact, two sides of the same coin). Even when it comes to the artistic and political milieu of the plays' composition, New Historicist critics tend to fight so shy of what they see as simplistic explanations[11] that their own posit a relationship which is barely graspable. Tennenhouse explains why he ignores specific events and prefers to see Shakespeare's career in terms of a general, broadly-based cultural and aesthetic shift demarcating the reign of James from that of Elizabeth: to see Shakespeare's history plays "as overt political texts that can be interpreted by reference to the historical source material [...] testifies to a belief in the distinction between literature and politics and so serves the interests of modern society by imposing this belief on the past" (p. 109). However, while he advances his own politically correct credentials here, his own account is, in fact, no less mystifying than those he demonises, for it offers no explanation of agency or process, but merely postulates shifts in sensibility so widespread as to be unanalysable, and consequently, presumably, unstoppable by any consciously willed means: "with the ascension of James we are not entering new semiotic territory even though there appears to be a widespread attempt on the part of the literate classes to revise the problematics of power" (p. 110). What does this mean? Who were 'the literate classes' (and how, incidentally, might gender as well as class affect their literacy), what was the state of their apprehension of concepts like 'the problematics of power', how did they arrive at this group decision, how was it disseminated, and why? When the leaders of the Easter Rising seized the Dublin Post Office in 1916, when any *coup*-organising general worth his salt commandeers the local television and radio stations, they show themselves acutely aware of one thing of which Tennenhouse appears to have a rather shaky grasp: you need to know *precisely* what, and where, the lines of communication are, before any sort of change can be effected. (A similar blindness to pragmatics is identified in Greenblatt's work by Michael Bristol, who comments shrewdly that "New Historicism seems weakest in its attempt to present an account of state power by means of a cultural poetics").[12]

Of course good New Historicist practice (Leah Marcus' *Puzzling Shakespeare: Local Reading and its Discontents* is a prime example) may well offer precisely such specifics. In Tennenhouse's account, however, grand cultural concepts substitute for more particular local details such as the clear relationship between *Henry V* and the Earl of Essex and the potential links between *Henry VIII* and Princess Elizabeth. Far from positing a false dichotomy between politics and literature, noticing such contemporary resonances would have formed an essential component of original audience response to plays and would have radically informed reception of them.[13] When he does descend to the specifics of history, however, Tennenhouse is at his least happy, for his grasp of it is fundamentally insecure. Elizabeth I, he declares, "used her power as a patron to affect the power of the ruling families and thus set economically-based political authority in opposition to that based on blood" (p.112); and when, dying, she named her successor, she thus "acted in accordance with a view of the crown as an object of property, which was therefore dispensed according to the will of its owner. By naming James rather than an English claimant, however, she also acted according to the law of primogeniture" (p. 114).

Both these statements fit Tennenhouse's thesis rather better than they fit the facts customarily accepted by historians. Who were "the ruling families", and, more fundamentally, in what possible sense could they be said to "rule"? Elizabeth herself - with advice, which she could sometimes choose to ignore - did the ruling; the suggestion that anybody else did simply ignores the political realities of sixteenth-century England. Similarly, by naming James as her successor Elizabeth was not, as Tennenhouse implies by picking up on his earlier construction of an opposition between inheritance and primogeniture in the will of Henry VIII, restoring a principle of primogeniture: the Suffolk line, which Henry had favoured over the Stuart one, had no surviving members of indisputably legitimate birth (the legality of Lady Catherine Grey's marriage to the Earl of Hertford, and hence the legitimacy of her two sons, having been brought into doubt by the lack of produceable witnesses), and James' dual descent from not one but two marriages of Margaret Tudor gave him the highest remaining quotient of Tudor blood in the land, thus making him the only likely heir. It was surely less a question of principle than of practicalities. The entire situation was problematic - as a modern Tudor historian comments, "when Richard of York claimed the Crown in the teeth of King Henry VI in 1460 [...] no law had decided whether the Crown was a title of a property, and the issue had to be resolved by wager of battle".[14] Given the appalling history of battles of varying decisiveness which followed, any attempt to clarify the issue definitively by a subsequent monarch would have seemed remarkably ill-advised, and as a result in the sixteenth century "the succession in England was governed not by law but by custom".[15] If Elizabeth I did indeed name James, then, her decision, made on her deathbed, in a seriously debilitated state, could well be seen less as a fully weighed constitutional statement - especially in view of her notorious refusal to indicate her successor earlier - but more as an action circumscribed by custom, and perhaps by a sense that she was actually doing little more than ratify an assumption which had long been shared by many of her councillors. Indeed the extent to which James' succession was considered the most probable outcome is best illustrated by the uncertainty surrounding the question of whether or not Elizabeth *did* name him: the evidence that she did so is - suitably enough - essentially an anecdote,[16] a fact which Tennenhouse passes over in silence, since certainty on the subject, however dubious, seems to suit him better.

Greenblatt's methods, although sharing a detectable family resemblance, are rather different. In place of the winds of change which sweep through Tennenhouse's argument, Greenblatt offers the minutely particular, which he recounts with intensely seductive charm and verve. It would be a deeply ungracious critic who failed to pay tribute to the engaging style and intimacy of his writing; nor can one suggest that he, like Tennenhouse, is ill at ease with history, since his ability to deploy evidence is startling. He is, in addition, a gifted close reader of the anecdotes with which his text is so pleasantly littered: his comments on Hariot's Algonquin episode seem to me (at the level of verbal elucidation at least) genuinely inspired.[17] Where I (rather regretfully) part company with

## New Historicism and History Plays                                             59

Greenblatt, however, is when he turns his attentions to the plays themselves, and I do so because I find his readings of them not only unconvincing but also, and much less forgiveably, uninspired, so that he does not even provoke engaged disagreement. Like all too many New Historicists, he is guilty of demonising older critics (Tillyard is the most notorious example) to enhance the perception of his own approach as new. Thus he writes of *1Henry IV* as being, in comparison with *Measure for Measure* and *Macbeth*, 'a play [...] in which authority seems far less problematical'.[18] Does it really? I have had first-year students who, without prompting, have recognised the Machiavellian aspects of Hal's performances. Can anyone be so insensitive to that radical ambiguity which seems always to present itself as the fundamental condition of the Shakespeare text?

Well, yes: apparently Tennenhouse can. He sees Shakespeare's treatment of Henry V as "hagiography" (p.120), and goes on to call him "Shakespeare's most accomplished Elizabethan monarch" (p.121) - rather missing the point that "Elizabethan monarch" is an odd term to apply to a man who reigned from 1413 to 1422. Greenblatt is certainly rather more sensitive than this to the less pleasant aspects of Hal's character, but when it comes to other areas of the text, this most modern of critics in fact begins to sound alarmingly old-fashioned: "We may find, in Justice Shallow's garden, a few twilight moments of release from this oppressive circumstantial and strategic constriction, but Falstaff mercilessly deflates them - and the puncturing is so wonderfully adroit, so amusing, that we welcome it" (p.39). What distinguishes this from a far older type of criticism, now denigrated as 'liberal humanism'? In a blind reading test, I would assign this passage on stylistic grounds, except for the one phrase "oppressive circumstantial and strategic constriction", to a Victorian critic, magisterial in his use of 'we', benign in his willingness to find pleasure even in the deflating of what he had previously found pleasurable. There is more zest in Greenblatt's invocation of Hariot's glossary of Algonquin vocabulary as a parallel to Hal's acquisition of canting, but ultimately he can push this analysis no further than Warwick has already done for him, in a passage which he quotes. When it comes to actual engagement with the texts, both Greenblatt and Tennenhouse fall decidedly flat; moreover, both subscribe to a tendency of devoting so much time to the exposition of their reading frameworks that the readings themselves can be only sketchily worked through.

A very different set of problems bedevils Emily Bartels' reading of Marlowe's *Edward II* in *Spectacles of Strangeness*. Her affiliation with the techniques of New Historicism is clear from the outset: in the introduction to the volume, she declares that "[t]o understand the historical and ideological import of [Marlowe's] representations is vital to an understanding of the cultural and individual self-fashioning of the Renaissance".[19] Her terminology pays obvious homage to Greenblatt's early book *Renaissance Self-Fashioning from More to Shakespeare*, a debt which she almost immediately avows at the same time as she seeks to register distance from certain aspects of Greenblatt's practice:

> My approach has clearly been shaped by new historicist criticism, but in arguing that Marlowe's plays are finally subversive my book offers an important exception to the new historicist tendency, still being reiterated even as it is beginning to be challenged, to read subversive texts as inevitably playing into the coercive ideologies they seem to resist. I also have attempted to historicize the plays in a way that gives a 'thicker description' of a complex cultural phenomenon.    (Introduction, p.xv)

Despite arguing for genuine subversion, however, she nevertheless follows standard New Historicist practice in several other respects. Assuming "the intense interconnectedness of theatrical and extra-theatrical discourse" (Introduction, p. xvi), she opens her reading of *Edward II* by explaining that "[b]efore turning to Marlowe, I want to consider how sodomy figured within the social discourses of the early modern period" (p.145). In itself, this might well be fruitful. Where Bartels' approach seems to me profoundly problematic, however, is in its resolute refusal to engage with any *other* discourses of the early modern period.

Unlike both Greenblatt and Tennenhouse, Bartels does indeed pay attention to the pastness of the past. Equally, she does instantiate a model of reality - as opposed to unceasing circulations of fictionality and textuality - against which she gauges the representative strategies of the Marlovian text. Looking, in many ways, more like an old historicist than a new, she repeatedly refers back to her preferred historical account of the reign of the 'real' Edward II as a way of grounding her discussion of Marlowe. It is perhaps eccentric to rely so heavily on the account of only one historian, but the work she cites (Natalie Fryde's *The Tyranny and Fall of Edward II, 1321-1326*) is published by Cambridge University Press, and thus benefits from an aura of respectability, as well as being relatively recent (1979). But what she consistently fails to acknowledge is that Marlowe's play and Fryde's historical account are not reworkings which can simply be held in parallel, for they are written for vastly different purposes and, above all, for vastly different historical periods. I have no idea what material circumstances shaped the composition and publication of Natalie Fryde's monograph, but I cannot suppose that the real danger of imprisonment and / or maiming if she failed to please the state authorities was one of them. For Marlowe, such potential consequences were by no means out of the question (as the eventual manner of his death might seem to suggest); equally, an eye on the political preferences of the prevailing regime undoubtedly informed the discursive strategies of Holinshed's *Chronicle*, the third text to which Bartels insistently harks back. One cannot reasonably read either Marlowe's or Holinshed's recensions of the reign of Edward II without remembering the dominant ideologies of the period for which they wrote.

And yet this is precisely what Bartels does. Leaning heavily on Fryde, as she willingly acknowledges in a footnote, she discourses blandly of "Edward II [...] whose reign was one of the most unstable in the history of the English monarchy [...] during Edward's time, the authority of the king (who was elected) had not yet been clearly established" (p.147). Edward II's reign was indeed disturbed, but as a contender for "one of the most unstable" it must find itself challenged by those of

Richard II, King John, Henry VI, King Stephen, Richard III, Henry III, and even, arguably, Henry VII (featuring no fewer than three impostors, one of whom, Perkin Warbeck, gave the crown quite considerable trouble), which perhaps tends to make the distinction seem less notable. As for the electivity of the kingship, this was theoretically true: but how much practical applicability did the idea have? After (and arguably including) the contention between Stephen and Maud, there was no claim for the kingship which did not include an argument based on genealogical inheritance; doubt about the correct inheritor was focused not on this principle but on the proper workings of primogeniture, usually in the absence of a son or in the face of the suspected adultery of a queen. Loades suggests that "Henry VI had a son of undoubted legitimacy when York was recognised as his heir",[20] but the point, for Elizabethans at least, was that the legitimacy of Edward of Lancaster was *not* undoubted: his mother, Margaret of Anjou, was widely believed to have taken a lover, and his alleged father to be an innocent incapable of his begetting. The Wars of the Roses were motivated not by a belief that the monarchy was elective but rather by a claim that, in bypassing the rights of Lionel of Antwerp's inheritrix in favour of a male cousin, the fundamental principles of heredity had been misconstrued. Even more to the point for Marlowe's audience, whatever debates had been generated about the succession to both Henry VIII and Elizabeth I, they had never involved the proposal of any candidate without a blood-claim, however remote.

Bartels herself seems less than convinced about the importance of electivity when she summarises Holinshed's views on Edward II:

> The deposition becomes a "lamentable ruine", brought about by those who "ought" to have showed their sovereign "dutifull love and obedience". Its only benefit is that it secures the line, the nobles otherwise threatening to bar Edward's son from the throne - insisting that "the people" "in respect of the[ir] evil will" (thus incriminated) "would not faile but proceed to the election of some other that should happilie not touch him in linage" [...] The supremacy of the monarch prevails, and the center of power remains secure. (p.149)

This comment performs, in fact, two functions, one effectively acknowledged, and the other not. Ostensibly, it reinforces Bartels' argument by providing evidence that the nobles, at least, had contemplated bestowing the throne against the principle of primogeniture, and that Holinshed knew this. Less obviously, but with at least equal force, it also registers Holinshed's own profound revulsion at such an idea. He, at least, privileges inheritance over election. And that, of course, is precisely what we would expect; for whatever the situation may have been understood to be in the fourteenth century, it had changed beyond recognition by the sixteenth. It would be a brave man indeed who flatly asserted, while a Tudor was alive, that the English monarchy was elective. It was hardly the kind of argument to which Elizabeth I, who so prided herself on her resemblance to her father and her grandfather, was likely to take kindly; indeed she repeatedly ordered Parliament not to concern themselves with the issue of the succession.

It is this Elizabethan context which Bartels consistently ignores in her discussion of Marlowe's redaction of the story of Edward II. There is, astonishingly, no mention at all in the book's index of Elizabeth I, although the Queen is referred to, passingly, in discussion of plays other than this one. At one point in her argument, she focuses on the nobles' use of excuses to hedge around their conduct:

> Instead of placing the power of the kingship at issue, the nobility (and historians siding with them) justified what might otherwise be labeled treason, the uncertainties in the power structure notwithstanding, 'by claiming that they were attacking not the king's proper authority but one perverted by the counsel of evil favorites'. Recountings of the reign that bring in the issue of sodomy follow suit. (pp.147-8)

In a footnote to this, she adds that "[i]nterestingly, as Fryde makes clear, this excuse was not unique to the opposition under Edward; throughout the medieval period, as the powers of kingship were being defined and contested, the same strategy was deployed" (p.202, fn. 21). Use of this classic apologia was not, however, confined merely to the mediaeval period; rather, it is a perennial feature of revolts that still persists after Marlowe's lifetime - the Essex rebellion, for instance, was aimed, at least nominally, not at the Queen herself but at the councillors (chief among them the Cecils) who had incurred the Earl's displeasure by, he felt, thwarting his prospects. Tudor political thought would be sharply aware of the significant distinction between revolts which aimed at the actual replacement of the monarch - like the moves to crown, variously, Lambert Simnel, Perkin Warbeck, Lady Jane Grey, and Mary, Queen of Scots - and those which aimed merely at producing a modification of policy, like the Pilgrimage of Grace; the two types of insurrection were treated in different ways (though one of the factors which made Perkin Warbeck peculiarly menacing to Henry VII was that his personal claims became interwoven with a Cornish anti-policy revolt).

When Holinshed recounts the nobles' use of this disclaimer, therefore, his narrative must inevitably be coloured by a sharp awareness of his readers' understanding of the precise status of such an assertion and of the reasons underlying its use. But in Bartels' account Holinshed seems surprisingly divorced from any such considerations or shaping context, as she remarks that "[t]hough Holinshed seems to switch allegiance several times from the king to the barons to the king, he supports the absolute power of the monarchy" (p.148) - as though any other stance were reasonably open to a historian writing under the Tudors. For some time now, speaking of "the need to avoid the censor" has, it is true, become virtually a knee-jerk reaction in discussions of Elizabethan drama; but that does not mean that it is better to ignore totally the constraints within which authors - historians as well as dramatists - had to work, as John Hayward was to find to his cost when his representation of Henry IV and Richard II proved to be too near the knuckle for Elizabeth I.

Occasionally, however, it is not only the use of context but of text itself that poses problems in Bartels' reading of *Edward II*. This is particularly true of her discussion of Isabella:

> Though it is Isabella rather than Edward who is accused of showing bad faith within the marriage, the question Holinshed asks of her - "what will not a woman be drawne and allured unto, if by evil counsell she be once assaulted?" - points glaringly though indirectly to Edward, to the one renowned for succumbing to such counsel and his "owne fansie and will." That this excoriation erupts within the account of the Spensers points the finger also at them, setting their position against the queen's, as if their relation to the one "that should be most deere unto hir" is somehow responsible for the division within the marriage. (pp.152-3)

I really think this is not fair play. The reading strategy being covertly deployed here has, unannounced, suddenly switched from a historicist to, effectively, a psychoanalysing one, using Holinshed's juxtapositions to argue not for chronological or thematic connection but an unspoken (and therefore, presumably, all the more powerful and deep-rooted) psychological association which, unknown to the unsuspecting author, has radically conditioned his text. The same denial (or mystification) of authorial agency underpins the suggestion that the rhetorical question which the misguided Holinshed thought he was addressing to Isabella was actually being fired by his unruly psyche at Edward. This postulates a Holinshed open to a quite remarkable degree of open-mindedness about gender identity.

Actually, it might well seem more germane to think of Holinshed as not being so spectacularly enlightened as to imagine the proverbial faults of women being equally present in men, but as more of a child of the cultural assumptions of his time (this is, after all, the way that New Historicist critics themselves have traditionally inscribed those they choose to write about). The image of a woman "by evill counsell [...] once assaulted" may seem to Bartels to be obviously suggestive of Edward, but to me it is much more directly reminiscent of Eve, and I think that it briefly but concisely evokes a number of Elizabethan commonplaces about the inherently fallible nature of woman. A contextualising reading would, therefore, seem to be much more valuable than a psychoanalysing one, especially a psychoanalysing one which wilfully ignores the cultural assumptions that go to shape and pattern the psyche (recent American feminist scholarship has been just as scathing about the transhistorical familial and affective structures posited by psychoanalysis as it has about the New Historicism's own notorious indifference to issues of gender). It seems particularly ironic that it is in the work of a female New Historicist writer that we meet such an extraordinary example of refusing to acknowledge the deeply inscribed inequalities which structure all Renaissance representations of gender, and of insisting that instead of being about what intuitively it *is* about, the passage must instead be using an apparent interest in gender to address some other issue.

It would, however, presumably be in vain to expect an informed account of Elizabethan ideologies of gender from Bartels, since we have already had the earlier comment that Holinshed

> nonchalantly announces the king's marriage almost immediately after describing Gaveston's arrival and influence at court and then later announces Gaveston's marriage just as nonchalantly. This assumption of compatability is not in and of itself so surprising since early modern marriages were not necessarily, exclusively or primarily, a matter of desire, especially in royal households. (p.152)

What "assumption of compatability"? Holinshed makes no such claim, and it would be odd if he did - odd, indeed, if the word or indeed the concept of compatability was present either in his emotional or his lexical vocabulary. Again, his text is being read for him to ensure that conjunctions of events which may have been motivated by many different sorts of narrative or thematic considerations are insistently led as yielding psychological truths. Bartels' own sentence then goes on effectively to deconstruct itself when she juxtaposes the supposed "compatability" with the disclaimer that "early modern marriages were not necessarily, exclusively or primarily, a matter of desire, especially in royal households". This is fair enough; but surely she understates the case. Enough work has been done on the emergent ideology of romantic love to show how fragile it was, and how extensively marriage theory was governed by discourses of place, obedience and control. It is hardly credible to assume, then, that just because Holinshed makes no comment on the marriages of either Edward or Gaveston this automatically implies that he must have assumed that they and their wives were going to live happily ever after. In a classic move of mystification, through the guise of uncovering the unspoken psychological truth of the text, this strategy has actually written onto it a quite inappropriate set of concerns which will serve the interests of its own reading procedure while masquerading as inherent.

The concentration on Holinshed has been, in typical New Historicist manner, merely a prelude to engagement with Marlowe proper. It is, however, unfortunate that since Holinshed has already been used as a means of contextualisation, there is still no attempt to situate *Edward II* within any other contemporary Elizabethan discourses or practices, even when these seem to be urgently required. Bartels comments, for instance, that "Edward's claims to absolute authority, against the dictates of his father and the advice of his peers, are as legitimate and as problematic as the nobility's assumption of 'right'" (p.159). But how do Marlowe's representations of this conflict relate to sixteenth-century debates on the nature of rule, being promulgated in Bodin, and made live issues by the vicissitudes of the reign of Henry VIII and their effect on the English succession? Similar resonances clamour for consideration when it comes to Edward's chief departure from tradition: "Edward has begun 'to slaughter noble men' (4.1.8), actions which historians have suggested as a legitimate foundation for revolt because he acted without advice and without precedent. (The nobility had never before been executed by a monarch)" (p.160). Despite the reference to "historians", the footnote is, once again, to Fryde alone, and, once again, the sixteenth-century framework for Marlowe's representation of this fourteenth-century ruler seems urgently relevant

Kings might never have slaughtered the nobility before, but they had certainly done so since. Amongst other victims, Henry VIII executed the Duke of Buckingham, his own great-aunt the Countess of Salisbury, his brother-in-law Viscount Rochford, the Earl of Surrey (whose father the Duke of Norfolk was also due to face the axe when Henry himself died) and numerous others of his Plantagenet kin; Edward VI's reign saw the beheadings of his uncles Thomas Seymour, Lord Sudeley, and Edward Seymour, Duke of Somerset; Mary Tudor's those of her cousin, Jane Grey, the Duke of Northumberland, and the Duke of Suffolk, and Elizabeth herself had, by the time Marlowe wrote, sent to the block her cousin the Duke of Norfolk and, of course, Mary, Queen of Scots. Such a catalogue of slaughtered nobles must surely colour the production and reception of Marlowe's representation of Edward II undertaking similar acts. Whatever the original meanings of the king's acts may have been, the possibilities for understanding them have been irrevocably shaped by the intervening Tudor purge of recalcitrant nobility. Moreover, even within the play the idea of the novelty of Edward's actions is considerably complicated when Kent, in a passage Bartels cites, "remind[s] them (and us) of another royal precedent dictating obedience to the king, bringing forth the example of his 'father's days' when Percy 'brav'd Mowberay in presence of the king' and for the affront '*should* have lost his head' [...; emphasis added] and would have, had not the king decided otherwise" (p.161).

Another case where Marlowe clearly writes of Edward in relation to sixteenth-century concerns is when, as in his representation of Doctor Faustus, he takes pains to stress his anti-clericalism. Bartels quotes Edward "vowing to 'fire' [the] crazed buildings of 'Proud Rome', to force 'the papal towers to kiss the lowly ground', and to fill 'Tiber's channel' 'with slaughter'd priests'" (p.171) - again, all without any reference either to the intersection here with anti-Catholic and, specifically, anti-Papal feeling in Marlowe's England, or to Marlowe's representation of such issues elsewhere in his work (let alone the ways in which such issues might have figured in his probable parallel career of spy). New Historicism is resolute in its refusal to privilege the literary and in its determination to recover the text's relationship to other forms of writing and of cultural circulations, but it is a pity if that leads to the ignoring of so prominent a 'figure in the carpet' as Marlowe's determined introduction of anti-Catholic polemic into so many of his plays, as well as his apparently extraneous introduction of Christianity as an issue in the peregrinations of Tamburlaine.

Most problematic of all, however, are the interpretations of the characters' sexuality which Bartels needs to offer to support her central reading of the play as concerned primarily with the speakability of sodomy. She comments of Act 4, Scene 1 that "what is clearly missing even late in the play, as all along, [...] is, in fact, certification of what 'Edward's looseness' really is" (p.160). This fits in, naturally, with her basic thesis that sodomy is essentially silenced and one can only rudimentarily discern an emergent discourse of homosexuality in the period. And yet, with or without certification, performance of the play suggests that the audience rarely has difficulty in understanding precisely what 'Edward's looseness' is. Gaveston, after all, is hardly coy on the subject in his early speeches; and audiences in theatres are accustomed to hearing far subtler hints than his. To suggest that, whatever other Elizabethan discourses may do, the play itself somehow silences sodomy, would need much greater substantiation than this bare assertion.

Equally striking is her treatment of Isabella, of whom she says, "[l]est we view this as a purely political marriage, like Gaveston's to Edward's niece, Marlowe gives Isabella a voice of desire that supersedes politics" (p.169). Again, feminist theory could offer a very different reading of Marlowe's representation of Isabella: rather than automatically and unproblematically 'superseding' politics, her deployment of "a voice of desire" could be seen as irresponsible, as dangerous, as reprehensible, and as placing her firmly within misogynist traditions of characterisation of women. After all, when Edward, in a passage on which Bartels comments, offers to hang a golden tongue round the neck of Isabella, this could well be seen as less a reward than an offensive labelling of her as 'My Lady Tongue', the emblematic opposite to the chaste woman who is represented with a lock and key, signifying her laudable silence, round her neck.[21] The act, indeed, offers Isabella herself as a "spectacle of strangeness"; and so, perhaps, does

Marlowe when he so markedly differentiates her voice from those around her. Just because our own culture's investment in ideologies of desire and romantic love invites us to privilege Isabella's affectively-oriented discourse over the play's representations of more (overtly) political speech, we should not assume that Marlowe would have shared our assumptions.[22]

In sum, we should not let knee-jerk recognition of what we take to be familiar blind us to that strangest source of wonder, the pastness of the past; and it is this elision of the texture of history, in favour of its alleged textuality, that seems to me the most besetting sin, and the most alarming trend, of the New Historicism, particularly in its dealings with history plays, which tend to be written by dramatists with both a more acute sense of the historicity of history, and a greater faith in its potential as a political tool, than the New Historicists themselves seem all too often to show.

In Ben Jonson's *Sejanus*, the annalist Cremutius Cordus is arraigned in the Senate and charged with the writing of politically unsound history. Analogous things happened to living historians in the Tudor and Stuart periods, most prominently to John Hayward, who dabbled in the murky waters of the reign of Henry IV and the usurpation of Richard II. Writers of Renaissance history plays were all too aware that historiography was a profoundly political act, and it was a practice they seem to have seen primarily as running *counter* to the interests of the state as a form of genuine subversion. New Historicism's own theorising of the uses of history allows for little registering of the rather different nuances of the Renaissance historian-dramatist's own theorising of his practice. Bartels, Tennenhouse and Greenblatt read Marlowe and Shakespeare; they even read (though with disputable levels of attention and accuracy) what Marlowe and Shakespeare read. But what they miss is the double-layering effect, the additional strangeness which makes the past's version of its past, and the constitutive structures and particularities of its practices of representing it, different from our longer-sighted overview of them. Doubly different, doubly distanced, the history which forms the New Historicism's subject was itself new once, and it told stories about its own history in ways which may be very different from the way we retell them now.

*Notes*

1. Frank Lentricchia, "Foucault's Legacy: A New Historicism", in *The New Historicism*, ed. H. Aram Veeser (London: Routledge, 1989), pp. 231-42, here p. 234.

2. I am grateful to Anita Roy of Manchester University Press for supplying me with these figures.

3. On the question of such differences see, for instance, Walter Cohen, "Political Criticism of Shakespeare", in *Shakespeare Reproduced*, edited by Jean E. Howard and Marion F. O'Connor (London: Methuen, 1987; reprinted Routledge, 1990), pp. 18-46; with rather different emphasis, Thomas Healy, *New Latitudes: Theory and English Renaissance Literature* (London: Edward Arnold, 1992), p. 61; and Don E. Wayne, "Power, Politics and the Shakespearean text: recent criticism in England and the United States", in *Shakespeare Reproduced*, pp. 47-67.

4. See, for instance, Frank Lentricchia, "Foucault's Legacy", Elizabeth Fox-Genovese, "Literary Criticism and the Politics of the New Historicism", Vincent Pecora, "The Limits of Local Knowledge", and, with a rather different emphasis, Judith Lowder Newton, "History as Usual? Feminism and the 'New Historicism'", all in Veeser's collection *The New Historicism*, and Steven Longstaffe, 'The Politics of the English History Play 1589-1605', unpublished D. Phil thesis, University of York, 1992.

5. Richard Wilson, *Will Power: Essays on Shakespearean Authority* (Hemel Hempstead: Harvester Wheatsheaf, 1993), p. 8; see also Jeffrey N. Cox and Larry J. Reynolds, *New Historical Literary Study* (Princeton: Princeton UP, 1993), p. 4.

6. Wilson, *Will Power*, pp. 16-17.

7. See particularly Joel Fineman, "The History of the Anecdote: Fiction and Fiction", in Veeser, *The New Historicism*.

8. See Lentricchia and Pecora in Veeser, *The New Historicism*. Lynda Boose makes the very interesting suggestion that it is, in fact, the Vietnam war that is particularly responsible for the mindset of New Historicism (see "The Family in Shakespeare Studies; or - Studies in the Family of Shakespeareans; or - The Politics of Politics", *Renaissance Quarterly*, 40 (1986), pp. 707-41, p. 738.

9. I refer particularly to Stephen Greenblatt, *Marvelous Possessions: The Wonder of the New World* (Oxford: Clarendon Press, 1991). On this see Howard Felperin, *The Uses of the Canon: Elizabethan Literature and Contemporary Theory* (Oxford: Clarendon Press, 1990), p. 121.

10. Leonard Tennenhouse, "Strategies of State and political plays: *A Midsummer Night's Dream, Henry IV, Henry V, Henry VIII*", in *Political Shakespeare: New essays in cultural materialism*, ed. Jonathan Dollimore and Alan Sinfield (Manchester: Manchester UP, 1985), pp. 109-28, here p. 112. All future references to Tennenhouse will be to this article and page numbers will be cited in brackets in the text.

11. See Louis A. Montrose, "Professing the Renaissance: The Poetics and Politics of Culture" in Veeser, *The New Historicism*, pp. 15-36, p. 18.

12. Michael D. Bristol, *Shakespeare's America, America's Shakespeare* (London: Routledge, 1990), p. 206.

13. See, for example, Lily B. Campbell, "The use of historical patterns in the reign of Elizabeth", *Huntington Library Quarterly*, 1 (1937-8), pp. 135-67, and A.H. Tricomi, "Philip, Earl of Pembroke, and the analogical way of reading political tragedy", *Journal of English and Germanic Philology*, 85 (1986), pp. 332-45.

14. David Loades, *The Politics of Marriage: Henry VIII and his Queens* (Stroud: Alan Sutton, 1994), p. 3.

15. Loades, *The Politics of Marriage*, p. 3.

16. Neville Williams, *Elizabeth I, Queen of England* (London: Weidenfeld and Nicolson, 1967), p. 352.

17. Though see the stringent critique of his use of both Hariot and Machiavelli offered by Brian Vickers, *Appropriating Shakespeare: Contemporary Critical Quarrels* (New Haven: Yale UP, 1993), pp. 250-7, and by Tom McAlindon in "Testing the New Historicism: 'Invisible Bullets' Reconsidered", forthcoming in *Studies in Philology*. I am grateful to Tom McAlindon for generously allowing me a copy of his essay before publication and to Rowland Wymer for arranging it. I have found both his and Vickers' comments on Greenblatt immensely informative. Where I part company from them is in being able to subscribe to admiration for Hal; the reasons for this are too lengthy to discuss here, but see my forthcoming "Fluellen's Name", in *Shakespeare Studies*, autumn, 1996, and also my forthcoming chapter on the history plays in *The Moment of Marriage in Shakespeare* (Macmillan, 1997).

18. Stephen Greenblatt, "Invisible bullets: Renaissance authority and its subversion, *Henry IV* and *Henry V*", in Dollimore and Sinfield, *Political Shakespeare*, pp. 18-47, p.29. In further references to this article page numbers will be cited in the text.

19. Emily C. Bartels, *Spectacles of Strangeness: Imperialism, Alienation and Marlowe* (Philadelphia: Pennsylvania UP, 1993), introduction, p. xv. All further references to Bartels will be to this book and page numbers will be cited in the text.

20. Loades, *The Politics of Marriage*, p. 3.

21. See Lisa Jardine, *Still Harping on Daughters* (Hemel Hempstead: Harvester, 1983), particularly pp. 48 and 57-8.

22. See esp. Dympna C. Callaghan, "The Ideology of Romantic Love: The Case of *Romeo and Julie*", in Dympna Callaghan, Lorraine Helms and Jyotsna Singh, *The Weyward Sisters:*

*Shakespeare and Feminist Politics* (Oxford: Blackwell, 1994), pp. 59-101, for very perceptive comment on the dangers of transhistorical readings of the ideologies of romantic love.

# TRUTH, HISTORY AND STAGE REPRESENTATION: THE *HENRY VI* PLAYS AT STRATFORD UPON AVON

## Michael Scott
### (De Montfort University)

For Francis Bacon writing his famous essay *Of Truth* it was clearly possible, from his position of Christian faith, to be able to pity jesting Pilate: "What is Truth; said jesting Pilate; And would not stay for an Answer". In Christian ideology Pilate turned his back on the very embodiment of Truth in the person of Jesus of Nazareth. Such security in a universality of faith is not the dominant ideology of the twentieth century but, nevertheless, as Bacon continues, there is an interest and perception evident in the essay even for a secular audience and also perhaps even a little irony:

> Certainly there be that delight in Giddinesse; and count it a Bondage, to fix a Beleefe; Affecting Freewill in Thinking, as well as in Acting. And though the Sects of Philosophers of that Kinde be gone, yet there remaine certain discoursing Wits, which are of the same veines, though there be not so much Bloud in them, as was in those of the Ancients. But it is not only the Difficultie, and the Labour, which Men take in finding out of *Truth*; Nor againe, that when it is found, it imposeth vpon mens Thoughts; that doth bring *Lies* in fauour: But a naturall, though corrupt Loue, of the *Lie* it selfe.[1]

The 'corrupt love of the lie itself' it might be argued, is the very essence of theatre. It has been so since drama's development in fifth century Attica, as is apparent, in one of our earliest theatrical records which tells of Solon's rebuke of Thespis:

> Thespis, at this time, beginning to act tragedies, and the thing, because it was new, taking very much with the multitude [...] Solon [...] went to see Thespis himself [...] act: and after the play was done, he addressed him, and asked him if he was not ashamed to tell so many lies before such a number of people; and Thespis replying that it was no harm to say or do so in a play, Solon vehemently struck his staff against the ground: "Ah",

said he, "if we honor and commend such a play as this, we shall find it some day in our business."[2]

Solon had a moral concern about the profession of lies as did Plato, but the theatre has continued on its way. When Peter Shaffer wrote his play on Mozart, *Amadeus*, a colleague of mine with a deep love of music was not alone in being indignant. There was no historical truth in the narrative Shaffer gave to Salieri, and yet the play, and later the film, seemed to affirm that Mozart's death was historically brought about by his jealous colleague. Though attacked by the historical (and musical) purists Shaffer's play was widely popular with an international audience. The same outrage did not occur with Robert Bolt's *A Man for All Seasons,* which praised Thomas More; but Edward Bond's *Bingo,* which depicted Shakespeare at the close of his life as a hard-hearted man of property, has not always found universal praise. What historical authority has Bond for depicting "the greatest of English poets" in such an unfavourable light?

The popular historian, Michael Wood, once implied during his brilliantly dramatic historical programmes on television that the present constructs its own history. It is a populist statement but ironically it has a certain currency in the context of debates on the new historicism. Brian Vickers instructively writes:

> New Historicism, like so many branches of contemporary criticism, is more interested in present theories than in the past. Hence the influence of Foucault's middle period work on power and knowledge, on discipline and punishment, as he moved from studying hospitals and clinics to prisons - as if the whole of human society consisted of those who devised and administered repressive institutions and those who suffered from them.[3]

The interpretation of history naturally implies choice. It involves the ideology of the historian within his own cultural context. No doubt E.M.W. Tillyard has been correctly criticised by the new historicists and others for his ideological naivety, but does the fact that Alan Sinfield or Jonathan Dollimore proclaim their own ideological intentions mitigate the bias in their scholarship?[4] It would be naive to

## The *Henry VI* Plays

think so. In January 1993 the former Chancellor of the Exchequer, Nigel Lawson, proclaimed Shakespeare to be a Tory, asserting that the dramatist espoused Tory values.[5] In December 1994 the former Home Secretary, Kenneth Baker, during the BBC's *Bard on the Box* series followed a Tillyardian line of belief in the chain of being, by quoting Ulysses' speech from *Troilus and Cressida:*

> Take but degree away, untune that string,
> And hark what discord follows  (1.3. 109-110)[6]

Baker affirmed that this demonstrated Shakespeare's personal belief in the order of things. He was immediately rebuffed by the current Director of the Shakespeare Institute, Stanley Wells, who argued that for anyone to say so was to engage in a fallacy. Shakespeare, Wells asserted, created a range of characters who had different viewpoints. We could not know from their lines Shakespeare's own philosophy. Yet in 1970 the former Artistic Director of the Royal Shakespeare Company, Peter Hall, reflecting on his renowned production (with John Barton) of the *Henry VI* plays, *The Wars of the Roses*, quoted exactly the same lines, noting:

> There is a difference between learning and understanding. As a student I never felt there was much life in this theory (of degree) - perhaps because I learnt it as a mechanical set of rules. But as I worked year in and year out on Shakespeare, I began to see it not as a relic of medievalism but as a piece of workable human pragmatism, humanitarian in its philosophy and modern and liberal in its application.[7]

In the same introduction, Hall also quoted a speech by the Labour politician Richard Crossman, made in 1964. Crossman stated:

> The truth is that in Shakespeare his histories came a great deal nearer to the real motives of our contemporary political world than those critics who viewed him through Victorian or Edwardian blinkers. The July plot (against Hitler) is Shakespearean tragedy precisely because it is concerned with the politics of naked power and the ethics of treason. The German who cannot be a good German without betraying his country has always understood Shakespeare better than the Englishman safe on his uninvaded island.[8]

Conservative or Labour, the urge to assert Shakespeare's historical truthfulness is always present; but what happens when history meets theatre in production?

A professional dramatist realises that theatrical effect relies as often as not on conflict. Shakespeare was clearly aware of this and, as is well known, was unafraid of altering historical facts in order to sharpen the dramatic situation. When, at the opening of *1 Henry IV*, Bolingbroke makes a comparison between Hal and Hotspur, a historically fallacious seed is sown for the play's dramatic effect:

> See riot and dishonour stain the brow
> Of my young Harry. O, that it could be proved
> That some night-tripping fairy had exchanged
> In cradle clothes our children where they lay,
> And called mine Percy, his Plantagenet!
> Then would I have his Harry, and he mine.
> But let him from my thoughts.
> (1.1. 84-90)

The passage does not just set forth the conflict between the King and his son, but also the rivalry between the two young nobles, Prince Hal and Hotspur. No "night-tripping fairy" could ever have exchanged Hal and Hotspur in their cradles. Historically it would have been impossible. Hotspur was of King Henry's generation, not of his son's, as Kenneth Muir reminds us, with reference also to Daniel's *Civil Wars* and the dramatic fight between the two "youths":

> Hal saves the King's life and fights with Hotspur in single combat, two points in which Daniel and Shakespeare improve on the chroniclers, although the dramatist might well have decided, without Daniel's example, to end the rivalry between Hal and Hotspur foreshadowed in *Richard II*, with such combat. The historical Hotspur was thirty-nine at the time of his death; Daniel and Shakespeare make him the same age as the prince.[9]

Shakespeare, whether or not he was following Daniel, was clearly ready to ignore the factual history of the chroniclers so as to make effective theatre. Interestingly enough, Muir in describing this fact uses the word "improve". Shakespeare "improved" on the chroniclers. Such critical language raises interesting issues. Did Shaffer, for example, "improve" on historical knowledge to establish the fictional conflict, to the point of death, between Mozart and Salieri? Did Robert Bolt "improve" on history in his portrayal of Cromwell and More in *A Man for All Seasons*?

Historical drama is not necessarily about history. Bond's *Bingo* concerns the reception and veneration of Shakespeare as an exemplar of universal virtues or truths through the centuries. Bond overtly rejects Ben Jonson's eulogy printed in the commendatory verses prefacing the *First Folio* (1623):

> Triumph, my Britain, thou hast one to show
>     To whom all scenes of Europe homage owe.
> He was not of an age, but for all time,
>     And all the muses still were in their prime
> When like Apollo he came forth to warm
>     Our ears, or like a Mercury to charm!     (Vss. 41-6)

In his essay "The Rational Theatre" Edward Bond writes "Shakespeare is not for all time, and even in his own time he was in many ways already out of date." [10] Thus in *Bingo* the contemporary dramatist creates an historical fiction, or rather a fictional history, to reduce current trends of deification by middle-class audiences which use Shakespeare to confirm and satisfy their own deep-seated bourgeois ideology. *Bingo* is not about history, but about the present. In writing in this way Bond merely speculates on possible historical scenarios. Shakespeare may well have done the same. The critical industry - of which the present writer is naturally a part - has thereby been given plenty of scope for further speculation, for the cut and thrust of academic argument. Geoffrey Bullough's scholarly eight volumes recording the sources of Shakespeare's plays[11] have helped spawn theses of conjecture, argument and counter-argument, as demonstrated again, for example, by Kenneth Muir writing on *Richard II:*

> It is often said that the published accounts of the reign of Richard II showed a Lancastrian bias, and it is implied that for dramatic reasons

Shakespeare was compelled to give a more sympathetic portrait of his hero. Yet it is obvious from Elizabeth I's identification of herself with Richard at the time of the Essex rebellion, the censoring of the deposition-scene in the early editions of the play, the difficulties which beset Hayward for his history of Henry IV (which begins with the deposition of Richard), and the unambiguous teaching of the *Homilies* that it would have been impossible for a dramatist to approve openly of Richard's desposition, even if he had wanted to do so - which Shakespeare did not. In fact, all the sources of the play exhibited considerable sympathy for Richard: Holinshed, after discussing Richard's virtues and vices, is outspoken in condemning the way he was treated.[12]

Unlike Bond, who publishes a preface to *Bingo* in which he states, for example, ".... I admit that I am not really interested in Shakespeare's true biography in the way a historian might be. Part of the play is about the relationship between any writer and society",[13] Shakespeare does not tell us what he did or did not "want to do". Neither does he tell us what he did or did not believe. Critics can only speculate and in that speculation reflect their own preconceptions with life, whether Tory or Labour, religious or secular, new historicist or cultural materialist.

This is no less true on stage in the production of Shakespeare's dramatic constructions of historical events. In 1963, the Royal Shakespeare Company, under the direction of Peter Hall, began what was to become a modern trend in the production of Shakespeare's history plays. This was to present the three parts of *Henry VI* together with *Richard III* as a cycle. The following year *Richard II*, 1 *Henry IV*, 2 *Henry IV* and *Henry V* joined the repertoire in an historically chronological order. *Richard II* opened 15 April, 1 *Henry IV* and 2 *Henry IV*, 16 April, *Henry V*, 3 June, 1, 2, 3 *Henry VI*, (adapted) 29 July and *Richard III* 20 August. Thus, medieval English history from the reign of Richard II to the accession of Henry VII could thereby be seen in its dramatic entirety at the Royal Shakespeare Theatre, through the year. Peter Hall and his companion directors John Barton and Clifford Williams were following the cyclic movement of history according to what Tillyard regarded as the two tetralogies.[14] But they were not

## The *Henry VI* Plays

following Shakespeare. The plays were certainly not written in such a narrative order and even if they had been, Hall and Barton were not intent on slavishly following the Shakespearean texts. In 1963 they had condensed the three *Henry VI* plays into two. They then produced *Richard III* as the concluding play of a cycle, which in total they termed *The Wars of the Roses*. The 12,350 lines which comprise the four original plays were reduced to 7,450, of which, Barton tells us, 6,000 came from the original texts leaving 1,450 newly written, mainly by Barton himself.[15] The primary reason for the adaptation was not intellectually thematic but commercial, as Barton records:

> We decided at the outset that if we were to stage the *Henry VI* plays at all we would have to condense the three plays into two. The decision was strictly practical. Although it is very much part of the Royal Shakespeare Company's policy to present the lesser-known plays in the canon, we have perforce to be cautious about the number of rarities we include in our repertory in a given year. Economically, it is essential for the company to play to large audiences. We have found more often than not our box-office returns depend not so much on the quality of a production, as on how well known a particular play happens to be [...] For this reason alone, to have performed the three *Henry VI* plays as they stand was out of the question.[16]

This financial expedient was justly rewarded, during the 1963 season, in the transfer to the Aldwych Theatre in January 1964, where the first all-day performance was given on 11 January, and then in the production's transfer back to Stratford to run on from "the second tetralogy". Later *The Wars of the Roses* were presented by the BBC and the book of the television presentation was published in 1970. Hall and Barton had clearly been successful in developing a theatrical event which was commercially attractive.

Simultaneously they also framed their cycles within the super-power politics of the 1960s. It was the era of the USA and the USSR sizing up to each other. The Cuban missile crisis had occurred in 1962 when the world had come perilously close to a nuclear holocaust in the cause of big power politics. Peter

Brook's production of *King Lear*, which played from 1962 to 1964 with Paul Scofield portraying the King in the context of Beckett's *Endgame*, reflected the absurdity, not only of human action, but of existence itself. By 1964 at the RSC's Aldwych Theatre, Brook was producing Peter Weiss' *Marat/Sade*, an anarchic catastrophe of intellectualism declined into violence, revolution, hatred, sexuality and madness. The world in these years was felt by many to be on the verge of destruction. The political stakes were high; and power, ever-present in the two mighty nuclear arsenals, was dreadful in its "fearful symmetry" (Blake). Intellectually, the Stratford directors were influenced by the Polish scholar, Jan Kott, whose book, *Shakespeare Our Contemporary*, they had read in manuscript. Kott, who had fought with the Polish army and had belonged to the underground movement during the Nazi occupation, was deeply aware of totalitarian despotism, conflict and tyranny. His reading of Shakespeare's history plays, often widely generalised in statement many of which have been attacked, most recently by cultural materialists and new historicists, was a reading that manifested the mid-twentieth century understanding of social victimisation at its most grotesque. In a particularly influential passage Kott wrote:

> There are no gods in Shakespeare. There are only kings, every one of whom is an executioner, and a victim, in turn. There are also living, frightened people. They can only gaze upon the grand staircase of history. But their own fate depends on who will reach the highest step, or leap into the abyss. That is why they are frightened. Shakespearean tragedy, unlike ancient tragedies, is not a drama of moral attitudes in the face of immortal gods; there is no fate which decides the hero's destiny. The greatness of Shakespeare's realism consists in his awareness of the extent to which people are involved in history. Some make history and fall victims to it. Others only think they make it, but they, too, fall victims to it. The former are kings; the latter - the king's confidants who execute their orders and are cog-wheels in the Grand Mechanism. There is also a third category of people: the common citizens of the kingdom. Grand historical events are performed on the fields of battle, in the royal palace and the Tower prison. But the Tower, the royal palace, and the battlefields are actually situated in England. That was one of the discoveries of Shakespeare's genius which helped to create modern historical tragedy.[17]

## The *Henry VI* Plays

This was the setting for *The Wars of the Roses* and the production reflected, in its design and emphasis the superpower world in which the commoners were pawns in the strife between their Lords for political supremacy. The power struggles were the dominant feature. Peter Hall wrote to John Barton as the latter was working on 1 *Henry VI*:

> The movement of the play seems to be governed by the idea of a pendulum swinging with general regression from the triumphs of Henry V. There isn't a central figure, and I do not believe you should try to make one. The movement of the play derives from the opposition of two principles, one patriotic and constructive, but *misguided*, the other destructive and selfish. There is a feeling of growing disaster. There's the antithesis and interplay between strife and concord, peace and war at home and abroad.
> To sum up I am as worried as you by this first play. Be bold.[18]

Peter Hall's mode of discourse in this letter seems to reflect the time of writing; Kennedy having to be bold in standing up to Khrushchev. The climate was one of coldness, of ideologies competing for total supremacy; a coldness demonstrated not only in the narrative script that Barton created, or the macho characteristics Hall demanded from his highly talented cast, but in the set itself, as the designer John Bury recalls:

> *The Wars of the Roses* was designed in steel - the steel of the plate armour - the steel of the shield and the steel of the broadsword. In this hard and dangerous world of our production, the central image - the steel of wars - has spread and forged anew the whole medieval landscape. On the flagged floors of sheet steel tables are daggers, staircases are axeheads, and doors the traps on scaffolds. Nothing yields: stone walls have lost their seduction and now loom dangerously - steelclad - to enclose and to imprison. The countryside offers no escape - the danger is still there in the iron foliage of the cruel trees and, surrounding all, the great steel cage of war.[19]

Bury's language echoes that of Hall as his seemed to echo that of the world in which he lived. It did not necessarily follow that of Shakespeare, but to a large extent that was admissible in what he was attempting to do. The plays had been contemporised, and in their condensed appearance they clearly struck a popular chord with the audience of the 1960s. In this production Shakespeare's history plays were not about history but about the present, not Shakespeare's present but Hall's.

It is interesting to note the development of the history play at Stratford since that time, especially the *Henry IV* plays. There have been productions of individual plays such as *Richard III* with, for example, Norman Rodway (1970), Ian Richardson (1975), Alan Howard (1980), and Anthony Sher's much acclaimed spider-like interpretation (1984), or *Henry V* with, for example, Kenneth Branagh's notable portrayal for Adrian Noble in 1984 which was so influential on Branagh's subsequent film version; however, there has also been a desire to keep to the large-scale historical event. This was seen particularly with Terry Hands' production of the three parts of *Henry VI* in 1977 and Adrian Noble's production of the three *Henry VI* plays condensed into two, *Henry VI* and *Edward IV* played in repertory with *Richard III* as *The Plantagenets* in 1988. What became evident comparing 1963/64 with these productions was the movement away from big-power politics.

By 1977 Terry Hands was stressing the fact that he was producing the plays in their Elizabethan texts. For him the Barton-Hall adaptation, though appropriate for the sixties, would look naive in the seventies. The characterisation for his cycle was not to be dominated, therefore, by power but by petty selfishness, the motives of the small-minded seeking supremacy for childish reasons.

Adrian Noble's 1988 audiences were again confronted with an adaptation, but this time one which stressed greed and ambition. Richard was biding his time, manipulating events for his own aggrandisement. As *Edward IV* closed, Anton Lesser's Richard of Gloucester swung round to the audience and spat out the word "Now". *Richard III* followed on in sequence, opening, of course, with the same word. Hands' production in the seventies stressed, in the pettiness of its strife, the political impotence of that era. The scene, for example, in 3 *Henry VI*, 2.5, in which the King witnesses the spectacle first of a son who has killed his father and

## The *Henry VI* Plays

then of a father who has killed his son in the civil wars was highly ritualised - the King unable to move, reflective of a country vacillating about its sense of direction. By 1988 the greed evident in Noble's was indicative of the dominating values of the Thatcherite decade. Once again the theatre was reflecting not so much the ideology but the climate of its contlemporary era and society. Thus in Adrian Noble's introduction to the printed text of his production we find that he saw the focus on the moral issues pervading the play. He does not specifically mention the Miners Strike or the Falklands War and the consequent moral questions surrounding the Thatcher premiership. But this discussion, particularly of the Joan of Arc episodes, is revealing since he categorises the black and white moral choices, evident in the era of "no U-turns":

> Joan, to the English, is a witch who uses demonic powers to defeat the otherwise invincible Talbot; however, to the French she is a great heroine, a peasant girl who humbles and chastens the callow and often hubristic French aristocracy and inspires the nation to victory ... A modern audience is faced with a simple question: who are right, the French or the English? Is she a witch or isn't she? Then, very late in the day we, the audience, are given privileged information, when Joan conjures the devil and demons appear on the stage. Joan goes to her death with no trial and no proof of witchcraft given. In this case, it becomes not an issue of right and wrong, but one of faith.[20]

A "no-U-turn" philosophy is precisely one of faith in the apparent knowledge of moral, social and political certainty. Noble did not have overtly to refer to Mrs Thatcher or the politics of the day. His production naturally revealed a commentary upon a philosophy based on the assured certainties of the moral and political pathway which had been determined. For the Britain of Mrs Thatcher the Argentinians were clearly in the wrong just as surely as the English regarded Joan of Arc of being guilty. The Civil Wars depicted in Noble's production between Lancaster and York were about greed. The Britain of the eighties was not far away.

The early 1990s produced two particularly interesting productions of the histories at Stratford, but both originally in the small theatre, *The Other Place*. In 1992 Sam Mendes produced *Richard III* on its own, with Simon Russell Beale as the King. The play opened in darkness with just the tap of a walking stick as Richard came into the claustrophobic arena. There was a single light bulb, and what ensued proved to be a grotesque relish in the cruelty Richard enacted. The costumes were dull, brown and shabby. These characters were members of the ruling power who could not be bothered about their dress. Even the Queen Elizabeth's red velvet gave an impression of menial practicality. Far gone was the concept of cold steel emphasising power. This was rather a production about bickering, a childishness which in its lack of self discipline allows tyrants to appear in the playground. Richard's final confrontation with Richmond took place in a sandpit. This was nothing more than the cruelties of infantile taunting and viciousness turned into the sexual and violent obscenities of adult life. Richard was unceremoniously strangled to death. As the two concluded their ridiculous fight in Richmond's success Stanley tossed the crown into the sand for the victor. Tyranny, no doubt, had been exposed, but so had the hollowness of political intrigue. Richmond waited for a little and then picked up the crown and, in the manner of the Gower Memorial Prince Hal pose, raised it above his head. Golden light ironically came through open doors emphasising not the glory of majesty but the degeneracy of squabble.

The production revealed another dangerous fact of political commentary and human comprehension. As Charles Spencer (*The Daily Telegraph* 13 August 1992) noted, Simon Russell Beale became attractive to his audience in the audacity of Richard's evil:

> His face is fleshy and corrupt, his manner horribly insinuating. Despite all your best intentions you find yourself, like Lady Anne in the sinister wooing scene, surrendering to his vile personality, both repelled and enthralled.

John Peter (*The Sunday Times* 16 August 1992) likewise was acute in his perception of Beale's portrayal in relation to public views of the career politician, "Like most professional politicians, he is an actor giving a life long performance, but like all good actors, he observes others rather than displays himself".

In 1994 Katie Mitchell produced *Henry VI: The Battle for the Throne* in a similar manner, again at *The Other Place*. This was principally 3 *Henry VI* with some augmentation from Parts One and Two. There was no steel to be found nor sand but rather wood-bark chippings and mud. There were medieval chants and songs and elements of Christian ritual which attempted to give order to the chaos. The cast was young, probably again because of economies demanded by company commercial policy, but in their youth they appeared to demonstrate deliberately a political and social loss of direction and consequently an attempt to find a stability which evaded them in the strife of war. If Mendes' production of *Richard III* was grotesque in representing the sexual perversion of tyranny, Mitchell demonstrated the confusion of adolescence in its entrapment by its own actions, its own historicity. With *The Battle for the Throne* we were three decades away from *The Wars of the Roses*. The era of the Shakespearean epic seemed to have passed. Despite its medieval setting we were actually in the horror of the age of Aids and the confusion of the Balkan peoples. Significantly 3 *Henry VI*, which in the early sixties might not have attracted audiences, was taken, in this admittedly small-scale production, on an acclaimed national and international tour.

Paul Taylor in *The Independent* actually entitled his review "The horror, the horror", perceiving the intensity of Mitchell's vision as related to *The Heart of Darkness* and the enduring political nightmare of war during the twentieth century. Whereas, as Irving Wardle noted in *The Independent on Sunday*, the *Wars of the Roses* revealed the power struggles in "post colonial Africa", this 1994 production reflected the civil wars of Rwanda and former Yugoslavia. It was a production in the tradition not of Hall, Barton, Hands and Noble but of the late Buzz

Goodbody's 1970 'strip cartoon' production of *King John*. Mitchell, as Wardle also commented, was seeing "through the boys' power games. Less 'Pow'! you might say, and more 'Spat'." No longer was the Royal Shakespeare Company exposing the spectacular nature of these history-war plays. It was rather giving a reduced view in keeping with a world movement antagonistic to big power politics and distrustful even of political caricature. Authority cannot be reduced to the comic strip. Political authority cannot construct some form of divine justification as an excuse for its existence and conduct.

Was Solon correct when he castigated Thespis for the lies of the stage? In my view he was not. He failed to understand that drama is in itself a language, a communication through metaphor to its audience about themselves and their society. The representation of history in stage production is rarely about the past. It attempts to communicate what perhaps we used to call truths. Not those truths which are enwrapped in myths people like to believe, but the truths of contemporary issues. Myths are not to be confused with the metaphors of the stage, although they may have their place in those metaphors. Likewise drama is not to be confused with truth itself. Rather it has to be seen as a form of language, a means of communication between people - author (alive or dead), director, actors, designers, audiences. The Royal Shakespeare Company has often been criticised for its experimentation with the Shakespearean text and for its contemporisation of production. Yet, unless it experiments, true communication through drama will not take place. Each production has to be created afresh for its contemporary society because the 'truth' is in the process of the dramatic communication itself. In front of Pilate, Christ kept silent for the most part. It was only when Christ spoke that Pilate turned away. Bacon may have scorned the Governor in the context of a belief in universality and, perhaps, we in the late twentieth century may do so still in the context of a belief in rational discourse. Certainly we should not turn away from the contemporary or the confrontationary in theatre but embrace it in its challenge to us to participate as an audience. The

## The *Henry VI* Plays

post-war productions of the *Henry VI* plays demonstrate that this still can be the case.

*Notes*

1. Francis Bacon, "Of Truth" in *The Essayes or Covnsells Civill and Moral* newly written, 1625 (London: Oxford UP, 1966), p. 5.

2. "Thespis Meets a Critic" in *A Source Book in Theatrical History*, ed. A. M. Nagler (New York: Dover Publications, 1959), p. 3. Taken from Plutarch, *The Lives of the Noble Grecians and Romans*, transl. John Dryden and Arthur Clough (New York: Random House, n.d.), p. 115.

3. Brian Vickers, *Appropriating Shakespeare: Contemporary Critical Quarrels* (New Haven and London: Yale UP, 1993), p. 218.

4. Jonathan Dollimore and Alan Sinfield, eds, *Political Shakespeare: New Essays in Cultural Materialism* (Manchester: Manchester UP, 1985), pviii, note that their approach is ideologically committed to "the transformation of a social order which exploits people on grounds of race, gender and class".

5. *The Independent on Sunday*, 3 January 1993.

6. Quotations from Shakespeare's plays are from *The Complete Works* edited Stanley Wells and Gary Taylor (Oxford: Oxford UP, 1988).

7. Peter Hall, Introduction, *The Wars of the Roses Adapted for the Royal Shakespeare Company from William Shakespeare's Henry VI, Parts I, II, III and Richard III* by John Barton in collaboration with Peter Hall (London: BBC, 1970), p. x.

8. Barton and Hall, pp. xi - xii.

9. Kenneth Muir, *The Sources of Shakespeare's Plays* (London: Methuen, 1977), pp. 93-4.

10. Edward Bond, "The Rational Theatre" in *Bond Plays: Two* (London: Methuen, 1978), p. x.

11. Geoffrey Bullough *Narrative and Dramatic Sources of Shakespeare*, 8 Vols (London: Routledge & Kegan Paul, 1958-75)

12. Muir, p. 53.

13. Edward Bond, Introduction, *Bingo : Scenes of Money and Death* (London: Methuen, 1974), p. vii.

14. See E.M.W. Tillyard, *Shakespeare's History Plays* (London: Chatto & Windus, 1951).

15. See Barton and Hall, p. xvi.

16. Barton and Hall, p. xv - xvi. The *Henry VI* plays had rarely been performed at Stratford until 1963. In 1889 Osmond Tearle directed *Henry VI Part One* taking the part of Talbot. In

1906 Frank Benson directed all three parts, opening on successive nights, 2nd, 3rd, 4th April. Benson played Talbot in Part One, Cardinal Beaufort in Part Two and Richard in Part Three. In the same season he directed *Richard III,* opening on 5 May, playing the title role. He also directed *Richard II,* 30 April, playing Richard; *Henry IV Part Two,* 1 May, playing Hal and *Henry V,* 2 May, playing the King. (In 1905 he had directed *Richard II, Henry IV Part One* and *Part Two* and *Henry V* on successive nights: 1, 2, 3, 4 May). Benson had earlier directed *Henry VI Part Two* in 1899 and 1901 taking the role of the Cardinal each time as he did again in 1909. Following this there were no further productions of *Henry VI* plays at Stratford until 1963.

17. Jan Kott, *Shakespeare Our Contemporary,* 2nd ed. (London: Methuen, 1967), pp. 16-17. From the outset Kott was unpopular with literary critics because of what they saw as a laxity in critical method. His work, however, appealed to the theatre. Subsequently he has found no significant place in the critical debates which have dominated the discipline of literary studies in recent years, but his influence on Shakespearean productions continues to be seen, much to the irritation of some cultural materialists.

18. Barton and Hall, p. xx.

19. John Bury, "The Set" in Barton and Hall, p. 236.

20. *The Plantagenets,* Adapted by the Royal Shakespeare Company from William Shakespeare's *Henry IV Parts I, II, III* and *Richard III* as *Henry VI, The Rise of Edward IV* and *Richard III His Death,* Introduction by Adrian Noble (London and Boston: Faber & Faber, 1989), p. x-xi.

# THE LIMITS OF MODERNITY IN SHAKESPEARE'S *KING JOHN*

### Steve Longstaffe
### (S. Martin's College Lancaster)

Deborah Curren-Aquino, summing up fifty years of critical engagement with Shakespeare's *King John*, identifies a radical break with earlier views of the play in "the tendency in post 1940 scholarship to describe *John* as ambivalent, ambiguous, suspicious, sceptical, questioning and ideologically subversive".[1] The form and tone of *John*, in other words, are recognisably modern. Few critics have gone as far as Sigurd Burckhardt, who in the 1960s asserted that the play documented Shakespeare's **own** modernity, defined as the recognition that order, or "justice and truth at the heart of things", was of human, rather than divine, origin.[2] Burckhardt's position, though not his confidence that he could show that "when he wrote *King John*, or quite possibly in writing it, Shakespeare became a 'modern'", is echoed in Virginia Vaughan's claim of 1989 that the play "like Shakespeare's other history plays" depicts a crucial point in the inauguration of "the relativism of the modern age".[3] But for the most part, writers on *John* have avoided such grand narratives of epistemological shifts, and found the play's modernity to be historically produced in a much more local way: as part of a Shakespearian negotiation with chronicle, source play, or the history play genre. What *John* is sceptical about, in other words, is other historical accounts of John's reign, especially regarding their relationship to what might still be termed Tudor ideology. For many critics, Shakespeare's *John* is in antagonistic relation to such "sources" as the anonymous Queen's Men's play *The Troublesome Reign of King John* and the 1587 *Holinshed*, interrogating the writing of history of which these two texts, and the history play as a genre, were part.

Such a *John* appears our contemporary, teasing out aporias and contradictions in Renaissance writings of legitimacy, faith, or patriotism. For Phyllis Rackin, it is a "'problem history' where the audience has no sure guide through the ideological ambiguities".[4] Larry Champion identifies it as "an open-ended chronicle play with historical process transformed into human process, stripped bare of Tudor providentialism and reduced to an individual self-interest that only in its best moments might be communally enlightened".[5] Guy Hamel argues that Shakespeare's "assault on formulas [...] reveals itself in almost every departure from *The Troublesome Reign*".[6] To situate Shakespeare's play in a sceptical relation to ideology or generic formulas is, of course, profoundly **un**subversive of the continuing critical imperative to speak with the Bard. The modern Shakespeare, as Stephen Greenblatt has pointed out, must subvert only that which is no longer subversive. The *John* worthy of modern critics' engagement is produced by a common critical strategy, which is most clearly visible in the conclusion of one of the play's editors that "it would be a crippling limitation of the power of *King John* to tie it too closely to the situation of the 1590s".[7] It is in its implication in the religious politics of the period of the Spanish war that *John* is most clearly un-modern; it is part of the wartime anti-Catholic polemic, something which has been played down in order to produce a modernity which legitimates a continual critical return to the play, and to a lesser extent, to Shakespeare.

It is not surprising that there has been relatively little interest in *John*'s brand of Protestant nationalism of late, for, as David Aers has pointed out, many influential contemporary critics of early modern writing "display a marked lack of interest in Christian traditions, Christian practices and Christian institutions".[8] Mid-century critics, following E. M. W. Tillyard's characterisation of the play as "but mildly Protestant in tone", stressed the "moderation" of the play's anti-Catholic sentiments, whilst identifying an assertion of Protestant nationalism.[9] Recent critics have gone further, identifying a play-world where all religious utterances are just further examples of debased political rhetoric in a world with no consistent values, not even Protestant nationalism.[10]

But how debased is this rhetoric? Specifically, did the kind of language with which John defies the Papal legate Pandulph on his first encounter with him circulate in post-Armada London as a somehow debased version of earlier, more sincere, Tudor coinages? To stretch the 1980s monetary rhetoric further, I suggest that, on the contrary, play rhetoric directed against foreign Catholics wishing to overthrow an English monarch was on the gold standard during this period of war with Spain. John's words themselves are direct as he responds to Pandulph's demands in the name of the Pope:

> Thou canst not, cardinal, devise a name
> So slight, unworthy and ridiculous,
> To charge me to an answer, as the pope.
> Tell him this tale; and from the mouth of England
> Add thus more, that no Italian priest
> Shall tithe or toll in our dominions;
> But as we, under God, are supreme head,
> So under Him that great supremacy,
> Where we do reign, we will alone uphold
> Without th' assistance of a mortal hand:
> So tell the pope, all reverence set apart
> To him and his usurp'd authority.[11]

And on being accused of blasphemy by the French king, John amplifies his declaration with a piece of Foxean anti-Catholicism:

> Though you and all the kings of Christendom
> Are led so grossly by this meddling priest,
> Dreading the curse that money may buy out;
> And by the merit of vild gold, dross, dust,
> Purchase corrupted pardon of a man,
> Who in that sale sells pardon from himself;
> Though you and all the rest so grossly led
> This juggling witchcraft with revenue cherish,
> Yet I alone, alone do me oppose
> Against the pope, and count his friends my foes. (3.1 88-97)

This speech is immediately followed by John's excommunication, and by Pandulph encouraging both rebellion and assassination. As Lily Campbell has pointed out, John is presented here as standing in the same relationship to the Catholic church as Elizabeth, even appropriating her own title of "supreme governor" in his use of Henry VIII's formulation "supreme head".[12] The clarity of John's position here is momentary, however; he does not reach these vituperative heights again. Indeed, he resigns his crown to Pandulph later on. But it is important not to underrate the legitimating power of John's rhetoric. Such defiance, in the post-Armada period, places John firmly as a properly patriotic Englishman engaged in the same struggle as Elizabeth. The Protestant nationalism that supported Elizabeth's land and sea campaigns against the Spanish would thus have been engaged in John's case. Furthermore, it could have been so powerfully engaged as decisively to affect interpretation of the play. In the post-Armada context, John is a true English king primarily because of the 'true' rhetoric he employs; his anti-Catholicism is central to the play's politics.

*King John* is consensually dated to the period between 1587, when the second edition of Holinshed appeared, and 1598, when Francis Meres mentioned in print a Shakespearian *King John*, though it is impossible to know whether that play was the one first printed in 1623.[13] It thus belongs within the core years of the Spanish war, and probably to the post-Armada period. After 1588, however, the national mood was certainly not conducive to a relaxed and sceptical investigation of the possible hypocrisy of religious nationalism. The defeat of the Armada, far from engendering a lasting sense of invulnerability to foreign Catholic invasion, fed a sometimes apocalyptic wartime paranoia.[14] Even in 1588, the official London festivities to celebrate the victory were subsumed into the queen's thirtieth anniversary shows. Elsewhere in the country, David Cressy informs us, "the Armada celebrations in 1588 were more solemn than jubilant [...] the festivities were conducted in a minor key".[15] London, though its strategic importance meant that it was carefully governed, had its share of hardship, and had to cope with returning soldiers threatening to loot Bartholomew Fair in 1589, and with royal demands for men, ships, and money at a time when the capital was also struggling with plague and dearth.[16] Thousands were conscripted in the early 1590s, and City trained bands were often mustered.[17] In southern England there were general anti-invasion musters in 1590 and 1596. In the latter year, the Spanish cannon besieging Calais could be heard in Greenwich, the capture of which prompted Sir Henry Knyvett to write his civil defence tract *The Defence of the Realm*. The Spanish raided Cornwall in 1595, and sent another Armada in 1597.[18]

Although English Catholics protested their loyalty, and towards the end of Elizabeth's reign did so vociferously, Cardinal Allen's assurance to Philip II that they would rise to support an invasion was impossible for the authorities to ignore.[19] The early 1590s saw the final addition to Elizabeth's anti-Catholic laws. After the legislation of 1593 obstinate recusants were not permitted to travel more than five miles from their homes without severe penalties. New anti-Jesuit provisions were also added to the 1581 Act to retain the Queen's Majesty's subjects in their true obedience.[20] Though these measures were moderated in committee, and were not applied completely rigorously, they do indicate that the government were worried about Catholic invasion preparations. The church, naturally, was hardly irenic at this time. Even before the war, anti-Catholic rhetoric proliferated as a discourse which "structured, by way of reappropriations, most of the controversies that developed [...] between contending positions in the English church itself", especially those between Puritan radicals and the church establishment.[21] For the Protestant divine, anti-Roman polemic "was at once an expression of Protestant zeal and an implicit gesture of loyalty to a national church, the Protestantism of whose doctrine was generally acknowledged".[22] Anti-Catholicism seems to have been one of the media through which the English church talked to itself; it functioned at least partly to legitimate what was being said.

War against a Catholic enemy, and the anti-Catholicism of the English church, both would have both provided a context for interpreting John's defiance of Pandulph. In addition, anyone familiar with recent historical accounts of John's reign would have expected to see him presented as a legitimate king undermined by circumstances and Catholic conspiracy. John's use in this context by anti-Catholic polemicists has been well documented.[23] Foxe's account in the *Acts and Monuments* limits itself to religious matters, and places John within the perspective of the struggle between the true church and antichrist. Holinshed's account emphasises that the contemporary sources are Catholic and therefore biased, "scarselie can they afoord him a good word [...] the occasion whereof [...] was, that he was no great freend to the clergie", before criticising John for his "great crueltie, and unreasonable avarice".[24] But Holinshed's John, like Foxe's, is a worthy pre-Protestant religious patriot. Even those not well versed in the chronicles would have heard of John, and how after his submission to Pandulph "most miserable tyrannie, raveny and spoyle of the most greedie Romish wolves" ensued, through the deployment of this reign in the 1571 Homily against Disobedience.[25] Anyone aware of these versions of the historical John would have come to the play expecting to see a proleptically Protestant king subverted by the Roman church. Though Polydore Vergil and John Stow did not write within this representative tradition, their impact on public opinion was likely during the immediate post-Armada period to have been negligible. John does appear in the *Huntington* plays of the later 1590s as a wicked tyrant, but in these plays there is no attempt to address the political agenda of *King John*. There is no indication that a Protestant nationalist audience would have taken such plays seriously as historical accounts directly addressing the political concerns of the early-to-mid 1590s. Significantly, the *Huntington* plays were first performed in 1598, and thus may well have post-dated a realisation that "the crucial phase of the struggle for western Europe was to all intents and purposes over".[26]

## Modernity in *King John*

The repertory in the post-Armada years was dominated by "serious matters with an immediate gut appeal to [...] militarism", in the words of Andrew Gurr.[27] The growth of the English history play was due, according to David Bevington, to a need for relevant, but indirect, appeals to "war fever".[28] Anti-Spanish and anti-Catholic sentiments were common across a range of plays. John's resistance to Pandulph in Shakespeare's drama would have functioned metonymically to link him to contemporary anti-Spanish and anti-Catholic sentiment, and to the Protestant histories and other polemical deployments of the historical John's reign. The ubiquity and strength of anti-Spanish and anti-Catholic sentiment, furthermore, could well have operated so as to produce a strong cathexis for these sentiments and their utterer in the play, conditioning responses to, and interpretations of, it. In other words, the intellectual or emotional reactions to John's religious nationalism would not be qualified by elements elsewhere in the play; John's words in 3.1 would themselves qualify the responses to the rest of the play, including some of its ambiguities, suspicions, scepticisms and questions.

Recent critics read John's rhetoric very differently. For many, the religious nationalism of his speeches function not to mobilise anti-Catholic and anti-Spanish sentiment, but to indicate that such a rhetoric, and such a mobilisation, is more fully present elsewhere, in the *The Troublesome Reign*. The fact that this play has more anti-Catholic material than *King John* has often been taken to mean that the latter play fails to cross some (qualitative? quantitative?) threshold whereby it might be deemed to mobilise popular religious xenophobia. Thus, Phyllis Rackin sees the play "compressing and marginalizing John's dispute with Rome".[29] For M. M. Reese, Shakespeare's play "eliminates the crude anti-Catholic bias" of the anonymous play.[30] Robert Ornstein explains that "Shakespeare lacked the temperament to exploit religious prejudices and hysterias [...] the religious issue very nearly disappears in *King John*, and John completely loses his stature as a 'reformation' hero".[31] John Blanpied agrees that "Shakespeare neutralises the anti-

Papal material, leaving John without a polemical base from which to borrow his authority".[32]

For many, the result of this compression, and consequent neutralisation and marginalization, is a play which, in the words of Virginia Vaughan, presents "politics, not polemics".[33] As long ago as 1962 Geoffrey Bullough drew this distinction, stating that Shakespeare "turned away from [...] sectarian propaganda to emphasise more purely political motives".[34] Such a construction of Shakespeare's *John* (and, of course, *John's* Shakespeare) as drawing a distinction between real politics and un-sophisticated (and explicitly anti-Catholic) rabble-rousing has received much critical support, though earlier writers attribute it to a Shakespearian distaste for "bias" or "rant", or a preference for complexity over simplicity, and later ones more to a textual refusal of the easy closure which a more foregrounded religious element would have allowed or perhaps necessitated.[35] The dominance of Christianity in Renaissance England is perhaps the most effective reminder of Renaissance difference; conveniently, Shakespeare manages to play down that difference and provide a transcendent scepticism for our age of suspicious reading.

As can be seen from Blanpied and Ornstein, the playing down of the religious element also means a John robbed of the legitimating power of religious nationalism. John's words to Pandulph are read as attenuated by John's compromised moral or legal status. Deborah Kehler states that "in the light of his false claim, John's use of divinity to serve his own ends is transparent", while for Philip Edwards "what seems an admirable quality of sturdy national courage is questioned by the moral quality of the speaker, and by his eventual fate in the play".[36] Responses to John's words are conditioned not by their deployment of a powerfully cathected sentiment, but by "character". Even those critics recognising the power of John's words conclude that they are an isolated and anomalous moment, "occasional choric greatness", or an effect "of efficiency, not magnanimity".[37] At best, for Larry Champion, the anti-Catholic John is just one of the "equally persuasive views of the usurper, the would-be murderer, the terror-stricken capitulator, the sufferer, the patriot, and the kingly defender of his nation".[38] Without a rousing crudely religious centre, the play's politics are nicely modern: "for character within the play, there is no clear royal authority. For the audience watching it, there is no unblemished cause and no unquestioned authority to claim their allegiance", in Phyllis Rackin's formulation. David Womersley, though he sees the play as clearly conservative in its conclusions, agrees that it "confronts the question of how one lives in a world without value".[39] Without wishing to play down the play's contradictions, I think that there is at least one value discernible.

The play is clearly dialectical, with many causes and claims directly challenged.[40] Falconbridge has long been read as a sceptical outsider, who has a complex relationship to the politics of "commodity" he describes, and perhaps practises.[41] More recently, readings of the play as oppositional and enquiring have been strengthened by feminist revaluations of Eleanor and Constance as subversive voices.[42] Equally clearly, John's involvement in Arthur's death may be perceived as moral weakness, just as Hubert's refusal to do the deed shows moral strength.[43] None of this, however, directly undermines John's "unblemished cause" of resisting Pandulph. Although he is criticised for much else within the play, the only voices raised against John's defiance are Pandulph's and those foreign kings' loyal to him, which is only to be expected, as they are the targets of John's ire.

The main reasons for the widespread critical perception of the play as modern in its politics are mentioned by Kehler and Edwards above: that John is illegitimate, that he is lacking in "moral quality", and that he later gives his crown, effectively, to the Pope. Of these, the "moral" argument is least persuasive. Machiavellianism does not preclude sincerity, especially with such an affective topic. Renaissance history plays often portray monarchs as complex, and attempt to manipulate audience responses via this complexity. Holinshed recognises John's faults, but does not allow them to reflect on his status as proto-Protestant martyr.

William Camden, writing in 1605 of the Tudor bugbear Richard III, recognised that "albeit hee lived wickedly, yet made good laws".[44] The other two points require more detailed engagement. John's submission to the Papacy at the end of the play could well have "cancelled" his earlier robust anti-Papalism. Through an analysis of the representative strategies used for John's cession I will argue that it may not have done so. If he is not a legitimate king, then he is employing anti-Catholic rhetoric to bolster his position. He need not be shown to believe his own words. If this were so, John's use of religious rhetoric is on a par as a cynical manipulation of language with Richard III's political use of witchcraft accusations in Shakespeare's play and the anonymous *True Tragedy of Richard III*.

John is not illegitimate just because his opponents say he is. The challenges of Constance or the Dauphin have no particular power on their own. Yet for many critics, whether or not they engage with *John's* "modernity", it is axiomatic that John is an illegitimate king, that he is a usurper in possession of the crown when the right lies with Arthur (and, some have added, the true kingliness with Falconbridge).[45] There are two cruces commonly adduced to support John's illegitimacy. Both can be read differently.

The first is a critical exchange in the play's first scene, where John and Eleanor discuss the implications of the French challenge just made on Arthur's behalf. Eleanor reproaches John for not dealing with the question sooner, as "This might have been prevented and made whole/With very easy arguments of love,/Which now the manage of two kingdoms must/With fearful-bloody issue arbitrate" (1.1.35-8). John replies "Our strong possession and our right for us", to which Eleanor retorts, "Your strong possession much more than your right,/Or else it must go wrong with you and me./So much my conscience whispers in your ear,/Which none but heaven, and you and I, shall hear" (1.1.39-43). Most critics follow Reese's conclusion that this shows that "John is king *de facto* and possession is his only 'right'", though Edna Zwick Boris points out that Eleanor is "not denying John's right but emphasising the practical aspect of his advantage

## Modernity in *King John*

over Arthur".[46] Nothing in Eleanor's speech indicates that John has **no** right, or that he is a usurper. Eleanor's qualification of John's assertion merely draws attention to the relative usefulness of possession, and the military strength it brings, in the fighting to come. Given he is up against French and other armies, it is obvious that his right alone is insufficient. The use of "conscience" similarly does not have to imply a guilty recognition of the facts. Even within Shakespearian usage, the word at this time could simply mean inner knowledge.[47] Eleanor does not wish others to hear because a public acknowledgement of the relative uselessness of John's right is inappropriate to the dignity of his court, especially just after he has been challenged by Chatillon. Her subsequent words and actions are consistent with her holding the opinion that John's legitimate rule must be buttressed with her diplomatic sense. She refers to the will of Richard I, which in Holinshed plainly entitles John to the throne, in her confrontation with Arthur's mother: "I can produce/A will that bars the title of thy son" (2.1.470-1). Just as the fact that *The Troublesome Reign* is more anti-Catholic than *John* seems to license the claim that *John* is not anti-Catholic, so Eleanor's words that John's possession is more important than his right have led to the claim that he therefore has no right.

The other key moment for John's illegitimacy, and for the play's exploration of the consequent instability of political legitimacy, is Falconbridge's reaction to Arthur's corpse at the end of the fourth act. Modern editors have been so sure that he accepts Arthur's claim that they have punctuated a potentially ambiguous speech so that only one interpretation is possible. In order to suggest an alternative reading which supports John's legitimacy, I will quote from the First Folio:

> Bast. Go, beare him in thine armes:
> I am amaz'd me thinkes, and loose my way
> Among the thornes, and dangers of this world.
> How easie dost thou take all *England* vp,
> From forth this morcell of dead Royaltie?
> The life, the right, and truth of all this Realme
> Is fled to heauen: and *England* now is left
> To tug and scamble, and to part by th teeth

> The vn-owed interest of proud swelling State:
> Now for the bare-pickt bone of Maiesty
> Doth dogged warre bristle his angry crest,
> And snarleth in the gentle eyes of peace:
> Now Powers from home, and discontents at home
> Meet in one line: and vast confusion waites
> As doth a Rauen on a sicke-falne beast,
> The iminent decay of wrested pompe.
> Now happy he, whose cloake and center can
> Hold out this tempest. Beare away that childe,
> And follow me with speed: Ile to the King:
> A thousand businesses are briefe in hand,
> And heaven it selfe doth frowne vpon the Land[48].    (4.3.139-55)

Editors of the recent Penguin, Oxford and Cambridge editions concur in seeing the fourth line as addressed to Hubert, who has now picked up Arthur as Falconbridge commanded, and in punctuating the passage so that "From forth ..." begins a new sentence.[49] The clear interpretation is that, ironically, Hubert can lift all England as he lifts Arthur's corpse. Arthur is referred to as "England" at 2.1.91 and 202 by Philip of France. All the life, truth and right of England, which resided in Arthur, has fled (like Astraea) to heaven, and all that remains for the country left behind is a dogfight over the remaining in bones of power. Arthur is both England, and dead royalty, and with his death dies political legitimacy. "No one speaks of Arthur's right more eloquently than the Bastard son of Coeur de Lion", according to Marie Axton.[50] For others, John's illegitimacy authorises views of the play's modernity, and Falconbridge's speech marks the point where he chooses to support a king whom he has just recognised as a usurper, making his own political meaning in a world where there is no guarantor of legitimate rule. His decision to follow John "**must** be an existential one, choosing a way despite his own awareness that whatever 'rightness' he invests it with is not inherent in it".[51]

It is possible, however, to read the speech differently. If the "thou" of the fourth line is not Hubert, but the heaven to which Arthur's soul has presumably fled, Arthur need not be acknowledged as rightful monarch at all. Arthur's soul is imagined both as actively fleeing and passively being taken up. Arthur's body, in a familiar metaphor, is a "realme" from which the ruler ("England", as Arthur is English) has gone. Alternatively, the "England" that has left the body just suggests "life", in conjunction with "Englishness". Either way, Arthur's right is to the realm of his own body. Falconbridge then shifts to the larger realm, also lacking a ruler, but for the different reason that "powers from home, and discontents at home" are in conflict. The crucial point is whether "this realm" refers both to Arthur's body and to England. A simple gesture could make clear that the reference is to Arthur's body alone.

Falconbridge is critical of John, but this need not impugn his legitimacy, as the terms he uses recall those used by the nobles disapproving of John's recrowning in 4.2. Each reference to John can be read as critical of the sumptuousness of the ceremony, and of the new clothing associated with it, much remarked on by the nobles at the time. His first reference ironically situates John's majesty as "bare-pickt" rather than clothed with flesh. "Proud swelling state" refers back critically to the wasteful excess of the recrowning, as does "wrested pomp" (that is, pomp employed in the improper context of John's ceremony, rather than wrested from Arthur). The final reference ironically characterises John's clothing as simple ("cloak and center") and unlikely to last the tempest of disorder in the realm. Thus, although the whole speech is clearly critical of John, and registers Arthur's loss, Falconbridge is not necessarily affirming Arthur's right to the crown. Falconbridge's words are difficult to understand, but an audience accepting John's legitimacy need not have understood him to challenge this right, and it is possible to imagine a performance which makes clear that John is legitimate King. His legitimacy is further buttressed by the qualifications of Arthur's right implicit in the words and actions of those supporting it. A claim supported by a man who carries on his back the spoils of a dead Richard I is not likely to have impressed an Elizabethan audience, even if they responded positively to the bemused and passive "boy" who at one point states "I would that I were laid low in my grave./I am not worth this coil that's made for me" (2.1.164-5).

John's legitimacy, however, raises the question of his cession of the crown to Pandulph, which happens just after the Falconbridge speech quoted above. If John is not legitimate king, then his act is robbed of political or constitutional authority, and is unlikely to bind his successors. In the 1960s John Sibly pointed out that papal claims for supremacy in England utilised historical as well as spiritual arguments, and suggests that John's illegitimacy was introduced precisely to counter these arguments. He begins from the premise that technically, John was not a usurper until Arthur's death, as he could still have resigned the crown when Arthur reached his majority, and sees Falconbridge's words before the recrowning as recognising that John is now a usurper:

> it is **immediately** after the 'flight to heaven' of any 'right' John may have had in the realm, that he 'surrenders' his crown. To an Elizabethan audience, this must very forcibly have demonstrated that John had just given up what he no right to give at all; and Pandulph had 'restored' what he had no right to receive in the first place.[52]

The cession of the crown is merely an index of the current balance of power, and for a Protestant audience devalues a morally bankrupt and/or illegitimate John still further.[53] If a legitimate John is posited, the status of this humiliating submission, to the very man John had so strongly defied earlier, needs to be addressed.

The mere representation of John's submission need not have functioned simply to condemn him, despite the commonsense appeal of this position. The *Homily Against Rebellion* draws different conclusions. Here John's submission to Pandulph is the clearest example, in its awfulness, of the chaos into which rebellion throws the country. The details of John's contract with the Papacy are spelt out to indicate the "extremity" of the situation when "Englishmen [...] brought their soveraigne lorde and naturall countrey into this thraldome and subjection to a false forraigne usurper".[54] John's legitimacy emphasises the indignity of his submission. Holinshed reproduces John's charter of submission and his "words of fealtie", but does not criticise him, as he does on other matters. Foxe is slightly more difficult to interpret. A paragraph of the 1563 edition, omitted from the 1583 second edition, explains John's reasons for submitting as fear of the French king, and the perception that nothing else "could be found to avoid the present destruction both of his person and the realm also". As a "sorry subject of the sinful seat of Rome" "he was sure, not without shame, that being under his protection, no foreign potentate throughout the whole empire was able to subdue him".[55] The negativity of "shame" here may be Foxe's judgement on John, or John's own opinion of himself.

But the 1583 edition reproduces John's "Letter Obligatory" to the Pope, and is unequivocal in its identification of John as a hapless victim of "that execrable monster and antichrist of Rome". Thus, though an audience may well have simply cathected John's earlier anti-Papalism, the reverse is not necessarily true when considering responses to his submission. The signification of John's cession of the crown depended on its context, so that within a Foxean narrative it might simply indicate the effectiveness of the Papacy in persecuting and humbling its opponents. It is also important to recognise that John's cession of the crown in Shakespeare's play employs different dramatic strategies to his earlier confrontation, and that these strategies may well have directed an audience towards a response the final result of which would be to confirm John as legitimate.

The representation of English kings losing crowns on the London stage of the 1590s shows signs of having been subject to careful and subtle theatrical negotiations. Though recent critics have retreated from the once-commonplace conclusion that because the 1608 quarto of Shakespeare's *Richard II* was the first to feature his deposition it must have been censored, there is still the possibility that the first quarto of 1597, or the play as performed, was cut, or that Richard's abdication/deposition was somehow 'unwritable' at this period.[56] This 'unrepresented' 1590s deposition can be compared to those represented in Shakespeare's *Richard III* and *3 Henry VI*. The 1595 quarto of the latter presents Henry's resignation of his throne to the joint protectors Warwick and Clarence in a scene half the length of its 1623 First Folio equivalent, in which Henry accepts the arrangement so that "the people of this blessed land/May not be punished with my thwarting stars" (4.6.21-2). The 1590s quarto "underrepresents", rather than omits, Henry's deposition. In *Richard III* deposition is directly represented only in a stage direction in which Richard fights Richmond and is slain. Although the visitations Richard receives in his sleep before the battle can be argued to be a displaced representation of a deposing tribunal, to whose conclusions Richard involuntarily assents, the death of the king in this instance is underrepresented in that it is a *fait accompli*.

'Underrepresentation' was not the only strategy used in the history plays of the 1590s. The 1591 quarto of *The Troublesome Reign of King John*. which covers much of the same ground as Shakespeare's play, follows Foxe and the *Homily* in representing John's recrowning at Pandulph's hands. As with the two earlier texts, its principal strategy is to attempt to limit interpretation by presenting the deposition/abdication as primarily signifying John's helplessness in the face of Popish prelates' persecutions, the final wrong turning in a Troublesome Reign. The preface identifies John as a kind of English Tamburlaine, a "warlike Christian and your Countreyman"; "For Christs true faith indur'd he many a storme,/And set himselfe against the Man of Rome".[57] This John, as in Shakespeare's play, defies Pandulph on their first meeting, and orders Falconbridge to ransack the abbeys, though *The Troublesome Reign* shows the action where Shakespeare only alludes to it. John recrowns himself in front of his nobles, explaining that he does this not because he has been deposed, but because he is checking the "assured witnes of your loves" in a ceremony to bind the nobles to him, (*Troublesome Reign*, 1555).

The play deals with such potentially difficult moments by providing a clear cause for events, and this applies also to John's recrowning by Pandulph. He prepares to meet the legate by assessing his situation under the Papal interdict, recognising that his sins are too great for him successfully to banish Popery (though he looks forward to it happening), and resolving to "finely dissemble with the Pope" (*2 Troublesome Reign*, 275) as the realm's chaos is caused by Papal interference. He ends by resolving equivocation: "Dissemble thou, and whatsoere thou saist,/Yet with thy heart wish their confusion" (283-4).

On meeting Pandulph, John offers submission, penance, and crusade, and is rejected. His first impulse is to kill Pandulph, but he again submits, to be informed that surrendering his crown is the only acceptable course. John resolves to fight rather than do so. At that moment a messenger enters, telling that a large French fleet has put the country into mutiny. On hearing this, John's resistance collapses. He later receives his crown back "as tenaunt to the Pope" (637), berates himself ("Shame be my share for yeelding to the Priest"), and in his last speech traces this act as increasing his troubles: "Since John did yeeld unto the Priest of Rome/Nor he nor his have prospred on the earth" (707, 1075-6).

The dramatic strategy of *The Troublesome Reign* is to try to contain the implications of John's submission to the Pope by inserting it into a master narrative, the course of the ancient struggle between Roman and native Christianity (Protestantism). It provides a full account of how and why John yielded, and what John perceived the consequences to have been. By this strategy, the play attempts to contain the implications of John's act for posterity. Because the causes of the deposition easily fit into the Foxean picture of the embattled proto-Protestant subverted by Papal wiles, to represent the deposition itself is not necessarily to provide a subversive undoing of John's status as proto-Protestant hero. This strategy might be called "directive representation": the deposition is shown, but attempts are made to limit an audience's perception of its meaning.

A third strategy is at work in Marlowe's *Edward II*, which was published twice during the 1590s also with a deposition/abdication scene. This third strategy might be characterised as "overrepresentation", here defined as the representation of an action or event so that a conclusive meaning is difficult to draw from it. It is not clear, for example, from Edward's abdication/deposition scene why he has given up the crown, whether he has a choice, or whether he is in a fit state to understand what he is doing. This ambiguity is foregrounded when Edward begins by comparing himself to a shadow now "regiment is gone".[58] He then asks if he must resign his crown as Mortimer will take it, is told that it will rather pass to his son, denies this, is asked again whether he will resign, gives his crown to Leicester, takes it back just until night, is asked again for it, refuses, gives it back to protect his son's right on a reminder from Leicester, calls upon another to take it from him, hands it over, and sends a handkerchief wet with his tears to queen Isabel. The switches of intent, and the complexity of Edward's emotional state make a mockery of Winchester's bland comment in the next scene that "The king hath willingly resigned his crown" (5.2.28). Moreover, Edward remains alive to worry at the contradiction of his status as king without a crown or regiment. Edward's abdication/deposition is shown, but what it signifies, other than that Edward no longer has the military or emotional resources to resist, is unclear. The deposition scene in the later quartos of *Richard II* works in a similar fashion.

*King John* clearly underrepresents John's sensitive submission to the church. Where *The Troublesome Reign* attempts to direct attention from the constitutional consequences by focusing on John's reasons for, and reactions to, his swearing fealty, *King John* takes only 65 lines (during which John also hears of the effects of Arthur's death upon the rebels) to cover the period between the first mention of the idea and Falconbridge's rejection of it as an "inglorious league". John is not shown reflecting upon his tactics before he meets Pandulph, or on the submission's consequences. Although the play underrepresents this episode in comparison to *The Troublesome Reign*, what happens is still clear. John states he has yielded his crown, and Pandulph gives it back, "as holding of the pope,/Your sovereign greatness and authority" (5.1.3-4). Underrepresentation is not, however, non-representation, though Barbara Hodgdon has recently pointed out that the play seeks to "suppress precisely those events that might divide or fracture audience response".[59] But the play can be read as recognising the problems even in underrepresenting John's submission, and that it attempts to contain the negative

## Modernity in *King John*

implications of this via overrepresentation. It does not follow the Foxean strategy of presenting the recrowning with minimal comment and leaving the reader to point the moral; rather, it makes it difficult to understand, and thus subject to recuperative qualification by John's easily intelligible speeches in 3.1.

Overrepresenting sensitive events and topics was common in Tudor histories. A. R. Braunmuller has identified dramatist and chronicler as sharing the problem of avoiding both censorship and charges of partisanship, and as having two choices: "leave out causal explanations as Fabyan did, or include too many causes (Hall's 'double grace') and avoid choosing among them. Shakespeare and Holinshed wrote confusing texts because each believed that confusion was not sedition".[60] Braunmuller's useful formulation of the available strategies is confirmed in Holinshed's preface to the reader: "I have in things doubtfull rather chosen to shew the diversitie of their writings, than by over-ruling them, and using a peremptory censure, to frame them to agree to my liking: leaving it nevertheless to each mans judgement, to controll them as he seeth cause".[61]

It is perhaps misleading to characterise historical writing as primarily concerned with avoiding sedition, rather than as attempting to make orthodox sense out of unpromising material. Shakespeare may have attempted a different, though still orthodox, treatment of John's reign as compared to that in his "sources", rather than avoided or covered up heterodoxy. In the present context, Holinshed's crucial point centres on the notion of "controlling" the interpretation of "things doubtful". Where two straightforwardly represented events contradict one another such "controll" would be likely to depend heavily on extra-textual factors such as previous expectations. Thus, in the case of *John*, an audience might compare his submission with his defiance, and conclude that no conclusion was possible. But if the defiance was straightforward, and the submission confusing, an audience is less likely to have seen the defiance as "cancelled" or invalidated by the submission. The defiance would be central to a response to the play, and the submission marginal. Though *John* underrepresents John's submission in comparison with other texts, the issues upon which an interpretation depend are overrepresented: the validity of a recrowning, whether John can give away his crown, and what significance such an action has.

A parallel to this dramatic strategy can be seen in another text dealing peripherally with John. Thomas Wilson, writing in 1600 of the state of England, states that it is "an absolute Imperiall Monarchy held neither of Pope, Emperor, nor any but of God alone, and so hath bene ever since the year of the World 2855, which was 1108 years before Christ".[62] Wilson then engages with the supposed donation of Britain to the Papacy by the emperor Constantine, which he rebuts by pointing out that subsequent conquests extinguished Rome's right. The only other threat to this independent England is John's submission: "after this, K John did resign the Crowne to Pandolphus, the Pope's legate, and did receive it againe from him, to hold it of the Pope, paying yearly a certain Tribute; but then is easily answered (though it be the Pops strongest clayme) that King John was but an usurper, and being distressed besides with the Barons' Warres, he was forced to do yt to have the Pope's help, but his act was never confirmed by the States of the Country and therefore frivolous".[63]

This passage, written for private circulation and not printed until 1936, stresses the constitutional importance of an engagement with John's submission, though this is not a question Holinshed, Foxe or the *Homily* addressed. Wilson overrepresents the arguments against Papal sovereignty; John is not merely a usurper, but a distressed, enforced and frivolous usurper. The tactic here is not to provide one conclusive refutation, but to produce the impression that the cumulative force of all explanations is strong enough to show John's submission as irrelevant to the current situation. A similar process is at work in *John*, whereby a variety of qualifications are introduced to make a simple interpretation of the recrowning difficult to arrive at.

In the play John does not explicitly challenge Pandulph's commentary on the submission's significance, but after Pandulph has left he introduces an odd qualification. Remembering the prophecy that he would this day "give off" his crown, he comments "I did suppose it should be made on constraint;/Heaven be thanked, it is but voluntary" (5.1.28-9). Given that one of the foci of *The Homily's* treatment of John's recrowning is on the indignity of the English king being forced to submit, this statement can be seen as an attempt by John to reiterate his independence of Pandulph, so that the recrowning is a tactic, a piece of equivocation meaning nothing to John. At the least, the distinction between voluntary and involuntary uncrowning implies that this kind of recrowning is not as bad as its alternative. This muddle can be read as either denoting John's personal muddle (he has lost the crown but tries to persuade himself he hasn't) or as a piece of obliquity for which there is no clear interpretation (though the implication is that the recrowning is not what Pandulph thinks it is). Falconbridge's prompt criticism of John's "inglorious league" (5.1.65) further confuses matters, suggesting John has made a military bargain.

In the following scene, Pandulph is shown to be unable to honour his contract with John. Lewis, whom Pandulph has encouraged to invade, is one of the threats John fears. His first words after the truncated recrowning ceremony are to enjoin Pandulph to go "to meet the French,/And from his holiness use all your power/To stop their marches 'fore we are inflamed" (5.1.5-7). Not only is Pandulph unable to provide what John needs; he is also met with a forceful declaration of royal independence of the Papacy: "I am too high-born to be propertied,/To be a secondary at control,/Or useful serving-man and instrument/To any sovereign state throughout the world/[...] must I back/Because that John hath made his peace with Rome?/Am I Rome's slave?" (5.2.79-82, 95-7). Thus, although Pandulph clearly presents the recrowning as signifying John's subservience to the Pope, it is followed by an obscure distinction drawn by John, Falconbridge's perception that a purely political league has been made, and Lewis' declaration that he (and by implication, John) is royal and thus nobody's "slave". Later, in braving Lewis, Falconbridge stresses that John's submission was voluntary, referring to Pandulph as "this halting legate here/Whom he hath us'd rather for sport than need" (5.2.174-5).

*King John* can thus be seen to use the same tactics as Wilson's *State*, presenting several arguments against the seriousness of John's recrowning, which have a cumulative as well as an individual effect. It might even be said that much of the last third of the play is constructed to contradict Pandulph's claims of the significance of the recrowning, for only two scenes before John receives the crown back from Pandulph, he recrowns himself, and is criticised for so doing. In Act 4 John enters "once again crowned" (4.2.1). Though his nobles defer to John's right to do as he likes, the ceremony is presented, in the words of Pembroke as "superfluous: you were crowned before/And that high royalty was ne'er plucked off,/The faiths of men ne'er stained with revolt/Fresh expectation troubled not the land/With any longed-for change or better state" (4.2.4-8). Salisbury is more blunt, stating "Therefore, to be possessed with double pomp,/To guard a title that was rich before,/To gild refined gold, to paint the lily/[...] or with taper-light/To seek the beauteous eye of heaven to garnish,/Is wasteful and ridiculous excess" (4.2.9-11, 14-16). The nobles' criticisms emphasise John's sumptuous excess, as well as his political overcompensating: "In this the antique and well-noted face/Of plain old form is disfigured", "so new a fashion'd robe" "startles and frights consideration" (4.2.21-22, 27, 25). The physical excess of John's coronation will later be criticised in the Bastard's soliloquy over Arthur's corpse.

But just as prominent are the political arguments. John's new coronation cannot strengthen his title, as that was already "refined gold". He is trying to increase the light of the sun (himself) with a candle. Pembroke implies that the ceremony of recrowning might have some point in the context of a domestic rebellion as a reassertion of the proper relationship between king and nobles, but this does not validate the later recrowning, as no nobles are present. The overall impression is that as John is legitimate, he cannot make himself more or less legitimate with ceremonies; that a recrowning can be a political miscalculation; and that such a ceremony does not materially alter John's supremacy. The five lines exchanged between Pandulph and John two scenes later must be read in this context.

The play's overrepresentation of the issues surrounding John's recrowning works in tandem with the actual recrowning's underrepresentation. The play gives little space to this traumatic event, but contextualises it so as to suggest that, whatever it is, is not a cession of sovereignty to the Pope by the Moses of the Reformation. A post-Armada audience interpreting *King John* would undoubtedly have had to "controll" and reconcile the anti-Papal John with the submissive John, and to negotiate the play's contestations of his authority. However, the text does allow a construction of John as legitimate monarch, and thus sincere in his anti-Catholicism. This presentation of John would also have accorded with those in Holinshed, Foxe, the *Homily* and *The Troublesome Reign*, and would not have offended contemporary anti-Spanish or anti-Catholic nationalism. The model offered by critics identifying the play as "modern", in contrast, situates the play as against the grain of most influential historical accounts, the predominant "war fever" of the theatrical repertory, and the likely mood of wartime London. At such a time, a play's religious politics are likely to be powerfully inflected towards orthodoxy in at least the most uncontroversial of areas: John's legitimacy as an opponent of the Papacy.

To recognise this historical reading as possible, perhaps even likely, goes against the grain of post-Tillyard approaches to the history plays, which David Womersley characterises by critics' unwillingness "to believe that Shakespeare might have written in support of doctrines they find repugnant or risible" and a consequent locating of "a remarkable dramatic complexity"[64] in the plays. The reinvention of the history plays described from a different perspective by Womersley and Curren-Aquino has helped to continue Shakespeare's dominance of the Renaissance canon as continually relevant politically, something which happens surprisingly frequently by the traditional critical/polemical tactic of presenting

Shakespeare, or his texts, as rising above the simplicity and polemic of contemporary "sources". I have attempted to show how it is possible to read *King John* as irrelevant to modern political concerns, and that in at least one important respect Shakespeare is not our "ambivalent, ambiguous, sceptical, questioning and ideologically subversive" contemporary.

*Notes*

1. Deborah Curren-Aquino, *King John: An Annotated Bibliography* (New York: Garland, 1994), p. xxvi.

2. Sigurd Burckhardt, "*King John:* The Ordering of this Present Time", *ELH*, XXXIII (1966), p. 133.

3. Burckhardt, 134; Virginia Vaughan, "*King John:* A Study in Subversion and Containment", in *King John; New Perspectives*, ed. Deborah Curren-Aquino (London and Toronto: Associated UP, 1989), p. 62.

4. Phyllis Rackin, *Stages of History: Shakespeare's English Chronicles* (London: Routledge, 1990), p. 66.

5. Larry Champion, *"The Noise of Threatening Drum": Dramatic Strategy and Political Ideology in Shakespeare and the English Chronicle Plays* (London and Toronto: Associated UP, 1990), p. 98.

6. Guy Hamel, "*King John* and *The Troublesome Reign*: A Reexamination", in Curren-Aquino (1989) p. 54.

7. Stephen Greenblatt, "Invisible Bullets", in *Political Shakespeare: New Essays in Cultural Materialism*, ed. Jonathan Dollimore and Alan Sinfield (Manchester: Manchester UP, 1985), p. 29; *King John*, ed. Robert Smallwood (Harmondsworth: Penguin, 1974), p. 12.

8. David Aers, "A Whisper in the Ear of Early Modernists", *Culture and History 1350-1600: Essays on English Communities, Identities and Writing*, ed. David Aers (Hemel Hempstead: Harvester Wheatsheaf, 1992), pp. 195-6.

9. E.M.W. Tillyard, *Shakespeare's History Plays* (London, 1944; repr. Harmondsworth: Penguin, 1986), p. 220; see also M.M. Reese, *The Cease of Majesty* (London: Arnold, 1961), p. 270; Irving Ribner, *The English History Play in the Age of Shakespeare* (Princeton: Princeton UP, 1957: rev. edn, London: Methuen, 1965), pp. 121-2; David Bevington, *Tudor Drama and Politics* (Cambridge, MA: Harvard UP, 1968), p. 200.

10. This argument is developed thoroughly in Deborah Kehler, "'So Jest With Heaven': Deity in *King John*", in Curren-Aquino (1989) p. 101.

11. *King John* ed E.A.J. Honigmann (London: Methuen, 1954), 3.1.75-86. Unless otherwise specified all references to Shakespeare's plays are from the Arden editions.

12. Lily Campbell, *Shakespeare's Histories* (San Marino, CA: Huntington Library Publications, 1947;3rd edn, London: Methuen, 1964), p.154.

13. C.W. Heiatt, "Dating *King John*", *N&Q*, xxxv (1988), p.463 dates the play to 1593/4; Roslyn Knutson, *The Repertory of Shakespeare's Company 1594-1613* (Fayetteville: Arkansas UP, 1991), p. 75 suggests 1596-97; L.A. Beaurline's edition of *King John* (Cambridge UP, 1990), p. 210 plumps for 1590; A.R. Braunmuller's edition (Oxford UP, 1989), p. 15 chooses 1595-96; Smallwood, p. 10 also supports 1593/4, and Honigmann, p. lviii 1590/1.

14. Carol Wiener, "The Beleagured Isle: A Study of Elizabethan and Early Jacobean Anti-Catholicism", *Past & Present*, LV (1971), pp. 52-3; R.B. Wernham, *After the Armada* (Oxford: OUP, 1984), pp. 453-60.

15. David Cressy, *Bonfires and Bells: National Memory and the Protestant Calendar in Elizabethan and Stuart England* (London: Weidenfeld & Nicolson, 1989), p. 119.

16. Peter Clark, "A Crisis Contained? The Condition of English Towns in the 1590s", in *The European Crisis of the 1590s* ed. Peter Clark (London: Allen & Unwin, 1985), p. 55.

17. Clark, p. 46.

18. R.B. Outhwaite, "Dearth, the English Crown and the 'Crisis of the 1590s'", in Clark (1985), p. 25; Henry Knyvett, *The Defence of the Realm* (Oxford: Clarendon Press, 1906).

19. A. Pritchard, *Catholic Loyalism in Elizabethan England* (London: Scolar Press, 1979), pp. 6-8, 12.

20. T.E. Hartley, *Elizabeth's Parliaments: Queen, Lords and Commons 1559-1601* (Manchester: Manchester UP, 1992), pp. 98-101.

21. Donna Hamilton, *Shakespeare and the Poetics of Protestant England* (Lexington: Kentucky UP, 1992), p. 4.

22. Peter Lake, *Moderate Puritans and the Elizabethan Church* (Cambridge: Cambridge UP, 1982), p. 6.

23. See Carole Levin, *Propaganda in the English Reformation: Heroic and Villainous Images of King John* (Lewiston/Queenston, NY: Edwin Mellen Press, 1988).

24. Raphael Holinshed, *Chronicles of England, Scotland and Ireland*, Vol. II (London, 1807; repr. New York: AMS Press, 1965), pp. 339, 319.

25. *Certain Sermons or Homilies (1547) and A Homily Against Disobedience And Wilful Rebellion (1570): A Critical Edition*, ed. Ronald Bond (Toronto and London: Toronto UP, 1987), p. 243.

26. Wernham, p. 555.

27. Andrew Gurr, *Playgoing in Shakepeare's London* (Cambridge: Cambridge UP, 1987), p. 135.

28. Bevington, p. 195.

29. Rackin, p. 187.

30. Reese, p. 270.

31. Robert Ornstein, *A Kingdom for a Stage* (Cambridge, MA: Harvard UP, 1972), p. 88.

32. John Blanpied, *Time and the Artist in Shakespeare's English Histories* (London and Toronto: Associated UP, 1983), pp. 100-101. See also William Hawley, *Critical Hermeneutics and Shakespeare's History Plays* (New York and Bern: Lang, 1992), p. 70.

33. Vaughan, 1989, p. 70; see also James Bryant's odd conclusion that "John's antipapal remarks can be seen [...] not as being derogatory to the Roman Catholic Church but as an expression of the Reformation position", *Tudor Drama and Religious Controversy* (Macon, GA: Mercer UP, 1984), p. 133.

34. *Narrative and Dramatic Sources of Shakespeare*, ed. Geoffrey Bullough (London: Routledge & Kegan Paul, 1962), Vol. IV, p. 22.

35. For the former stance, in addition to Bullough, Reece and Ornstein cited above, see Marie Axton, *The Queen's Two Bodies: Drama and the Elizabethan Succession* (London: Royal Historical Society, 1977), p.108; Philip Edwards, *Threshold of a Nation* (Cambridge: Cambridge UP, 1979), p. 115, and Bevington, p.198. For the latter position, see Hawley, p. 70; Champion, p. 96; Hamel, p. 55.

36. Kehler, p. 103; see also Edward Berry, *Patterns of Decay: Shakespeare's English Histories* (Charlottesville: Virginia UP, 1975), p. 115.

37. Reese, p. 275; Emrys Jones, *The Origins of Shakespeare* (Oxford: Clarendon Press, 1977), p. 239.

38. Champion, p. 96.

39. Rackin, p. 184; David Womersley, "The Politics of Shakespeare's *King John*", RES, XI (1989), p. 502. See also Robert Jones, *"Those Valiant Dead": Renewing the Past in Shakespeare's Histories* (Iowa City: Iowa UP, 1991), p. 60 and Beaurline, p. 51.

40. Douglas Wixson, "'Calm words folded up in smoke': Propaganda and Spectator Response in Shakespeare's *King John*", *Shakespeare Studies*, 14 (1981), pp. 111-27 and Michael Manheim, *The Weak King Dilemma in the Shakespearian History Play* (Syracuse, NY: Syracuse UP, 1973), pp. 116-60.

41. Since at least James Calderwood's "Commodity and Honour in *King John*", UTQ, XXIX (1960), pp. 341-56.

42. Juliet Dusinberre, "King John and embarrassing women", *Shakespeare Survey, 43* (1989), pp. 37-52; Carole Levin, "'I trust I may not trust thee': Women's Visions of theWorld in

Shakespeare's *King John*", in *Ambiguous Realities: Women in the Middle Ages and the Renaissance*, ed. Carole Levin and J. Watson (Detroit: Wayne State UP, 1987), pp. 219-34; Rackin, pp. 146-200.

43. A topic of interest since at least Adrien Bonjour's "The Road to Swinstead Abbey: A Study of the Sense and Structure of *King John", ELH*, XVIII (1951), pp. 253-74.

44. William Camden, *Remains Concerning Britain*, ed. R. Dunn (Toronto and London: Toronto UP, 1984), p. 246.

45. See John Elliott, "Shakespeare and the Double Image of *King John*", *Shakespeare Studies*, I (1965), p. 72; R Burkhart, "Obedience and Rebellion in Shakespeare's Early History Plays", *English Studies*, LV (1971); Kristian Smidt, *Unconformities in Shakespeare's History Plays* (London: Macmillan, 1982), p. 73; John Loftis, *Renaissance Drama in England and Spain* (Princeton: Princeton UP, 1987), p. 74; Bonjour, p. 257; Reese, p. 263; Manheim, p. 131; Edwards, p. 115, Levin, 1987, p. 221; Hamilton, p. 43; Berry, p. 115; Bevington, p. 243; Honigmann, p. xxvii; Beaurline, p. 47; Hawley, p. 64; Hodgdon, p. 27; Robert Jones, p. 48; Rackin, p. 162; Kehler, p. 103; Dusinberre, p. 44.

46. Reese, p. 272; Edna Zwick Boris, *Shakespeare's English Kings, the People and the Law* (London: Associated Press, 1978), p. 133.

47. *Cymbeline*, 1.6.114-6.

48. *Mr William Shakespeare's Comedies, Histories and Tragedies*, facsimile prepared by H. Kökeritz (New Haven and London: Yale UP, 1954), pp. 17-18.

49. Honigmann's Arden edition is closest to the First Folio, substituting an exclamation mark for its question mark; his notes indicate that the 'England' of the fourth line refers to both Arthur and the country.

50. Axton, p. 109.

51. Robert Jones, p. 60; see also Womersley, p. 502 and Smallwood, p. 38.

52. John Sibly, "The Anomalous case of King John", *ELH*, XXXIII (1966), p. 421.

53. Emrys Jones, p. 256, Robert Jones, p. 57; Calderwood, p. 97; Donjour, p. 264; Champion, p. 92.

54. Bond, p. 243.

55. *Acts and Monuments*, Vol. II (London: Seeley Burnside & Seeley, 1843), p. 332. I have checked that this passage is not present in the 1583 edition.

56. J. Leeds Barroll, "A New History for Shakespeare and His Time", *SQ*, XXIX (1988), pp. 441-64.

57. *The Troublesome Reign of King John*, ed. Bullough, "To the Gentlemen Readers", p. 72. All quotations from *The Troublesome Reign* are from this edition.

58. *Edward the Second*, ed. W Moelwyn Merchant (London: Benn, 1967), 5.1.26.

59. Hodgdon, p. 30.

60. A.R. Braunmuller, "*King John* and Historiography", *ELH*, LV (1988), p. 318.

61. Holinshed, "Preface to the Reader". [*Chronicles*,Vol. II].

62. Thomas Wilson, *The State of England Anno Dom 1600*, ed. F. Fisher, *Camden Miscellany, XVI* (London, 1936), p. 1.

63. Wilson, p. 2.

64. Womersley, p. 499.

# *HENRY V* AND THE CHIVALRIC REVIVAL

## Robin Headlam Wells
### (University of Hull)

"O for a Muse of fire!" What more appropriate way to begin an epic celebration of England's greatest warrior-king than an invocation to Mars, the baleful god of war with 'famine, sword and fire' straining like leashed greyhounds at his heels (Prol. 1-8)?[1] Praised by his contemporaries as the flower of knighthood,[2] the historical Henry V was the epitome of English chivalry; and chivalry is essentially a martial ideal, a code of values that glorified military prowess as the supreme achievement of the virtuous knight.[3] For the medieval chevalier like Shakespeare's Duke of Exeter (4.6.7-32) death on the battlefield in the arms of a brother soldier while in the service of his liege is a consummation devoutly to be wished.

It is this chivalric ideal that the "warlike Harry" epitomizes. Shakespeare's holy warrior has "an aspect of iron" (5.2.239); his god is a 'God of battles' (4.1.285); and when he invades France he comes "In thunder and in earthquake, like a Jove" (2.4.100). Even as a wooer, he loves "cruelly" (5.2.211). But despite the celebratory tone of the Prologue, *Henry V* is no simple endorsement of chivalric ideals. The history of chivalry in late medieval and early modern England is a complex one, and Shakespeare's play embodies the ambivalent attitudes towards war and military heroism which that history inevitably reflects.

Flower of chivalry

Henry V is chiefly remembered for his extraordinary victory at Agincourt. But hardened at an early age to the rigours of border conflict, he showed a passion for war and a contempt for "the cursyd vice of slouthe and ydlenesse"[4] even before he became king. Shortly before his accession he commissioned a translation of the greatest war story of the ancient world. The result was John Lydgate's *Troy Book*, a translation of Guido delle Colonne's *Historia Destructionis Troiae*. Like Shakespeare, Lydgate begins his story with an invocation to Mars, patron of chivalry and the "causer [...] Of werre and stryf":

> O myghty Mars, that wyth thy sterne lyght
> In armys hast the power & þe my3t,
> And named art from est til occident
> The myghty lorde, the god armypotent,
> That, wyth schynyng of the stremes rede,
> By influence dost the brydel led
> Of cheualry, as souereyn and patrown ...
> Now help, o Mars, þat art of kny3thod lord,
> And hast of manhod the magnificence![5]

In his prologue to the *Troy Book* Lydgate explains that it was Henry's own enthusiasm for "verray kny3thod", "the prowesse of olde chiualrie" and "al that longeth to manhood" that was responsible for the prince's interest in the Troy story (I. 69ff.).

Though Henry's early death meant that his political vision, enshrined in the Treaty of Troyes (1420), of a joint kingdom united under English rule would never be realized, it did wonders for his heroic reputation. As Edward Hall writes in his *Chronicle*, Henry's "fame by his death as liuely florisheth as his actes in his life wer sene and remembred".[6] Already by the middle of the fifteenth century he had become part of English national mythology. When William Worcester wrote a book supporting Edward IV's renewal of the war with France he recalled Henry's "gret manhode" and exhorted Edward to remember the "victorious conquestis of youre noble predecessour".[7] And as Henry himself had hoped to inspire patriotic sentiments by making the Troy story available to English readers, so Worcester, in urging his countrymen to take up arms, adjures them to recall the siege of Troy as an example of true chivalry:

> let be brought to mynde to folow the steppis in conceitis of noble courage
> of the mighty dedis in armes of the vaillaunt knight Hector of Troy,

whiche bene enacted in the seige of Troy for a perpetuelle remembraunce of chevalrie.[8]

Contemporary opinion about Henry and his policies was divided.[9] Thomas Hoccleve, while praising Henry as the "floure of Chivalrie",[10] concludes his epideictic *Regement of Princes* with a philippic on the evils of war between Christian states.[11] Even Lydgate, despite the militaristic tone of his invocation to the *Troy Book*, seems to have had reservations about his patron's military ideals. At the end of Book IV he interpolates a long complaint addressed to Mars, the "first meuer of anger and of hate", deploring the ruinous consequences of war (IV. 4440ff.), a theme that he repeats in the concluding lines of the *Siege of Thebes*,[12] written, significantly, after the Treaty of Troyes when contemporaries had good reason for thinking that Henry's policies had been completely vindicated. Modern historians continue to disagree about Henry's character and achievements. M.H. Keen sees Henry's reign as a "record of tremendous English achievement".[13] But G.L. Harriss argues that his "messianic streak" led to "unjustifiable aggrandizement which was beyond English resources to sustain and which would ultimately face England with the crisis of its failure".[14] Desmond Seward, Henry's harshest modern critic, claims that "for all his brilliance, Henry V's ambition ended by bankrupting and discrediting his son, and by ruining his dynasty".[15]

Henry's reputation as the mirror of Christian chivalry owes much to his brother Humphrey, Duke of Gloucester, who commissioned the Italian historian Tito Livio to write his life (*Vita Henrici Quinti*), to the anonymous *Gesta Henrici Quinti* and to William Worcester, author of the chauvinistic *Boke of Noblesse*. In the sixteenth century the myth of Henry as the "floure of kynges passed"[16] was kept alive by the chroniclers Fabyan, Grafton, Hall and Holinshed. Their patriotic view of Henry found ready acceptance in militant Protestant circles, and is reflected in the crudely jingoistic *Famous Victories of Henry V*. When a new play about Henry appeared shortly after the *Famous Victories* was first printed, describing how the country's youth, gripped by war fever, abandons the "silken dalliance" of peace to follow the "mirror of all Christian kings" into battle (*H5*, 32.chorus.1ff.), it was clear that the Henry myth was in no danger of being allowed to die. At least that is what many twentieth-century critics of Shakespeare's play have assumed. For J.H. Walter Shakespeare's Henry combines the character and action of the epic hero with the moral qualities of Erasmus' Christian prince;[17] for Norman Rabkin he is "the kind of exemplary monarch that neither Richard II nor Henry IV could be, combining the inwardness and the sense of occasion of the one and the strength of the other with a generous humanity available to neither";[18] for Gary Taylor he is "a study of human greatness".[19]

It is true that Shakespeare's portrait of Henry is in many ways a notably sympathetic one. Henry's rhetoric is exhilarating; his courage in battle is exemplary; his piety seems indisputable and his honour bright. By the final scene of the play any lingering doubts about the legitimacy of his claims to France are easily forgotten in the superficially playful charm of the wooing of Katharine. When even the French king and queen seem delighted with "brother England" and the terms of his proposed alliance, what reason is there to doubt the integrity of this now plain-speaking soldier with a heart that "never changes, but keeps his course truly" (5.2.161-2)? But, as many critics have pointed out, this concluding scene of international and domestic harmony, almost like a comedy in its stylized conviviality,[20] is profoundly ironic. Unlike the typical romantic comedy, which ends with an unfulfilled promise of future happiness, the final chorus of *Henry V* takes us back to a future that is already past. We know all too well that not one of Henry's hopes will be realized: Katharine will never be a "soldier-breeder"; the king himself will not live to see old age; the peace between England and France will hold only a few years. As the chorus reminds us of the English blood that will soon be shed, it is difficult to suppress memory of all the other disquieting events we have witnessed in the play: the scheming clergy so eager to support a war that is conveniently in their own interests; Henry's brutal threats to the citizens of Harfleur; the patently unsatisfactory argument with Williams; the cold-blooded killing of the prisoners. Was Shakespeare, as one modern historian has suggested, the "prisoner of his time",[21] endorsing the militaristic views of the war party in Elizabethan politics? If so, then why did he apparently go out of his way to sow doubts in our minds concerning the integrity of his hero and the wisdom of Henry's policies?

The chivalric revival

To suggest that Shakespeare was the intellectual prisoner of his time is to imply that Elizabethans were united in their endorsement of the militaristic values that Henry V stood for in the popular imagination. This is not true. A brief review of changing attitudes towards the chivalric ideal in fifteenth- and sixteenth-century England may go at least some way towards explaining the anomalies in Shakespeare's play.

*Henry V* was written at a time when chivalric values, after a period of self-conscious anti-militarism, were once more in fashion.[22] Originating in the Middle Ages as the code of values of a military aristocracy, chivalry placed paramount emphasis on physical courage and military prowess as the guarantors of justice and honour. Where this involved dynastic rights of the kind that were at issue in the Hundred Years War, chivalry provided justification for aggressive international action. In exhorting Edward to defend his territorial rights, William Worcester appeals to "ye noble Englisshe cheualrie [...] to take armes and enterprinses, seeing so many good examples before yow of so many victorius dedis in armes done by youre noble progenitoures".[23] One of chivalry's most enduring legacies to the future was the honour code, a system of values characterized above all by a stress on competitive assertiveness. As Mervyn James explains, the honour code both legitimized and provided moral reinforcement for "a politics of violence".[24] It was this medieval code of values that the Essex circle hoped to revive. To his admirers the Earl of Essex was a symbol of national pride, the "Faire branch of Honor" and "flower of Cheualrie".[25] The earl was the centre of a dissident aristocratic movement that wanted to reform the commonwealth and restore military values to a society grown generally "unwarlicke, in love with the name, and bewitched with the delight of peace".[26] Drawing on the aristocratic charisma of its leader, it called for a return to the heroic values of the past. In doing so it was self-consciously rejecting a generation of anti-chivalric thinking.

With changing methods of warfare and the gradual disintegration of the feudal system of land tenure in which chivalry was rooted, the old martial values were in decline at end of the fifteenth century. "O ye knyghtes of Englond", complains Caxton in his *Book of the Order of Chyvalry* (an expanded translation of Ramón Lulls' *Libre del Orde del Cauayleria*) "where is the custome and usage of noble chyvalry that was used in those days".[27] What Arthur B. Ferguson calls "The Indian Summer of English Chivalry" is the literary rearguard action of men like Malory and Hawes, who wanted to revive an antiquated system of values that bore increasingly little relationship to contemporary social and military reality. By the second decade of the sixteenth century, that system was effectively dead. What had killed it was humanism.[28]

Fundamental to Renaissance humanism is a new sense of historical change. For the generation of More and Erasmus, a medieval culture of violence had no place in the new world of enlightened civic humanism. The sword and shield of Erasmus' Christian knight are those, not of the medieval warrior, but of St Paul's metaphoric "armour of God" (Eph. 6:13).[29] Erasmus is the most uncompromising of the sixteenth-century pacifists.[30] He concedes that war may be justified under exceptional circumstances, for example a Turkish attack against a Christian state. But wars between Christian states are inexcusable. In a barely concealed attack on the expansionist policies of the young Henry VIII, Erasmus denounces such wars as unmitigated folly:

> Almost all wars between Christians have arisen from either stupidity or wickedness. Some young men, with no experience of life, inflamed by the bad examples of our forbears told in the histories that fools have compiled from foolish documents, and then encouraged by flatterers and stimulated

by lawyers and theologians, with the consent and connivance of bishops, and even at their desire - these young men, I say, go into war out of rashness rather than badness; and then they learn, to the suffering of the whole world, that war is a thing to be avoided by every possible means.[31]

Erasmus' friend More, though equivocal as always, was clearly satirizing chivalric attitudes when he described how the Utopians despise the notion of honour in battle, counting "nothynge so much against glorie, as glory gotten in war".[32] As C. S. Lewis disapprovingly puts it, "the military methods of More's Utopians are mischievously devised to flout the chivalric code at every turn".[33] The powerful influence of Erasmus' thinking can also be seen in Sir Thomas Elyot's *The Governour*. Though not a pacificist, Elyot upholds the humanist emphasis on the primacy of learning. Comparing social values in the modern world with the "doctryne of aunctent noble men", he claims that the reason for the decay of learning in the modern world is contempt for education among the aristocracy. Elyot's model of princely virtue is Henry I, known as Henry Beau Clerke for his learning. Contrasting him with his brother Robert, "a man of moche prowesse, and right expert in martial affayres", Elyot praises Henry as the superior leader because his wisdom and learning enabled him to add "polycie to vertue and courage".[34] In drawing up a scheme of education for a newly emerging governing class Elyot omitted from his list of physical exercises suitable for noblemen any discussion of the tournaments that for Castiglione's courtier are a way of acquiring martial prowess.[35] For Elyot honour is to be won, not through battle, but through public service. The purpose of studying "morall philosophie" is to create a just society based on "vertues, maners, and ciuile policie".[36] Later in the century Elizabeth's tutor Ascham showed a similar scorn for the militaristic element in medieval chivalry when he complained that Malory's *Morte D'Arthur* was nothing but "open mans slaughter and bold bawdrye".[37]

It was the pacifist element in English civic humanism with its contempt for chivalric values that Sidney, and later Essex, wanted to reform. Though it cannot be said that the sixteenth century saw very significant advances in the social position of women, humanist education did at least provide the foundation for sexual equality: as Elizabeth's own example showed, women could also be scholars. By contrast, the honour code is unequivocally masculine; its appeal is, as William Worcester puts it, to "corage, feersnes, manlinesse and strength",[38] sentiments that are echoed by the Elizabethan armorist Gerard Legh when he defines honour as "glory gotten by courage of manhood".[39] In his *Apologie* of 1598 Essex compares the unheroic present with the "those former gallant ages" when England did not hesitate "to atchieve great conquests in France".[40] When Essex wrote his *Apologie* the simmering rivalry between the two main factions in the Privy Council was rapidly approaching crisis point.[41] On one side were the Cecils, astute and scheming politicians, but concerned above all to preserve peace, both at home and abroad. On the other was Essex, arrogant, mercurial, paranoid and desperate for military glory. Where the Cecils instinctively favoured civilian rule, Essex would have liked to have done away with civil magistracy altogether and to have replaced it with martial law. His dream was a military society ruled by an aristocratic élite. Matters came to a head with the Treaty of Vervins (May 1598): the Cecils urged acceptance of Spain's proposals; Essex, hoping no doubt that history would repeat itself and that a war faction would once again triumph as it had done in 1513, insisted on an all-out offensive against the dominant power on the continent: "now, now is the fittest time to make warre upon the Spaniard," he wrote in the *Apologie*.[42]

If the glamorous and bellicose young Henry VIII was a source of practical inspiration for the Elizabethan war faction, the great Lancastrian ancestor on whom he conspicuously modelled himself[43] enjoyed an almost mythical reputation in the popular mind. For the Essex faction Henry V was the perfect symbol of national pride. Here was not only an an inspirational type of what Lydgate calls "the prowesse of olde chiualrie", but also an embodiment of just the kind of aggressive military action that Essex himself so passionately advocated. Samuel Daniel, who praises Essex in the *Civil Wars* as a rare example "Of ancient honor

## Henry V

neere worne out of date",[44] imagines the ghost of Henry V returning (like Hamlet's father) to reprove the present age for its neglect of the "wondrous Actions" of the heroic past. In defending Henry's campaigns, he puts the emphasis, not on the reassertion of hereditary rights, but on "ioyes of gotten spoyles", "thoughts of glorie" and "conquests, riches, Land, and Kingdome gain'd" (V, stanzas 1, 3, 40). For Essex's admirers the "dreadful and yet lovely" Henry was the supreme example of chivalric heroism, inspiring both "terror and delight" (V, stanza 2).

Such blatantly militarist sentiments inevitably attracted criticism. There is, of course, always a danger of reading modern assumptions into the debates of the past. But if our own century has particular reason to be wary of charismatic military leaders, the sixteenth century was both fascinated and repelled by the cult of the megalopsyche. As Paul Siegel argues, humanists were fully aware of the opposition between their own ideal of honour through public service and commitment to civic ideals, and what they regarded as a false cult of neo-chivalric honour.[45] Sidney's friend Hubert Languet is typical of those humanists who had profound reservations about the culture of violence fostered by militant Protestantism. Warning him of the temptations of seeking honour through military achievement, Languet wrote to Sidney: "It is the misfortune, or rather the folly of our age that most men of high rank think it more honorable to do the work of a soldier than of a leader, and would rather earn a name for boldness than for judgment".[46] Essex received similar, though less friendly, advice from the Privy Council when it debated the Spanish peace proposals in 1598. Warning the Earl of the dangers of his obsession with war, the treasurer reminded him of the psalmist's prophecy: "Men of blood shall not live out half their days".[47]

When Shakespeare wrote *Henry V* the revival of chivalric military values had not yet reached its farcical anticlimax in the Essex rebellion. But as the final chorus allusions to the Earl's anticipated return from Ireland indicate, Essex and the values for which he stood were the subject of angry political argument.[48] By beginning the play with an invocation, not to one of the nine liberal arts, but instead to the patron god of chivalry, attended by "famine, sword and fire", Shakespeare was giving a sure signal that he meant to engage with the topical matter of martial versus eirenic values. Cultural Materialism suggests that the question that criticism should ask about Shakespeare's plays is whether they are for or against authority; as Jonathan Dollimore puts it, do they "reinforce the dominant order, or do they interrogate it to the point of subversion?"[49] But topical though it was in the late 1590s, neo-chivalric militarism is not an issue that will divide along simple authoritarian versus populist lines. Essex was certainly the centre of a dissident party that threatened Elizabeth's authority. But the rebellion of 1601 was an aristocratic, not a populist movement. As in 1513, the main beneficiaries of a land war in Europe would have been a nobility eager for offices and appointments as well as the usual financial spoils; for the common soldier the reward of victory would no doubt have been much like that of Pistol: no honours and titles, but a life of begging and stealing (5.1.74-83). In his recent Arden edition of *Henry V* T.W. Craik refers to Essex as a popular hero.[50] Though it is true that the earl was lionized by his followers, it is clear from the self-defensive tone of his *Apologie* that his love of war aroused deep suspicion among his opponents; indeed his sanity was seriously doubted.[51] When he made his ill-fated march on the City in February 1601 the people of London, instead of rallying to his cause, stood by in silent amazement as he led his little cavalcade up Fenchurch street crying "for the Queen, for the Queen".[52] Rather than asking whether Shakespeare is "for" or "against" Henry as a representative figure of authority, it would probably make more sense to consider what this exceptionally ambivalent play has to say about the factional issue so clearly announced in its opening lines.[53]

War and chivalry

Modern criticism is divided on the question of whether the play wants us to see Henry V as Christian hero or deceitful Machiavel. Because Henry is a natural autocrat, post-structuralist historicism sees him, perhaps predictably, as the latter. In one of his most influential essays[54] Stephen Greenblatt argues that throughout the three plays in which he appears Henry is a Machiavellian "juggler" and "conniving hypocrite". The final play of the series, says Greenblatt, "deftly registers every nuance of royal hypocrisy, ruthlessness, and bad faith".[55] Ruthless Henry undoubtedly is, but to accuse him of bad faith is to deny him his most outstanding and most dangerous characteristic, namely his frank and single-minded fidelity to his cause.

For Greenblatt *Henry V* is a classic instance of the way authority produces and contains subversion. Insofar as it is concerned to illustrate a transhistorical paradigm of power politics, Greenblatt's essay is, strictly speaking, a-historicist. For all its rhetorical persuasiveness, it suffers from the inevitable limitations of its analogical methodology. When flexible use is made of the text,[56] and when external appeal is made, not to proven source material or contemporaneous political debate, but to unconnected "reiterations" of an *a priori* principle, it becomes difficult either to prove or disprove his thesis. A more truly historicist case for seeing Henry as a dissimulating Machiavel has recently been made by Steven Marx.[57] The idea of the benign Machiavel using deception for the good of the state is not a new one in Shakespeare criticism.[58] But Marx goes, not just to Machiavelli, but to one of Machiavelli's own sources for his political analogues. Noting the presumably intentional parallel between the miracle of Agincourt and God's deliverance of Israel (the "Non nobis" that Henry orders to be sung after the battle is the Latin title of Psalm 115 celebrating the defeat of the Egyptian armies at the Red Sea), he argues that the Old Testament provided Renaissance humanists with a political history as rich and revealing as those of the classical world. Citing a number of biblical figures who use trickery to defeat their enemies, Marx suggests that Shakespeare shows Henry deliberately and cynically using holy war as a political device to inspire faith in his followers and credulity in his enemies.

Based as it is on proven sources rather than on tendentious readings of entirely unconnected texts, Marx's argument is a much more powerful one than Greenblatt's. But again the play itself does not provide convincing support for the claim that Henry is unscrupulously manipulating religion for political ends. Modern historians speak of the historical Henry's "messianic streak"[59] and his religious bigotry.[60] Even Allmand, his most admiring biographer, describes him as "a man with an obsession".[61] Shakespeare's Henry also has that obsessive, single-minded zeal that is characteristic of many religious converts.

It is true that in *Henry IV* the prince uses deception to enhance his reputation, announcing at the beginning of Part 1 that he will "falsify men's hopes" by "redeeming time" when people least expect it (*1H4*, 1.2.204-10). Whether or not his reformation at the end of Part 2 is authentic, he appears, when we see him at the beginning of *Henry V*, to have all the characteristics of the reborn Christian. From the conversation between Canterbury and Ely in the first scene we learn that Henry does indeed seem to be the "new man" described by the sixteenth-century chroniclers:[62]

> Never was such a sudden scholar made;
> Never came reformation in a flood,
> With such a heady currance, scouring faults;
> Nor never Hydra-headed wilfulness
> So soon did lose his seat, and all at once,
> As in this king (1.1.32-7).

As well as showing an impressive grasp of theological and political matters, the reborn king is a compelling orator, especially on the subject of war. "List his discourse of war," says Canterbury, "and you shall hear / A fearful battle rend'red you in music" (1.1.43-4). It is Henry's passion for war that particularly interests the bishops. Seeing in this a way out of the church's own problems, Canterbury makes the king an offer: if he will guarantee the security of church lands, the clergy will support a re-opening of the war against France. But before Henry will agree to this proposal he insists on satisfying himself that he does have a legitimate claim to the French crown. The ground is thus prepared for the notorious debate on Salic Law.

If it was Shakespeare's intention to portray Henry as the mirror of Christian kings and to justify his aggressive military policies, Canterbury's exposition of Salic Law seems an odd way of going about it. To establish the legality of Henry's claim to France Shakespeare could easily have had a group of courtiers discussing the Plantagenet dynasty. One of them might begin by reminding the court that English kings had ruled the Angevin empire since time immemorial (that is to say, since the 11th century); another might say that Edward III had a better claim to the French throne than anyone else, better certainly than Philip VI; a third might rejoin that Philip's confiscation of the Duchy of Aquitaine in 1337 was quite illegal; a fourth might point out that when Henry's father met the Dukes of Berry, Bourbon and Orléans in Bourges in 1412 all had agreed that Aquitaine was rightfully English. All this could have been done quickly and emphatically. Alternatively, Shakespeare could have followed the example of the *Famous Victories of Henry V* where the question of Henry's legal claims to France is dealt with in two sentences. In response to the king's request for advice Canterbury simply says "Your right to the French crown of France came by your great-grandmother, Isabel, wife to King Edward the third, and sister to Charles, the French King. Now, if the French King deny it, as likely enough he will, then must you take your sword in hand and conquer the right".[63] What could be simpler? The king has a clear legal right and he must defend it.

By contrast, Shakespeare reproduces more or less word for word from Holinshed a forensic argument of such tortuous casuistry that no theatre audience could possibly follow it. Holinshed's own view of Canterbury's tactics comes across fairly clearly. Winding up what Holinshed calls "his prepared tale", the Archbishop shifts to a different register as he exhorts Henry to "advance forth his banner to fight for his right" and "spare neither bloud, sword, nor fire" in defence of his inheritance. Parliament responds to this emotive rhetoric with cries of

"Warre, warre; France, France". Carried away by its own jingoism, the House forgets the more mundane question of church lands and votes enthusiastically for war. Holinshed comments dryly: "Hereby the bill for dissoluing of religious houses was cleerelie set aside, and nothing thought on but onelie the recovering of France, according as the archbishop had mooved".[64]

With his keen interest in the unscrupulous use of political oratory – *Julius Caesar* was probably written in the same year as *Henry V* – Shakespeare clearly saw the dramatic potential of such material. But if Canterbury's motives are dishonourable, this does not mean that Henry is necessarily a conniver. Indeed he is insistent that the archbishop explain the crown's legal position "justly and religiously" (1.2.10). Warning him not to "fashion, wrest, or bow" the facts to suit convenience (14), Henry soberly reminds the court of the consequences of going to war. In contrast to Canterbury's casuistical exposition of Salic law, the king's response is a simple question: "May I with right and conscience make this claim?" (96). As in Holinshed, Canterbury's reply is an emotive appeal to national pride:

> Gracious lord,
> Stand for your own; unwind your bloody flag,
> Look back into your mighty ancestors.
> Go, my dread lord, to your great-grandsire's tomb,
> From whom you claim; invoke his war-like spirit ... (100-4).

Taking up the archbishop's theme, Ely urges Henry to think of "exploits and mighty enterprises" (121). Unlike Hamlet, whose reaction to an appeal to dynastic honour is an impassioned declaration of vengeance, Henry remains cool, quietly reminding the court of the need to prepare, not only for a foreign campaign, but also for the possibility of an attack from Scotland. The debate concludes with the Archbishop's emollient parable of the bee hive. Obedience to the rule of nature, says Canterbury, is the key to social harmony: just as members of a bee hive work together under the direction of a king, so national success depends on each member of society working for the common good.

*Henry V* 133

Canterbury's parable is meant as an illustration of the general principle that Exeter has just stated in the preceding speech. "Government," says Exeter,

> though high, and low, and lower,
> Put into parts, doth keep in one consent,
> Congreeing in a full and natural close,
> Like music (180-3).

Musical harmony is a key metaphor in political debate in this period.[65] In formulating their constitutional arguments both apologists for and critics of the crown appeal to the laws of a nature whose characteristic feature is "harmonicall agreement" and "due proportion". As the encyclopaedist Pierre de La Primaudaye explains,

> A citie or ciuill company is nothing else but a multitude of men vnlike in estates or conditions, which communicate togither in one place their artes, occupations, workes, and exercises, that they may live the better, & are obedient to the same lawes and magistrats ... Of such a dissimilitude an harmonicall agreement ariseth by due proportion of one towards another in their diverse orders & estates, even as the harmonie in musicke consisteth of unequal voyces or sounds agreeing equally togither.[66]

That Exeter's appeal to these familiar Pythagorean principles should make Canterbury think of bees is not in itself surprising. The association is conventional. The *inscriptio* of an early 17th-century emblem illustrating the principles of social harmony explains that

> As busie Bees unto their Hive doe swarme,
> So do's th' attractive power of *Musicke* charme [...]
> This *Harmony* in t'humane *Fabricke* steales
> And is the sinewes of all Common-weales.[67]

The significant thing about the archbishop's little clerical homily is not its content – which is conventional enough – but the context in which it is made and the lesson that Canterbury draws from it. The mythological figure who embodies Exeter's harmonist principle is Orpheus. As Puttenham explains, Orpheus' legendary ability to tame wild beasts with his music is a figure for the civilizing influence of the arts and their ability to restrain the brutal passions of our fallen nature.[68] His antithesis in Renaissance mythography is Hercules. Orpheus is a symbolic representative of the arts of peace, Hercules those of war.[69] Both figures are claimed by mythographers as founders of civilization and represent opposing ideals of community.[70] The irony of Canterbury's speech is that he should appeal to harmonist principles, not in order to defend the Orphic arts of peace, but to argue for war. In what seems no less of a *non sequitur* than Hector's abrupt *volte face* at the end of his eloquent exposition of natural law in *Troilus and Cressida* (2.2.163-93), the archbishop concludes his parable of social harmony with a call to arms: "Therefore to France, my liege" (1.2.213).

Behind Canterbury's speech lies a long debate on the arts of war and peace.[71] At the end of the play there is another reminder of that debate. In an extended natural image, ironically of great beauty, the Duke of Burgundy reflects sadly on the way peace, the "nurse of arts", has been "mangled" by war. As nature reverts to wildness, so humanity seems to return to its primal savagery:

> as our vineyards, fallows, meads, and hedges,
> Defective in their natures, grow to wildness;
> Even so our houses and ourselves and children
> Have lost , or do not learn for want of time,
> The sciences that should become our country;
> But grow, like savages - as soldiers will,
> That nothing do but meditate on blood ... (5.2.54-60).

But Henry, unlike the effeminate Richard II, is no "nurse of arts". Above all he is a holy warrior. Having satisfied himself that he has good legal and religious grounds for going to war, he announces his decision. With calm deliberation he declares that once France is his he will either bend it to his will or "break it all to pieces" (224-5). When the French ambassadors arrive he informs them that he is "no tyrant, but a Christian king". J.H. Walter has shown that Shakespeare knew Erasmus' *Education of a Christian Prince* well and was probably working closely with it when he wrote *Henry V*.[72] But Henry's notion of what it means to be a Christian king could not be more different from Erasmus'. For Erasmus clemency is one of the prince's cardinal virtues.[73] So too is it for Shakespeare's Portia. If mercy "becomes / The thronèd monarch better than his crown" it is because "It is an attribute of God himself" (*The Merchant of Venice*, 4.1.184-90). By contrast, Henry sees himself as the scourge of a vindictive God. In retaliation for the Dauphin's insult, Henry tells the ambassadors to warn their prince that

> his soul
> Shall stand sore charged for the wasteful vengeance
> That shall fly at them; for many a thousand widows
> Shall this his mock mock out of their dear husbands;
> Mock mothers from their sons, mock castles down;
> And some are yet ungotten and unborn
> That shall have cause to curse the Dauphin's scorn.
> But this lies all within the will of God,
> To whom I do appeal; and in whose name,
> Tell you the Dauphin, I am coming on,
> To venge me as I may and to put forth
> My rightful hand in a well-hallow'd cause (282-93).

It would be difficult to think of a more aptly ironic comment on such cold savagery than Exeter's "This was a merry message"(298).

Dramatically the whole scene is of crucial importance in establishing one of the play's central thematic concerns, that is, the dangers of single-minded idealism. Many critics and historians – including, I suspect, Holinshed – are suspicious of Canterbury's motives. Legally his arguments may be sound,[74] but the effect of his speech is not to clarify matters but to confuse them. That Henry himself seems to be satisfied with the archbishop's exposition of Salic Law does not mean that he is a "conniving hypocrite". What we see in this scene is a king first confirming that he has a "well-hallow'd cause", and then coolly and openly informing his enemies what they can expect if they dare to oppose his will. The truly frightening thing about him is the sense he has of the absolute rightness of his cause. Having "whipp'd th' offending Adam out of him" (1.1.29), he is now a man driven by a powerful sense of missionary zeal. Though he claims to be a Christian king, it is really Mars who is his true god, and Henry is his scourge.

By contrast, the clergy with whom he deals are not idealists inspired by a divine mission, but cynical politicians who are prepared to see England go to war rather than lose their lands. Defending Canterbury's speech against the usual charges of tedium and incomprehensibility, Gary Taylor argues that the archbishop's performance is "both comprehensible and dramatically necessary": comprehensible because Elizabethans were apparently interested in Salic Law and were used to listening to long speeches, and dramatically necessary because if you want to build up to a thrilling climax (Henry's riposte to the Dauphin) you have to begin at a low pitch.[75] Taylor needs to defend the archbishop's speech because he believes that Shakespeare approved of Henry's policies and wanted to justify them. Dramatically, however, what comes over most strongly in these crucial opening scenes is not the transparent justice of Henry's cause, but the inherent danger of unholy alliances between unscrupulous cynicism and single-minded idealism, a motif that Shakespeare was later to develop to devastating effect in another tale about an idealistic soldier and a Machiavellian cynic.

But Henry is no Othello; a steely self-control is one of his most impressive characteristics. It is not just that he is good at mastering his feelings; as he admits when he learns of the killing of the luggage boys, normally he is simply not prone to strong emotions. But in this case anger is an entirely appropriate response. The other occasion when he allows his anger to show is in the argument with Williams.

The disguised king who shows his true humanity by mingling with his people in a brief interlude of benevolent deception is a common motif in Elizabethan fiction.[76] It is just such a stereotype that the chorus evokes as he asks us to imagine Henry passing among his "ruin'd band" of soldiers and raising their spirits with his "cheerful semblance and sweet majesty" (4. Chorus, 40). But the reality is rather different. Instead of cheering his men, Henry quarrels with them, provoking Bates to call him and Williams a pair of "English fools" (4.1.220). It is

Bates who triggers the argument by innocently suggesting that at a moment like the present the king is probably wishing he were anywhere but at Agincourt. Henry tells him that, "his cause being just and his quarrel honourable" (127), it is unlikely that the king would want to be anywhere else. Bates is not interested in challenging the point, but Williams immediately picks it up: "But if the cause be not good, the king himself hath a heavy reckoning to make" (133-4).

We thus return to the play's central politico-religious problem. In an apocalyptic image of dismembered bodies joining together at the day of judgment, Williams speculates on the horror of dying unattended on the battlefield in the knowledge that wives and children are left unprotected and debts unpaid. If the cause for which these men are about to die is not a good one, he says, "it will be a black matter for the king that led them to it" (133-45). Unknowingly Williams has touched on something that is dear to Henry's heart. Little wonder that he becomes angry, for who is Williams, a common soldier, to question the scourge of God? Henry's response is a long speech absolving the king of any responsibility for the souls of men who die with "irreconciled iniquities" (156); such men, he tells Williams, cannot expect to escape the wrath of God, for "war is his beadle, war is his vengeance" (174-5). Williams and the king are clearly talking at cross purposes: one is thinking about soldiers dying with unprotected dependents; the other is concerned to obey the will of a vindictive "God of battles". Henry's theology is harsh and, so far as Williams is concerned, irrelevant. But it is not pronounced in bad faith. If Henry fails to answer Williams' worries it is because he is apparently incapable of understanding the concerns of a common soldier. As he admitted when he threatened the citizens of Harfleur with "heady murder, spoil, and villainy" (3.3.32), "What is it then to me" if the innocent suffer? "What is't to me?" (15; 19). Henry's mind is on loftier things than the sufferings of common people. As we hear him pray to his God of battles at the end of the scene there is no question of his sincerity. Henry's fault is not "juggling" hypocrisy, but a missionary idealism that is incapable of doubting its own validity. If there is a moral in this play it must be "beware of men with visions".

The debate with Williams does not show Henry to good advantage. But the following morning he is in his true element. His rallying cry to his troops in the Crispin's day speech is not a piece of cynical bravado, but an expression of unaffected joy in doing the one thing that, for the chevalier, gives meaning and purpose to life:

> We few, we happy few, we band of brothers;
> For he to-day that sheds his blood with me
> Shall be my brother (4.3.60-2).

For the medieval knight war provides the ultimate test of his virtue; it is something for which his whole training in the chivalric arts has been a preparation. This is why Henry tells Westmoreland that he would not wish for any additional men, since that would diminish the glory of the hour:

> I would not lose so great an honour
> As one man more, methinks, would share from me
> For the best hope I have. O do not wish one more! (31-3).

War does not just provide a test of a knight's prowess; to die well is his supreme reward. Johan Huizinga quotes a passage from Jean de Bueil's *Le Jouvencel* (c.1466) that captures wonderfully the idealized sentiments that war is capable of inspiring:

> It is a joyous thing, is war [...] You love your comrade so in war. When you see that your quarrel is just and your blood is fighting well, tears rise to your eye. A great sweet feeling of loyalty and of pity fills your heart on seeing your friend so valiantly exposing his body to execute and accomplish the command of our Creator. And then you prepare to go and die or live with him, and for love not to abandon him. And out of that there arises such a delectation, that he who has not tasted it is not fit to say what a delight it is. Do you think that a man who does that fears death? Not at all; for he feels so strengthened, he is so elated, that he does not know where he is. Truly he is afraid of nothing.[77]

Idealization of battle is the very core of medieval chivalry. It is the knight's moment of true glory. Exactly the same sentiments as those described by Jean de Bueil are expressed in Exeter's account of the deaths of Suffolk and York in Act 4, Scene 6. This speech is a moving piece of theatre. In dramatic contrast to the disorder and confusion among the demoralized French (scene 5), we are now given a picture of heroic self-sacrifice and sublime emotion as two noble warriors, brothers in chivalry, are united in death. Exeter reports how, tenderly kissing the torn and bleeding face of his companion in arms, York cries

> 'Tarry my cousin Suffolk.
> My soul shall thine keep company to heaven;
> Tarry, sweet soul, for mine, then fly a-breast;
> As in this glorious and well-foughten field
> We kept together in our chivalry' (4.6.15-19).

Holding Exeter's hand, the dying York asks him to commend him to the king. Then he kisses the lips of his dead companion once more;

> And so espous'd to death, with blood he seal'd
> A testament of noble-ending love (26-7).

No conventional love scene in Shakespeare is so affecting. Indeed so powerful is Exeter's story that even Henry is almost moved to tears - almost, but not quite (4.6.33-4). If this battle scene had been written in the fifteenth century it might just have been possible to take it seriously. A century later it is the purest kitsch.

As if to signal the fact that Exeter's romantic chivalry is no more than theatrical sentimentality, this mood of maudlin heroism is abruptly broken by an alarum signalling that the French have regrouped. With brutal efficiency Henry immediately orders the prisoners to be killed. Since the prisoners are actually on stage at the time the order is given, Gary Taylor is probably right in suggesting that the killing would have taken place in front of the audience.[78] Whether or not circumstances on the battlefield at Agincourt meant that it was tactically necessary to kill the prisoners is something that no theatre audience would have time to consider. Dramatically, though, its impact is stark. This time it is Gower who provides the commentary. Supposing, wrongly, that Henry had ordered the killing of the prisoners in retaliation for the slaughter of the luggage boys, he says, "O, 'tis a gallant King!" (4.7.10).

## The dangers of idealism

One effect of the meeting between Henry and his bishops at the beginning of the play is to make us warm to Henry's integrity. Confronted with such blatant cynicism, it is not difficult to admire the man of honour. As Robert Ashley writes in a treatise entitled *Of Honour* (c.1600):

> By honour are vertues kindled and incouraged, by honour are vices eschewed, by honour ignoraunce, error and folly, sloth and sluggishness, hatred and fear, shame and ignoraunce, and all evill affeccions are alayed.[79]

Henry is a man inspired by a heroic ideal. At Agincourt his integrity and his valour are set off to even greater advantage by the foolish boasting of the Dauphin (3.7). When the man of honour is as gifted an orator as Henry, the combination of missionary zeal and impassioned eloquence is almost irresistible. Against our better judgment we respond to his inspiring words, forgetting for the moment the cruel reality behind the noble rhetoric. Yet repeatedly the play brings us back to that reality. Even as the Act 2 Chorus describes how England's youth are fired with thoughts of war, and "honour's thought / Reigns solely in the breast of every man", he tells us that they follow Henry to battle like "English Mercuries" (2, chorus 3-4; 7).

Mercury is, of course, the messenger of the gods, noted both for his celerity and for his eloquence (not a quality normally associated with soldiers). But like so many of his Olympian clients he has a double nature. He is both peacemaker – the caduceus is a symbol of peace, order and government – and thief.[80] Is Henry a peacemaker or a thief? It depends on one's point of view. Lydgate described the historical Henry as a "prince of pes" resolving an ancient dynastic dispute (*Troy Book*, V. 3416); Shakespeare's Henry also sees himself as a peacemaker. Ironically it is on the eve of a battle in which some ten thousand men are about to lose their lives that Henry reflects on his peacemaking role. As he ponders the cares of office he thinks ruefully how the peasant little knows "what watch the king keeps to maintain the peace" (4.1.279). But Erasmus saw Henry's campaigns as a classic example of the folly of attempting to extend territory. To him the chivalric ideals that endorsed them were simply a means of promoting war under a veneer of glory.

What Shakespeare thought about Henry we can only guess. However, it is interesting that, having given us a heroic image of chivalrous English warriors setting off to do battle for their country's honour, he immediately produces some English Mercuries of a rather different kind. The subplot of *Henry V* looks very much like a parody of the play's heroic main plot.[81] Its characters are pilferers, fools and braggarts motivated by self-interest and an absurd sense of 'manly' pride. The ironic parallel between Henry's exploits and those of his soldiers is underlined by Fluellen's comparison of him to Alexander the Great: "If you mark Alexander's life well, Harry of Monmouth's life is come after it indifferent well" (4.7.33-4). There are several allusions to Alexander in the play (1.1.46; 3.1.19; 4.7.13ff.). But the anecdote from Alexander's life that is most damaging to Henry is the general's meeting with a pirate he has taken prisoner. In St Augustine's version of the story Alexander asks Dionides how he dare "molest the seas". Dionides replies: "How darest thou molest the whole world? But because I doe it with a little ship onely, I am called a theefe: thou doing it with a great Nauie, art called an Emperour".[82] In the light of Erasmus' deprecation of war between neighbouring rulers when disagreements could easily be settled by arbitration,[83] Bardolph's complaint at the pointless brawling of his companions sounds very much like an oblique comment on his betters. As Nym and Pistol quarrel over a meaningless point of honour, he asks: "why the devil should we keep knives to cut one another's throats?" (2.1.88-9).

If, as Fluellen says, "there is figures in all things" (4.7.35), we have to ask what the function of these sub-plot scenes is with their foolish squabbling, petty thieving and preposterous heroics. Is it to show Henry's "gret manhode"[84] to advantage, revealing "true things by what their mock'ries be" (4, Chorus, 53)? or is it to suggest that for all Henry's noble rhetoric his foreign policy is merely thievery on an international scale? Paradoxically it is both. In his study of medieval chivalry Huizinga suggests that "the quest for glory and honour goes hand in hand with [...] hero worship".[85] Only by evoking a sense of the extraordinary glamour of the chivalric ideal in such a way as to make us experience for ourselves the irresistible appeal of its rhetoric is it possible to show the true danger of charismatic heroism.[86] Gary Taylor is right to describe *Henry V* as a study of human greatness. His contemporary biographers were unanimous in seeing him as the flower of English chivalry. But the question that the play forces audiences – both sixteenth-century and modern – to ask is whether the world can afford heroes of this mould.

Compared with Richard II, Henry is a model of kingly authority. But though his own sense of the indisputable rightness of his cause is beyond question, historians have not been unanimous in endorsing that view. One scholar describes his legacy as "a false ideal of foreign conquest and aggression, a reckless contempt for the rights and feelings of other nations, and a restless incapacity for peace".[87] Whatever we may think of the ethics of Henry's policies, their practical result was national impoverishment, both economic and artistic. (In contrast to the literary glories of Richard's reign Henry's is an artistic waste land.) In a study of military leadership John Keegan writes of the sterility of the heroic society. A society that is preoccupied with "the repetitive and ultimately narcissistic activity of combat" is incapable of developing to the full its creative and artistic potential. Keegan's conclusion is that humankind "needs an end to the ethic of [military] heroism in its leadership for good and all".[88]

# Henry V

There are, of course, other kinds of heroism. Having anatomized the warlike Herculean hero in a series of tragedies,[89] Shakespeare turns, at the end of his career, to an entirely different kind of leader. Like the idealized James, for whom he is an epideictic model of both praise and warning, Prospero is a reluctant pacifist who learns that "the rarer action is / Is in virtue than in vengeance" (5.1.27-8). Above all Prospero is a type of the creative artist. By contrast, the heroes of the martial and political tragedies are destructive figures. They are charismatic leaders who are either responsible for the collapse of the state whose safety they are supposed to be guarding, or else place it in extreme jeopardy. Like them, Henry V is a profoundly paradoxical figure, a national hero who is indirectly responsible for a national disaster.

*Notes*

1. Quotations from Shakespeare are from *The Complete Works*, ed. Peter Alexander, London: Collins, 1951.

2. In the Envoy to his *Troy Book* John Lydgate praises Henry as the "sours & welle" of knighthood, see *Lydgate's Troy Book*, edited by Henry Bergen, 4 vols (London: Early English Text Society, 1906-35), V.1. Thomas Hoccleve describes him as the 'welle of honur' and 'flour of Chivalrie', *Hoccleve's Works*, 3 vols, edited by Frederick J. Furnival, (London: Early English Text Society, 1892-7), 1.41.

3. See Maurice Keen, *Chivalry*, New Haven and London: Yale UP, 1984; J. Huizinga, *The Waning of the Middle Ages*, (1924; repr. Harmondsworth: Penguin, 1982), chapter 4; Malcolm Vale, *War and Chivalry: Warfare and Aristocratic Culture in England, France and Burgundy at the End of the Middle Ages*, London: Duckworth, 1981.

4. *Lydgate's Troy Book*, Prol. 83.

5. Ibid., 1.ll.1 7; 36 7.

6. *Hall's Chronicle*, (1548; repr. London, 1809), p. 113.

7. William Worcester, *The Boke of Noblesse*, with an introduction by John Gough Nichols, (London: J.B. Nichols, 1860), p. 20.

8. Ibid. p.20.

9. J.R. Lander, *Conflict and Stability in Fifteenth-Century England*, (London: Hutchinson, 1969), p. 61.

10. See above, note 2.

11. *Hoccleve's Works*, 3.192-3.

12. *Lydgate's Siege of Thebes* III.4645ff., 2 vols, ed. by Axel Erdmann and Eilert Ekwall (London: Early English Text Society, 1911-1930) II, 191.

13. M.H. Keen, *England in the Later Middle Ages: a Political History* (London: Methuen, 1973), p. 377.

14. G.L. Harriss, ed., *Henry V: the Practice of Kingship* (Oxford: Oxford UP, 1985), pp. 24; 209. See also Harold F. Hutchison, *Henry V: a Biography* (London: Eyre & Spottiswoode, 1967), pp. 222-4.

15. Desmond Seward, *Henry V as Warlord* (London: Sidgwick & Jackson, 1987), p. 218.

16. *Hall's Chronicle*, p. 113.

17. J.H. Walter, ed., Introduction to Arden edition of *Henry V* (London: Methuen; Cambridge, MA.: Harvard UP, 1954), p. xvi.

18. Norman Rabkin, *Shakespeare and the Common Understanding*, (1967; repr. Chicago and London: Chicago UP, 1984), p. 98. However, Rabkin later revised this view: see *Shakespeare and the Problem of Meaning* (Chicago and London: Chicago UP, 1981), pp. 33-62.

19. Gary Taylor, ed., Introduction to *Henry V*, (Oxford and New York: Oxford UP, 1982), p. 72.

20. In *Shakespeare and the Common Understanding*, pp. 99-100, Rabkin compares the play to a comedy.

21. Christopher Allmand, *Henry V* (London: Methuen, 1992), p. 434.

22. See Arthur B. Ferguson, *The Chivalric Tradition in Renaissance England*, Washington, London and Toronto: Folger Shakespeare Library, 1986. See also Sydney Anglo, ed., introduction to *Chivalry in the Renaissance* (Woodbridge: Boydell Press, 1990), pp. xi-xvi; Ferguson, *The Indian Summer of English Chivalry: Studies in the Decline and Transformation of Chivalric Idealism*, Durham, NC: Duke UP, 1960; Richard C. McCoy, *The Rites of Knighthood: The Literature and Politics of Elizabethan Chivalry*, Berkeley, Los Angeles and London: California UP, 1989); Roy Strong, *The Cult of Elizabeth*, London: Thames & Hudson, 1977; Frances Yates, *Astraea: The Imperial Theme in the Sixteenth Century* (London and Boston: Routledge & Kegan Paul, 1975), pp. 88-111.

23. Worcester, *The Boke of Noblesse*, p. 29.

24. Mervyn James, *Society, Politics and Culture: Studies in Early Modern England*, (1978; repr. Cambridge: Cambridge UP, 1986), p. 309.

25. Edmund Spenser, *Prothalamion*, 146, *The Poetical Works*, edited by J.C. Smith and E. de Selincourt (London, New York and Toronto: Oxford UP, 1912), p. 602.

26. Robert Devereux, Earl of Essex, *An Apologie of the Earl of Essex* (London, 1598), Sig.D2$^v$.

27. Ramón Lull, *The Book of the Ordre of Chyvalry*, transl. William Caxton (c.1483-5), (London: Early English Text Society, 1926), p. 122.

28. The following paragraph is largely based on Ferguson, *The Chivalric Tradition in Renaissance England* (see above, note 22).

29. Desiderius Erasmus, *Enchiridion Militis Christiani: An English Version*, ed. Anne M. O'Donnell, SND (Oxford: Early English Text Society, 1981), ch. 2, "The wepons of a chrysten man", pp. 41-55.

30. See Philip C. Dust, *Three Renaissance Pacifists: Essays on the Theories of Erasmus, More, and Vives* (New York: Peter Lang, 1987), pp. 13-61.

31. *The 'Adages' of Erasmus*, edited with a translation by Margaret Mann Phillips, (Cambridge: Cambridge UP, 1964), p. 348.

32. Thomas More, *Utopia*, with an introduction by John O'Hagan (London and Toronto: Dent, 1910), p. 91.

33. C.S. Lewis, *English Literature in the Sixteenth Century Excluding Drama* (London, Oxford and New York: Oxford UP, 1954), p. 29.

34. Sir Thomas Elyot, *The Boke Named the Governour*, ed. Foster Watson, (London: Dent, 1907), p. 49.

35. Baldassare Castiglione, *The Book of the Courtier*, transl. Sir Thomas Hoby, ed. W.H.D. Rouse (London: Dent, 1928), p. 41.

36. *The Governour*, p. 69.

37. Roger Ascham, *The Scholemaster* in *English Works*, ed. W.A. Wright (Cambridge: Cambridge UP, 1904), p. 231.

38. Worcester, *The Boke of Noblesse*, p. 9.

39. Gerard Legh, *The Accedens of Armory* (1562; repr. London, 1597), fol. 13.

40. *An Apologie*, Sig. D3$^v$.

41. See Wallace T. MacCaffrey, *Elizabeth I: War and Politics 1588-1603* (Princeton: Princeton UP, 1992), pp. 153ff.; see also R.D. Wernham, *The Making of Elizabethan Foreign Policy, 1558-1603* (Berkeley, Los Angeles and London: California UP, 1980), passim.; John Guy, *Tudor England* (Oxford and New York: Oxford UP, 1988), pp. 439ff.

42. *An Apologie*, Sig. D4.

43. See Dominic Baker-Smith, "'Inglorious glory': 1513 and the Humanist Attack on Chivalry" in *Chivalry in the Renaissance*, ed. Anglo (see above, note 22), p. 135.

44. Samuel Daniel, *The Civil Wars*, II. stanza 130, ed. Lawrence Michel (New Haven: Yale UP, 1958), p. 312.

45. Paul N. Siegel, "Shakespeare and the Neo-Chivalric Cult of Honor", *The Centennial Review*, 8 (1964), p. 43.

46. Hubert Languet, *The Correspondence of Sir Philip Sidney and Hubert Languet*, edited by S.A. Pears (London, 1845), p. 138.

47. Quoted by MacCaffrey, *Elizabeth I: War and Politics*, p. 516.

48. What Shakespeare intended by the allusion to Essex is an unresolved puzzle. Was it a provocative reminder of Essex's popularity? or a warning of his ambitions? or was it, as Annabel Patterson suggests (*Shakespeare and the Popular Voice* [Cambridge, MA and Oxford: Blackwell, 1989], p. 87) a 'well meant' attempt at mediation between the queen and her general? Since the play was presumably written before Essex had disgraced himself in Ireland, the latter suggestion does not seem plausible. Given the unreliability of the Chorus as a commentator (see Andrew Gurr, ed., Introduction to *King Henry V* [Cambridge: Cambridge UP, 1992], pp. 6-16) it would seem more likely that Shakespeare was making a discreetly ironic comment on militaristic values by comparing one well known model of chivalric honour with another.

49. Jonathan Dollimore, "Critical Development: Cultural Materialism, Feminism and Gender Critique, and New Historicism", in *Shakespeare: a Bibliographical Guide*, ed. Stanley Wells (Oxford: Clarendon Press, 1990), p. 414.

50. T.W. Craik, ed., Introduction to *King Henry V* (London and New York: Routledge, 1995), p. 3.

51. P.M. Handover, *The Second Cecil: The Rise to Power 1563-1604 of Sir Robert Cecil, later first Earl of Salisbury*, (London: Eyre & Spottiswoode, 1959), p. 187.

52. Handover, p. 222; Robert Lacey, Robert, *Earl of Essex: An Elizabethan Icarus*, (London: Weidenfeld & Nicholson, 1971), p. 290.

53. The standard work on Shakespeare and war is Paul Jorgensen, *Shakespeare's Military World*, (Berkeley and Los Angeles: California UP, 1956). For an important recent discussion of Shakespeare's treatment of militarism see Steven Marx, "Shakespeare's Pacifism", *Renaissance Quarterly*, 45 (1992), pp. 49-95.

54. Arthur F. Kinney describes "Invisible Bullets" as "perhaps the most important and surely the most influential essay of the past decade in English Renaissance cultural history" (*Rogues, Vagabonds and Sturdy Beggars: A New Gallery of Tudor and Stuart Rogue Literature*, ed. Kinney (Amherst, MA: Massachesetts UP, 1990), p. 1.

55. Stephen Greenblatt, *Shakespearean Negotiations: The Circulation of Social Energy in Renaissance England* (Oxford: Clarendon Press, 1988), pp. 41; 56.

56. On Greenblatt's rhetorical strategies, analogical method and flexible treatment of texts see Tom McAlindon, "Testing the New Historicism", *Studies in Philology*, 92 (1995), Fall issue.

57. Steven Marx, "Holy War in *Henry V*", unpublished paper read at the annual conference of the Shakespeare Association of America, Albuquerque, 1994.

58. John F. Danby, *Shakespeare's Doctrine of Nature: A Study of 'King Lear'* (London: Faber & Faber, 1961), pp. 81-101.

59. Harriss, *Henry V,* (note 14 above), p. 24.

60. Lander, *Conflict and Stability in Fifteenth-Century England.* Lander describes Henry as "a bigot of near-heroic mould whose intense religiosity equalled only his intense legalism over feudal property rights" (p. 58).

61. C.T. Allmand, "Henry V the Soldier, and the War in France" in *Henry V*, ed. Harriss, p. 129. Cf. Lander, who writes of 'the obsessive character of his kingship' (*Conflict and Stability*, p. 208).

62. For discussion of Pauline allusions in Henry IV see J.A. Bryant, "Prince Hal and the Ephesians", *Sewanee Review*, 67 (1959), pp. 204-19; D.J. Palmer, "Casting off the Old Man: History and St Paul in Henry IV", *Critical Quarterly*, 12 (1970), pp. 267-83. See also Robin Headlam Wells, *Elizabethan Mythologies: Studies in Poetry, Drama and Music* (Cambridge: Cambridge UP, 1994), pp. 44-62.

63. *The Oldcastle Controversy: Sir John Oldcastle, Part I and the Famous Victories of Henry V*, Revels Plays edn., ed. Peter Corbin and Douglas Sedge (Manchester and New York: Manchester UP, 1991), p. 175.

64. *Holinshed's Chronicles*, 3.66.

65. See Headlam Wells, *Elizabethan Mythologies*, pp. 6-7 and passim.

66. Pierre de La Primaudaye, *The French Academie* (London: 1586), p. 743.

67. *The Mirrour of Maiestie: or, The Badges of Honovr* (1618), facsimile copy ed. Henry Green and James Croston (London:, 1870), Sig. F2. The beehive analogy is a commonplace in classical, medieval and Renaissance political writing (see J.H. Walter's notes on 1.2. in his Arden edition of *Henry V*, p. 22). As Andrew Gurr has shown in the *Education of a Christian Prince*, which Shakespeare is known to have used when he was writing *Henry V*, Erasmus uses the beehive analogy to caution the prince against the temptation to enlarge his territories see "*Henry V* and the Bees' Commonwealth", *Shakespeare Survey*, 30 (1977), pp. 61-72.

68. George Puttenham, *The Arte of English Poesie*, ed. by Gladys Dodge Willcock and Alice Walker, (Cambridge: Cambridge UP, 1936), p. 6

69. In the *Boke of Noblesse* William Worcester says that the labours of Hercules "were writen in a figure of a poesy for to courage and comfort alle noble men of birthe to be victorious in entreprinses of armes" (p. 21).

70. Puttenham follows Horace *(Ars poetica,* 391-401) in representing Orpheus, together with Amphion, as the founder of civilisation, see *The Arte of English Poesie*, p. 6). But in *The Arte of Rhetorique* (ed. G.H. Mair (Oxford: Clarendon Press, 1909) Thomas Wilson ascribes this role to Hercules (Sig.Avii). In the famous pacifist essay "Dulce bellum inexpertis" Erasmus refers to Hercules as the founder of war. See *The 'Adages' of Erasmus,* (see above, note 31),. p. 317.

71. See Dust, *Three Renaissance Pacifists*.

72. Introduction to *Henry V*, (note 17 above), pp. xvii-xviii.

73. *The Education of a Christian Prince*, (note 67 above), p. 209.

74. See Theodor Meron, *Henry's Wars and Shakespeare's Laws: Perspectives on the Law of War in the Later Middle Ages* (Oxford: Clarendon Press, 1993), p. 27ff.

75. Introduction to *Henry V*, (note 19 above), pp. 34-8.

76. Anne Barton, 'The King Disguised: Shakespeare's *Henry V* and the Comical History' in *The Triple Bond: Plays, Mainly Shakespearean, in Performance*, ed. Joseph G. Price (University Park and London: Pennsylvania State UP, 1975), pp. 92-117.

77. *The Waning of the Middle Ages*, p. 73.

78. Introduction to *Henry V*, (note 19 above), p. 32.

79. Robert Ashley, *Of Honour*, ed. Virgil B. Heltzel (San Marino, Ca.: The Huntington Library, 1947), p. 30.

80. On Mercury as a symbolic representative of peace, government and control see Douglas Brooks-Davies, *The Mercurian Monarch: Magical Politics from Spenser to Pope* (Manchester: Manchester UP, 1983), p. 2; see also Edgar Wind *Pagan Mysteries in the Renaissance* (London: Faber, 1958), p. 91n2. On his thieving habits see the Homeric *Hymn to Hermes*; see also Ovid, *Metamorphoses*, II.685ff.; II.815ff.

81. Graham Bradshaw writes brilliantly on what he calls 'dramatic rhyming' in *Henry V* in *Misrepresentations: Shakespeare and the Materialists* (Ithaca and London: Cornell UP, 1993), pp. 63-80.

82. St Augustine of Hippo, *Of the Citie of God*, trans. J. Healey (London, 1610). For this point I am indebted to Janet M. Spencer, 'The Execution of Justice and the Justice of Execution: Criminalizing Wars of Conquest in *Henry V*', unpublished paper read at the annual conference of the Shakespeare Association of America, Albuquerque, 1994.

83. *The Education of a Christian Prince* (above, note 67),. pp. 252-3.

84. See above note 7.

85. *The Waning of the Middle Ages*, p. 68.

86. One of the most persuasive analyses of charismatic heroism and its dangerous power is Joseph Conrad's: see Robin Headlam Wells, '"The question of these wars': *Hamlet* in the New Europe" in *Shakespeare in the New Europe*, ed. Michael Hattaway, Derek Roper and Boika Sokolova (Sheffield: Sheffield Academic Press, 1994), p. 105. Emrys Jones discusses charismatic heroism in *Scenic Form in Shakespeare,* Oxford: Clarendon Press, 1971. A theatre audience, says Jones, is a "charmed crowd": just as a crowd can turn law-abiding citizens into credulous barbarians, so intelligent, civilized people become susceptible in the theatre to feelings which in other circumstances they would probably disown (pp. 6; 132).

87. Charles Plummer, ed., Introduction to Sir John Fortescue, *The Governance of England* (London: Oxford UP, 1885), p. 8.

88. John Keegan, *The Mask of Command* (London: Jonathan Cape, 1987), pp. 312-3; 350.

89. See Eugene M. Waith, *The Herculean Hero in Marlowe, Chapman, Shakespeare and Dryden,* London: Chatto & Windus, 1962.

# HISTORY'S SIR THOMAS AND SHAKESPEARE'S ERPINGHAM

## Christopher Smith
### (University of East Anglia, Norwich)

Apart from having his portrait drawn by Holbein,[1] there is perhaps no way an Englishman from the past could hope to have his character more memorably preserved for posterity than by figuring, no matter how briefly and in however altered a form, in a Shakespeare history play. Mentioned but once in *Richard II* (2.2.283), as a mere name in a list, Erpingham speaks briefly in only two short episodes in the first scene of Act IV of *Henry V*, saying more in the first than in the second and uttering just fifty-two words in all; he is also the subject of passing conversation between these two appearances and, after this, is finally mentioned in a stage direction as coming on stage "with all his host", but on this occasion he has nothing to say.[2] Such an exiguous role earns Erpingham no more than incidental reference even in Mahood's recent study of 'bit parts' in Shakespeare,[3] and one might wonder whether allusion might not be more appropriately made not so much to portraiture proper as rather to another genre favoured in Elizabethan and Jacobean times, the miniature. But, unlike the vast majority of the delightful works of Hilliard and Oliver, Shakespeare's Erpingham is a figure in a background whom we shall, moreover, be well advised to see within a perspective.[4]

Sir Thomas (as he will be styled here even before he was knighted, in order to distinguish him for the Shakespearean character, who will be called Erpingham throughout except in direct quotation from *Henry V*) served the Lancastrian cause long and loyally, and was duly rewarded for his pains.[5] He was born in 1357 into a family that claimed to have held property around the north Norfolk village of Erpingham since the Conquest,[6] and about the time of his father's death in 1370,[7] he followed his example and entered the service of John of Gaunt, who held land in the nearby manor of Aylsham.[8] It was the start of an arduous career. He first appears to have given satisfaction when suppressing rebellion in Norfolk and then in Middlesex in the early 1380s, and in the middle of the decade, already a knight bachelor, he went out with John of Gaunt on his expedition to Spain. In the early 1390s he embarked on yet more challenging assignments:[9] he accompanied the Earl of Derby, John of Gaunt's son, on his two campaigns in Lithuania, at the end of the second crossing Europe with him and continuing on to Palestine, though it seems probable he was denied the ultimate satisfaction of going with him to Jerusalem.[10] When his master was banished from the kingdom, Sir Thomas formed part of the retinue that loyally left England with him and remained with him on the continent. He was still with him when he returned to claim the throne. The esteem in which Sir Thomas was held was shown by his appointment as one of the commissioners who received Richard II's resignation of the crown. In 1400 Henry IV gave him the office of chamberlain to the royal household and the year after also made him a Knight of the Garter,[11] which meant that he could display in St George's Chapel, Windsor, his arms: vert, an inescutcheon argent within an orle of martlets argent.[12]

For the next few years Sir Thomas remained a trusted servant of the crown, despite suspicions of Lollardry,[13] and although he was perhaps to some degree eclipsed towards the end of the reign of Henry IV, he came to the fore again after the accession of the new king.[14] Though advanced in years by now, he not only accompanied Henry V on the taxing Agincourt campaign,[15] commanding the archers on the battlefield,[16] where two of his own men fell,[17] but continued to undertake duties in France for some time after. Sir Thomas died in 1428 and was buried in Norwich Cathedral, on the north side of the presbytery. His most impressive memorial is the grand gate leading into the Cathedral Close that bears his name; there is a complex (if sadly eroded) display of heraldry that bespeaks his family history and his religious affinities,[18] including the arms of the Trinity that were displayed at Agincourt.[19] In a niche at the top of the gate may be seen the kneeling figure of the bearded Sir Thomas, complete with the Garter below the right knee and the knightly spurs; most probably it was not, however, placed there originally, but, having been removed from his tomb at an earlier date, was set up here in the early eighteenth century.[20] Though Sir Thomas remains, then, a presence in Norfolk and Norwich,[21] it is true to say that he is known to the wider world as Shakespeare's Erpingham.

Shakespeare's treatment of Sir Thomas, like his handling of history generally, is free. Perhaps it would be better to say that when dealing with the past he accords greater importance to remaining true to his vision of event and character as he interprets them than he does to the accurate and impartial presentation of what is recorded by historians, whose task is different from that of the creative writers. Those are entitled to the same licence, subject to inner coherence, plausibility and public acceptability, in fashioning recorded fact in accord with their conception as in rearranging personal experience. Historians have one task, writers another, even if they borrow from history. So there is no need for alarm if we see that there are differences between the Sir Thomas whose career we have just sketched and the Erpingham who appears so briefly in *Henry V.* All the same, it is enlightening to note what use Shakespeare made of the material that forms the basis for this minor character in his play.[22] That the inclusion of Erpingham was a deliberate choice appears to be indicated by the fact that Erpingham does not figure in the cast list of *The Famous Victories of Henry the Fifth*, the earlier chronicle play with which Shakespeare was familiar.[23]

It is plain that in *Henry V*, a play that in its minor roles parades a gallery of rich characters typifying various British traits, Erpingham is introduced to embody the older generation, whose wisdom and steadiness the king values after the extravagances of his salad days, now that he is, in the words of a chronicler who was close to him "aetate iuvenis sed maturitate senex".[24] Perhaps even the very great disproportion of the extent of their roles can also be taken as a measure of the differences between Hal's excessive devotion to Falstaff and Henry's more appropriate and more measured, though still warm relationship with the aged knight. Thomas M. Cranfill places Erpingham in the context of a broader study of 'old heroes' in Shakespeare's works, suggesting these were characters with whom the dramatist had a deep sympathy.[25] With reference to the Royal Shakespeare Company's centenary production of *Henry V*, the comment was made that "It is interesting that for the first time in three plays, an old man of the previous era actually approves of Henry."[26] However that may be, it is enough now to note how much Shakespeare emphasises Erpingham's age.

When the character first appears on stage, Shakespeare immediately directs our responses to him by making the king greet him as "old Sir Thomas Erpingham" (4.1.13). This reinforces an impression the audience will have already gained from his body language and his "good white head", and when the king, strictly unnecessarily, mentions his hair the point is stressed yet further. Then the king goes on to comment that the knight might prefer a more comfortable bed than the hard ground, and this very considerateness hints once again at old age and the weariness of the flesh that often goes with it. In this context the language of Henry's generalisations about the way the mind can revive the body keeps up the insistence on the theme:

> ...when the mind is quicken'd, out of doubt
> The organs, though defunct and dead before,
> Break up their drowsy grave. (4.1.20-22)

It is as if the king, with Erpingham before him, can hardly avoid the vocabulary of mortality. After this, not only does the episode end, as Erpingham departs, with the king describing him as "old heart", but a little later, Williams also uses, as if no other were available, the adjective "old" when speaking of the knight.

The theme of age goes, however, hand in hand with that of honour. Erpingham is invariably referred to by his full name and title. Moreover, it is notable how many times the adjective "good" is used in speeches addressed to him or concerned with him. Cumulatively the effect is to create an impression of praiseworthiness.

> Good morrow, old Sir Thomas Erpingham:
> A good soft pillow for that good white head
> Were better than the churlish turf of France. (4.1.13-15)

And 'good' will be the second word Henry uses in his next speech in which the knight is praised in a generalisation: "'Tis good for men to love their present pains." (4.1.18) In the context of so many repetitions of 'good', Erpingham's own use of the comparative degree of the same adjective in a reply that in any case redounds to his credit is all the more striking: "This lodging likes me better, / since I may say, 'Now lie I like a king'." (4.1.16-17) Shakespeare, as if intent on stressing the link between goodness and age in the knight that we have already noted, gives the following words to Henry when later in the scene Erpingham informs him that his nobles are looking for him: "Good old knight, / Collect them altogether at my tent..." (4.1.292-3). And it is tempting to interpret "I'll be before thee" (4.1.294) as a hint that the young monarch can walk more quickly than his interlocutor.

The theme of goodness is, moreover, reinforced by being contrasted with the 'churlish' in "the churlish turf of France". OED does cite, along with other, later evidence, Barnaby Googe's translation of Heresbach's *Husbandry* some twenty years before *Henry V* as evidence for interpreting 'churlish' in collocations with soil and tillage as meaning simply 'hard'. Yet it would be hard to deny that at the time this was most likely taken as a figurative use of a term whose primary meaning was still sensed; and that is how Shakespeare employs the word, for instance, in *Troilus and Cressida*: "as valiant as the lion, churlish as the bear, ..." (1.2.21). In the circumstances of a play full of praise for English chivalry, Erpingham will, then, rise as nobler yet when compared with the "churlish turf" of France, particularly if an allusion to the four elements can be seen within the line. The impressions gained when first we see Erpingham are strengthened when

Williams, in simple tribute, echoes his monarch's estimation by calling the knight "a good old commander and a most kind gentleman".

Many have been content to see Erpingham simply as the embodiment of the view that old age has, in Tennyson's phrase, "yet his honour and his toil". There are, however, some puzzles in his role. This may be seen even in a simple piece of stage business. Henry's borrowing of Erpingham's cloak is, of course, a homely realistic detail that readily yields symbolism in a Judaeo-Christian tradition stretching back to the Second Book of Kings and is an apt emblem of Henry's readiness to slough off his old self and assume a new, more responsible personæ. But is not a reciprocal piece of business needed too? For the king simply to take Erpingham's cloak - and his request is not, in all conscience, one that could readily be refused - and not to hand the knight his in return would be an action bespeaking an indifference to the welfare of the aged captain at dead of night that would have been entirely at odds with the solicitude that has just been expressed verbally.[27] With modern actors. an exchange of cloaks might cost a valuable moment of stage time, but in Shakespeare's age the players would have been more adroit at handling these garments, so the action would not have been unduly delayed for what would appear to be a necessary gesture.

If this is detail, the interpretation of Erpingham's most famous line is quite an important issue: "... I may say, 'Now lie I like a king.'" Generally this is interpreted as the witty riposte of an indomitable old fire-eater turned courtier who, in a way that is often thought typically English, copes with a tense and difficult situation with a laugh, using, as Craik points out, the common expression in its literal sense for humorous effect. Gurr is, it seems, alone in espying that the other meaning of 'lie' is appropriate too, only to be called "perverse" by Craik for his pains. Whether or not Gurr is well-advised to found his argument on "Henry's perversion of the proverb about ill neighbours" a few lines previously, his reading none the less has much to commend it, particularly in a drama full of wordplay by an author who could rarely resist a quibble. The best reason for admitting a second meaning for the word "lie" is found in the simple fact that we soon see the king knows perfectly well that Erpingham should not be taken literally. When Williams enquires what Erpingham thinks of the army's "estate", Henry replies unhesitatingly: "Even as men wrecked upon a sand, / that look to be washed off the next tide." (4.1.97-8) That could scarcely be more explicit: he admits readily that this veteran with experience that is more valuable than some of his fellows' displays of book learning can recognise full well that the situation is very dangerous indeed. When Bate asks whether Erpingham has "told his thought to the king", the very form of his question indicating that he is expecting the strongly negative reply he is given: "No; nor it is not meet he should." (4.1.100)

In the light of these exchanges we may return to Henry's remark on Erpingham's exit: "God-a-mercy, old heart, thou speak'st cheerfully." (4.1.34) Indeed he does, But, unless we are to accept the unlikely hypothesis that the truth of the matter dawns on Henry only later, which would suggest a certain slow-wittedness, and also suppose that the old soldier is, as Gurr calls him, simply "a model of cheerfulness", then the conclusion cannot be avoided that the king knows there is a gap between what Erpingham appears to be saying and what he really means. But such disingenuousness would quite undermine the honest character of "good" Erpingham. So it is more satisfactory to interpret "lie" in the sense of "uttering an untruth", not to deceive the person to whom it is addressed, but rather in order to establish, with a quibble opaque to mere bystanders, a moment of covert understanding between the experienced captain and his youthful commander when both of them appreciate the need to cloak the truth from those whose hearts are not so stout.

An even more intriguing puzzle arises from the role given - or more precisely - not given to Erpingham. Arguments from omissions are notoriously difficult, but in this instance Shakespeare's departure from what was not only well attested but also very commonly known fact is so striking as to invite speculation that history has been distorted in order to allow room for an alternative interpretation. In writing *Henry V* Shakespeare has played down the role of the archers at the Battle of Agincourt, preferring to make much not only of other weaponry but also of a different class of warriors.[28]

Whether contemporary with the events or written in the aftermath of them or in the modern era, all historical accounts of the Hundred Years War stress the importance of the longbow in securing victory for the kings of England.[29] The generalisation holds too for the Battle of Agincourt where Sir Thomas is credited not only with the highly responsible task of marshalling the archers but also with the highly dramatic gesture of hurling into the air his warder (or staff) and bidding his troops prepare to shoot their arrows with the cry "Nestroque".[30] Precisely what those syllables meant has remained an enigma, but the French soon had cause to regret the action they commanded. What is found in histories is echoed in ballads:[31]

> Agincourt, Agincourt!
> Know ye not Agincourt?
> Where English slu and hurt
>    All their French foemen?
> With our pike and bills brown,
> How the French were beat down,
>    Shot by our bowmen.

Or:

> Our English archers discharged their shafts
>    As thicke as hayle in skye
> & many a Frenchman on the feelde
>    That happy day did dye.

The same theme is repeated by Roger Ascham in *Toxophilus*, in which Henry V is praised as "a prince pereless and moste victorious conqueroure" whose battle were won by the longbowmen.[32] Yet, though the role of the archers in the Hundred Years War cannot have been a secret to anybody in late Tudor England, Shakespeare chose to make nothing of it in *Henry V*.

In part the reason may have been military. Impressive though the deeds of the archers may have been in the Hundred Years War,[33] it was being recognised more and more as the sixteenth century wore towards its close that the longbow was an obsolete weapon. The military historian Cruickshank sums up the matter: "By far the most important military development in Elizabeth's reign was the victory of fire-arms over the older missile weapon, the longbow. It was by no means an easy victory. It was achieved slowly, in the face of considerable technical and financial difficulty and bitter opposition from some professional soldiers."[34] Henrician archery legislation in the early 1540s was an attempt to stop the spread of opinion against the longbow; and that it was followed by further attempts to enforce shooting practice during Elizabeth's reign may be interpreted not so much as attempt to reinforce her father's policy but as an admission of its relative failure. No doubt published in an attempt to curry favour at court after the promulgation of the first laws, Ascham's *Toxophilus*, however important its status in the development of English prose, was too literary to turn the tide.[35] Its publication history is significant too. It was first published in 1547, and new editions were called for in 1560 and 1583. That is a more than respectable record, but, for our purposes, it is important to note that there was no further occasion for printing the text in the Early Modern period. Romantic nostalgia for the longbow - for that is what it really amounted to - is shown in its true light when the professional commanders at Tilbury in 1588 angrily threw away the bows that were sent them at the Council's command.[36] Arrows could still kill, of course, as is shown, for instance, in the continuing use of the bow for sporting purposes,[37] and there were attempts even as late as 1612 to enforce new archery laws. But in warfare morale can be readily undermined by what is considered out-of-date equipment, and by the end of the sixteenth century no English commander would be confident his men would not let him down if they were armed with longbows.

*Henry V* clearly rejects the historical fact of the importance of the longbow in the Hundred Years War. The reasons may well be, at least in part, changes in military opinion and practice. It is notable, however, that, amidst a number of references in the play to equipment, in which the longbow is conspicuous by its absence, the only form of protection that receives any commendation - even in the reverse form of condemnation by the French nobility who mistakenly ridicule it (e.g. Orleans's speech, 3.3.137-9) - is the heavy steel helmet that had, by the end of the sixteenth century, replaced the all-over plate armour which had been developed specifically as protection against arrows.

But we need to go beyond such purely technical aspects, though they would no doubt appeal to at least a proportion of Shakespeare's initial audiences, especially any aristocratic patrons with military pretensions. To stress, as did historians and ballad writers alike, the role of the archers at Agincourt was, in effect, to ascribe the triumph, not to the aristocracy, but to the archers, who were, in many ways, "base, common and popular". In fact they were, in large measure, not even English, but Welsh, and that, from certain angles, could seem yet worse. Asking why Erpingham is denied Sir Thomas's most celebrated historical role as commander of the archers and going on to enquire into the suppression of the importance of the longbow in the Hundred Years War cannot, then, but reinforce the opinion that Shakespeare has reorganised his material, programmatically, one might say, in order to glorify the role of the nobility of England.[38] This makes *Henry V* what Giorgio Melchiori has taught us to call "a Garter play".[39]

Erpingham's role is so short, it is difficult to trace any particular trends in its interpretation on stage. Thomas L. Berger, after showing most interestingly how the drama might have been performed with a cast of a bare thirteen actors, suggests the actor playing Erpingham might also have doubled as Fluellen, the French king and Beaumont.[40] Even if that conclusion is accepted – and, as Berger himself scrupulously admits, it has been challenged – there are arguments against accepting the view that any particular dramatic impact would have been made. Doubling was so common a practice in Shakespeare's theatre that comparisons, possibly of an ironic nature, might well have not been made in the way that they sometimes are in modern productions, where the audience will tend to think that the director is seeking to make particular points by deciding to double certain roles.[41] Besides, cloaked, in a white wig and doubtless bearded to emphasise his age, and adopting suitable body language, Erpingham would hardly have been recognisable as the actor taking other parts in the play. If, for authenticity or experimentally, doubling were essayed in a modern production, the dimming of the lighting for the first part of Act IV would, of course, again tend to militate against recognition.

Theatrical performance is notoriously evanescent, and there have, it may readily be granted, been few playgoers who have concentrated their attention on Erpingham when watching or recording their impressions of *Henry V*. This gives especial interest to two highly regarded film versions, Lawrence Olivier's 1944 Two Cities production and Kenneth Branagh's 1987 screen adaptation for Renaissance Films. Following Shakespeare, Olivier does not bring on Erpingham until the night before Agincourt. The role is entrusted to the paunchy Morland Graham, and his arms, on the left shoulder of his cloak, serve to identify him visually in the film almost as well as they might have done in the fifteenth-century campaign. His "now lie I like a king" is accepted at face value and with a ready laugh by monarch and his nobles alike. But Henry's commentary, like his remark "thou speak'st cheerfully" is omitted, and though he borrows Erpingham's cloak, the possibility of monarch and knight exchanging them is not envisaged. Not only is the appreciation of Erpingham preserved in the later exchanges with the soldiers, but after the knight has summoned Henry back to join his nobles, he accompanies him as he returns through the camp, looking in at the tents where mass is being celebrated. This involves some slight departure from the implications of Shakespeare's text, but there are significant corresponding benefits. Silent, as in the play, but very much in evidence as a background figure with what, in this situation, we may call the English host, Erpingham is part of the audience for the battle speech. Finally we see him again, identified by his arms, as the soldiery marches off after the fighting.

All this is worthy enough, but Branagh is notably more inventive in a manner that is, moreover, entirely responsible both to Shakespeare and to history.[42] While Erpingham is given no words that Shakespeare had not assigned to him in the original play, his part is developed plausibly and consistently in the light of an awareness of Sir Thomas's place in history. Much is in fact added by making Erpingham's not just a walk-on part late in the play, but by showing the knight rather as a character who is present throughout and who shares in the responsibility for what takes place since he has lent tacit support to the plan to invade France.

Erpingham, played by Edward Jewesbury, is first seen in the play in the presence chamber (1.2.). With his full head of white hair, though no beard, with a trimmer figure than Morland Graham's and with his chain of office conspicuous against his smarter costume, he is an elder personage in an assembly where others are younger and emphasis is placed upon Henry's youthfulness. The courtiers are seated in stalls on the king's left and right; Erpingham's place, not insignificantly, is on the right-hand side, and only Exeter and Westmoreland are seated higher. As the Archbishop expounds his case, Erpingham turns to the two nobles and nods his head in vigorous approval. Plainly he sides with the war party. Later, after the dismissal of the French ambassador, Branagh conveys Henry's determination by striding off. As the courtiers follow him, the aged Erpingham has to bestir himself to keep up the pace.

It is in the Southampton council chamber (2.2.) that Erpingham is next seen.[43] Throughout the early discussions he stands behind Exeter, grave, tense, but approving. In the moment when it seems the traitors may resist arrest, Erpingham does not advance to take part in the scuffle. Instead, he stands, protectively, by the king. For this scene Erpingham, like the others, has donned his coat of arms, and though the tinctures are distorted by a quirk of studio lighting, so that the vert is shown correctly only towards the end, armorial bearings will henceforth reinforce the identification of the character.

At Harfleur (3.1.), where Sir Thomas took part in the negotiations at the surrender,[44] Erpingham is first seen standing beside the king as he returns from the breach on his white charger. Next we espy him standing behind Exeter and Westmoreland, clearly inspired by the monarch's rallying cry. No doubt in order to facilitate character recognition, Branagh has the entire cast bare-headed throughout this episode (apart from Fluellen in 3.2.), though historically it seems unlikely those engaged in the fighting would have been so ill-advised as to have dispensed with the helmets about which there is so much talk in the play.

Act 4 is naturally Erpingham's high point, We first glimpse him sitting on the ground beside Exeter by a camp fire while the Chorus is still setting the scene. The episode in the English camp at Agincourt (4.1.) opens with the king's greeting to Erpingham, which is followed by the exchange about the churlish turf. Lines 18-23 of Henry's response are, however, cut: he responds only with "Humph" before asking the knight for the loan of his cloak. Erpingham volunteers to accompany the king through the camp (l.29), but the offer is declined. Erpingham then pronounces the line "The Lord in Heaven bless thee, noble Harry" with deep emotion. Indeed, it is so profound that some may sense something of an incongruity when Henry replies: "God-a-mercy, old heart! Thou speak'st cheerfully." Then the king wanders away through the camp.

The exchanges about Erpingham between Bates and Henry are retained in their entirety (4.1.94-100). A little later, during his soliloquy (4.1. ca. 273) Henry walks past a cart. On it we see first a shield with his arms, next another with Erpingham's; then we realise that the cart (like those we have seen at the end of 3.7. after Mountjoy's departure) is loaded with arrows.

As the day dawns, Erpingham tells the king that his nobles are seeking him (ll. 291-2), and, calling him "good old knight", the king asks that they should be told to assemble at his tent. A nod of acquiescence, in lieu of the prosaic "I shall do't, my lord", saves a few moments.[45] Just before the battle Erpingham is seen again, once more beside Exeter and Westmoreland, and at the end of the St Crispin speech he joins with nobles and common soldiery alike in the cheer. But after all have knelt and crossed themselves before the combat begins, it is noticeable that he is less athletic than his comrades in arms.

Perhaps following Olivier rather than Shakespeare, Branagh makes good cinematic action out of the archers' preparations, with Erpingham bustling about, plainly concerned if not obviously in charge, as stakes are driven and sheaves of arrows are distributed. When Erpingham hands Exeter his mace we have, in the invention of a little bit of business, an emblem of the knight's role in the play. Then, as battle commences, comes Branagh's major and most significant piece of apt inventiveness. There is tension as the French charge, and the most striking expression of it comes with a shot of Erpingham's face in extreme close-up, filling the entire screen. One interpretation might be that he is simply frightened, but there is another that is a richer and more rewarding hypothesis. It is that this old soldier who has seen much fighting in a long career and has no illusions about the extent of his own involvement in the questionable decisions that led up to the campaign and who is deeply concerned for the welfare of the house he serves has a true appreciation of the horrors that are to come. That the play contains Harry's great moment of anagnorisis in his personal agony in the night is a commonplace. With fine help from Michael Williams, Branagh makes Bates' intervention into something hardly less powerful. And now, in a powerful piece of what is in effect silent cinema, Erpingham too is shown to have come to a full realisation of a situation for whose creation he is to a degree responsible and from which it is questionable whether there can be any escape.

Branagh's inventiveness is not yet exhausted. He has Erpingham go at the king's behest to succour the Duke of York, appear to hear Llewellyn lament over the slaughter of the boys (4.8.) and listen with emotion to the tally of slaughter.

More strikingly still, and fully in keeping with his position in the household, Erpingham joins with Westmoreland and others to bear York's corpse from the field. At the conference at Troyes, Erpingham appears once more, in what we come to see more than once is his normal position, as a senior presence respectfully backing up the royal family. All in all, Branagh has developed Erpingham's role from a bit part to quite a central one, not by distorting the Shakespearean material but by developing it imaginatively in the light of the role Sir Thomas played in history.

Nothing would be more absurd than trying to promote Erpingham's role to make it central to the play, yet it is clear that even in the small compass of his part there is much of interest, even possibly of controversy. Olivier and Branagh ignore the ennoblement of *Henry V* that may be regarded as epitomised in the banishment of the archers from the play; they have, each for different reasons, chosen to bring out the popular and nationalistic aspect of the play, contrasting it with the effete ineffectualness of the French aristocracy. This makes for good theatre, but only at the cost of some distortion of Shakespeare. Though Sir Thomas and Erpingham are only relatively distantly related, consideration of the original and the stage character has, however, been revealing about Shakespeare's interpretation of the whole saga of Henry V. As for the historical Sir Thomas, a man clearly much devoted to the perpetuation of his name in stone and heraldry, if he were ever, by some miracle, able to discover that his character has been altered so that it could be pressed into the service even of a theatrical memory of the Lancastrian monarch he had served so staunchly, there seems little reason for doubting that he would, as ever, still lie content.

*Notes*

1. Frantisek Dvorak, *Drawings: Holbein*, St Paul, Minnesota, 1985.

2. For this article the 'base text' has been *King Henry V*, ed, T.W.Craik, The Arden Shakespeare, Third Series, London: Routledge, 1995; I have also consulted, with profit, *The Life of Henry the Fift*, ed. F.J.Furnivall, The Old-Spelling Shakespeare, London: Chatto & Windus, 1912; *Henry V*, ed. Gary Taylor, The Oxford Shakespeare, Oxford: Clarendon Press, and *King Henry V*, ed. Andrew Gurr, The New Cambridge Shakespeare, Cambridge: Cambridge UP, 1992. I must also acknowledge my debt to Joseph Candido and Charles R. Forker, *'Henry V':* *An Annotated Bibliography*, The Garland Shakespeare Bibliographies, New York: Garland, 1983.

3. M.M. Mahood, *Bit Parts in Shakespeare's Plays*, (Cambridge: Cambridge UP, 1992), pp. 67-8.

4. Graham Reynolds, *Nicholas Hilliard and Isaac Oliver*, London: HMSO, 1971; a few miniatures (e.g. Nos, 38, 54, 57 and 124, formerly thought be of Sir Philip Sidney) show their subject in a significant or characteristic setting, but these are exceptions in a genre that prefers to depict a head or at most head and shoulders against a featureless background.

5. Overlooked when the first volumes of *The Dictionary of National Biography* were compiled, Sir Thomas was accorded an entry, by A.F. Pollard, in the *First Supplement*.

6. If the family had indeed come over with the Conqueror, one wonders why it took its name from the north Norfolk village whose existence is attested as early as 785 under the Saxon form of 'Erpingaham' Eilert Ekwall, *The Concise Dictionary of English Place-Names* (Oxford: Clarendon Press, 1960), under 'Erpingham'.

7. It was only in about 1415, i.e. after the Agincourt campaign, that Sir Thomas had set in the floor of the parish church of St Mary, Erpingham, a fine brass in memory of his father showing a figure armed from head to foot, Nikolaus Pevsner, *North-East Norfolk and Norwich,* The Buildings of England, Harmondsworth: Penguin, 1962, and Muriel Clayton, *Catalogue of Rubbings of Brasses and Incised Slabs* (London: HMSO, 1968), p. 38. The church also once had a brass to the memory Sir Robert de Erpingham, grandfather to Sir Thomas, who most likely had this set here too, see Richard Butler-Stoney, *The Church of St Mary, Erpingham*, no place: Church Tours, 1994.

8. Charles B. Jewson, *People of Medieval Norwich* (Norwich: Jarrold, nd), p. 82.

9. J.L. Kirby's *Henry IV of England*, London: Constable, 1970, provides, within the framework of a biography of the king, a sketch of this phase in Sir Thomas's career in more than twenty passing references.

10. See *Expeditions to Prussia and the Holy Land made by Henry, Earl of Derby (afterwards King Henry IV), in the years 1390-1 and 1392-3, being the Accounts kept by his Treasurer*, ed. L. T. Smith, Camden Society, NS 52 (1894).

11. He was appointed in the place of Thomas Beauchamp, 4th Earl of Warwick, who was degraded upon conviction for treason, see G.F. Boltz, *Memorials of the Order of the Garter*, (London: Pickering, 1841), p. 195. Pickering's statement (p. clvi) that Erpingham was "slain" in 1428 is not supported by other authorities.

12. Joseph Foster, *The Dictionary of Heraldry* (London: Bracken, 1902, repr. 1989), p. 78; W.H. St John Hope, *The Stall Plates of the Knights of the Order of the Garter, 1348-1485* (Westminster: Constable, 1901), see Plate XLII; Edmund H. Fellowes, *The Knights of the*

*Garter, 1348-1939, with a Complete List of the Stall-Plates in St George's Chapel, Windsor*, Historical Monographs relating to St George's Chapel Windsor (London: SPCK, 1939), p. 19; Grace Holmes, *The Order of the Garter Stall Plates, 1348 to 1984*, Historical Monographs relating to St George's Chapel, Windsor Castle, No.16 (Windsor: Oxley, 1984), pp. 55 and 158.

13. His presence at Sir Charles Oldcastle's execution has provoked much speculation, see, e.g., J.D.Griffith, *Henry V* (London: Baker, 1935), p. 138.

14. The basic source for all to do with Henry V remains J.H. Wylie, *Henry V*, 3 vols, Cambridge: Cambridge UP, 1919.

15. For a military persepective on the matter, see Lieutenant-Colonel Alfred H. Burne's *The Agincourt Campaign*, London: Eyre & Spottiswoode, 1956.

16. A key source is Sir Harris Nicolas, *History of the Battle of Agincourt* (1833), London: Pordes, 1971; see p. 346 for Sir Thomas and his "retenu" of fourteen men-at-arms, one of whom died at Calais, and forty seven archers.

17. One of them was called John Calthorpe, whose name, surely significantly, is also that of a north Norfolk village close to Erpingham (Wylie, II, p. 196).

18. Personal heraldry and religious symbolism are likewise mingled in the famous Erpingham cope, see Donald King, "A Relic of 'Noble Erpingham'", *Victoria and Albert Museum Bulletin*, IV:2 (1968), pp. 59-64.

19. See Nicolas, coloured plate opposite p. 404.

20. I must particularly thank Mr Tony Sims who, with real scholarly generosity, has kindly allowed me to consult his unpublished BA dissertation, "The Church Gate of the Norwich Cathedral Priory: An Examination of the Architectural Style and Decoration, the Patronage and Purpose", University of East Anglia, Norwich, 1990.

21. It would, however, be wrong to attribute to Sir Thomas himself the most conspicuous display of his arms in Norwich, between each of the clerestory windows on the south wall of the nave of St Andrew's Hall, formerly the Blackfriars Church (clearly seen in plate 31 of Andrew Kent, *Norwich in Pictures*, Norwich: Jarrold, 1971). The heraldry was put there, doubtless as a filial tribute, by Sir Thomas's son, Friar Robert, see Helen Sutermeister, *The Norwich Blackfriars* (Norwich: City of Norwich, 1977), p. 21.

22. The question of Shakespeare's sources for *Henry V* has been exhaustively explored, e.g. in *Narrative Sources of Shakespeare*, IV, *Later English History Plays: King John, Henry IV, Henry V, Henry VIII*, London: Routledge & Kegan Paul, 1962; my object here is not to add to the list of sources, but to see how the material has been used.

23. William Wells, *The Famous Victories of Henry the Fifth: A Critical Edition*, unpubl. PhD dissertation, Stanford University, 1935.

24. *Gesta Henrici Quinti*, ed Frank Taylor and John S. Roskill, Oxford Medieval Texts (Oxford: Clarendon Press, 1975), p. 2.

25. Thomas M. Cranfill, "Shakespeare's Old Heroes", *Texas Studies in Literature and Language*, XV. 2 (Summer, 1973), pp. 215-30.

26. *The Royal Shakespeare Company's Production of 'Henry V' for the Centenary Production of the Royal Shakespeare Theatre*, ed. Sally Beauman (Oxford: Pergamon, 1979), p. 176.

27. An analogy might be the insistence of Sir Ralph Abercromby, dying after the Battle of Alexandria, that the soldier's rough blanket on which he had been laid should be returned without delay to Duncan Roy of the 42nd, see *The Oxford Book of Military Anecdotes*, ed. Max Hastings (Oxford: Oxford UP, 1985), p. 187.

28. For a clear modern account of the battle, and the role of the archers in it, see Christopher Hibbert, *Agincourt*, London: Batsford, 1964.

29. For a standard treatment of the Hundred Years War, see Anne Curry, *The Hundred Years War*, London, Macmillan, 1993.

30. Wylie (II, p. 156), rather boldly, chooses to interpret the famous cry without more ado as "Knee! Stretch!"

31. See *Bishop Percy's Folio Manuscript: Ballads and Romances*, ed. J.W. Hales and F.J. Furnivall (London: Tübner, nd), II, pp. 159-73 and 595-9.

32. Roger Ascham, *Toxophilus* in *English Works*, ed. W.A Wright, Cambridge English Classics (Cambridge, Cambridge UP, 1904), pp. vii-119; see p. 54.

33. For surveys of the entire field of archery, see W.F. Paterson, *Encyclopedia of Archery*, London: Hale, 1984, and Robert Hardy, *Longbow: A Social and Military History*, London: Stephens, 1992.

34. C.G. Cruickshank, *Elizabeth's Army*, 2nd ed. (Oxford: Clarendon, 1966), p. 102. See too Robert Hardy, "The Longbow" in *Arms, Armies and Fortifications in the Hundred Years War*, ed. Anne Curry and Michael Hughes (Woodbridge: Boydell, 1994), pp. 161-82.

35. L.V.Ryan, *Roger Ascham* (Stanford: California UP, 1963), esp. pp. 49-81.

36. Lindsay Boynton, *The Elizabethan Militia (1558-1638)*, (London: Routledge and Kegan Paul, 1967), p. 212.

37. See "Playing Bows and Arrows", Chapter 8 of Hardy's *Longbow*: both shooting at targets and also at game became gentlemen's pastimes in the seventeenth and eighteenth centuries.

38. Writing at much the same time as Shakespeare, Michael Drayton, however, found no difficulty in accommodating both the archers and Sir Thomas in heroic evocations of Agincourt; see *Works*, ed. J.W.Hebel (Oxford: Blackwell for Shakespeare Head, 1961), II, pp. 375-78 and III, pp. 9-72 (especially ll.1265-72 and 1441-8).

39. Giorgio Melchiori, *Shakespeare's Garter Plays*, Newark: University of Delaware Press, 1994.

40. Thomas L, Berger, "Casting *Henry V*", *Shakespeare Studies*, xx (1988), pp. 89-104.

41. John C. Meagher, "Economy and Recognition: Thirteen Shakespearean Puzzles", *Shakespeare Quarterly*, 35:1 (1984), pp. 7-21, opines, however, that the doubling is significant.

42. William Shakespeare, *Henry V: An Adaptation by Kenneth Branagh*, London: Chatto & Windus, 1989.

43. Historically, the arrest took place not at Southampton, where the trial, in which Erpingham took part, was subsequently held, but in Portchester Castle, see *Gesta Henrici Quinti*, p. 19, and T.G. Pugh, *Henry V and the Southampton Plot of 1415* (Gloucester: Sutton, 1988), p. 123.

44. Griffith, p. 171.

45. The same episode was omitted in the Royal Shakespeare Company's production of *Henry V*. "The Erpingham sequence, which we cut, seems merely mechanical. At a time when acting was different it may have served as a bridge for the actor between the end of the soliloquy and the beginning of the prayer. Today it is in danger of breaking not just the concentration of the actor, but also that of the audience. Naturalistic bridges are really not necessary to communicate changes of thought, either on stage, or in life. A clanking figure would have been a gross intrusion, and would almost certainly have produced a barrage of released-tension-coughing - timed precisely to drown the vitally important "O God of battles" that follows immediately after" (Beauman, p. 185).

# "POSSESSED WITH RUMOURS": POPULAR SPEECH AND *KING JOHN*

### Dermoth Cavanagh
### (University of Northumbria)

This essay is concerned with rumours as an expression of popular political attitudes in early modern England. It then compares the action of such scandalous tale-telling to theatre and particularly to Shakespeare's orchestration of historical material in *King John*. *King John* is of particular interest for this approach in that it exemplifies how key elements of popular opinion can be diffused in a text where the populace is not substantially represented. To examine this, *King John* will be read as both manifesting a concern with the power of rumours and as a play whose theatrical effects function in ways analogous to rumours. This is to say that *King John* does not simply reinforce the concern of the Tudor government with the chaotic potential of irresponsible language. Indeed, important components of its theatrical design and the forms of speech released within it act, as I will argue, rumours do: to heighten critical awareness of the reality of political conduct. *King John* does not use history as an admonitory political fable about the risks of undisciplined speech, indeed it is in the shocked and angry voices of marginalised groups – the words of women, children, prophets and the illegitimate – that the clearest perceptions of the political process are articulated. However, any comprehensive reading of the play must also acknowledge some qualification of its imperative to present a satirical account of authority. In particular, the Bastard's development manifests a compensatory tendency to bring 'irregular' speech and attitudes into conformity. The dramatic success of this containment of critical speculation is debatable, but its presence, at least, needs to be acknowledged.

The spectre of rumour is regularly evoked in Tudor theatre, and usually its occurrence is a symptom not only of the crudity and fickleness of mass opinion, but of a failure of authority.[1] This allows for some complexity of political effect: the existence of volatile public opinion can be traced back not simply to the credulity of the mob, but to the weakness of a political order which has allowed doubts over its legitimacy to gain substance. In Act 4, Scene 2 of *King John* we see something of this ambivalent quality of rumours. This scene describes the onset of the calamities that will destroy the King: the internal disaffection created by John's (presumed) assassination of his young nephew, Arthur (his rival for the throne); the commencement of the French invasion, on the grounds of John's illegitimate status, backed by Papal interdiction; the sudden death of Eleanor, John's mother. It begins with the disquiet of the court at John's need to undergo another coronation. At this point, the Messenger brings both the certain news of Eleanor's death and the rumoured death of Constance (Arthur's mother) who "in a frenzy died/Three days before; but this from rumour's tongue/I idly heard - if true or false I know not" (4.2.122-4).[2] Now the Bastard enters – significantly having apprehended another troublesome speaker, the prophet Peter of Pomfret – and describes the growing agitation of the kingdom:

> But as I travelled hither through the land
> I find the people strangely fantasied;
> Possessed with rumours, full of idle dreams,
> Not knowing what they fear, but full of fear. (4.2.143-6)

Hubert himself now arrives at court and describes in more precise detail the spreading ripples of scandal:

> Young Arthur's death is common in their mouths,
> And when they talk of him, they shake their heads,
> And whisper one another in the ear.
> And he that speaks doth grip the hearer's wrist,
> Whilst he that hears make fearful action
> With wrinkled brows, with nods, with rolling eyes.
> I saw a smith stand with his hammer, thus,
> The whilst his iron did on the anvil cool,
> With open mouth swallowing a tailor's news,
> Who with his shears and measure in his hand,
> Standing on slippers which his nimble haste
> Had falsely thrust upon contrary feet,
> Told of many thousand warlike French

> That were embattailed and ranked in Kent.
> Another lean, unwashed artificer
> Cuts off his tale and talks of Arthur's death. (4.2.187-202)

In these images of arrested action we see the power of rumours: the regulating patterns of work-discipline are disrupted by their disorientating effect. "Young Arthur's death is common in their mouths" – by sharing its suspicions the populace uncovers the concealed design of authority. Moreover, this description of rumour's social agency is congruent with theatrical effect. Just as rumours transform the attention of the "smith", the "tailor", the "lean unwashed artificer", so their report interferes with the scene designed by the King: the sympathies of the audience are drawn to the truths that inhere within disaffected speech. Despite the hostile and dismissive presentation of the people's fears manifested by those who bear them to court – the Messenger only listens "idly" to "rumour's tongue"; the Bastard hopes that the country *is* afflicted with groundless apprehensions – the rumours *are* correct. The King *has*, at the least, attempted to arrange for Arthur's destruction; an invasion is in progress. The prophecy of Peter of Pomfret that John will yield up his crown on Ascension Day is vindicated in 5.1 when the King re-submits to Papal authority.

The swirl of prophecy and rumour in the kingdom confirms, rather than distorts, what we have seen of public actions and events in *King John*. The political world's grounding in "commodity" and the struggle for sectional advantage have already aroused hostile commentary from those scandalised by it. (See, for example, 2.1.561-98 and 3.1.83-95) The first three acts have conducted us through a world of unalloyed political opportunism where principles are ruthlessly subordinated to self-interest. Amid the collective cynicism and bad faith, force is revealed as the ultimate arbiter of 'right' and an accumulating awareness of the pursuit of sectional interests informing 'high' politics is expressed by those most appalled by it: Constance and Blanche, Arthur, the Bastard, the common people.

It is in such confirmations of the facts of *realpolitik* that *King John's* meaning is often located and it has become customary to interpret the play as an expression of political disenchantment.[3] Sigurd Burckhardt argued that *King* John embodies the relativist discovery that the Elizabethan world picture was false and therefore the most stable social order is only a particular political arrangement (116-43). Burckhardt claimed, influentially, that "when he wrote *King John*, or quite possibly in writing it, Shakespeare was or became a 'modern' ..." (117). Distanced in time, the play appears to be released from the inhibitions intrinsic to a treatment of the fifteenth century narrated in Shakespeare's other English history plays. Subsequent criticism has concurred with this: Emrys Jones has analysed the play's 'deviously ironical construction ... designed to produce an effect of frustration' (234); Eamonn Grennan describes *King John* as "an experience which must call into doubt the whole historical enterprise" (34) and another commentator speaks of its impulse to "sardonically deflate the heroics of politics" (Watson, 123). This sense of the play as disseminating a disruptive knowledge of the artificiality of social processes is condensed in the introduction to the recent Oxford edition of the play:

> By representing the contentious, mystified passage of property, power, and legitimacy from generation to generation, *King John* dramatises - and thus both demystifies *and* makes unfamiliar - some of the most intensely serious cultural assumptions in late Tudor England. (Braunmuller, 38)

Clearly, this tradition of emphasising *King John's* exposure of pragmatism and duplicity has increased understanding of its range of implication. The reputation of King John, in the sixteenth-century, has been identified as especially good terrain for the exploration of such ambiguous political feelings. Reformation intellectuals had revised the historiography of the reign precisely to demonstrate both the contingency of apparently immutable social arrangements and the manipulation of the past for ideological purpose (see Levin). John's depiction as a cruel impious tyrant in the medieval chronicles was seen as a distortion which typified the contaminating influence of Catholicism on society. As Tyndale put it:

> Consider the story of King John, where I doubt not but that they [i.e. the priests) have put the best and fairest for themselves and the worst of King John: for I suppose they make the chronicles themselves. (Quoted from Elliot, 66)

John's reign had been resuscitated at the Reformation as an inspiration in the struggle for national independence from Rome, and his tragic capitulation to Papal authority had been hallowed by Protestant martyrology as prefiguring Tudor monarchical supremacy. However, by the late sixteenth century, the King's heroic dimensions had been diminished by more considered historical evaluations: Foxe had acknowledged John's manifold weaknesses, and Holinshed had included some disparaging detail concerning John's cruelty and deviousness (see Levin). As John R Elliott has pointed out:

> there were two, quite distinct 'books' of the reign of King John existing side by side in Shakespeare's century, in one of which John was portrayed as a villainous failure, in the other as a national hero. (65)

To any sophisticated interest then, King John could provide a compelling example of how convictions concerning a given monarch's reputation could be produced by the manipulation of popular opinion, as well as demonstrating how vulnerable this could be to sceptical consideration. Undoubtedly, Shakespeare adapts material from the alternative historical tradition that recorded John's scheming, viciousness and instability.

However, it is also important to acknowledge and explain some countervailing strategies in the text that attempt to reorient political responses into a less sceptical mode. It has been shown that a long performance tradition established *King John* as a thumpingly patriotic spectacle and a play with a tragic – rather than satiric – effect in its treatment of the King's fate (see Waith; Beaurline, 1-23; Hodgdon, 32-5). Before we dismiss this understanding of the play as a product of a naive and mystified patriotism, it may be worth granting it some correspondence with now underrated elements of the dramatic design. For example, after Constance' s exit at 3.4.105 – after her devastating speeches of betrayal and bereavement at the fate of Arthur – no more women's voices are heard in the play. Similarly, the child who appears in the final scene is the previously unseen Prince Henry – John's son and heir – who mourns his father' s death with gravity and compassion (5.7.13-24). These alterations to the tenor of speech are most strongly marked in the Bastard's growing patriotic resolution and loyalty to John. The play does manifest some wariness over its politically destabilising effects and this can be explored in its re-creation and reshaping of popular political disaffection, especially as they are articulated in rumours.

The OED reminds us that the term 'rumour' had more forceful connotations of uproar and tumult in early modern English, drawn from its association with social disturbance. By the late fifteenth century, its relatively neutral use as a general term for popular discussion of important people or issues had been overlaid with much more pejorative implications. By the sixteenth-century a rumour is primarily a "loud expression or manifestation of disapproval/protest" which can circulate around a "noted/distinguished person/thing".

This accrual of new meanings reflects the social necessity to define and regulate the disturbing capacities of popular speech in post-Reformation culture. In the context of a society with only an irregular and uncoordinated system of communication – where the 'news' could often be delayed and wildly out-of-date – the power of rumour as a potentially irresponsible source of information was a matter of increasing concern to the government. In the classification of rumour, one can perceive a characteristic stigmatising and surveillance of the 'irrationality' of popular opinion. From the 1530s onwards a stream of proclamations were issued against rumours and rumour-mongers, and considerable judicial resources were expended on their detection, particularly derogatory information concerning the monarch and other key members of the elite.

This is clearly apprehensible in the Treason Act of 1534, which was used in the prosecution of rumour-mongers, makers of political prophecies, and seditious speakers of various kinds. The Act is notable for being both the first major redefinition of treason for over two centuries and for the principal terms of this redefinition being its inclusion of speech and writing (Elton, 286-7).[4] In the previous statute of 1352, treason could only be committed as an act (assassination, assault, rape); this was now enlarged to include the actual or symbolic harm done to the royal person by words:

> any person or persons [...] do maliciously wish or will or desire by words or writing, or by craft imagine invent practise or attempt, any bodily harm to be done or committed to the King's most royal person, the Queen's or their heirs apparent, or to deprive them or any of them of the dignity title or name of their royal estates, or slanderously & maliciously publish & pronounce, by express writing or words, that the King our Sovereign Lord should be heretic schismatic Tyrant infidel or Usurper of the Crown [...] being thereof lawfully convicted according to the laws and Customs of the Realm, shalbe adjudged traitors. (*Statutes*, Henry VIII, c 13)

Treason can now occur at the level of representation, or, more accurately, misrepresentation, in the public circulation of words which deprive the monarch and his or her heirs of credit, honour, and legitimacy and which therefore cause other subjects to misrecognise him or her. It is this concern with the establishment of the reputation of the élite and the forces which may impugn or detract from its value that animates legislative procedures.

In 1554 these edicts were codified in "An Acte against sedityous Woordes and Rumours":

> That no Man shoulde bee so hardye to contryve speak or tell any false Newes lyes or other such lyke false thinges of Prelates Dukes Earles Barons and other Nobles and Peares of the Realme, or of the Chancelour Treasure Clerck of the Pryvie Seale Stewarde of the Kynges Householde Justices of thone Bancke or of thother, or of any greate Officers of this Realme. (*Statutes*, Mary, c3)

The Act of 1554, brought scurrillous rumours – which could be either spoken or printed – under the category of sedition. Here the penalties were often severe. Spoken sedition was punished by the pillory and the cutting off of both ears (or, for those who could afford it, a £100 fine and three months imprisonment). For repeating another's sedition the penalty was the pillory and the removal of one ear. Loss of the right hand was the penalty for written sedition. Second offences were subject to life-imprisonment and the confiscation of all property. In 1581, under Elizabeth, the legislation on seditious rumours was toughened, principally by the introduction of the death-penalty for second offences and the inclusion of those who wished for or spread rumours of the Queen's death or speculated on how long she might live (Samaha, 64-5).

It is this need for more powerful mechanisms by which illicit words and perceptions can be regulated that animates the categorisation of rumour as a form of speech which interferes with desirable norms of political recognition. As one Henrician proclamation puts it: rumours are "feigned contrived, and forged tidings and tales [...] neither dreading God nor his highness" (*TRP*, I, 11). Yet, it is in this latter attribution of a speech without dread, that one can begin to take rumours as seriously as the Tudor state did and detect how important components of popular mentalities are being expressed within them.

An awareness of broader historical and social processes may both provide a context for, and heighten the significance of, this re-definition of cultural norms regarding speech. Sixteenth-century governments paid increasing concern to the regulation of social conduct with the aim of ordering its potentially de-stabilising implications (see Kent, 41-71). Symptomatic of this was a heightened concern with popular speech, especially with its scurrillous, abusive capacities. In his *Description of England* (1587), William Harrison remarked that the talk "of the inferior sort is now and then such as savoureth of scurrility and drunkeness" (Emmison, 70). By 1611, William Vaughan lamented that "detractions, defamations, perjuries, and idle speeches become now-a-dayes more rife than in former times" (Sharpe, 3). Such observations manifest a much wider social concern over the characteristics of the popular mentality and its propensity towards undisciplined reflection and irreverence.

Clearly, there was a growing anxiety amongst the early modern élite about the nature and attitudes of subordinate groups. Notoriously, the poor and rootless were increasingly imbued with qualities normally associated with external or demonic threats; Sir Thomas Browne wrote of "that great enemy of reason, virtue and religion, the multitude, that numerous piece of monstrosity [...] confused together make but one great beast" (Hill, 301). Lower-class mobility was seen as transmitting disaffection, transients are apprehended as vagabonds, "lawless beasts", "the very filth and vermin of the commonwealth" who travel for "vile, wretched and filthy purposes". (Slack, 24-5). In a detailed study of early modern vagrancy, A. L. Beier observes that in the period "vagabondage was defined as a social and political danger much like witchcraft ... Destitute, rootless and masterless, he [the vagrant] seemed part of a conspiracy to destroy society" (12).

This relates to what Paul Slack has uncovered in his work on early modern poverty, when he speaks of

> the emotions of fear and disgust which mounted in the early sixteenth century ... the aura of dirt, pollution and peril which was firmly attached to the Tudor poor ... It is as if social boundaries were being redrawn and proper, respectable society being newly and more tightly defined. (23-4)

Slack argues that one hallmark of the early modern is a shift in attitudes towards the poor, that is, from medieval social theory, which tended to regard the poor as objects of charitable obligation (and even admiration), towards a stigmatising conception of the poor as a threat to the good of the social order. Early modern commentators began to make distinctions between the 'deserving' and 'undeserving' poor and to argue for the preponderance of those who were idle and politically disaffected. Such subjects required detection, condemnation and punishment, rather than alms and sympathy. One symptom of this group was perceived to be their disordered speech. As one commentator put it, alms should be given to the elderly and ill, but not those who "be impatient, and [...] revenge [their] wrongs with execrations and curses" (Slack, 22). One can relate these new definitions and attitudes to the insecurities of a society undergoing unprecedented transformation and division.

Again this process may be considered in terms of a reordering of the power relationships between élite and subordinate groups. Antony Fletcher and John Stevenson have helped provide a context for explaining such legislation by elucidating a key social process of the period: the penetration of local communities by processes of central administration and their integration into 'national' standards often defined in opposition to popular traditions. The political relationship between rulers and ruled is increasingly defined in terms of the management and containment of the governed (1-40). In the demarcation of respectable from illicit speech, one can see the fashioning of a new set of 'offences' which permit the cultural reinforcement of new social boundaries and also the management of popular mentalities: the governing élite is increasingly sensitive towards a public temper which is hostile to innovation and more immune to monarchical charisma. The apparently random elaborations and distortions of rumour seem as closely aligned to popular fear, anger and aspiration.

At their simplest, rumour-mongers are detected as those who take a malicious delight in spreading scandalous tales of social 'realities', especially those concerning the behaviour of prestigious figures. For example, in August 1536, Sir William Hoo, a Sussex vicar, was reported to Thomas Cromwell for spreading a rumour. This consisted of his explanation of the current changes in religious belief and practice being tolerated by Henry VIII. Hoo had explained that the Reformation promoted by the "children of the Devil" was being furthered in this way: they that rule about the King make him great banquets and give him sweet wines and make him drunk, and then they bring him bills, and he putteth his sign to them". (*L&P*, Henry VIII, XI, 126). This small instance of a scandalous tale being investigated helps to document the increasing anger of the Tudor government with rumour-mongering: the spreading of culpably erroneous information.

Although rumours circulate around many events and personages, those that concern monarchical behaviour are inevitably treated most seriously and recorded more fully. For example, rumours of Henry VIII's scandalous sexual appetite persisted throughout his reign. In September 1537, Maurice Bull was imprisoned for spreading a tale about a man who "rode by the way and a fair wench behind him" and his encounter with the king who "took the wench from him and had his pleasure of her, and thus he said the King lived in adultery" (*L&P*, Henry VIII, XII; ii, 243). The potential volatility of rumours is evidenced in this presentation of the king as an adulterer, a scandalous tale that could have more serious implications. In June 1535, Thomas Jackson, a Yorkshire chantry priest, was indicted for claiming that the King was not only living in adultery with Anne Boleyn but had previously kept both her and her mother as mistresses: "and now he hath married her whom he kept afore and her mother also" (Elton , 300).

A consideration of several tales disseminated about Elizabeth can make some of the capacities of rumour more vivid and also demonstrate further common elements in popular attitudes towards authority. One can see some important implications in the frequent indictment of those who transmitted or welcomed rumours of the monarch's death. Rumours of Elizabeth's imminent demise were frequent in her last years and were stringently monitored as evidence of public disaffection. In 1584 Walsingham received reports concerning Jeffrey Leeche who had "declared the Queen would not live half a year" (*CSPD*, Elizabeth, 1581-90, 206). "Mutinous rumors" of the Queen's actual death and a resulting civil war were rife in Cornwall in 1599 and blamed on one William Crowsyer, who affirmed "that her majesty was dead, and that an army was in the field about London, wherein Her Majesty's picture was brought forth, but she was not there in person" (*CSPD*, Elizabeth, 1598-1601, 296).

In each of these cases we see another common strategy of the state's explanation of the persistence of rumours: they originate in the treasonous temper of individuals who wish to defame the monarch. Like her father, Elizabeth endured a constant flow of scandalous rumours concerning her sexual improprieties, and the circulation of such rumours was seen as a harbinger of more serious forms of political discontent. This became most disturbing when they concerned her giving birth to illegitimate children. In 1581 Henry Hawkins was indicted for saying "that my Lord Robert hath had five children by the Queene, and she never goeth in progress but to be delivered" (*CSPD*, Elizabeth, 1581-90, 12). Dionisa Deryck was convicted in Essex in 1590 for spreading the following seditious rumour about the Queen, saying she

> hath already had as many children as I, and that two of them were yet alive, one a man child and the other a maiden child, and the others were burned [...] my Lord of Leicester was the father and wrapped them up in the embers of the chimney which was in the chamber where they were born. (Emmison, 42)

It is the proximity of these kinds of idle tale-telling to political sedition that is so threatening to the Tudor state. Scurrillous rumours are not simply the expression of a debased laxity of imagination, but manifest a more truculent form of uninstructed social hostility. When Edward Fraunces's speculations on the realities of the Queen's private life were reported in 1598, his political attitudes were simultaneously made plain:

> the Queen [...] had three bastards by the noblemen of the Court, two sons and a daughter, and was herself base born; and added that the land had been happy if Her Majesty had been cut off 20 years since, so that some noble prince might have reigned in her stead. (*CSPD*, Elizabeth, 1581-90, 137).

One way of recognising a rumour is through its presumption with the reputation of authority; as another proclamation puts it, they present "things and facts sounding to the dishonour and slander of the King's most royal majesty [...]

and other the King's most honourable council ..." (*TRP* I, 281). All of these rumours bring into the public domain illicit knowledge of private 'facts' which impugn the reputation of the monarch, rendering their authority provisional or even illegitimate. Characteristically, 'official' Tudor thinking ascribed rumours to a minority of agitators seeking to inflame popular opinion by wild exaggerations or to demoralise it with scare-stories. In Proclamation after Proclamation we hear of "devilish and slanderous persons", "light and perverse persons", "lewd and vagrant persons" united only in their treasonous irresponsibility.[5] Yet, the dynamics of how rumour circulated can be recovered as both oblique and direct evidence of popular political anxieties. As Alistair Fox has observed of prophecy, they "alert us to the existence of a very large substratum of opinion underlying the more visible outcrops of Tudor political thought" (94). In the existence of rumours, the early modern élite perceived a persistently hostile commentary on its actions: the circulation of rumours was indicative of more entrenched forms of public cynicism, The increase in the circulation of slanderous speculations is, as Pauline Croft has commented, indicative of "rising alienation from court life and values which can be discerned from the 1590s" (60).

Rumours testify to what Patrick Collinson terms, in another context, "the other [,] non-adulatory face of Elizabethan politics" (43) and in their reflection on monarchic instability, hypocrisy and self-interest one sees the existence of a public temper which remains uncharmed by monarchic charisma, intransigent to admonition. Rumours are a component of what Bakhtin terms "spheres of unpubliciscd speech", where "all the dividing lines between objects and phenomena are drawn quite differently than in the prevailing picture of the world" (121). In their redrawing of social relations, rumours present a counter-image of authority, expressing collective doubts over its probity and entitlement to obedience. At their most threatening they act as an unregulated channel of information which rivals the government's presentation of policy and events.

For early modern government, rumours were a form of speech profoundly implicated in attitudes of obstinacy and resistance. They embodied a popular description of society that refused to conform to the official version of events. Rumours can be located as part of a wider struggle about political truth between authority and subordinate groups – what it consists of; who should define it; what are the consequences of its plural definition. If Hughes and Larkin are correct in identifying the Tudor period as a key stage in the evolution of political sovereignty, then we can see in the government's acute reactions to rumours the transition from a "condition of very real, if unclearly defined limitations, to a modern reality of sovereignty which resists limitation." (xxxvii).

The relationship between the volatility of popular speech and the Elizabethan theatre has already been articulated in contemporary theory. Critics such as Stephen Mullaney have familiarised us with a sense of the 'place of the stage' on the margins of Tudor culture and its receptivity to other forms of liminal phenomena in which the vulnerability of the social structure is expressed. Michael D Bristol has urged us to see how theatre embodied the energy and initiative of collective life in ways which inevitably constituted a critical reflection on containment and domination. In *Vagrant Writing*, Barry Taylor pursues the relationship between the 'idle' speech and actions of vagrants and theatre as an order of representation which evades regulation by any comprehensive moral discourse.

There is much in this analysis to reconsider how the popular stage both increased its social compass and extended its range of political enquiry by adopting the modes of popular speech. Theatre could recreate both the infectiously irreverent appeal of rumours and permit indulgence in reflections that were at least partially freed from constraint. One of the key sources of antagonism rumours presented to authority was the difficulty inherent in identifying their source. Rumours characteristically seeped around the mechanisms of social regulation and control, as one proclamation puts it, they are "whispered and secretly spread abroad by uncertain authors, in markets, fairs, and alehouses, in divers and sundry places of this realm" (*TRP* I, 281). Similarly, as the City authorities soon discovered, it was difficult to determine who exactly was responsible for a play's effects - dramatist, actors, audience, theatre-owner.

This equivalence between theatre and rumours as forms of marginal discourse which granted a disturbing latitude of political perception was identified in the period. As early as the minority of Edward VI, a proclamation was issued "Enforcing Statutes against Vagabonds, Rumor Mongers, Players, Unlicensed Printers" (1551). Rumour-mongers and "players of interludes" are classed together amongst those who "dispute of his majesty's affairs [...] without consideration or regard to the quiet of the realm" (*TRP* I, 371).[6] In an Injunction issued in the first year of Elizabeth's reign, one again sees the close association between the need to license plays and seek the apprehension of those who:

> hath invented, bruited, or set forth any rumors, false and seditious tales, slanders, or makers, bringers, buyers, sellers, keepers, or conveyors of any unlawful books, which might stir or provoke sedition... (Chambers, IV, 265)

Anti-theatrical discourse repeatedly circulated the same set of anxieties and apprehensions that sought the extirpation of rumour. Geoffrey Fenton's *A Forme of Christian Pollicie gathered out of French* (1574), is a typical statement of such attitudes:

> Great then is the error of the magistrate to give sufferance to these players, whether they be minstrels, or interluders who on a scaffold, babbling vain news to the slander of the world, put there in scoffing the virtues of honest men [...] There often times are blown abroad the public and secret vices of men, sometimes shrouded under honourable personage, with infinite other offences ... (Chambers 1923, IV, 195)

Like rumours, plays are seen as a discourse of disclosure where scandalous knowledge is disseminated without politic consideration.

This capacity of the theatre to compel attention on terms less conditioned by deference was reflected on within plays themselves. The most famous and expansive instance of this is in Shakespeare's Induction to *2 Henry IV*, where Rumour speaks in ways which explicitly call attention to its embodying of important principles of theatrical practice:

> Open your ears; for which of you will stop
> The vent of hearing when loud Rumour speaks?
> I, from the Orient to the drooping West,
> Making the wind my post-horse, still unfold
> The acts commenced on this ball of earth.
> Upon my tongue continual slanders ride,
> The which in every language I pronounce,
> Stuffing the ears of men with false reports.
> I speak of peace while covert enmity,
> Under the smile of safety wounds the world;
> And who but Rumour, who but only I,
> Make fearful musters and prepar'd defence,
> Whiles the big year, swoln with some other grief,
> Is thought with child by the stern tyrant War,
> And no such matter? Rumour is a pipe
> Blown by surmises, jealousies, conjectures,
> And of so easy and so plain a stop
> That the blunt monster with uncounted heads,
> The still-discordant wav'ring multitude,
> Can play upon it. But what need I thus
> My well-known body to anatomize
> Among my household? (Induction, 1-22)[7]

Here the same cluster of elements we find identified for regulation in Tudor proclamations are distinguished. The speech is flooded with plurals – ears, acts, tongues, slanders, reports – it is the mass impact of rumours that is being stressed and their galvanising effect. Rumours are powerful, volatile, and distort events; they are endlessly resourceful in their ability to possess an audience, speaking "every language". However, rather than disapproval, this is a major source for an excited involvement in the possibilities offered by this experience. As John Blanpied points out, Rumour is "implying that the audience ("my household"), even in consenting to hear the play thereby consents as well to aid him in his business of spreading "continual slanders"; "false reports"" (212). The theatre is where Rumour's ability to generate collective imaginative conjecture is most powerfully liberated, along with the promise of subversive insight secreted within its fabrications: "I speak of peace while covert enmity,/Under the smile of safety wounds the world". Rumour's thrilling capacity to license an unpredictable series of reactions to a given narrative is singled out as the audience's most vivid theatrical experience. The audience's own "surmises" will be released along with other forms of disruptive speculation. Rumour serves as an appropriate induction to a play where an assured set of political loyalties will be difficult to maintain, where even the most apparently trustworthy story will be conditioned by doubts concerning its integrity.

However, if Rumour is identifying – and even to some degree celebrating – the Elizabethan theatre as a plural and volatile discourse that can undermine a normative hierarchy of responses, it is also undermining itself. There are some paradoxical effects in this proclamation of a space where truth and falsity will be difficult to distinguish. The latitude of speculation offered is simultaneously defined as prone to the inaccuracy rehearsed in official Tudor condemnations of rumour. If Rumour's household is indeed the theatre, it is compromised by the characteristic forms of perception it encourages: the audience is also alerted to the credulity that can be exploited in its own suggestibility. It has been argued that in *2 Henry IV* instinctive identifications with the sound of irreverent and undisciplined speech are ultimately exhausted and an audience is prepared more effectively for a voice that will impose coherence and control (See Greenblatt, 21-65). *King John* is another play which adapts the irreverent potential of the popular voice and where one is also asked to evaluate the reconstruction of speech and attitudes around conventional norms.

It is clear from the opening of *King John* that the play is engaged in formulating a dramatic language that articulates disquiet at the standards of court conduct. Certainly, in Act 1 of *King John*, Shakespeare forestalls the directing authority of Protestant myth by building on both the 'rumours' about King John – those semi-official glimpses of the King's unheroic inadequacies – and by inventing an 'exaggerated' extraneous narrative around the 'facts' of the reign. The effect of this is to disrupt the sympathetic disposition of an Elizabethan audience towards King John. Here, the king is constantly displaced from the centre of attention by more compelling figures – his mother, Eleanor; the Falconbridge family. John's speech is curiously colourless and his actions continually compromised. This is most vividly expressed in the sharp exchange between John and Eleanor concerning the tenuousness of his claim to the throne:

> King John    Our strong possession and our right for us.
>
> Eleanor    Your strong possession much more than your right,
> Or else it may go wrong with you and me ...  (1.1.39-41)

Similarly, the invented story of the Falconbridge family farcically replays the process by which legitimacy and succession are secured. Both main and sub-plots concern competing claims for just entitlement to land; both depend on settling the order of precedence between two brothers; both suggest that one brother possesses the land that might equally well belong to the other. Moreover, an awareness of how the political actions of the élite are dependent on pragmatism is pervasive; John's enforcement of justice and distribution of honour is shown as erratically prone to favouritism in the sudden elevation of the Bastard; and it is of a piece with the Plantagent behaviour we hear of in Richard the Lionheart's arrangements to cuckold his nobles. As with rumours, Act 1 enacts a sequence of diminutions of monarchical credibility; the political stature of John's regime is depleted by presenting its corrupt antecedents and fraudulent legitimacy.

This construction of an audience response which resists the conventional entitlement of the monarch to deferential understanding is consolidated by an alignment with the Bastard's understanding of events. In Act 1 his 'spontaneous' responses are deployed in sympathetic contrast to the callow pedantry of his brother and the cynically convoluted rhetoric of the court. Moreover, this identification is established around his heedlessness of decorum and unillusioned delight in the contingency of experience. In the soliloquy which crowns his triumphant rise in social prestige, the Bastard exposes those techniques of self-presentation by which the impression of superior social status is managed:

> A foot of honour better than I was,
> But many a foot of land the worse.
> Well, now can I make any Joan a lady;
> 'Good den, Sir Richard.' - 'God-a-mercy, fellow.'
> And if his name be George, I'll call him 'Peter';
> For new-made honour doth forget men's names:
> 'Tis too respective and too sociable
> For your conversion          (l. 1. 182-9)

Moreover, this irreverent perception of élite identity as a theatrical deception is sensationally endorsed in the hypocrisy that prevails throughout the struggle between France and England over the legitmacy of John's claim to the throne. Intriguingly, in the ethical contortions performed by the opposing protagonists – the pacts made and un-made; the same subjects alternately flattered and coerced – it does become difficult to maintain a coherent allegiance to the English cause. As the Bastard's speech on 'commodity' defines it, the same squalid principles drive the political machine whether it is French, Papal, or English (2.1.561-98).

This is how the Bastard functions in the play: the reckless talker, the scandalised commentator on the duplicity of public life. Similarly, much of *King John* shares the effect of rumours, acting as a defamatory speculation on the illicit nature of authority. Clearly, both his role and the sardonic design of the play can be aligned with Annabel Patterson's view that 'the popular voice was in fact represented in Elizabethan and Jacobean England, despite or because of its political silencing, as a cultural tradition of protest' (32). However, the development of the Bastard's political knowledge is not simply described in terms of a gradually accumulating cynicism which contributes to his – and, by extension, the audience's – emancipation from deference. His reappearance in Act 4 after his journey through the kingdom alerts us to a new current in his speech that responds to the division of the nation. Similarly, his encounter with the treasonous nobles furthers his recoil from those who act on the suspicion of court-scandal. At the end of Act 4, the Bastard's sense of principle is reconstructed in an act of commitment to the King. After his meditation on the coming apocalypse of war – "the imminent decay of wrested pomp" – he tersely decides "I'll to the king" (4. 3. 139-59). The Bastard does not abandon his knowledge of John' s weak claim to the throne, nor is he sure that the King has not been responsible for the murder of Arthur, but such doubts no longer spark his derision: the Bastard's recklessness is finally transformed into an unillusioned act of faith in time of crisis.

In Act 5, the Bastard learns to pursue what he now perceives as the national cause, rather than his own. Barbara Hodgdon has used Jonathan Dollimore's analysis of "transgressive reinscription" in Renaissance theatre to describe the peculiarities of the Bastard's role:

> marginal to the power structure, he seeks to be reinscribed within it but, once incorporated, he remains at its fringes, able to demystify and subvert its operations ... in *King John* however, where the King himself turns kingship upside down, the Bastard serves to protect the institution he embodies from further taint." (28)[8]

This conservative movement in the play is figured most powerfully in the self-abnegation with which he refuses the opportunity of command, despite the King's drastic psychological collapse. The Bastard's renewal in these terms also revitalizes hitherto inert habits of political response in the audience. As the play drains away other scandalised voices – those of women, prophets, children – they are replaced by the emotional maturation of the Bastard: the willing self-discipline of his own anarchic impulses when confronted by anarchy in the realm. An indulgence in defamatory cynicism, is called to account all the more powerfully when those sentiments have been so radically expressed and found wanting. The Bastard's speech is reordered towards the articulation of collective norms – anti-French and Papal slander; the need for kingly resolution.

The heroic note is most effectively struck after its long disappearance in the play when the Bastard kneels to the previously unseen Prince Henry and expresses a loyalty for which there is no cause beyond the hard-learned necessity for obedience:

> And happily may your sweet self put on
> The lineal state and glory of the land!
> To whom with all submission on my knee
> I do bequeath my faithful services
> And true subjection everlastingly. (5.7.101-5)

How much emphasis one gives to the Bastard's 'conversion' is debatable and could find different emphases in different productions. The alarming circumstances that besiege all the characters make such a gesture tentative, perhaps a desperate reaction to incipient chaos or to more malign forms of political restraint. Still, this distancing from some of the attitudes expressed by the play's scandalised voices is present. Whereas in others of Shakespeare's English history plays – for example, both parts of *Henry IV* – one can detect a much more emphatic confirmation of the veracity of popular scepticism, *King John* manifests a tentative handling of the critical energies of popular speech.

*Notes*

1. Compare Octavius Caesar's rueful reflections in *Antony and Cleopatra* on the sympathy accruing to his rival Pompey through "men's reports":

> The common body
> Like to a vagabond flag upon the stream,

Goes to, and back, lackeying the varying tide,
To rot itself with motion. (1.4. 44-7)

*Antony and Cleopatra*, ed. M. R. Ridley (London: Methuen, 1965).

2.  This and all subsequent quotations are from *King John*, ed. L. A Beaurline (Cambridge: Cambridge UP, 1990).

3.  See, for example, many of the contributions to a recent collection of essays on the play "*King John*": *New Perspectives*, ed. Deborah T. Curren-Aquino (Newark: Delaware UP, 1989), especially Virginia M. Vaughan, "*King John*". A study in subversion and containment", 62-75; Phyllis Rackin, "Patriarchal history and female subversion in *King John*", 76-90; Dorothea Kehler, "So jest with heaven: Deity in *King John*", 99-113.

4.  For a more detailed account of the general context to which this piece of legislation belongs, see John Bellamy, *The Tudor Treason Law* (London: Routledge & Kegan Paul, 1979), especially pp. 29-36.

5.  See *Tudor Royal Proclamations*. ed. Paul L. Hughes and James F. Larkin, (New Haven: Yale UP, 1964-69), Vol. 1, 168; 229; 281.

6.  Peter Roberts has recently analysed Elizabethan concerns over players: "Elizabethan players and minstrels and the legislation of 1572 against retainers and vagabonds" in *Religion, Culture and Society in Early Modern Britain*, ed. A. Fletcher and P. Roberts (Cambridge: Cambridge UP, 1994), pp. 29-55.

7.  *King Henry IV. Part II*, ed. A. R. Humphreys (London: Methuen, 1966).

8.  For Jonathan Dollimore's use of this term see "Subjectivity, Sexuality and Transgression: The Jacobean Connection", *Renaissance Drama*, n.s. 17 (1986), pp. 53-81, especially 57-8.

*Abbreviations*

| | |
|---|---|
| CSPD, Elizabeth | *Calendar of State Papers, Domestic Series, of the Reigns of Edward VI. Mary, Elizabeth, 1547-1625.* Ed. Robert Lemon and Mary Anne Everett Green. 12 vols. London, 1856-72. |
| L&P, Henry VIII | *Letters and Papers. Foreign and Domestic of the Reign of Henry VIII.* Ed. J. Gardiner, J. S. Brewer and R. H. Brodie. 21 vols. London, 1862-1910. |
| Statutes | *Statutes of the Realm.* Ed A. Luders et al. 11 vols. London, 1810-28. |
| TRP | *Tudor Royal Proclamations*, Ed. Paul L. Hughes and James F. Larkin. 3 vols. New Haven: Yale UP, 1964-69. |

*Works Cited*

Bakhtin Mikhail. *Rabelais and His World*. Transl. Hélène Iswolsky. Cambridge, MA: MIT Press, 1968.

Beaurline, L. A. Introduction. *King John*, ed. L. A. Beaurline (Cambridge: Cambridge UP, 1990), pp. 1-57.

Blanpied, John W. "'Unfathered heirs and loathly births of nature': Bringing History to Crisis in *2 Henry IV*". *English Literary Renaissance*, 5 (1975), 212-31.

Bristol, Michael D. *Carnival and Theater: Plebeian Culture and the Structure of Authority in Renaissance England*. London: Methuen, 1985.

Braunmuller, A. R. Introduction. *King John*, ed. A. R. Braunmuller. (Oxford: Clarendon Press, 1989), pp. 1-93.

Burckhardt, Sigurd. "*King John*: The Ordering of This Present Time". In *Shakespearean Meanings* (Princeton: Princeton UP, 1968), pp. 116-43.

E. K. Chambers, *The Elizabethan Stage*, 4 vols. Oxford: Clarendon Press, 1923.

Collinson, Patrick. "The Monarchical Republic of Queen Elizabeth I", *Elizabethan Essays*. (London. The Hambledon Press, 1994), pp. 31-57.

Croft, Pauline. "The Reputation of Robert Cecil: Libels, Political Opinion and Popular Awareness in the Early Seventeenth-Century". *Transactions of the Royal Historical Society*. 6th series, 1 (1991), 43-69.

Elliot, John R. "Shakespeare and the Double Image of King John". *Shakespeare Studies*, 1 (1965), 64-84.

Elton, G. R. *Policy and Police*. Cambridge: Cambridge UP, 1972.

Emmison, F. G. *Elizabethan Life. Vol I: Disorder*. Chelmsford: Essex County Council, 1971.

Fletcher, A., and John Stevenson. Introduction. *Order and Disorder in Early Modern England*. Ed. Fletcher and Stevenson (Cambridge: Cambridge UP, 1985), pp. 1-40.

Fox, Alistair. "Prophecies and Politics in the Reign of Henry VIII". In *Reassessing the Henrician Age: Humanism, Politics and Reform 1500-1550*. (Oxford: Basil Blackwell, 1986), pp. 77-94.

Greenblatt, Stephen J. "Invisible Bullets". In *Shakespearean Negotiations: The Circulation of Social Energy in Renaissance England*. (Oxford: Clarendon Press, 1988), pp. 21-65.

Grennan, Eamon. "Shakespeare's Satirical History: A Reading of *King John*." *Shakespeare Studies* 11 (1978), 21-37.

Hill, Christopher. "The Many-Headed Monster In Late Tudor and Early Stuart Political Thinking." In *From the Renaissance to the Counter-Reformation*. Ed. Charles H. Carter (London: Jonathan Cape, 1966), pp. 296-324.

Hodgdon, Barbara. *The End Crowns All: Closure and Contradiction in Shakespeare's History*. Princeton: Princeton UP, 1991.

Jones, Emrys. *The Origins of Shakespeare*. Oxford: Clarendon Press, 1977.

Kent, Joan R. "Attitudes of members of the House of Commons to the regulation of 'personal conduct' in late Elizabethan and early Stuart England", *Bulletin of the Institute of Historical Research*, 46 (1973), 41-71.

Levin, Carole. *Propaganda in the English Reformation: Heroic and Villainous Images of King John*. Lewiston, New York: Edwin Mellen Press, 1988.

Mullaney, Steven. *The Place of the Stage: License, Play and Power in Renaissance England*. Chicago: Chicago UP, 1988.

Patterson, Annabel. *Shakespeare and the Popular Voice*. Oxford: Basil Blackwell, 1989.

Samaha, Joel. "Gleanings from Local Criminal-Court Records: Sedition Amongst the 'Inarticulate' in Elizabethan Essex". *Journal of Social History*, 8 (1975), 61-79.

Sharpe, J.A. *Defamation and Sexual Slander in Earl Modern England: The Church Courts at York*. York: Borthwick Institute of Historical Research, 1980.

Slack, Paul. *Poverty and Policy in Tudor and Stuart England*. London: Longman, 1988.

Taylor, Barry. *Vagrant Writing: Social and Semiotic Disorders in the English Renaissance*. Toronto: Toronto UP, 1991.

Waith, Eugene. '*King John* and the Drama of History'. *Shakespeare Quarterly*, 29 (1978), 192-211.

Watson, Donald G. *Shakespeare's Early History Plays*. London: Macmillan, 1990.

# *CORIOLANUS* AND THE TRAGIC USE OF HISTORY

## David Farley-Hills
### (Emeritus Professor University of Wales, Swansea)

The first of Shakespeare's Roman tragedies, *Titus Andronicus*, differs markedly from his three later Roman plays in having little, if any, basis in history. In contrast, *Julius Caesar* (1599), *Antony and Cleopatra* (1606)[1] and *Coriolanus* (1608) stick very closely to their classical sources and if anything progressively so as the series continues. In *Coriolanus* this is not just a matter of fidelity to the principal sources in Plutarch (via North's translation of Amyot's French version) and in Livy, but of a faithfulness to the 'feel' of republican Rome that Dryden (who was in a good position to know) is said to have called "truly great and truly Roman".[2] T.J.B.Spencer, who quotes both Dryden's and Pope's approval of the play's sense of Roman history, endorses their judgement with enthusiasm: "... to write *Coriolanus* was one of the great feats of the historical imagination in Renaissance Europe".[3]

It may be coincidental, but I think it is not, that contemporary neo-classical theory was advocating a necessary connection between tragedy and history. By neo-classical theory I refer to the critical work of those Italian writers of the sixteenth century, (gradually becoming known to the English as the century came towards its close), who were developing new theories of literature, and notably drama, based on Aristotle's *Poetics*, (with an admixture of Horace and Donatus) and classical, especially Senecan, practice. It is usually assumed that Shakespeare, as a practical man of the theatre, was not much interested in critical theory; I find this assumption improbable. I am not suggesting that Shakespeare was an avid reader of the neo-classical theorising of the likes of Minturno, Trissino, Giraldi and Castelvetro, though he was certainly reading a lighter side of Giraldi in preparation for *Othello*, *Measure for Measure* and (probably) *King Lear*, possibly in Italian.

We can take it for granted, too, that he had read Sir Philip Sidney's *Apology for Poetry*, which summarises and discusses ideas of the new criticism.

But you no more needed to imbibe neo-classical dogma by reading these theoretical texts in Jacobean England than you need to have read *Of Grammatology* now in order to know something of 'post-structuralism'. Shakespeare was, after all, one of the principal actors in that *cause célèbre* of neo-classicism on the Jacobean popular stage, the production of Jonson's *Sejanus* (probably initially for the Court) late in 1603. It is even possible that Shakespeare helped Jonson write the stage version of the play, for Jonson mentions a "second pen" that had "good share" in preparing it for the public stage;[4] although Chapman is usually cited as the likely collaborator (on very little, if any, evidence), it seems more likely that a Globe play would be supervised by its chief playwright than by a man who had (conspicuously) no relationship with Shakespeare's company. It was transferred to the Globe on the re-opening of the theatres in 1604. Jonson's address "To the Reader", published in the quarto version of the play in 1605, makes it quite clear (if Shakespeare hadn't noticed) that the occasion was meant to be a show of neo-classical strength, and although Jonson says he has not been too careful of the mere "formes" of neo-classicism, he prides himself in particular on what he calls his "truth of argument",[5] that is, his fidelity to his historical sources. This is massively reinforced by extensive annotations of the text proclaiming his classical authorities.

Jonson's increasing interest in neo-classical dogma can be traced from the rather sceptical comments on the neo-classical "lawes" by Cordatus ("the Authors friend") in the Induction of *Every Man out of his Humour*(1599)[6] to the wholesale surrender to the "lawes", "as best Criticks have designed" in the prologue to *Volpone* (1606).[7] *Every Man out of his Humour* was also one of Shakespeare's selections for the Globe (as indeed was *Volpone*), for it is inconceivable that Shakespeare did not have a major say in what went on to the Globe stage, and we have Rowe's word for it that he took a special interest in Jonson's early career as a dramatist.[8] *Every Man out of his Humour* was one of the first plays for the new theatre and must have been performed shortly after the production of *Julius Caesar*, which may well have inaugurated the opening of the play-house in the autumn of 1599. It is unlikely that Shakespeare's choice of a classical subject, treated with some neo-classical decorum, and Jonson's discussion of fashionable literary theory coupled with a claim to be following in the steps of the *vetus comoedia*[9] (Induction, 1.232) are unrelated.

The quickening of Shakespeare's interest in Italian neo-classicism would seem to follow natural from the move of the Globe playhouse to the South Bank and the opportunities thus opened up of attracting the "wiser sort" (to use Gabriel Harvey's phrase) from across the river in Westminster and the Western suburbs of London. Things Italian had never been more fashionable, and both Marston (whose mother was of Italian extraction) in the newly opened Paul's Boys' playhouse, and Chapman at Blackfriars were quick to exploit the fashion. We learn from *Hamlet* (F, 2.2.335ff.) that one of the boys' companies was causing Shakespeare some concern at the time. Both these rivals adapted Italian plays. Chapman's Blackfriars' play, *May Day* (c.1602) follows Alessandro Piccolomini's *Alessandro* fairly closely, while the sub-plot of the *Gentleman Usher*, also a Blackfriars play, is taken from a story by Antonio Benevieni, one of the several Italian neo-platonic writers with whose work Chapman was familiar. His knowledge of Italian comedy is further evidenced by his mentioning the title of four plays in his dedication to *Widow's Tears*. He also tried his hand at neo-classical tragedy for Blackfriars in *Bussy d'Ambois* at about the same time as Jonson was producing *Sejanus*

Marston makes use of Sforza d'Oddi's *Morti Vivi* in writing *What You Will* for Paul's Boys and even includes part of a scene in Italian in *Antonio and Mellida* (4.1.191ff.). Chapman and Marston were shortly to join forces with Jonson to write the comedy of *Eastward Ho*, which, among other things, pokes fun at Shakespeare's Gothic tragedy, *Hamlet*, especially in one scene (3.2) now usually attributed to Chapman. Here Chapman introduces us to a character called Hamlet, who is footman to the play's nymphomaniac heroine (called Gertrude). The point of Chapman's satire is that *Hamlet* breaks all the best neo-classical rules in showing wanton heroines (Ophelia's bawdy thoughts are mocked) and a hero who is incompetent at the two things most valued in the neo-classical hero: love and action. Chapman's Hamlet even fails, after much trying, to succeed in obtaining a coach for his mistress, Gertrude, while she criticises him for failing (unlike her other footman) to provide her with "milk" (3.2.44).

Shakespeare had perhaps called down this neo-classical wrath for being flippant about a neo-classical play on the Trojan war, that Hamlet admired, but that turned out to be "caviare to the general" - the lubricious Hamlet even has the cheek to praise the play for omitting "sallets in the lines to make the matter savoury". *Hamlet* was an immense success, whereas *Sejanus* was at first a failure (which must have rubbed salt in Jonsonian wounds); but the tide of history (more literally then than the modern cliché allows) was clearly with Jonson and Chapman; Shakespeare, in the late Roman plays, recognised this as he strove increasingly to please not only the wiser (and more fashionable) sort in general, but, from time to time, the wisest fool in Christendom in particular.

In his article on the sources of *Sejanus*[10] Richard Dutton gives a brief mention of Castelvetro's view "that a pure fiction in tragedy is ludicrous" (quoting G. Giovanni), but to regard Castelvetro as "representative" is to simplify the matter considerably. The view that tragedy is to be distinguished by its fidelity to history from comedy, which is largely fictive, gradually hardens into dogma as Italian neo-classical doctrine develops in the sixteenth century. It is already to be found in the highly influential late classical commentary on Terence by Donatus, where we read: "the events of Comedy are always fictitious, those of tragedy are often true and taken from history".[11] It originates in Aristotle's discussion of the distinction between poetic and historical truth in Chapter IX of the *Poetics*, where, although he starts by arguing for the essential difference between poetic and historical truth, he goes on to say that in practice comedy is mostly based on fiction,

In tragedy, on the other hand, the authors keep to the names of real people, the reason being that what is possible is credible. Whereas we cannot be certain of the possibility of something that has not happened, what has happened is obviously possible, for it would not have happened if this had not been so.[12]

Unfortunately, these convoluted remarks became steadily more convoluted in neo-classical explication. In spite of Aristotle's opening remarks in the chapter, and in spite of his later assertion that "it would be absurd" to confine tragedy to the traditional stories and his pointing to examples of fictional tragedies, neo-classical commentary increasingly came to assert that tragedy must be true to historical sources. Trissino, for instance, in Book V of *La Poetica* (1562) summarizes Aristotle fairly accurately and comes to the conclusion that it is enough that the main action is true ("che la summa della fatta sia vera").[13] He comes to this conclusion, however, by converting Aristotle's descriptive account of Greek drama into the prescriptive: you are advised to seek actual names and true actions in writing tragedy ("si convenien cercare nomi veri, et attioni vere").

Giraldi, in the *Discorso sulle comedie e sulle tragedie* (1554), wavers a little, but comes eventually to the opinion that tragedy should deal in historical fact (though his own tragedies are as often as not fictional). We find the fully fledged dogma in Castelvetro's *Poetica d'Aristotele* (1570) where Aristotle is roundly condemned for not making it quite clear that tragedy must always be based on historical fact:

> As tragedy must tell of the action of a king, it follows that such action must really have happened, for we cannot create a king, who never existed, by our imagination, nor can we attribute actions to such a king; indeed we cannot even attribute to a really historic king actions which he never performed: for history would give us the lie.[14]

There was general agreement that tragedy must deal with royal events in a suitably decorous manner. It was Castelvetro, incidentally, who established the dogma that there must be unity of place, one of the rules Jonson assures us he has obeyed in *Volpone*.

Not all of Jonson's contemporaries shared his enthusiasm for the new historicism; indeed others preferred to follow Aristotle (and Sidney) on this matter, rather than the neo-Aristotelians. Marston, for instance, takes an Aristotelian stand in the address "To the General Reader" prefacing his tragedy *Sophonisba* (c.1606) when he declares: "Know that I have not laboured in this poem to tie myself to relate anything as an historian, but to enlarge everything as a poet." Dekker makes a similar declaration to his readers (perhaps with his old enemy in his sights) in writing of his *Whore of Babylon* (1607): "know that I write as a Poet, not as an Historian, and that these two doe not live under one law". In his address to Sir Thomas Howard prefacing *The Revenge of Bussy D'Ambois* (c.1610, printed 1613) Chapman pointedly asks:

> And for the authentical truth of either person or action, who (worth the respecting) will expect it in a poem, whose subject is not truth, but things like truth? Poor envious souls they are that cavil at truth's want in these natural fictions ...

Chapman, however, was one of the friends who came to Jonson's support (as did Marston) by writing commendatory verses on the play when *Sejanus* was published in 1605. The most interesting of these verses is by a certain "Ev. B.", who tells us he was at the performance of the play at the Globe when it provoked "the Peoples beastly rage". Many in the audience (he says) did not know whom to blame most, the vulgar for rejecting it, or the author for exhibiting it in such company.[15] The same suggestion that there was a marked difference in response between the vulgar and the gentry is made in William Fennor's *Descriptions*, 1616:

> But sweet Poesye
> Is oft convict, condemn'd, and iudg'd to die
> Without iust triall, by a multitude
> Whose iudgements are illiterate, and rude.
> Witnesse *Sceianus*, whose approved worth,

> Sounds from the calme South, to the freezing North
> [...] With more then humane art it was bedewed,
> Yet to the multitude it nothing shewed;
> They screwed their scurvy iawes and look't awry,
> Like hissing snakes adiudging it to die:
> When wits of gentry did applaud the same ...[16]

Jonson, then, may have had a *succès d'estime* among those who mattered, even if the stinkards disapproved. Shakespeare had seemingly misjudged his audience's respectability, assuming it to be "wiser" than it was when he accepted *Sejanus* for the Globe, and this may explain why he waited more than four years before trying out his own neo-classical tragedy at around the time when the King's Men were re-opening Blackfriars to play to a more exclusive *clientèle*.

Although both *Antony and Cleopatra* and *Coriolanus* are firmly based in their historical sources, there is a marked difference in the way the historical material is handled in the two plays. *Coriolanus* is markedly closer to the requirements of neo-classical theory than the earlier play. There is not only an unmistakable unity of tone that the earlier play deliberately avoids as it contrasts the worlds of Rome and Egypt, but also a determination to restrict place (to Rome and its wider environs) and time (events are given the feel of compact continuity which neo-classicism required at this stage of its development), requirements flouted in *Antony and Cleopatra* more conspicuously than in any other of the Roman plays. Shakespeare also keeps much more closely to his historical sources in *Coriolanus* than is his custom in the English history plays.

Shakespeare had, of course, used historical sources many times before. In his English history plays he often adheres fairly closely to his historical sources, but in every case adds fictional material and so embellishes his sources that the plays become a mixture of fact and fiction that makes them more fiction than fact. If we take *Richard II* (1595-6) as a representative example of Shakespeare's use of English history in tragedy, we can compare it both with Jonson's handling of his sources in *Sejanus* and with *Coriolanus* to illustrate the difference between the neo-classical respect for historical accuracy and the much freer use of sources in the earlier play.

*Richard II* is based on the last two years of Richard's life, from April 1398 to March 1400, as told in Ralph Holinshed's *Chronicles of England, Scotland and Ireland* (in the edition of 1586-7).[17] As in *Sejanus* and *Coriolanus*, the material is selected and re-arranged for dramatic purposes. Shakespeare omits, for instance, the whole of Holinshed's account of Richard's campaign in Ireland and how Richard was tricked by the Earl of Northumberland on his return through Wales. This latter omission was possibly made "to avoid showing Bolingbroke in a bad light by making his envoy behave treacherously".[18] Shakespeare also adds considerably to the historical material, as in the scene in which Richard sends Bolingbroke into exile (1.3), where the part played by John of Gaunt, with minor exceptions, "is entirely invented".[19] The end of the scene may have been inspired (thinks Ure) by Shakespeare's reading of Lyly's *Euphues*.[20]

The additions to Holinshed include Shakespeare's conception of the character of John of Gaunt (which may have been influenced by Froissart's *Chronicle* and/or the anonymous play *Thomas of Woodstock*), most of the part of Queen Isabel ("in Holinshed, as in history, she was a child of eleven"),[21] the Duchess of York's behaviour in 5.3, ("again Shakespeare's invention"- Ure), the whole of the Garden scene, 3.4, the part played by the Earl of Northumberland and "much of the character and behaviour of Richard, especially in the last two acts".[22] It is worth remarking about this last example that the most that was generally conceded by neo-classical theorists was (as in Trissino) that even if there were some fictional characters allowed in tragedy the principal figures and events should be true to history. *Richard II* can be seen as a patchwork of history and authorial invention, the main purpose of which is to create a compelling dramatic spectacle in sight and sound for the Elizabethan audience, to hold a mirror up to the audience's nature, rather than to reflect accurately the life and times of the Plantagenet king.

The aims of neo-classical tragic theory were not greatly different from this, though there is considerable disagreement between different theorists about whether the main purpose of tragedy (as well as comedy) was moral (as Giraldi thought)[23] or aesthetic (as Castelvetro tends to argue).[24] There is, however, a marked difference in the means involved in that end, between Shakespeare's promiscuous mixture of fact and fiction in *Richard II* and the neo-classical methods as exemplified in *Sejanus* and *Coriolanus*. *Sejanus* is obsessively concerned with "truth of argument". It follows closely books I-VI of the *Annals* of Tacitus, translating passages such as Tiberius' speech (I, 454-502) and Cordus' defence before the Senate (III, 407-60). Jonson, however, recognises the need for adaptation and compression for dramatic purposes, for he was as aware as his most recent editor that the function of the dramatist is not the same as that of the historian.[25] Other sources are used, such as Suetonius' *Life of Tiberius*, to fill out the portrait of Tiberius, while the account of the fall of Sejanus, missing from the defective Book V of the *Annals*, is supplied from Dio Cassius' *History of the Roman People* (books LVII and LVIII), Juvenal's Tenth Satire and Claudian's *Against Rufinus*. Further sources used include Plutarch's *Moralia*, Seneca's tragedies and Lucan's *Pharsalia*, with some considerable use made of Machiavelli's *Prince* and *Discourses on Livy*.

Occasionally Jonson even departs altogether from his historical sources (and history), when, for instance, he has Silius commit suicide in the course of his trial in the Senate (3.1.319-39) - an act of violence, incidentally, countenanced in neo-classical tragedy by such events as the killing of Sulmone by Orbecche in Giraldi's *Orbecche* (5.3.116-32). Jonson also manipulates the historical chronology by having Cordus arraigned in the same scene (3.1) when historically his trial took place about a year after Silius' death. For other departures from the historical records the reader is referred to the account of Jonson's handling of his sources in the edition of the play by Philip Ayres.[26]

Jonson's use of time (but not place) is freer than most neo-classical theorists thought proper, for Aristotle's observation that generally "tragedy tries [...] to keep within a single revolution of the sun, or only slightly to exceed it" (*Poetics*, Chapter V) was acceded to, but the requirement gradually became narrower and more prescriptive. In Castelvetro it had become: "the time of the representation and that of the action represented must be exactly coincident".[27] The action of *Sejanus* takes place in various parts of Rome, and Herford and Simpson point out that the time covered by the events of the play encompasses several years historically and that Jonson's plot presupposes the passing of several days at the least; time, for instance, to allow Sejanus to travel to Campania and back between Acts 3 and 4, and there is a further delay of more than a day before Sejanus' fall in Act 5.[28] Jonson admits that he has not followed "the strict laws of time" in the play,[29] but in any case it would be wrong to think of neo-classical theory as rigid and invariable at this date, there was considerable disagreement among different theorists and a great deal of independence from Aristotle. Jonson is possibly thinking specifically of Castelvetro, whose views increasingly prevailed as the new century advanced.

If we compare Shakespeare's handling of his sources in *Coriolanus* with Jonson's in *Sejanus* and his own in *Richard II*, it is clear that his late tragedy conforms much more closely to the method of *Sejanus*. Like *Sejanus*, *Coriolanus* has one principal source in Roman history. This is "The Life of Caius Martius Coriolanus" in Plutarch's *Lives of the Noble Grecians and Romans*.[30] Like Jonson, though not so extensively, Shakespeare uses supplementary sources, notably for Menenius' speech on the relation of the belly to the rest of the body (1.1.95-153), which makes use of Philemon Holland's translation of Livy's *Ab Urbe Condita*, and (possibly) of his translation of Plutarch's *Moralia*, William Camden's *Remaines* and William Averell's *A Marvellous Combat of Contrarieties* (1588). Like *Sejanus*, *Coriolanus* makes use, not merely of the incidents recounted in the sources, but of the words in which such incidents are described in North's translation of Plutarch's

*Life*.[31] Such verbal echoes are rare in Shakespeare's earlier plays, though they are to be found in *Antony and Cleopatra*.

The sources of *Coriolanus* are thus followed with considerable fidelity, with only those changes that help convert prose narrative into effective verse drama. It is particularly noticeable how closely Shakespeare has followed the sequence of events in Plutarch's narrative (as Bullough's annotation of the *Life* clearly shows).[32] At the same time his concern to concentrate the events can be seen in such details as the omission of all reference to the 30 days to consider his terms that Coriolanus gives the first Roman delegation who come to him to urge him to return to Rome.[33]

Some characters (notably Menenius and Aufidius) are expanded considerably from their role and character in Plutarch. Volumnia is given a far more commanding role in the play as the strongest influence on Coriolanus' character, and there are adjustments and additions to the roles of Valeria and Cominius. There are some changes, too, in the chronology; Shakespeare compacts the various riots of the people recorded in Plutarch into one and generally concentrates the action. He adds touches here and there: Coriolanus enters Corioles alone, not with North's "very fewe men to helpe him", and the dramatist invents the warm welcome the hero receives from the people of Rome on his return from the victory. A more important change is that Coriolanus' attempt to abolish the tribunate and stop the supply of corn after he has been denied the consulship, as recorded in North, is suppressed (to prevent Coriolanus from seeming petty and vindictive).

There is, perhaps, a tendency for Shakespeare to present Coriolanus in a better light than Plutarch does. He omits, for instance, the speculation that Coriolanus tries to trick the Romans into war,[34] and such references in Plutarch as those to Coriolanus' lack of learning and reason[35] and "rough and unpleasant" speech,[36] as well as other adverse criticisms, are omitted or toned down. Even so, the picture Shakespeare gives of Coriolanus is essentially that presented by

Plutarch. There are times when North's language shows through in the play in an extraordinary transmutation, as when "oh mother, sayed he, you have won a happy victory for your countrie, but mortal unhappy for your sonne" becomes:

> O mother, mother!
> What have you done? Behold the heavens do ope,
> The gods look down, and this unnatural scene
> They laugh at. O my mother, mother! O!
> You have won a happy victory to Rome;
> But for your son, believe it, O, believe it,
> Most dangerously you have with him prevail'd,
> If not most mortal to him.      (5.3.182-9)

Shakespeare nonetheless did not follow the passages at the end of Plutarch's *Life* when the Romans celebrate their escape from destruction by building a temple to the goddess Fortuna in honour of Volumnia and Virgilia. Plutarch (somewhat sceptically) tells how the ladies pay for a statue of the goddess and have it placed in the temple, where a miracle occurs: the statue speaks to the ladies and sweats and weeps blood. Shakespeare leaves out all but a bare mention of the building of a temple to Fortune (5.3.207) and proceeds immediately to the death of Coriolanus at the hands of Aufidius. The tendency to play down references to the supernatural can be seen elsewhere in the play: Shakespeare omits, for instance, the sequence in Plutarch where Titus Latinus recounts an ominous dream to the Senate and undergoes a miraculous cure there.[37] He also omits the delegation of priests and soothsayers that Rome sends to plead with Coriolanus.[38]

This secularisation and de-mystification of the events is all the more remarkable because it is a tendency in all of Shakespeare's other late plays to dwell on the marvellous. In *Antony and Cleopatra* not only does Shakespeare include that mysterious scene in which the tutelary god Hercules is heard leaving his ward (4.3), but the play abounds in mythologising references and the marvellous is relished, not least in the Queen of Egypt herself. *Macbeth*, which probably comes between the two Roman plays,[39] is dominated by occult forces, not to mention the "Tales, Tempests and such like drolleries" of the late plays.

Ben Jonson was understandably scornful of such Shakespearean backsliding. For neo-Aristotelian theorists (like Jonson) disapproved of such Gothic tendencies (although gods and goddesses were allowed to appear in human form) on the grounds that to be mimetic, action and character had to cultivate verisimilitude. In contrast to the neo-Platonists among the neo-classicists (such as Chapman) who held a mystical view of poetry and a vatic view of the poet, the neo-Aristotelians favoured a down-to-earth view both of the function of poetry and its manifestations, a contrast that Castelvetro makes explicit:

> Aristotle did not believe poetry to be a special gift of God, granted to one man rather than another, like the gift of prophecy, and such similar unnatural privileges not shared by others. And without doubt, he sets out to reprove openly that opinion which some have attributed to Plato, that poetry is inspired in men by a divine rage. Which opinion had its origin and birth in the ignorance of the vulgar and has been cultivated and fostered by the pride of poets for this reason and in this manner.[40]

Jonson had initially followed the neo-Platonists, and his conversion can be traced, not only by the increasing interest he shows in neo-Aristotelian theory, already mentioned, but, over the same period, by a parallel change in his views on poetry and the drama. As late as *Poetaster* (1601) he had the poet Ovid express an allegiance to "sacred poesie [...] the queene of soules"[41] that, the play suggests, is shared by its author. When he came to revise *Every Man in his Humor* (c. 1606) he suppressed the vatic speech by the old play's hero Lorenzo Junior in praise of Poesie "Blessed, aeternall, and most true devine",[42] and provided a prologue proclaiming the neo-Aristotelian unities, promising men rather than monsters in the characterization and:

> ... deedes, and language, such as men doe use;
> And persons, such as *Comoedie* would chuse,
> When she would shew an Image of the times,
> And sport with humane follies, not with crimes.[43]

In theory at least, realism had come to take the place of myth.

So in *Coriolanus* history predominates over myth, the gods stand aloof from the play, they look down and laugh at the "unnatural scene" of Coriolanus' capitulation. This is a curious description of a scene where Coriolanus has, at last, shown the weaknesses of his human nature - by human standards he has at last acted naturally. But by the standards of the gods, and so of the ideal nature of man, he has shown himself weak and unheroic; by showing himself to be a mere man, he has lost that *virtus* which Plutarch had earlier described as the "valliantnes [...] honoured in Rome above all other vertues".[44] In becoming a man, Coriolanus has ceased being a neo-classical hero. Shakespeare's ending thus exposes a contradiction at the heart of neo-classical theory: that the demand for historical truth to life (verisimilitude) conflicts with the tendency towards idealising the hero.

Castelvetro makes it clear that to be a tragic hero not only involves being of exalted birth and being "above the average", but of obeying rules of conduct that are different from those of ordinary men:

> The characters of tragedy are quite different from those of comedy. Tragic characters are regal and have exalted spirits and are haughty, and what they want, they want excessively, and if an injury is done to them, or if they are led to understand it might be done to them, they do not run off to the magistracy to complain of the aggressor, nor suffer the injury patiently, but take the law into their own hands according as their will dictates, and out of revenge they kill both strangers and blood relatives, and in desperation not merely blood relatives, but even themselves. For such persons, being of royal estate, which is reputed the height of human felicity, and with the power to avenge themselves for the injuries done to them, are not subject to contempt or mockery by the mediocre, nor do they feel the loss of small things, nor suffer it, nor does marriage or the satisfaction of amorous desires add to their pleasure, living, as one can say they do, in perpetual married bliss and amorous satisfaction, so that to create more happiness necessitates reducing their happiness or at least that they fall into misery or a low state with a spectacular leap. But characters in comedy are poor in heart, keen to obey magistrates and live under the law, and suffer injuries and harm and run to officials begging them to obtain redress by means of the law, for the sake of their

reputations, or compensation for the damage; they do not take the law into their own hands, nor go about killing relatives or themselves or others for the reasons that kings would kill for.[45]

This lurid and amoral view of the tragic hero (well exemplified, incidentally, in Chapman's *Bussy d'Ambois*) is refined in *Coriolanus* into something beyond Castelvetro's imagination, but the resemblance is still unmistakable. Castelvetro sees tragedy as essentially an aesthetic phenomenon, and it is likewise a feature of Shakespeare's tragedy that moral judgements are left in abeyance - as they are not in Plutarch - so that the tragedy is allowed to reside in the irony that Coriolanus dies in becoming human and resigning that *virtus* which the Romans regard as "the name of vertue selfe". The play is nicely balanced between praise and blame, so that the dominating mode is, as in *Sejanus*, one of irony. This ironic detachment is aided by Shakespeare's presentation of the hero from the outside, as it were, again in accordance with neo-classical practice; there are no extended soliloquies, so the audience hears little of Coriolanus' inner feelings. For this reason modern critics' attempts to psycho-analyse are particularly mistaken: "drama does not imitate men in action to discover their characters".[46] The Aristotelian emphasis on action produces a tragedy where events tend to dictate character, rather than character dictating events.

There is much else in *Coriolanus* either by accident, but much more likely by design, that would satisfy the neo-classically minded. Women are given that dignity that (in Giraldi's view) should prevent the inclusion of any but those of noble birth ("women in tragedies, as well as being of regal status, must be grave, prudent and sagacious [...] because they are used to being among the great and men of wisdom and by continual conversation with such appear as other women cannot").[47] Their conversation should accordingly be without blemish, there should be "no sallets in the lines to make the matter savoury". No play in the Shakespeare canon is freer from such indecorum than *Coriolanus*.

The language generally has a controlled and austere toughness that it shares with both Jonson's and Chapman's neo-classical tragedies. Even the amount of violence on stage is, by Shakespearean standards (and the requirements of his audiences, no doubt) strictly controlled - fighting yes, but only one death at the end of the play and that both Jonson and Giraldi would tolerate for the new drama. By the standards of French neo-classicism in the later seventeenth century many features of *Coriolanus* would be (and were) unacceptable. John Dennis, for all his expressed admiration of the play, thought its "wild confusion" needed regularising in *The Invader of His Country*, published in 1720,[48] but neo-classicism meant something much more flexible and less constrained in the Jacobean period than it subsequently became. Giraldi, for instance, as a practical man of the theatre, writes in the *Discorso* "the judicious author should not revere the ancients so much that he copies their vices", and he defends his play *Didone* against the complaint that he has included too many characters, with the argument that "if perhaps I have departed from Aristotle's rules to some extent, in conforming with the customs of our own age, I have done it following the example of the Ancients, for Euripides works his plots very differently from Sophocles and the Romans very differently from the Greeks".[49]

If, as has been argued,[50] the play was written for the newly-vamped Blackfriars theatre its audience there would surely have recognised it as a triumphant attempt to out-Roman even the redoubtable Jonson and (as Ide argues) that other notable classicist of the popular theatre, George Chapman.

*Notes*

1. See my dating of the play, "The Position of *Antony and Cleopatra* in the Canon", *Notes and Queries*, 238:2 (June 1993), pp. 193-7.

2. John Dennis, *Letter to Sir Richard Steele*, 26 March, 1719. Quoted by T.J.B. Spencer, "Shakespeare and the Elizabethan Romans", *Shakespeare Survey*, 10 (1957), p. 27.

3. *Shakespeare Survey*, 10, p. 35.

4. *Sejanus* ed. C.H. Herford and P. Simpson, *Ben Jonson* (Oxford: Clarendon Press, 1932), Vol. IV, 351.

5. *Sejanus*, Ed. Herford/Simpson, IV, 350.

6. *Every Man out of his Humour* ed. C.H. Herford and P. Simpson, *Ben Jonson* (Oxford: Clarendon Press, 1927), III, 436.

7. For a more detailed account of Jonson's interest in, and relation to, neo-classical theory, see my articles: "Jonson and the Neo-Classical Rules in *Sejanus* and *Volpone*", *RES*, ns 46, No.182 (1995) pp.153-73, and "Ben Jonson and the Italian Neo-Classical Theorists", *Journal of Anglo-Italian Studies* [University of Malta], 3, (1993), pp. 52-60.

8. Nicholas Rowe, *Some Account of the Life etc. of Mr William Shakespear (1709)*, in *Eighteenth Century Essays on Shakespeare*, ed. D. Nichol Smith, (Glasgow: James MacLehose, 1903), pp. 7-8.

9. *Every Man out of his Humour*, ed. Herford/Simpson, III, 436.

10. Richard A. Dutton, "The Sources, Text, and Readers of *Sejanus*: Jonson's 'Integrity of the Story'", *MP*, 75 (1978), pp. 182-3.

11. See Laurence Lerner, *Shakespeare's Tragedies* (Harmondsworth: Penguin, 1968), p. 300.

12. Aristotle: *On the Art of Poetry*, transl. by T.S. Dorsch in *Classical Literary Criticism*, (Harmondsworth: Penguin, 1965), p. 44.

13. Giovanni Giorgio Trissino, *La quinta e la sesta divisione della poetica* (Venice: Andrea Arrivabene, 1562), facs. ed. (Munich: Wilhelm Fink, 1969), p. 10v.

14. H.B. Charlton, *Castelvetro's Theory of Poetry*, (Manchester: Manchester UP, 1913), p. 113, (Charlton's translation is, as usual, rather free). The reference is to Lodovico Castelvetro, *Poetica d'Aristotele* (Vienna: Gaspar Stainhofer, 1570), publ. in facs. (Munich: Wilhelm Fink, 1967), p. 104v. The Italian reads: "... se [la favola della tragedia] dee contenere attione reale seguita che contenga attione avenuta e certa, e d'un re, che sia stato, e che si sappia che sia stato, conciosia cosa che non ci possiamo imaginare un re che non sia stato ne attribuirgli alcuna attione, e quantunque sia stato e si sappia che sia stato non possiamo attribuirgli attione che non gli sia avenuta."

15. *Ben Jonson*, ed. Herford/Simpson, (Oxford: Clarendon Press, 1952), XI, 317.

16. *Ben Jonson*, ed. by Herford/Simpson, (Oxford: Clarendon Press, 1950), IX, 190-1.

17. My account of the sources of *Richard II* is taken largely from Peter Ure's Arden edition of the play (London: Arnold, 1961; Ure's scene-by-scene account of the sources is particularly useful) and Geoffrey Bullough's *Narrative and Dramatic Sources of Shakespeare*, 8 vols (London and New York: Routledge, 1957-75), III, 355-82.

18. Bullough, *Narrative and Dramatic Sources*, III, 363.

19. Ure, headnote to 1.3.

20. Ure, headnote to 1.3.

21. Ure, Introduction, p. xxxii.

22. Ure, Introduction, pp. xxxii-xxxiii.

23. In the Prologue to *Cleopatra*, for instance, he declares: "[tragedy] purges mortal souls of vices and makes them desire virtue only" ("Purga da'vittii gli animi mortali,/E lor face bramar sol la virtute").

24. Castelvetro, *Poetica*, p.16v "... poetry was invented solely for pleasure and amusement" ("... la poesia sia stata trovata solamente per dilettare, e per ricreare"). And see Charlton, *Castelvetro's Theory of Poetry*, pp. 66f.

25. Ben Jonson, *Sejanus His Fall*, ed. Philip Ayres (Manchester: Manchester UP, 1990) Introduction, p. 37.

26. *Sejanus His Fall*, ed. Ayres, pp. 10-16.

27. Charlton, *Castelvetro's Theory of Poetry*, p. 84; for the Italian see Castelvetro, *Poetica*, p. 31v.

28. *Ben Jonson*, ed. Herford/Simpson, IX, 585.

29. "To the Reader" l.7, *Sejanus*, ed. Herford/Simpson, *Ben Jonson*, IV, 350.

30. This account of the sources of *Coriolanus* is mostly taken from Philip Brockbank's Arden edition (London: Arnold, 1976), pp. 29-35.

31. See, for example, Brockbank's note on 5.3.94f: Volumnia's great speeches are close renderings of the versions in North.

32. Geoffrey Bullough, *Narrative and Dramatic Sources*, V, 505-49.

33. Bullough, V, 534.

34. Bullough, V, 530. Marginal Note: "Martius Gaius craftie accusation of the Volsces."

35. Bullough, V, 519.

36. Bullough, V, 522.

37. Bullough, V, 528-9.

38. Bullough, V, 535.

39. See my article, "The Position of *Antony and Cleopatra* in the Canon", *Notes and Queries*, 238:2 (June 1993), p. 196.

40. *Poetica*, pp.35v-36r. The Italian reads: "Aristotele non haveva opinione che la poesia fosse dono spetiale di dio conceduto ad uno huomo piutosto che ad un altro, come e il dono della profetia et altri simili privilegi non naturali, et non communi a tutti. Et senza dubbio intende anchora che nol faccia apertamente di riprovare quella opinione che alcuni attribuiscono a Platone, che la poesia sia infusa negli huomini per furore divino. La quale opinione ha havuta origine, et nascimento dall'ignoranza del vulgo, et e stata accresciuta, et favorata dalla vanagloria de poeti per queste ragioni et in questa guisa."

41. *Poetaster*, 1.2.231-2, ed. Herford/Simpson, *Ben Jonson*, IV, 216.

42. *Every Man in his Humor*, Q (1601), 5.3.317, ed. Herford/Simpson, *Ben Jonson*, III, 285.

43. *Every Man in his Humor*, F (1616) Prol. 21-4, ed. Herford/Simpson, III, 303.

44. Bullough, V, 506.

45. *Poetica d'Aristotele*, p.123v. (cf Charlton's paraphrase, *Castelvetro's Theory of Poetry*, pp.107-8). The Italian is as follows: "... altre sono le persone della tragedia, et altre sono le persone della comedia. Quelle della tragedia sono reali, et hanno gli spiriti maggiori, et sono altiere, et vogliono troppo quello, che vogliono, et se è loro fatta injuria, o si danno ad intendere che sia loro fatta, non ricorrono a magistrati a querelarsi dello'ngiuriante, ne comportano la'ngiuria patientemente, ma si fanno da se ragione, secondo che l'appetito loro detta, et uccidono per vendetta i lontani e i congiunti di sangue, et per disperatione non pure i congiunti di sangue, ma talhora anche sestessi. Alle quali persone essendo esse poste nello stato reale, che è reputato il colmo della felicita humana, et potenti a vindicarsi degli oltraggi fatti loro, non si fanno scorni, o beffe mezzane, ne essi sentono danno di roba leggiere, ne è loro fatto, ne per nozze, o per adempimento di desideri amorosi s'augumenta la loro alegrezza, dimorando essi, si puo veramente dire in perpetue nozze et in continui solazzi amorosi, in guisa che per fare nascere l'alegrezza conviene che loro si sciemi della felicita, o almeno che essi caggiano in manifesto pericolo, che la felicita sia per iscemare. Et per far nascere la tristitia conviene, che trabocchino in misero o in basso stato col salto molto memorevole. Ma le persone della comedia sono di povero cuore, et avezze ad ubidire a magistrati, et a vivere sotto le leggi et a sopportare le'ngiurie ei danni et a ricorrere agli ufficiali et supplicandogli che facciano per mezzo degli statuti loro restituire il loro honore, o ammendare il danno, non si fanno ragione da se, ne trascorrono ad uccisioni de'parenti o di sestessi o d'altri, per le cose per le quali vi trascorrono i re ...".

46. Charlton, *Castelvetro's Theory of Poetry*, p. 102. The reference is to Castelvetro, *Poetica*, p. 19v.: "Ne e vero che gli huomini rassomiglianti rassomiglino gli huomini occupati ['|n attione per iscoprire i costumi...".

47. *Discorso*, edited in *Scritti estetici di G.B. Giraldi Cintio* (Milan: G.Daelli, 1864), p. 104. The Italian reads: "... le donne delle scene tragiche possono essere, quanto alla real qualità conviene, gravi, prudenti e accorte [...] perchè tuttavia elle stanno nelle grandezze, e tra persone gravi, e possono elle dalla continua conversazione apparar quello che le altre donne non possono...".

48. See Brockbank's edition, p. 77.

49. *Discorso*, ed.cit. p. 93: "... non dee giudizioso scrittore dar tanto di riputazione alla autorità degli antichi che voglia anco imitare i lor vizi ...". Also "Lettera su *Didone*", *Tragedie*, (Venice: Giulio Cesare Cagnacini, 1583), p. 155: "Et se forse in qualche parte, mi son partito dalle regole, che da Aristotile, per conformarmi co'costumi de'tempi nostri, l'ho io fatto coll'essempio de gli antichi, perche si vede, che altrimente diede il pricipio alle sue favole Euripide che Sophocle, et con altro modo disposero le loro favole i Romani, [...] che i Greci."

50. Richard Ide, *Possessed with Greatness* (London: Scolar Press, 1980), p. 170.

# INSTRUMENTS OF DARKNESS: *MACBETH*, OVID, AND JACOBEAN POLITICAL MYTHOLOGIES

**by Zara Bruzzi**
**(Brunel University College)**

In 1581, a law was passed against various forms of witchcraft thought to be practiced against Queen Elizabeth, including "prophecying" and "conjurations" to discover "how long her Highness should live, and who should reign after her decease, and what changes and alterations should thereby happen".[1] Elizabeth Tudor died in 1603, and by the time *Macbeth* was written, in 1606, it was, it seems, not only permissible but fashionable to reinvent prophecies from Scottish history foretelling the accession of King James VI of Scotland to the throne of England, thereby turning a matter of turbulent speculation into one of the fulfilment of a divine plan for the advancement of the house of Stuart: a new monarch, a new dynasty, a new royal mythology.[2]

This essay is concerned with Ovidian myth in relation to the construction of political mythologies, and is thus divided into two sections: an initial investigation of Ovidian myths of demonic women in *Macbeth*, followed by a speculative analysis of the political use to which these myths are put within the context of Jamesean discourse and propaganda (including suggestions of anti-Elizabeth bias) at the beginning of his reign. In this regard, perhaps one of the most significant aspects of the change of ruler was the question of gender. During Elizabeth's reign, courtly panegyric fostered the construction of a (virginal) feminine that was numinous, divine, endowed with mystical and magical majesty. Elizabeth was widely identified with the triple goddess Cynthia/Diana/Hecate, and courtly devotion to her was expressed as the Petrarchan impasse of obsessional love for an all-powerful but unattainable object of desire which destroys the lover/subject as

Diana did Actaeon; but Elizabeth also represented herself as a maternal figure. Her cult thus contained within it the potential for a fantasy of Elizabeth as an omnipotent and destructive mother (as in Raleigh's *The Ocean to Scinthia*); and some texts of the 1590s - notably John Donne's *Elegies*, Ovidian epyllia (including *Venus and Adonis*) - seem to give expression to that anxiety by ridiculing chastity and/or controlling female sexuality, including that of powerful goddesses, by reasserting male dominance. James's royal discourse, on the other hand, based on "Roman styles and patriarchal claims", was more reassuring to a patriarchal society: "as the Father of his fatherly duty is bound to care for the nourishing, education, and vertuous government of his children, even so is the king bound to care for all his subjects"; "I am the Husband, and all the whole Isle is my lawfull Wife; "I am the Head, and it is my Body".[3] The logic of Jamesean metaphors is that subversion might be expressed as female transgression, disobedience, irrationality, and that, as Peter Stallybrass observes, political transgression could be linked with the demonic:

> If kingship is legitimated by analogy to God's rule over the earth, and the father's rule over the family and the head's rule over the body, witchcraft establishes the opposite analogies, whereby the Devil attempts to rule over the earth, and the woman over the family, and the body over the head.[4]

Fantasies of a nurturing father and an omnipotent, destructive mother provide the central antithesis of Janet Adelman's psychoanalytic account of *Macbeth*: "the whole play represents in very powerful form both the fantasy of a virtually absolute and destructive maternal power and the fantasy of absolute escape from this power". She argues that the witches' "power of cosmic coercion is rewritten [in Lady Macbeth] as the power of the mother to misshape or destroy the child". Moreover, Adelman argues, the murder of Duncan destroys the only defence against this fantasy: for Duncan is not only a benevolent paternal figure, but also, as the fount of nurturance in the play, an almost maternal figure, and hence an androgynous figure, a benign father/mother. Malcolm's victory over

Macbeth, aided by the English, constitutes the restoration of the power of the father to Scotland.[5]

It is striking how strongly Adelman's thesis (even given her reservations about Duncan as a satisfactory father figure) seems to confirm James's descriptions of his own role as king. There is a rather startling element of androgyny in *Basilicon Doron*, for example, where James asserts that he is the kingdom's "loving nourish-father" and gives to the nation "nourish-milke".[6] It seems possible that the tensions and contradictions in *Macbeth* which recent controversy over the play's political alignment have highlighted might, in part, be attributed to the tensions of the times, the wrench from one royal regime to another, and attempts to exorcise the old and establish the new by means of a distinctive mythology. There might also, however, be indications of realignments of royal policy. My interest in the possibility that *Macbeth* not only participated in, but also helped to formulate, a recognisably Jamesean mythology has been influenced by several recent investigations of relations between the Shakespearean text, source, political thought, and public event. Although David Farley-Hills does not discuss *Macbeth* in *Shakespeare and the Rival Playwrights*, his thesis that Shakespeare's post-1600 writing undergoes "extraordinary changes and re-directions", experimental and disparate, in contrast with the "remarkable consistency" of earlier work, could equally well be applied to the play. Farley-Hills attributes the change to the pressure of competition from new dramatists and new dramatic fashions, such as that for neo-classicism; but a reiterated theme, if unstated cause, which runs through the book is the presence of the new monarch, King James, and the influence of his political writing on dramatic texts of the time. In *Witches and Jesuits*, Gary Wills places *Macbeth* firmly within Jacobean public event and contemporary writing, by arguing that the play belongs, alongside John Marston's *Sophonisba*, Thomas Dekker's *The Whore of Babylon*, and Barnabe Barnes' *The Devils Charter*, to the genre of Gunpowder play: "The typical Gunpowder play deals with the apocalyptic destruction of a kingdom (attempted or accomplished), with convulsions brought about by secret "mining" (undermining), plots and equivocation. And witches are active in this process".

However, there are striking differences as well as likenesses between the plays grouped together by Wills; and David Norbrook, in an essay I will be considering later on, makes a case for the significance of George Buchanan, James's tutor and opponent of hereditary monarchy, as being a provocative choice of source for *Macbeth*, raising issues of monarchical theory in particular, and more generally of the significance of the tension that may lie between sources and dramatic reworking. It seemed that Norbrook's argument concerning sources from Scottish history might also apply to classical allusions in *Macbeth*: R.K. Root finds greater discrimination in citation of classical texts in Shakespeare's post-1600 writing, such as the construction of a "mythology of horror" in *Macbeth*. It seemed possible, therefore, that the Ovidian myths that I find present in *Macbeth* participate in an intricate structure of allusions to classical and contemporary myth in the play which together constitute a remarkable contribution to early Jacobean political mythologies.[7] This essay explores that possibility.

*Ovidian myths*

Curiously, some of the classical sources of *Macbeth* confirm the presence of the fantasies of destructive female power which Adelman discusses. Much attention has been paid to the Senecan influence on *Macbeth*, but there are elements of the play which could strike the reader of Ovid as indicative of Ovidian qualities: the observed paradox at the heart of the play, for instance, that the hero is presented simultaneously as criminal and as victim; the recent preoccupation with the presentation of the feminine in the play as transgressive, monstrous.[8] There are two Ovidian myths which I will argue are significant influences on the play: the tale of Tisiphone, a witch and one of the Furies, told in Book IV of the *Metamorphoses*, and the terrible spell she casts on Ino and Athamas; and that of Medea, witch and murderess, told in Book VII.

## *Macbeth* and Jacobean Political Mythologies

In the tale of Tisiphone, the fury departs for earth, accompanied by personifications of Madness and Terror, Grief and Dread, to destroy an entire royal family. The effect of her enchantment is to drive Ino and Athamas into a pseudo-Bacchic frenzy during which they slaughter their children. Deluded into thinking he is hunting a lioness and her cubs, Athamas snatches their baby son from his mother's arms and dashes his brains out on a rock. Ino then jumps off a cliff clutching their other child. This tale, rather than that of the infanticide of Medea, would seem to be the source for Lady Macbeth's lines:

> I have given suck, and know
> How tender 'tis to love the babe that milks me.
> I would, while it was smiling in my face,
> Have plucked my nipple from his boneless gums
> And dashed the brains out, had I so sworn
> As you have done to this. (1.7.54-8)[9]

The origin of the tale of Ino and Athamas is one of divine jealousy, that of the queen and mother of the gods, Juno, for a new young god, Bacchus. The story thus resembles quite closely that of *Hercules Furens*, one of the Senecan sources of *Macbeth*, where the presiding influence is also that of a jealous Juno, resentful of the deification of her sexual rivals' children. Similar emphasis is put on the unwelcome new god, Bacchus, like Macduff "ripped/ From out his mother's womb", though the main emphasis is on Juno's deadly hatred of Hercules and his heroic victories.[10] She summons the Furies to drive him to madness, which causes him to murder his wife and children, mistaking them for those of his enemy, the tyrant Lycus. Hercules, like Athamas, dashes his son's brains out.[11] Both tales seem, in the emphasis put on the jealousy of Juno as agent of infanticide, to confirm Adelman's sense of "a virtually absolute and destructive maternal power" in the play's imaginative origins.

The Tisiphone episode would seem to be more than an occasional influence in *Macbeth*. Her snakes inflict mental poison - "it was the minde that felt the cruell stings" - and she brings with her a deadly poison brewed in Hades: "strange hallucinations and utter forgetfulness, crime and tears, mad love of slaughter, all mixed together with fresh blood, brewed in a brazen cauldron", which she pours over the doomed couple.[12] The potion has been recognised as a source for the witches' brew, the rituals of their charms;[13] and "strange hallucinations" and "purpose whole inclinde/To cruell murther", as Golding's translation puts it, are integral to the play. Macbeth's mind is full of scorpions; his insomnia and terrors are simultaneously horrifyingly specific in the suffering depicted and vague in origin, as are the hallucinatory effects generally: "a voice" cries "Sleep no more!". Similarly, there are strikingly vivid personifications, Pity, seeling Night, wither'd Murther, that belong to no clear system of allegory, which contribute to the paranoid dislocation that is one of the play's strongest effects. Macbeth's "restless ecstacy" originates in chronicle material, in Buchanan's accounts of Macbeth's and King Kenneth's tortured consciences; and specific passages expressing that guilt derive from Seneca. But the episode of Tisiphone seems to provide a synthesis of elements picked out from disparate sources from which to develop a rhetoric of guilt and mental pain, and of destruction through supernatural possession. Above all, the tale seems to suggest the perverse claustrophobia of the play; for Ovidian narratives of chthonic enchantments depict the enclosure of their victims within an exclusive environment of emotional extremes, alienated and obsessional, which persists until their predestined destruction is completed.

The motif of infanticide resonates through *Macbeth* with terrible variations: "birth-strangled babe", "sow [...] that hath eaten/ Her nine farrow". Macbeth is increasingly obsessed with his own and others' heirs, with the obliteration of families, which suggests that Lady Macbeth's vaunt marks the transition from comprehensible fantasy to frenzied crime, her metaphor transposed to Macbeth's action. There are suggestions of Bacchic madness in the text: "have we eaten of the insane root?", "that which hath made them drunk hath made me bold". The inscription of the Tisiphone episode into *Macbeth*, like that of *Hercules Furens*, reinforces the play's ambiguity, suggesting that Macbeth (and Lady Macbeth) are victims of supernatural possession of an uncontrollable kind, their criminal careers impelled by forces imposed from without. In *Macbeth*, tragedy as personified, or embodied, by the (transgressive) feminine offers a cruel pattern of incitement to recognition and enactment of illicit desire – only to betray and destroy it. *Macbeth* is also concerned with personal culpability, however, and the principal Ovidian influence on this aspect of the play would seem to be the tale of Medea, which adds the motif of parricide to that of infanticide.[14]

At the beginning of her story, Medea is a typical Ovidian heroine. Many of the episodes in the *Metamorphoses* concentrate on passion of a monstrous or forbidden kind which focuses particularly on women;[15] and Ovid's rhetorical technique for presenting the transforming imperatives of sexual obsession is the extended soliloquy spoken by women about to commit a sexually inspired 'crime': Medea about to betray her father and country for love of Jason; Scylla also about to betray her father and embattled country for love of the enemy, Minos; Byblis obsessed with incestuous passion for her brother; Myrrha about to commit incest with her father.[16] Medea's soliloquy is taken as the paradigmatic example in John Velz's study of the Ovidian soliloquy in Shakespeare; and although he focuses principally on Tarquin and, to a lesser extent, Angelo in *Measure for Measure*, the features he identifies in Ovid may be found in Macbeth's soliloquies in the opening scenes of the play. As Velz observes, the effect of Ovidian soliloquies is "of the old self questioning a newly discovered stranger".[17] After meeting the weird sisters, Macbeth encounters a horrified recognition of hitherto unacknowledged thoughts of murder, which a new self recognises as "black and deep desires": "To know my deed, 'twere best not know myself". Shakespeare appears to be experimenting with metamorphosing the intense transgressive eroticism of Ovid's tragic heroines into the obsessional criminality of the hero.[18] Also suggestive of Medea is the vacillating process of decision-making imposed by the recognition of conflicting identities. The effect of Medea's self-interrogation is to make her decide in favour of filial duty; but on seeing Jason again, a surge of renewed passion decides her to betray her fatherland. The sequence is reminiscent of Macbeth's probing of the advantages of, and moral objections to, the murder of Duncan; his decision not to proceed; and his capitulation to Lady Macbeth's persuasions. His dilemma and decision resemble Medea's: "Desire persuades me one way, reason another. I see the better and approve it, but I follow the worse".[19]

The more overtly influential episodes from the tale of Medea are those of the rejuvenation of Aeson and the murder of Pelias. In the former episode, Jason asks Medea whether she can renew the youth of his aged father, Aeson. After praying to Night and to Hecate for aid, Medea gathers herbs and boils them in a pot, to which she adds a typically Ovidian catalogue of grisly ingredients, fragments of dismembered creatures. The "withered bough" she stirs the brew with develops green leaves and berries, and where drops spill over onto the ground, flowers and grass spring up. She then slits Aeson's throat, empties out his blood, fills it with her potion, and he immediately recovers his youth. Details of this episode seem to be distributed through *Macbeth*. The rituals surrounding Medea's invocation to Hecate (so fully invoked in *The Tempest*), the boiling and bubbling of her cauldron, and its grotesque ingredients, have long been associated with the weird sisters.[20] The eerie, morally confusing, conjunction of creation and destruction here, the interlacing of red with green, blood with planting, the slaughter of old age with the restoration of youth to power, seem suggestive of similar juxtapositions in *Macbeth*.

The murder of Pelias is much more concentrated in its influence. Medea persuades his daughters to cooperate with a similar scheme of rejuvenation, but deceives them by omitting the necessary magic ingredients. In this episode Medea shows herself to be both a "juggling fiend" and an "instrument of darkness". To reinforce her claim to be able to renew their father's youth, she puts on a show for them wherein she slays the oldest of their rams, and plunges it into her magic cauldron, from which it emerges as a new-born lamb. It is difficult to say whether there is any connection between this grotesque incident and the apparition scene in

*Macbeth* (although clearly both belong to a similar tradition of sorcery); but Medea's combination of honest and deceptive magic, tricking the daughters of Pelias into a murder she has persuaded them is a filial duty, has obvious affinities with the weird sisters' equivocation with Macbeth. Moreover, Medea's contemptuous treatment of the daughters of Pelias is strikingly reminiscent of Lady Macbeth's reaction to Macbeth's change of heart, charging him with cowardice and indecision, "Letting 'I dare not' wait upon 'I would'/ Like the poor cat i'th'adage": "wherefore stand ye doubting thus like fools" (or in a modern version "Why do you hesitate now, you laggards?") she chides them when they recoil from striking; and when they do stab their father, they avoid looking at their deed:

Yet was not any one of them so bolde that durst abide
To looke upon their father when she strake, but wride aside
Hir eyes: and so their cruell handes not marking where they hit
With faces turnde another way at all aventure smit.

(Perhaps, again, a modern translation, "none could bear to see her own blows" provides a clearer rendering.)[21] The description seems to be a possible source for Lady Macbeth's "That my keen knife see not the wound it makes" (1.5.51), indeed for the pervasive textual expansion into encounters and denials between eyes and hands in *Macbeth*, "The eye wink at the hand", "Scarf up the tender eye of pitiful Day"; Lady Macbeth's later revelation that "Had he not resembled/ My father as he slept I had done't" repeats the idea of a daughter unable to stab her father while looking at him; and Ovid's account of the draining out of the old mens' blood coincides with the emphasis on the horror of the sight of blood in the play: "Yet who would have thought the old man to have had so much blood in him?" (5.1.37-38).

As well as occasional resonances of the tale through the play, there seems to be a series of moments which invite comparison between Lady Macbeth and Medea. The first of these is in Act 1, Scene 5. There are, in Lady Macbeth's invocation of the spirits, strong reminders of a similar invocation by Seneca's

Medea to Hecate (as Inga-Stina Ewbank has pointed out) where she exhorts herself to "Exile all foolysh Female feare, and pity from thy mynde" as she steels herself to slaughter her children (though there are Ovidian elements here as well, the echo of Ovid's daughters of Pelias already suggested; and Lady Macbeth's figuration of surrender to cruelty as physiological change is also Ovidian).[22] In the following scene Lady Macbeth would again seem to be deliberately compared to Medea, when Duncan arrives at Inverness castle. The audience has previously heard her declaring that "the raven himself is hoarse/ That croaks the fatal entrance of Duncan/ Under my battlements". But to Duncan "this castle hath a pleasant seat", and Banquo comments on the nesting martlets:

> This guest of summer,
> The temple-haunting martlet, does approve
> By his lov'd mansionry, that the heaven's breath
> Smells wooingly here: no jutty, frieze,
> Buttress, nor coign of vantage, but this bird
> Hath made his pendent bed, and procreant cradle. (1.6.3-8)

Medea is linked with nesting swallows in one of Geffrey Whitney's emblems which shows a statue of Medea slaying a child, and a swallow, "whoe did suspect no harme", and "Hir Image likes", building its nest there (Plate I). The motto reads, *Ei, qui semel sua prodegerit, aliena credi non oportere*, and the moralizing second stanza reads:

> Oh foolishe birde, think'ste thow, shee will haue care,
> Vppon thy yonge? [...]
>   Thow arte deceaude, and arte a warninge good,
>   To put no truste, in them that hate theire blood.[23]

Recognition of the emblem is not crucial, or even central, to an understanding of the scene. The textual juxtaposition of menace and misplaced trust is sufficiently striking on its own. But Banquo's speech seems to extend beyond the irony of the immediate dramatic situation. Its effect is unexpectedly elegiac, evoking a familial tenderness already under attack, reinforcing the association of Duncan with a rhetoric of nurture. His vulnerability is further emphasised by the entrance of Lady Macbeth. To a member of the audience familiar with Whitney and Seneca, the motif of Medea would be beginning to emerge perceptibly here, I suggest, even though the strongest reference to Ovid's Medea, and the explicit introduction of the motif of infanticide, do not occur until the following scene.

In Act 1, Scene 7, in addition to Lady Macbeth's resemblance to Medea in her manipulative rhetoric, her prefiguration of Duncan's murder also has some details in common with Ovid's description of the murder of Pelias. In Ovid, "a death-like sleep held the king, his body all relaxed, and with the king his guards, sleep which incantations and the potency of magic words had given".[24] Although Lady Macbeth's version is fuller, the drugging of the chamberlains with "wine and wassail", and their "drenched natures" lying "as in a death" seem quite strongly reminiscent of the murder of Pelias. Reiteration of the motif of sleeping grooms in the murder scene, and Macbeth's account of their confused waking "As they did see me with these hangman's hands" (2.2.27), recalls (more distantly) the same Ovidian episode, the bewildered waking of King Pelias as his daughters stabbed him, "streaming with blood [...] half-mangled": "daughters mine what doe ye? who hath put/ These wicked weapons in your hands?"; and the association is possibly strengthened by the reaction of his daughters: "their courage left them, their hands fell", leaving Medea to complete the deed.[25]

As Geoffrey Bullough points out, despite hints in the chronicles, Lady Macbeth is largely Shakespeare's creation. In Boece, Buchanan and Holinshed, both Donwald and Macbeth have ambitious wives. Closest to Lady Macbeth's words are those of Macbeth's wife in Boece, who charges him with cowardice, not daring to attempt the "thing with manhede and curage quhilk is oferit to him be benevolence of fortoun".[26] In Holinshed's account of the murder of King Duff, both Donwald and his wife plie the chamberlains with drink, after which she persuades her reluctant husband to order the murder. A significant aspect of the tale of the murder of Pelias seems to be, as with the episode of Tisiphone, that it synthesises elements otherwise only found in disparate sources. Duncan's murder is not shown on stage; but that censored, central event, which a series of fragmented accounts forces us to imagine, seems close to the narrative sequence of the murder of Pelias: drugged sleep, the entrance of Medea with Pelias' daughters into his chamber, their fear to strike, Medea's prolongued harangue, their reluctant stabbing of their father, his waking, Medea finishing the crime off because of his daughters' distress.

Allusions to Medea in *Macbeth* seem very selective, concentrating on her as an exemplar of evil.[27] Her witchcraft is transferred, with that of Tisiphone, into the ritualistic and rhythmic chants of the weird sisters which dismember existing form and subvert the stabilility of language and law, thus associating the feminine with anarchic, archaic and dangerous forces, and creating a new mythology of political disruption. Moreover, the apparently deliberate comparison of Lady Macbeth to Medea emphasises her "fiend-like" qualities, her deviation from the role of dutiful subject, wife and mother. Yet Lady Macbeth also echoes Medea's victims, as a daughter shrinking from parricide, eventually maddened by her role of accomplice. Macbeth, too, plays the woman, victim of Medea-like persuasion, but also Medea herself, hesitating at first between doubt and desire, love and horror, and later hardening into proliferating acts of murder. If Ovid's tales contribute to the demonisation of the feminine in the play, they also contribute to its psychological complexity, to the conflicting drives towards criminality and compassion within and between Macbeth and Lady Macbeth. In this sense, they contribute to the depiction of the terrible price to be paid in terms of human suffering and spiritual deterioration for the crime of regicide.

On the other hand, traces of the tale of Ino and Athamas suggest that regicide is a form of madness, a manifestation of possession, where distinctions between the ordained and the voluntary are confused: "Some say he is mad".[28] At the end of the play, Macduff, holding aloft Macbeth's severed head, announces that the time is free. Macduff has never encountered the witches, and knows nothing of the mental world inhabited by Macbeth from the moment the sisters greet him, plagued by voices, visions, terrors and, ultimately, an empty despair, from which decapitation releases him. The time is not free for Macbeth while he lives. He is "cabin'd, cribb'd, confin'd", not only by demonic female forces, human and supernatural, but also by his commitment to the ideology of legitimacy which he attacks. His murders are motivated by an attempt to capture a future which he is unable to believe belongs to him, and are thus, of necessity, inconclusive, potentially endless. For to have children, to produce heirs, gradually becomes a metaphor for the legitimacy to which he has no access. As Susanna Hamilton has observed, the assertive action of the Macbeths takes place against "the stasis of an inescapable, predestined scheme which allows them no genuine self-assertion at all".[29] This is the pattern of the tale of Tisiphone, of Ovid's tales of chthonic enchantment, which seem to be given a political, indeed a specifically providentialist, force in *Macbeth*.

*Political mythologies*
The myths of infanticide and parricide which I have been investigating would seem to participate in James's patriarchal rhetoric of royalty.[30] They seem to give narrative form to subversions of metaphors of kingship as husband and father of the people, the rational head of the irrational body. Moreover, they are myths which would appear to endorse a loyalist view of the gunpowder plot, in which, as James claimed to Parliament, the conspirators had planned to eliminate not only the monarch, but his entire family, and countless others. For myths of (insanely or inexplicably wicked) infanticide and parricide, especially of tales associated with transgressive or demonic women, mythologise regicide as family crime. As Goldberg observes:

> With the language of family, James made powerful assertions. He rested his claims to the throne in his succession and based Divine Right politics there as well [...] identifying his prerogative with the production of a

legitimate male successor. That is, unlike his Tudor predecessor, James located his power in a royal line that proceeded from him.[31]

In this sense, *Macbeth* seems a prophetic dystopia of events recently averted (and, in James's view, averted by his personal astuteness) as well as an exemplar from the past.

However, *Macbeth* is not the first play in which Shakespeare alludes to the myth of Medea in a political context. As Ewbank has reminded us, Medea's infanticide had been invoked by Shakespeare much earlier, in *2 Henry VI*, when Clifford (another character who, like Lady Macbeth, undergoes a stony metamorphosis) claims that he will chop up a child of the house of York into "As many gobbets" "As wild Medea young Absyrtus did".[32] The representation of power as a family matter was not a Jacobean innovation. *3 Henry VI* shows historical and emblematic instances of infanticide and parricide; but Shakespeare's central image of civil war is familiar from the Tudor homilies, which characterised civil war in these terms. After Mary Queen of Scots gave birth to James as her legitimate heir, there was such strong fear of war over the succession, that Parliament petitioned the Queen to nominate her heir unless, by leaving the question open to dispute, she become the "parricide" of her nation.[33] It is easy to forget the anxiety and uncertainty over the royal succession that Henry VIII's irregular matrimonial career, and the childlessness of his children (whose legitimacy his successive marriages had made dubious), had created, and which the accession of James had brought to an end. The memory and fear of civil war also pervade *Richard II*, a play which anticipates the themes and metaphors of *Macbeth*, the emphasis on the slaughter of children, the reiterated figuration of England as a green land, a demi-paradise, that will be overwhelmed by a tide of blood, even Richard's metaphor of night as a cloak for "murthers, treasons, and detested sins" which the sun of the day, the monarch's return, will expose. The difference between *Richard II* and *Macbeth*, however, is that Richard's vision proves a delusion, whereas *Macbeth* reaffirms the validity of the association of legitimate rule with day, and treason and murder with night; and whereas *Richard II* anticipates the horrors of the Wars of the Roses, the cancelling of the green by the red, in *Macbeth* the process is reversible. A re-greening of the land occurs with the march of Malcolm and Edward's troops on Dunsinane.

Thus, from one perspective, *Macbeth* can be seen as developing the themes and metaphors for civil war from the history plays, and extending earlier association of the myth of Medea with political violence. On the other hand, the psychology of the murderous usurper, within which is inscribed an Ovidian rhetoric of desire as conflict between compulsion and self-loathing, is given a mythic horror unequaled in the more sceptical climate of the history plays. Moreover, there is no parallel to the triumphalist close to *Macbeth* (except in the triumph of Richmond in *Richard III*, a play with which *Macbeth* has often been compared). It is, perhaps, in this emphatic, baroque contrast between the darkness of usurping guilt and the light of legitimate rule that the innovatory, Jacobean quality of the play is to be found. For the restoration of light and green were integral to Stuart mythology in the early years of James's rule. James already featured as Neoplatonic light in Ben Jonson's *The Masque of Blackness* (1605), and Thomas Campion's *The Lord Hay's Masque* (1607) features the transformation of barren gold trees to elaborately foliated green ones which eventually regain the form of knights under the rays of the sun, the kingly influence. The masque celebrated the marriage of a Scot to an Englishwoman, and the union of the English and Scottish crowns under James. The metamorphosis of the trees, assisted by Flora and Zephirus, obviously, in context, invokes a hermetic spring, the flowering of a new reign; but the Ovidian fiction that they were originally men transformed into trees by Cynthia as punishment for an attempt to marry one of her nymphs, and Flora's emphasis on the "hallowed and immortall flowers" of marriage in contrast to "winter's wrath and cold mortalitie", seems not only to constitute an allusion to Elizabeth's actual conduct towards her courtiers, but also to imply that James's provision of heirs contrasted favourably with her barrenness, and that there thus is a visual pun on tree, signifying family tree as well as plant.[34] (The masque also seems to imply a perception of Elizabeth's power as emasculating.) The tree motif is anticipated in *The Masque of Blackness* (1605) where Queen Anne personated fertility as one of the nymphs presenting a golden tree laden with fruit.

Marion Lomax's observation that there are iconographic links between *The Lord Hay's Masque* and *Macbeth* is thus intriguing, particularly her suggestion that the iconography of the masque's trees relates in some way to those in *Macbeth*.[35] D.J. Gordon, in his analysis of the depiction of the apotheosis of James painted by Rubens on the Whitehall ceiling, identifies the figure of the crowned infant as an allegory of the birth of the union of the English and Scottish crowns. James had proclaimed himself King of Great Britain in 1604 (the title accorded to him in the dedication of *The Lord Hay's Masque*), and Gordon cites a passage from the Bishop of Bristol's tracts of around 1604/5 in support of James which identify the union of England and Scotland as a child, a new birth, and with the triumph of Protestantism and peace over Babylonian discord and war.[36] Graham Parry notes that in 1604 Andrew Willet, in a sermon entitled *Ecclesia Triumphans*, endorsed the policies of peace and union, comparing James to David and to Solomon, associating James with "the cedar tree sheltering the country, his children being the branches and green shoots", and anticipating the apocalyptic triumph of Protestantism in Britain to the end of recorded time and the Second Coming.[37] Thus the apparition of the crowned child holding a tree in *Macbeth* might be interpreted as echoing royal iconography prominent in the opening years of James's reign, and the prophetic vision might suggest, at least to some members of an audience, the triumph of Banquo's heir as well as Duncan's. (Even the branches of Birnam Wood might have carried resonances of royal iconography at the time, although, of course, the peacefulness of James's accession contrasted strongly with Malcolm's accession by military invasion.) In the context of the gunpowder plot, the emphasis in *Macbeth* on children, and references to, and incidence of, infanticide, reinforced by invocations of the monstrous crimes of Athamas, Ino, and especially, Medea, have an obvious applicability to this aspect of Jamesean mythologies as well, both to his real children, his fruitful family tree, and to his metaphoric child of peace and union.

Any discussion of the political context of *Macbeth* is made conjectural by the fact that we only have the the play in revised form, and cannot be sure what was in the original text;[38] but the details of Jamesean iconography in the play discussed above seem to suggest a strong focus on royal concerns around 1604 to 1606. The informing presence of the myths of Tisiphone and Medea that I have argued for might also lead one to speculate, *pace* Forman and Nosworthy, that the witch episodes, even if considerably enhanced during the play's revision, were an integral part of the play's original conception.[39] Indeed, in the light of the argument in *Witches and Jesuits* for witchcraft as an intrinsic element of the "Gunpowder play" genre, it is difficult to think otherwise.[40] However, Wills does not investigate differences between the representation of witchcraft in the texts he cites, nor does he consider possible Jacobean modifications to representations of Catholicism as witchcraft. For associating Catholicism with witchcraft was not a Jacobean innovation: Elizabethan Protestantism had done so from the beginning of the reign. John Foxe, for example, in his *Acts and Monuments*, perhaps the most influential document in the popularisation of apocalyptic Protestant mythology, lists, among Roman abuses, necromancy and sorcery.[41] But the misogyny of anti-Catholic propaganda which attributed a dangerously seductive allure to Roman practice, figured by bedizened temptresses, was, in radical Protestant tradition, counterbalanced by a numinous female figure representing the purity of the true church.[42] The contrast emphasised differences of doctrine and liturgy, ritual and vestments.

James's attitude to Catholicism was rather different. After the Hampton Court conference of 1604, he had little sympathy with Puritan aspirations; and although he had been frustrated in his intentions to reconcile Protestant and

Catholic when he acceded to the English crown (and his broken promises most probably accelerated Catholic despair) James's and Cecil's overall policy was a more conciliatory attitude to confessional division than that of militant Protestantism. Peace with Spain had been signed in 1604, and James was, in his parliamentary address immediately after the discovery of the plot, careful to remind members that it was

> the work of a few fanatics, not of the English Catholics as a whole. It was true that no sect of the heathen, though they worshipped the very Devil, preached, as did some Catholics, that kings should be murdered and governments overthrown. Yet many Catholics were good men and loyal subjects, and only the guilty should be punished.[43]

James is formulating his own demonology of Catholicism here. His target is the Papacy, which had released Catholics from allegiance to a non-Catholic monarch and sanctioned invasion and assassination of heretic rulers, his intention to split English Catholics from a spiritual allegiance to the Pope which conflicted with their loyalty to him. Royal discourse shifts the emphasis from religious difference to political difference, the dividing distinction being one of attitudes to absolutism and the authority of the monarch, whereas in Elizabethan Protestantism monarchy and religion were virtually indivisible, as the queen was consistently mythologised as protectress, personification even, of the Protestant cause. The contrast in attitude may be illustrated by comparing two "Gunpowder plays", Barnabe Barnes's *The Devil's Charter* (acted before the king at court), where the devil is displayed on stage "in his pontificalls", and Thomas Dekker's *The Whore of Babylon*, which retains the traditional Foxean antithesis between the wicked Empress of Babylon and the virtuous Elizabeth as Titania, the Fairie Queene. In Dekker's text the centre of wickedness is Catholicism. The Whore is depicted as waited upon by pontiffs and kings, and the play retains a militantly Protestant political stance. In Barnes's text the centre of wickedness is the devilish Pope Alexander VI. Presentation of the Pope as the heart of evil was closer to James's position, as may be seen, for example, in a pamphlet which echoes the official version of the gunpowder plot, *The True Testimonie of a Faithfull Subject*, which links the evils of "civill dissention" with the machinations of the Pope, and treachery and rebellion against King James with witchcraft.[44]

There may be a similar renegotiation of mythologies of Catholicism in *Macbeth*. The combination in the play of the emphasis placed on the outrage of regicide, the ideological unacceptability of the act even to its perpetrators, the terrible punitive suffering they consequently endure, with the division of evil between unseen but ever-present diabolical powers, their actively subversive agents, and simple human wickedness, may suggest a subtext concerned with the choice between loyalty to the monarch or the treachery advocated by the Papacy and its proselitising agents. But the suggestion remains undefined, ambiguous. This quality of suggestive indeterminacy, of refusal, even, to identify witchcraft with Catholicism, and the inscription of an Ovidian rhetoric of the mental conflict surrounding unnatural crime, gives Macbeth a quality of psychological expansiveness, a space in which to investigate the ironies and compulsions inherent in the topic of religio-political allegiances, which would be closed by traditional myth and established attitudes to Catholicism. Ambivalence is necessary to the plot and, I would argue, to the political situation. If the weird sisters are, as witches, instigators of disorder and destruction, enemies of kingly rule, as sibyls they anticipate James's triumph. This ambiguity might be seen to reflect inevitable conflicts surrounding James's accession in relation to Catholicism; for he inherited his claim to the English throne from his mother, Mary Queen of Scots, in whose name Elizabeth's right to the English throne was challenged, who in her turn had Mary executed for treason. Henry Paul is doubtlessly right to attribute the family tree/tree puns of Stuart mythology to Scottish histories and the myth of Stuart descent from Banquo. It is possible that, as he argues, Bishop John Leslie's diagrammatic 'Banquo tree' is an immediate source for tree metaphors in *Macbeth*.[45] However, it would seem more significant than Paul allows that Leslie's is a Catholic text, printed in Rome. In 1584, Leslie had written a tract in defence of the right of Mary and James to inherit the English throne after Elizabeth's death, supporting his claim for them on the basis of an argument for "government by succession of princes" rather than election, and warning of the dire effects of the latter system:

> The trueth of this matter will more euidently appear, if you deeply consider what iniuries and calamities the people of that country is forced to endure, where an vsurping Tyranne, not by right of succession, laufull heir vnto his aunceator, but by ambition & stronghand violently intrudeth hym selfe vpon an other mans right & possession. For suche a one, (by vexing his subiectes with continuall fear, & oppressing them with wicked exactions, and more wicked morders) sticketh not to subuert all lawes of God & man, to the ende that he may rule all alone. Thus whiles he most cruelly tirannizeth ouer his subiects, and they most mortally doe hate hym: what mischiefes and miseries do not burst in vpon any nation by suche a desperate head and suche discorde of membres?[46]

James's *Basilicon Doron* (which has a long section on usurping tyrants), Leslie's text and *Macbeth* would, though with very different emphases, seem to belong to a common discourse concerning hereditary monarchy. Moreover, Leslie warns of a war of succession, looking back to the Wars of the Roses and arguing that the succession of Mary and James will deliver England "from all ciuill warres and Barbarous crueltie". There is little here for James to disagree with. Leslie even argues for union between Scotland and England. He does so, however, by arguing for reunification under the old religion, Catholicism, and this was not a view James could agree with. The emphatic Protestantism of the English texts supporting James's policy of union cited above suggests that a Stuart myth, appropriated by Catholic polemic during Mary's lifetime, is being reappropriated for Calvinist James. The ambiguity of the witches in *Macbeth*, in that they are simultaneously evil and truthful prophets of the future, could be accounted for by this struggle.

A possible further reason for the ambiguity of the witches in *Macbeth* is provided by David Norbrook, especially as Leslie's pro-Marian polemics were in direct ideological conflict with Buchanan's philosophy of monarchy. Norbrook's reading of the play is that, although its topicality is most plausibly linked to the gunpowder plot, its political concerns are much broader, engaging, possibly under pressure from James (but by no means unproblematically) with Buchanan's hostility to hereditary monarchy as expressed in his history of Scotland, written to justify the overthrow of Mary Queen of Scots. Particularly relevant is Norbrook's argument for the connection between anti-absolutism and witchcraft:

> Witches could be seen as special enemies of monarchs because they claimed for themselves the kind of divine, quasimagical authority that absolute monarchs were trying to concentrate in their own hands. Witches were doubly heinous in claiming any kind of active power for the weaker sex. It is not surprising, then, that Bodin, a major theorist of monarchical authority and one opposed in principle to rule by women, should have written against witches. James's eagerness to take up the campaign against witches reflects his general concern to be in the vanguard of European monarchical theory, which implied, by the 1590s, a heightened insistence on the dignity of monarchy.[47]

Whether or not the king had the specific influence on *Macbeth* which Norbrook implies, it is quite possible that the emphasis on witchcraft in the play implies a simultaneous concern both with Catholicism and with enemies of the rights of hereditary monarchs; for, as Sommerville has observed, "from the 1590s onwards the equation of popery with anti-absolutist theories became one of the commonest themes in English political writing" and works such as Buchanan's, though written by Protestants, were criticised for expressing views which were regarded as popish.[48] Ovid's tale of Medea, so barbaric and isolated, so mysteriously aberrant, so insistent on her crimes against fatherland, fathers and children, provides an appropriate analogue of subversive activity against the patriarchal family's head, its royal father and husband, while avoiding any clarification of the political source of outrage.

My suggestions concerning the formulation of a new Jamesean discourse of witchcraft might explain the connection between *Macbeth* and Jonson's *The Masque of Queens*. The witches in *The Masque of Queens* are much less ambiguous than those in *Macbeth*, much more obviously the king's enemies; for they are purely allegorical figures, representing such qualities as Malice, Impudence, Slander, Mischief, thus keeping criticism of the monarch unspecific, but implying any sort of opposition is diabolically inspired. Of interest in connection with *Macbeth* is their leader, the Dame, who is both witch and fury, and who cites both Ovid's and Seneca's Medea in her invocation to "fiends and furies, if yet any be/ Worse than ourselves" to come to her aid to reduce the universe to chaos (quite unavailingly - the witches are comically ineffectual). The whole of the antimasque is reminiscent of *Macbeth*, but some of the Dame's lines seem to be particularly so:

> I hate to see these fruits of a soft peace,
> And curse the piety gives it such increase.
> Let us disturb it then, and blast the light;
> Mix hell with heaven, and make Nature fight
> Within herself; loose the whole hinge of things,
> And cause the ends run back into their springs.[49]

Given the uncertainty of the date of the revision of *Macbeth*, the play's relationship to *The Masque of Queens* is as problematic as that between *Macbeth* and Middleton's *The Witch*. It is possible that the witches in the Folio *Macbeth* are modelled on Jonson's; but it is also possible that Jonson was influenced by *Macbeth*. (He drew on earlier sybilline tradition for *The Masque of Augurs* [1622], promising to James a long line of princes at a time when the Spanish marriage crisis was at its height, and radical Protestant criticism of the king intense.) "Moreover, Jonson had delivered the stunning court spectacular, *Hymenaei*, at the beginning of 1606, celebrating the Jamesean topics of union, royal fruitfulness and peace, and James's survival of the gunpowder plot. The court masque might already have been pushing the public theatre towards emulation; and the spectacular introduction of Jamesean themes and iconography which I have argued for in *Macbeth* might well, in turn, be Shakespeare's response to Jonson's earlier success."

References to peace regularly encode the monarch in Jonson's masques; but *The Masque of Queens*, performed on February 2, 1609, might be interpreted as showing particular concern with foreign policy and relations with Catholicism at a time when peace in Europe was very much on the agenda. There were complex negotiations for a peace between Spain and the Netherlands throughout 1608. James's traditional sympathy for the absolute rights of rulers, which rendered his attitude towards the Netherlands ambiguous, was at this time coloured by the pamphlet war he was personally involved in with the Papacy over the legitimacy of the Oath of Allegiance imposed on British Catholics as a result of the gunpowder plot. On behalf of Pope Paul V, Cardinal Bellarmine reasserted the spiritual supremacy of the Papacy, and after James published his riposte, *An Apologie for the Oath of Allegiance* in 1608, Bellarmine published a letter from James written in 1599 hinting at the possibility of his conversion to Catholicism. The consequences were grave embarrassment to James and the indignation of Scottish Presbyterians, which was only resolved by inducing the Scottish secretary, Lord Balmerino, to take the blame.[50] Thus the king was embattled with both Catholics and Presbyterians (a similar combination to that proposed as the political context of *Macbeth*), and the masque's emphasis on the power of writing to bestow fame seems to establish its concern with the pamphlet war. The picturesque malignancy of the witches in *Macbeth* might have struck Jonson as a model that he could cite, amplify and fashion to his own purposes at this juncture.

If Jonson's early masques seem to be concerned with James's advocacy of union and his struggles with the Papacy, they also appear to be concerned with denigration of the power of women, implicitly that of Elizabeth. The power of the warrior queens in *The Masque of Queens* is symbolic only; and Bel-Anna (that is, Jonson's patron and James's queen), although combining all the other queens' virtues in her person, attributes all "the luster of her merit" to the light of the king.[51] It is striking how, particularly in Jonson's early masques, in keeping with the presentation of the monarch as the only fount of light, Neoplatonic enlightenment, the feminine tends to be disempowered, overshadowed. It is literally blackened in his first commission for Queen Anne, *The Masque of Blackness*, performed on Twelfth Night, 1605. Anne and her ladies masquerade as Ethiops burned black by the sun, who have been prophetically informed by their moon-goddess, Aethiopia, (subsequently referred to as Diana in the text) that they may be magically whitened by the purer waters of Britannia, and the refulgence of its sun, the monarch. So the myth of the three-personed goddess, central to the cult of Elizabeth as Cynthia, Phoebe, Diana, Hecate, the myth that constructed a woman ruler as a numinous ideal, that of radiant and mystical chastity, is emptied of its political significance. It is the monarch, Britannia's sun, whose beams "shine night and day, and are of force/ To blanch an Ethiop, and revive a corse".[52] There seem to be similar hints of a dismissal of Elizabeth's role as saintly virgin in the following year's court masque, *Hymenaei*. The presiding deity is Iunio, Juno, goddess of marriage and union. In the ensuing barriers there is a curious dispute between Truth and Opinion who support marriage and virginity respectively, which culminates in the triumph of Truth; and the arguments for virginity inevitably suggest, at that date, the mythologies of Elizabeth: "The moon when farthest from the sun she shines/ Is most refulgent; nearest, most declines". In "virgins [...]/ Depend on no proud second, are their own/ Center and circle, now and always one" it is possible to hear an echo of Elizabeth's motto, *Semper eadem*, translated by Helen Hackett as "Always one and the same".[53] The role of Cynthia as magical opponent, as impediment to union and fertility, in the the following year's masque, that for the marriage of Lord Hay, has already been mentioned.

New monarchs liked to make clear that the kingdom was under new management. Elizabeth did the same to Mary, though her claim to legitimacy was based on her role as the instrument of god in the restoration and preservation of the Protestant religion. Indeed, this was the only defence that could be found to justify a woman ruler by such obdurate Calvinists as Knox and Foxe, and Calvin himself.[54] Under James, there were two principal politico-religious agendas:

James's own, which centred on Britain as a discrete empire, allied to a policy of peace in Europe, peace with Spain, and a reconciliation of confessional difference, encouraged by royal marriages. The other, in support of which the myth of Elizabeth as the Virgin Queen had been constructed, was the policy of militant Protestantism, enmity with Spain, and active support for European Protestantism. The debate continued throughout James's reign.[55] The implicit attacks on Elizabeth in the courtly texts I have been discussing could be read as constituting a declaration of opposition to the policies of the militant Protestant faction. I sense they may be more. Towards the end of Elizabeth's reign, a profoundly patriarchal ruling class had become tired of subservience to a woman. Her government, the French Ambassador noted, was "little pleasing to the great men and nobles, and if by chance she should die, it is certain that the English would never again submit to the rule of a woman".[56] In the masques considered here, which imply criticism of Elizabeth, there is, I suggest, a hidden agenda of criticism of the concept of a woman in power.

It seems possible that there is a similar subtext to *Macbeth*. Within the mythic origins of the play is the motif, as has been seen, of a new young god displacing an older goddess.[57] *Macbeth* closes, as other critics as well as Adelman have argued, with a strong sense of relief at the restoration of patriarchal rule, and liberation from a regime dominated by malignant female powers. As political myth, these powers would seem to symbolise the various enemies of (Protestant) hereditary right; but the emotional logic of the association of Jamesean iconography with Malcolm's triumph might also suggest an exorcism of the previous regime. Shakespeare's portraits of women in power are often disturbing: Queen Margaret, Tamora, the "unnatural hags" Goneril and Regan. In the political unconscious of the play, especially at a time when the new dynasty had been threatened, it is, perhaps, possible to discern relief that, with the accession of James, male authority had been restored to the English monarchy, and that the time was, in 1606, free from the perceived danger and impropriety of the rule of a woman.

*Notes*

I am grateful to the Northern Network and London Renaissance Seminars for the opportunity to discuss this paper at formative stages, and to friends and colleagues for helpful suggestions, particularly Tony Bromham and Margaret Healy.

1. Peter Stallybrass, "*Macbeth* and Witchcraft" in *William Shakespeare: Macbeth*, New Casebooks, ed. Alan Sinfield (London: Macmillan, 1992), 25-38, here 26-7.

2. The first dramatisation of the legend in James's reign appears to have been in Dr. Matthew Gwynne's playlet *Tres Sibyllae*, performed on James's visit to Oxford in 1605; see Henry N. Paul, *The Royal Play of Macbeth* (New York: Octagon Books, 1978), pp. 17-24.

3. Jonathan Goldberg, "Fatherly Authority: The Politics of Stuart Family Images" in *Rewriting the Renaissance: The Discourses of Sexual Difference in Early Modern Europe*, ed. Ferguson, Quilligan and Vickers (Chicago and London: Chicago UP, 1986), pp. 3-32 (p. 3).

4. "*Macbeth* and Witchcraft", see note 1 above, pp. 27-8.

5. Janet Adelman, *Suffocating Mothers: Fantasies of Maternal Origin in Shakespeare's Plays, Hamlet to The Tempest* (London and New York: Routledge, 1992), pp. 130-47 (here 131 and 137-8).

6. Jonathan Goldberg, "Speculations: *Macbeth* and Source" in *Shakespeare Reproduced: The Text in History and Ideology*, ed. Jean E. Howard and Marion F. Crawford (New York and London: Methuen, 1987), pp. 242-64 (p. 258).

7. See David Farley-Hills, *Shakespeare and the Rival Playwrights 1600-1606* (London and New York: Routledge, 1990*)*, esp. p. 5; Gary Wills, *Witches and Jesuits: Shakespeare's 'Macbeth'* (New York and Oxford: Oxford UP, 1995), esp. p. 9; David Norbrook, "Macbeth and the Politics of Historiography" in *Politics of Discourse: The Literature and History of Seventeenth-Century England*, ed. Kevin Sharpe and Steven N. Zwicker (Berkeley and London: California UP, 1987), esp. p. 79; R. K. Root, *Classical Mythology in Shakespeare* (New York: Gordian Press, 1903, repr. 1965), repr. 1965), pp. 12-13.

8. For Senecanism in *Macbeth* see Robert S. Miola, *Shakespeare and Classical Tragedy: The Influence of Seneca* (Oxford: The Clarendon Press, 1992), J.A.K. Thomson, *Shakespeare and the Classics* (London: Allen and Unwin, 1952). Kenneth Muir offers a succint survey in *The Sources of Shakespeare's Plays* (London: Methuen, 1977), pp. 211-14.

9. J.M. Wood, "Lady Macbeth's Suckling", *Notes and Queries* NS 13 (1966), p. 138. The occurrence of two identical words in the *Macbeth* passage and Arthur Golding's translation of the Athamas episode would seem to make the source certain: "smyling" and "dasht": "He snatched from betweene/ The mothers armes his little babe *Loearchus* smyling on him [...] and dasht his tender head/ Against a hard and rugged stone": *Shakespeare's Ovid: Arthur Golding's*

*Translation of the Metamorphoses*, ed. W.H.D. Rouse (London: Centaur Press, 1961), Book IV, ll. 636-40, p. 94. This is the translation used unless indicated otherwise. A modern translation has been used where it seems that Shakespeare is closer to the Latin text. Citations from *Macbeth* are from the revised Arden Shakespeare. ed. Kenneth Muir (London: Methuen, 1972).

10. Seneca, *Mad Hercules*, transl. Frank Justus Miller, in *The Complete Roman Drama*, 2 Vols (New York. Random House, 1942), II, p. 474.

11. *Mad Hercules*, p. 492.

12. Ovid, *Metamorphoses*, 2 vols, transl. Frank Justus Miller, Loeb Classical Library, 3rd edn rev. by G.P. Goold (Cambridge, MA, and London: Loeb, 1977), I, 213, henceforward referred to as *Loeb*. I have used a modern translation here, as the Golding is not clear at this juncture: he has "desire of gadding foorth abroad' for "erroresque vagos' which Miller in the Loeb edition renders as "strange hallucinations" (I, 213) and Innes in the Penguin edition as "vague hallucinations"; see *The Metamorphoses of Ovid* transl. Mary M. Innes (Harmondsworth: Penguin, 1955), p. 107.

13. See Edgar I. Fripp, *Shakespeare Man and Artist*, 2 vols (London: Oxford UP, 1938, repr. 1964), I, p. 108, and James O. Wood, "Fillet of a Fenny Snake", *Notes and Queries*, NS xii (1965), pp. 332-3.

14. In this context, it is perhaps worth recalling that Euripides' *Medea* compares her to Ino: Euripides, *Medea and Other Plays*, transl. Philip Vellacott (Harmondsworth: Penguin, 1963, repr. 1971), p. 56. There is an important mythic link between Ino and Medea, also connected with infanticide. The golden fleece which Medea helped Jason to obtain was that of the golden ram upon which Ino's stepchildren escaped from her murderous intentions.

15. Female sexuality is frequently presented as unwelcome, degrading even, an overwhelming force of nature in the *Metamorphoses*: see William Keach, *Elizabethan Erotic Narratives: Poetry and Pathos in the Ovidian Poetry of Shakespeare, Marlowe and Their Contemporaries* (Hassocks: Harvester Press, 1977), Chapter 1.

16. F.P. Wilkinson, *Ovid Recalled* (Cambridge: Cambridge UP, 1955), pp. 205-6.

17. John W. Velz, "The Ovidian Soliloquy in Shakespeare", *Shakespeare Studies*, 18 (1986), 1-24, here p. 5.

18. E.A.J. Honigmann describes Macbeth's introspection as "'inward-looking honesty": "[Macbeth] appeals to us as his own accuser, so that we can participate simultaneously with his moral and his criminal nature": *Shakespeare: Seven Tragedies - The Dramatist's Manipulation of Response* (London: Macmillan, 1980), p. 138.

19. *Loeb*, I, p. 343.

20. See, for example, John Upton, *Critical Observations on Shakespeare* (London: G. Hawkins, 1746), p. 51; Fripp, p. 108; H.R.D. Anders, *Shakespeare's Books* (New York: AMS Press, 1965), p. 38.

21. Golding, Book VII, ll. 437-41; *Loeb* I, p. 367.

22. Inga-Stina Ewbank, "The Fiend-like Queen: A Note on *Macbeth* and Seneca's *Medea*" in *Aspects of Macbeth: Articles Reprinted from 'Shakespeare Survey'*, eds Kenneth Muir and Philip Edwards (Cambridge: Cambridge UP, 1977), pp. 55-7.

23. Geffrey Whitney, *A Choice of Emblemes* (Leyden, 1586), p. 33. One of Whitney's cited sources is Ovid. The nesting swallow, however, he attributes to an epigram by the (very) minor French poet Borbonius, or Nicolas Bourbon. It is difficult to know how widely the emblem was known. It might have drawn on a familiar tradition. Caroline Spurgeon points out that 'martin' was a slang word for 'dupe', used as such by Greene and Fletcher, and that Shakespeare refers to the building martlet in a context of deceptiveness in *The Merchant of Venice*, 2.9.29: *Shakespeare's Imagery and What It Tells Us* (Cambridge: Cambridge UP, 1935, repr. 1990), pp. 187-8.

24. *Loeb*, I, p. 365. See p. 364, ll. 328-30 for the Latin: "iamque neci similis resoluto corpore regem/et cum rege suo custodes somnus habebat,/ quem dederant cantus magicaeque potentia linguae".

25. *Loeb*, I, p. 367, Golding, Book VII, ll. 446-7. There are few verbal echoes to link the two texts at this juncture: perhaps Lady Macbeth's "Was the *hope* drunk,/ Wherein you dressed yourself" catches Medea's "that ye doe not feede/ A fruitlesse *hope*" (Golding, ll. 431-2).

26. *Narrative and Dramatic Sources of Shakespeare*, ed. Geoffrey Bullough (London and Henley: Routledge & Kegan Paul, 1978), VII, p. 437.

27. In catalogues of good and bad women, the reputation of Medea varied: she was sometimes commended for her skill as a sorceress, but more frequently listed in misogynistic tracts as an example of female wickedness for her family crimes: see Linda Woodbridge, *Women and the English Renaissance: Literature and the Nature of Womankind, 1540-1620* (Brighton: Harvester Press, 1984), e.g. p. 119.

28. David Norbrook's suggestion that Shakespeare's political stance was close to that of Montaigne, whose belief in the "'irredeemably irrational elements in human motivation" led him to a position of sceptical conservatism, trusting custom and tradition more than reason, may be hinted at in the irrational frenzy of evil in *Macbeth*: Norbrook, pp. 98-9.

29. Susanna Hamilton, "'The charm's wound up': Reference Back in *Macbeth*", *English*, XXXV, No. 152 (Summer 1986), pp. 113-19 (here 116-17).

30. J.P. Sommerville has argued that the patriarchal discourse of absolutism was increasingly influential from the 1590s onwards, and Norbrook argues that it influenced James's thinking on monarchical theory under pressure from republican theorists; see "*Macbeth* and the Politics of Historiography" (see note 7) and J.P. Somerville, *Politics and Ideology in England 1603-1640* (London and New York: Longman, 1986), pp. 27-39.

31. Goldberg, "Fatherly Authority", pp. 4-5. See Paul for an account of the Gunpowder Plot, and also Wills for details of topical reference in *Macbeth*.

32. *2 Henry VI*, 5.2.57-60. Ewbank suggests rightly, I think, that the story is "already associated with a particular kind of destructiveness", and that the allusion owes more to Seneca than to Ovid: Ewbank, p. 58.

33. Richard A. McCabe, *Incest, Drama and Nature's Law 1550-1700* (Cambridge: Cambridge UP, 1993), p. 123.

## Macbeth and Jacobean Political Mythologies

34. Thomas Campion, *The Discription of a Maske, Presented before the Kinges Maiestie at White-Hall, on Twelfth Night last, in honour of the Lord Hayes, and his Bride* (London, 1607), B3r.

35. Even if one cannot accept Lomax's argument that *Macbeth* supercedes *The Lord Hay's Masque*, she is surely right in suggesting that the texts belong to the same iconographic tradition: see Marion Lomax, *Stage Images and Traditions* (Cambridge: Cambridge UP, 1987), Chapter 3.

36. D.J. Gordon, "Reubens and the Whitehall Ceiling" in *The Renaissance Imagination*, ed. Stephen Orgel (Berkeley and London. California UP: Berkeley and London, 1975), pp. 38-41: "(except we will smother the childe of Union in his first birth,) both English and Scottish, will soone heare him sound aloude into the whole world, that all great Britaine is like Jerusalem, which is, as a City, at unity with it selfe; and Babilon, even division, disorder, discord" (p. 40).

37. Graham Parry, *The Golden Age Restored: The Culture of the Stuart Court, 1603-42* (Manchester: Manchester UP, 1981), pp. 231-2. Parry also links Willet with *Macbeth*: "The heirs of James 'shall be continued to the end of the world, we trust', says Willet, uttering a hope that was widely shared, and which was expressed, for example, in *Macbeth*, through the vision of the heirs of Banquo (of whom James was one); p. 231.

38. As Nicholas Brooke has recently observed, too much credence cannot be attached to Simon Forman's account of the performance at the Globe in 1610/1611, as he seems to remember little of the play after the appearance of Banquo's ghost, and fails to mention the apparitions or their prophecies: "'they must surely have been in the original play"; see *The Tragedy of Macbeth*, ed. Nicholas Brooke, The Oxford Shakespeare (Oxford: Clarendon Press, 1990), p. 66.

39. J.M. Nosworthy seems inclined to trust Forman absolutely, and to attribute the presence of the Folio witches to the influence of *The Masque of Queens* and *The Witch*: see *Shakespeare's Occasional Plays* (London: Edward Arnold, 1965), p. 18. But see the note on Nicholas Brooke's view above.

40. See, in particular, *Witches and Jesuits*, Chapter 2, pp. 35-49.

41. John Foxe, *Acts and Monuments* (London, 1576), "To the true and faithfull congregation of Christes uniuersall Church", p. ii verso. Reginald Scot's *The Discoverie of Witchcraft* (London, 1584) is another text which associates the superstitious worship of Catholics with belief in witchcraft.

42. Again, the myth is to be found in Foxe, as early as *Christus Triumphans: Comoedia Apocalyptica* (Basel, 1556), and the true and universal church is later linked with Elizabeth in the *Acts and Monuments*. The tradition persisted, of course, into the Jacobean era, as in the Appendix to Thomas Tuke's *Treatise against Painting and Tincturing of Men and Women* (London, 1616), p. 42, which speaks of "this old Roman *Iesabel*" and accuses the Church of Rome as being "the Mother of spiritual fornications, magicke, sorcerie, and witchcraft".

43. David Harris Willson, *King James VI and I* (London: Jonathan Cape, 1956), pp. 223-6. I do not intend to suggest that James should be identified with Duncan. James prided himself on his foresight which frustrated the plot, in direct contrast to Duncan, who is easily duped. But failings in Duncan's character and regime do not necessarily imply subversive intent on Shakespeare's part, which seems to be the view of some modern critics.

44. R. V[enner], *The True Testimonie of a Faithfull Subiect...*, n.d. [1605], A8r, B4r, B4v, B5r. The pamphlet refers to "Gowries treason" as well as the gunpowder plot. For comment on *The*

*Whore of Babylon* as oppositional text, see Kathleen E. McLuskie, *Dekker and Heywood: Professional Dramatists* (Basingstoke and London: Macmillan, 1994), p. 51. The devil may be found in his pontificals in *The Divils Charter* (London, 1607) ACTUS 5, SCEN. Ultima, l. 3069.

45. Paul, pp. 162-82.

46. John Leslie, *A Treatise Tovvching the Right, Title and Interest of the Most Excellent Princesse Marie, Queene of Scotland, And of the most noble king Iames, her Graces Sonne, to the succession of the Croune of England* (1584), A2r-v.

47. "Macbeth and the Politics of Historiography", p. 105.

48. Sommerville, p. 44.

49. *Ben Jonson: The Complete Masques*, ed. Stephen Orgel (New Haven and London: Yale UP, 1969), ll. 132-6, p. 127. All citations from Jonson are from this edition.

50. Samuel R. Gardiner, *History of England from the Accession of James I to the Outbreak of the Civil War, 1603-1642*, 10 vols (London: Longmans, Green, 1885), II, Chapter XI; Willson, Chapter XIII.

51. Orgel, pp. 134-36.

52. Orgel, p. 56.

53. Orgel, p. 101; Helen Hackett, *Virgin Mother, Maiden Queen* (London: Macmillan, 1995), p. 81.

54. Christopher Haigh, *Elizabeth I* (London & New York: Longman, 1988), Chapter I.

55. S.L. Adams, "Spain or the Netherlands? The dilemmas of early Stuart foreign policy" in *Before the Civil War: Essays in Early Stuart Politics and Government*, ed. H. Tomlinson (London: Macmillan, 1983), pp. 79-101.

56. Carolly Erickson, *The First Elizabeth* (London: Macmillan, 1983), p. 388. For disillusionment with Elizabeth in the 1590s, see Hackett, Chapter 6.

57. Macduff's strange birth is present in Holinshed; but, as has been seen, it is echoed by the birth of Bacchus, alluded to in classical texts cited in *Macbeth*.

# *MACBETH* AND THE SOCIAL HISTORY OF WITCHCRAFT

### B. J. Sokol
### (Goldsmiths' College, London)

> A sailor's wife had chestnuts in her lap,
> And mounch'd, and mounch'd, and mounch'd:
> "Give me", quoth I: --
> "Aroynt thee, witch!" the rump-fed ronyon cries.
> (*Macbeth*, 1.3.6-8).

1

The ways we understand the 'witches' in *Macbeth* may be both clarified and enlivened by social historical investigations. Extensive recent research into the actual phenomena of witchcraft accusations in late sixteenth- and early seventeenth-century Europe reveals widespread patterns that suggest how witches may have been perceived by Shakespeare and his original audiences. Not only do these historical insights concerning the very elaborate social, intellectual and psychological matrix of early modern witchcraft help us to overcome the anachronistic or fanciful notions found in some critics writing on *Macbeth*, but they may also allow us to see important aspects of the play freshly, with a newly sharpened focus.

We shall not concentrate here on the relationship between the 'witch' scenes of *Macbeth* and the gender issues crucial to the play,[1] just touch on them at the outset. While the play raises questions about Macbeth's and Duncan's versions of masculinity, and while Lady Macbeth pleads to be 'unsexed', we find Shakespeare's weird sisters (as opposed to those in his sources) ugly and bearded. Some recent studies addressing psychological aspects of witchcraft and questioning the 'constructedness' versus the 'biologically determined' nature of gender and gender relations, help to elucidate this nexus.[2] Also in relation to 'family values', the witches in *Macbeth* place in their cauldron "Finger of birth-strangled babe,/ Ditch-deliver'd by a drab" (4.1.33-4), a detail of dismemberment that should be counterpoised with Macbeth's imagined powerful "Pity, like a naked new-born babe,/ Striding the blast" (1.7.21-2), and aligned with his later murder of children. The precise choice of ingredients for the "gruel thick and slab" is elucidated by a recent witchcraft study which shows how particularly horrid persecutions of alleged witches evidenced the authorities' extreme spite against familial nurturance, affection and pity.[3]

Such psychological matters are integral to the play, but must, being outside the purview of social history, be passed over here. On the other hand, the singing and dancing witch choruses of the Hecate scenes (*Macbeth*, 3.5 and 4.1.39-43) are almost certainly extra-Shakespearean interpolations, and will be ignored without regrets.[4] What we shall concentrate on is emerging evidence that, despite widespread confusions and equivocations concerning witchcraft in Shakespeare's period, European witchcraft fears and accusations presented a fairly uniform general tendency. With some exceptions, these did not derive 'from above' in the form of centrally controlled or politically motivated scapegoating or persecution. They arose rather 'from below' during "moments of crisis" in which "small communities"[5] projected into alleged witches the anxiety, anger, fear, and despair accompanying an inexorable waning of serviceable traditions of local good will. The decline of humane traditions was not in any way felt to be *caused* by witches; on the contrary, the individuals accused of malign witchcraft were more than likely among the chief *victims* of a palpable draining of mutuality out of communal life. They attracted suspicion because, either explicitly or implicitly through their situations, they cried out against a denial of traditionally expected benefits, or even attempted by threats to extort them. That is to say, suspected witches were typically attention-drawers or guilt-causers concerning changes with causes beyond the scope of the communities in which accusations occurred.

A wide range of historical corroboration of such a pattern will be described presently. But first I should like to emphasise that the witch fears locally *felt* and the social unease these feelings expressed were not consciously acknowledged as bearing any before-and-after or cause-and-effect relation. Similarly, in *Macbeth* unnatural events such as an owl hawking a falcon, or horses eating horses, or the apparition of three weird sisters on a heath, *precede* the unnatural regicide. Nevertheless they may express how Macbeth's tyranny devastates traditional prosperous human relations – feasting, for instance, or nurturing children. Externally we may judge social stress or change to cause the psychology of occult fears, but as a dramatic 'objective correlative' witch activity in *Macbeth* is neither a cause nor consequence of events, but rather symbolises the internal states that lie at the core of the play.

2

The aim, then, will be to use the insights of historical research to help elucidate what Shakespeare may have meant to communicate through his presentations of three 'weird sisters' in *Macbeth*. Is it possible that they were adopted simply as handy theatrical devices? Ever since Kyd's Elizabethan box-office hit *The Spanish Tragedy* began with a shocking ghost-spirit parley, and notably since the appearance of the scene-setting ghost in *Hamlet*, dramatic forays into the spirit world served the Shakespearean theatre well as plot – 'establishing' devices, sinister pace setters, and sensational attention getters.[6] Are we now in danger of over-interpreting a theatrical ploy or convention?

Certainly, we know well the sensationalist drawing powers of the supernatural. But rather than attuning us to Shakespeare's usage, the present-day marketable qualities of the occult may tend to mislead us. In regard to witchcraft, even some modern scholars have "approached their material with a mixture of romanticism and indignation, of fascination and horror".[7] However, much serious recent work has studiously avoided a judgmental stance, soberly reviewing the documents and records of witch accusations in pursuit of their complex meanings.

First let us consider some sources of distortion. Since the decline, in the western world, of a *general* belief in witchcraft, artistic, commercial and propagandist motives have repeatedly sensationalised witches in a train of fictional and 'factional' productions.[8] For a gem of the genre we may consider a Pendle Borough Council brochure promoting the region to visitors under a heading: "Strange tales of witchcraft still linger beneath Pendle Hill". This coyly if tamely suggests that "mystery still surrounds" the "true story" of ten Lancashire women and one man hanged for witchcraft in 1612, asking "Were they really [...] possessed with evil powers?".[9] The banality of such witch-touting, eliciting the dubious thrills of residual superstition, is starkly opposed to the reality of early modern witchcraft practice and persecution. The commercial viability of the 'merrie Englande with hornes' genre indeed indicates a possible, though by no means insurmountable barrier in modern sensibility to parts of *Macbeth*.

A kind of sensationalism attuned to Jacobean sensibilities is deliberate in Shakespeare's 'Scottish Play',[10] but *Macbeth* is a serious work of literature in its vivid witchcraft scenes, which were shaped also by deeper thematic matters. To pursue these thematic matters, while our responses are nagged by our age's neo-paganism, commodified spookiness, and propagandist appropriations, requires careful inquiry.

It is not easy now to imagine how witches were seriously consulted, feared, bribed, and sometimes prosecuted (although, for interesting reasons, not very often executed) in Shakespeare's sophisticated England. Intellectual history reveals a complex early modern debate over whether witchcraft phenomena were real, impostures, impossibilities, or symptoms of mental aberration. This debate was not at all straightforwardly divided on lines between rationality and irrationality, nor even did it concern generally agreed upon practices or offences. Where it existed, religiously dislocating and politically dangerous scepticism about the 'reality' of witchcraft was typically partial and/or equivocating. And where belief in the reality of witchcraft was maintained, there was great variability, even contradiction, in the definitions and categorisations of magical activities. We will explore how Shakespeare's peculiarly mixed presentation of the 'witches' in *Macbeth* synthesises some of the most agreed upon, and analyses some of the most debated polarities in the multifarious views of his age.

3

It is noteworthy that term 'witch' appears often in the Folio speech prefixes and stage directions, but not in any spoken lines of the text except once, when the first sister angrily remembers the retort of the uncharitable "ronyon". The precise meaning of the young woman's "Aroynt thee, witch!" is still an unresolved crux;[11] but, as we shall see, it and its dramatic context correspond to the most typical of actual English witchcraft accusations.

In this and some further aspects the prophetic sisters of *Macbeth* resemble the 'actual' witches popularly accused in Shakespeare's age; yet in other ways they are quite different. Indeed, the brevity of their stage appearance notwithstanding, the 'weird sisters' are creatures of tremendous and deliberate ambiguity. It is explicit in their deceiving equivocations, manifest in their ungendered countenances, and implicit even in the report of the play in Simon Forman's diary. Forman's play-going diary for 1611 describes the apparitions seen by Macbeth and Banquo as "3 women feiries or Nimphes".[12] Holinshed more complexly describes an apparition of "three women in strange and wild apparell, resembling creatures of the elder world", who were regarded "at the first but some vain fantasticall illusion by Mackbeth and Banquho". But, some of their prophesies fulfilled, "afterwards the common opinion was, that these women were either the weird sisters, that is (as ye say) the goddesses of destinie, or else some nymphes or feiries".[13] Holinshed's shifting and qualified ("common opinion") evaluation gives an ambiguous hint of imposture or delusion;[14] in *Macbeth* this is rendered in Banquo's doubts, including "Or have we eaten on the insane root?".

Further ambiguity arises in Forman's and Holinshed's joint use of the term 'nymphs'. In Forman's supposedly first-hand account, Macbeth's "secret, black and midnight hags" are thereby transformed from 'foul' to 'fair', for 'nymphs' were always for Shakespeare (and, according to the *OED*, for his age) alluringly or at least attractively feminine. The problem of how to reconcile the most usual gender of witches with the three sisters' bearded faces, allied with the fact that they were probably never played by women before 1888,[15] suggests gender-related issues outside our scope, but also focuses attention once more on the question of their exact natural or supernatural status.

Like several contributions in a long literary critical debate on this question,[16] the newer historical knowledge of witchcraft also indicates that it cannot be answered with exactitude. Uncertainty is inevitable because the 'witch' of Shakespeare's period never belonged to a neatly-defined category. Thus scholars have debated distinctions between English witches, Scottish witches, continental witches, villagers' maleficent witches, intellectuals' demonic witches, popular white witches, the sceptics' illusionary witches, and so forth. Anthropologically oriented researchers even construct complex definitional graphs preliminary to recording concrete historical data.[17]

The need for such classifications arises due to several factors. Despite theological injunctions, many people in Shakespeare's time held that, in addition to bad or dangerous witches, there were various sorts of good ones; in fact, many people employed them as we do doctors, personal advisors or therapists. Others vehemently decried such practices, while still others in various ways questioned the actuality of witchcraft. Shakespeare himself jocularly mocks traditional village 'wise women' in *The Merry Wives* 4.5. 25 and 53 and *Twelfth Night* 3.4.97. That is to say, he places them in ridiculous dramatic situations, showing no outright condemnation but little respect.[18] On the other hand, the charitable physician Cerimon in *Pericles* appears to be a white witch. Paulina in *The Winter's Tale* also hints that she may be a good witch,[19] and in *The Tempest*, Prospero may be said to practice theurgy or white magic.[20] This late usage of Shakespeare was daring, for there were strong contemporary objections to white witchcraft, for instance by mainstream physicians perhaps jealous of competition.[21]

In his *Daemonologie* (1597) King James himself totally condemned all forms of magic;[22] but again ambiguity arises, for, as historians have long noted, James changed his activities from the pursuit of Scottish witches to the pursuit of witchcraft impostures and false accusations after he arrived on the English throne.[23] Perhaps on a parallel path, Shakespeare frequently refer to 'real' witch malevolence in earlier plays, but in *Othello* (1.2.63-75 and 1.3.60-4), *Pericles* (2.5.49) and *The Winter's Tale* (2.2.67-115 and 4.4. 426-7) exposed misguided anger behind false accusations of witchcraft.[24] (Yet Shakespeare's Late Plays feature not only theurgy, but also foul and envious Sycorax.)

The varied footings on which members of Europe's learned or authoritative classes came to intervene in order to moderate or prevent witchcraft prosecutions are the subject of several interesting investigations.[25] Yet before the intellectual tide began to turn to general scepticism (in most Western European countries around the end of the seventeenth century) only very few thinkers openly expressed doubts about the reality of witchcraft.[26] Opinions in this tricky area of ideology were mainly kept ambiguous, lest they attract unhealthy notice. Attitude shifts were insinuated, not stated. So King James's *Daemonologie*, setting out to contradict the sceptics Weyer and Scot,[27] argued that melancholy delusions cannot explain witch phenomena (pp. 29-30). Nevertheless it has been claimed that, following the 1602 Mary Glover case in London, James approved (or even inspired) Edward Jordan's thesis that her possession by witchcraft was a medically explainable mental delusion.[28] It is perhaps no wonder, if even kings were not explicit, that Stuart Clark finds it striking "how few examples there are" in Europe "at each end of the spectrum ranging from total acceptance of all demonic claims - where we find only Bodin and perhaps Remy [...] - to total rejection - where we find only Reginald Scot and his English followers".[29]

The explanation of this intellectual fence-sitting was that in learned (as opposed to popular) opinion witchcraft was taken to involve diabolical compacts, not merely magical harming or *maleficium*. If an educated person were explicitly sceptical they would risk the label 'Saducee'[30] or denier of the spirit world. Presumably without any conscious cowardice, the rational physician Sir Thomas Browne in 1642 still wondered "how so many learned heads should so far forget their metaphysicks, and destroy the ladder and scale of creatures, as to question the existence of spirits: for my part I have ever believed, and do now know, that there are witches".[31]

4

That Shakespeare, as a dramatic poet, did not have to express anything explicit about his own philosophy[32] does not mean that he was intellectually disengaged when he depicted the witches in *Macbeth*. If his three "sisters exhibit a combination of characteristics - human and supernatural, Classical and contemporary",[33] this was a fair mirror of the current state of ambiguity about the nature of their species.[34] Moreover, Shakespeare reflects a more than local awareness in his allusions to un-English witch activities and punishments.[35] In his England, death by burning was a punishment only for treason,[36] yet burning for witchcraft heresy is noted in both Parts of *King Henry IV* and in *The Winter's Tale*, as well as serving as a metaphor in *Romeo and Juliet* 1.2.91 and *King Lear* 3.2.84. In *The Winter's Tale* Shakespeare also implicitly mirrors the charge of witches' night flying, a legal charge that was virtually unheard of in England.[37]

Although Shakespeare was aware of exotic witch heresies, in his England, Keith Thomas tells us:

> witchcraft to most men was still an activity - doing harm to others by supernatural means - not a heresy. This can be seen in the wording of the Acts of Parliament which first made witchcraft a statutory offence.

What is striking is that no reference to a diabolical compact is made in either of the first two.[38]

Thomas adds to this that the final "1604 statute [...] never satisfied the zealots, who would have liked to impose the death penalty for any type of magical activity whatsoever",[39] indicating an area of sharp controversy. Resulting complex tensions over witchcraft are, I believe, cunningly negotiated in *Macbeth* by means of its mixed presentation of the ambiguous sisters.

At the very start of the play the three witches are arranging their next *meeting*, a possible pointer to an un-English coven.[40] But this hint is undermined because they are not summoned by Satan or a sub-devil to meet in large numbers or in groups of thirteen. Nor do they descend to kissing diabolical posteriors in blasphemous church rituals, or other famous communal pranks.[41] Their practices accord better, in tone and deed, with the image of English witches given by Barbara Rosen: "... in English courts and English superstition [they] turned out to be stubbornly independent and anti-social- one might almost say, irreligious".[42]

Thus, when they meet in 1.3, the (only) three witches of *Macbeth* do not plot heresy, caper or blaspheme, but rather compare their doings like mischievous village gossips, sociably addressing each other as 'sister'. This term of address may imply a zealous association, but perhaps not, for accusations of solely maleficent witchcraft often extended to multiple members of one family.

A recent authoritative survey summarises how in several ways English witchcraft was "peculiar":

> English witches did not fly. They did not go to sabbath. They did not copulate or make pacts with the devil, or make powders and ointment, with the bones of murdered infants [...] They were not accused of being heretics, but of harming their neighbour's cows. They were not tortured or burned.[43]

On the whole, therefore, Shakespeare's swine-killing sisters in many respects closely resemble 'actual' English witches. They lack, however, one important characteristic of English witches as presented in Alan Macfarlane's thoroughly researched investigations into Essex witchcraft. He has shown that English witches never congregated from afar or were strangers to their alleged victims, who were, on the contrary, almost always long-standing neighbours of less than five miles distance.[44] Indeed, so mundane was Essex witchcraft that official accusations often occurred only after years of informal complaints. Thus, 'real' English witches were not at all the sort to appear suddenly to strangers. They were well-known locals, not apparitions like those first amazing Macbeth and Banquo within Holinshed's "laund"(forest clearing), or on Shakespeare's "blasted heath"

Christina Larner tells us that also with regard to Scotland, where persecutions of diabolical witchcraft were relatively much more frequent and severe than in England, we can "forget about thundering torrents, impenetrable mists and high mountains [...] the places where the accused [witches] confessed to having met with the Devil were crossroads, barns, mills and churches".[45]

Ignoring such historical information, while attempting to expose modern "accommodations of one aspect of the play to [later] prevailing attitudes", Alan Sinfield wittily if speciously claims that:

> For many members of Jacobean audiences, witches were a social and spiritual reality: they were as real as Edward the Confessor, perhaps more so [...] Latterly we have adopted other ways with the Witches [of *Macbeth*] - being unable, of course, to contemplate them, as most of Shakespeare's audience probably did, as phenomena one might encounter on a heath.[46]

But, as we have seen, 'real' English witches were never popularly contemplated as extraordinary apparitions of strangers on heaths.

In another supposedly 'materialist' reading of the witchcraft in *Macbeth*, also showing more wit than historical substance, Terry Eagleton claims that the witches are "the heroines of the piece".[47] He is defiantly anachronistic in claiming this, although he locates the witches' "style" within an historical materialist bifurcation:

> There is a style of transgression which is play and poetic non-sense, a dark carnival in which all formal values are satirized and deranged; and there is the different but related disruptiveness of bourgeois individualist appetite, which, in its ruthless drive to be all, sunders every constraint and lapses back into nothing. (p. 5)

In accordance with his positive assessment of the first of these types of 'transgression', Eagleton holds that the three witches are wholly admirable:

> As the most fertile force in the play, the witches inhabit an anarchic, richly ambiguous zone both in and out of official society [...]They are poets, prophetesses and devotees of female cult, radical separatists who scorn male power and lay bare the hollow sound and fury at its heart. (p. 3)

Such an assessment of the 'positive value' of the witches in *Macbeth*, Eagleton humorously alleges, would naturally occur to "any unprejudiced reader - which would seem to exclude Shakespeare himself, his contemporary audiences and almost all literary critics." (pp. 1-2). There are hints here of a conscious parody of historicist readings. Still, Eagleton seriously claims there is a fascinating and valuable "subversiveness" in witchcraft (p.4).

This claim applies to *Macbeth* notions about witchcraft that, although found in many modern critical writings, were never entertained in Shakespeare's age. These suggest that witchcraft was not only expressive of, but also actively expressed, social discontent. This derives from a confusion of the inversion truly provable in contemporary ideas about diabolical witchcraft[48] with forms of active social subversion.[49] The likewise untenable notion that early modern witches pursued a "female cult", or alternative religion "both in and out of official society", finds no support in historical scholarship except in the long-discredited 1920s theories of Margaret Alice Murray.[50]

5

The investigation of local and popular aspects of European witchcraft has been a rapidly enlarging field since the 1970s, and there is no sign of abatement. This proliferation of fine-grained studies, fortunate for us, arises, no doubt, from a wish to explore the personal relations, emotional lives, and the fortunes of the historical majority who had less than exalted rank or dynastic importance. These studies constitute a body of historical scholarship which is generally less concerned with theological, intellectual, legal and governmental involvements with witchcraft - matters suggesting 'social control' as it were from 'above' - than with how witchcraft was experienced popularly 'from below' in villages or towns. Thus the main focus of this scholarship is on one half of the social process in which a European witch "began her career in the farmyard as an enemy of her neighbour, and ended it in the courts as a public person, an Enemy of God and of the godly society".[51] Such an historical focus is especially valuable for the student of *Macbeth*, not only because seventeenth-century English law and judicial practice concerning witchcraft showed a far less than the average degree of emphasis on ideological control.[52] As Larner, a major contributor of 'social control' models for witchcraft phenomena, has pointed out: "to stress the importance of political activity and elitist ideas may not explain the persecution in any psychological depth, but it does at least account for its appearance at a specific point in time".[53] Such diachronic accounting is, of course, historically invaluable. But a synchronic understanding perhaps more psychologically 'in depth' might well be the more enlightening about specific artistic uses.

Suitable explanations 'in depth' are suggested by the particular model for English witchcraft accusations which Larner was thinking about when she wrote the above. This model was proposed in the early 1970s by Keith Thomas and his student Alan Macfarlane. It was derived by using the analytic methods of social anthropology following extensive historical research. As such, it positively corroborated and historically rooted what was described by Richard Kieckhefer in another context as 'one of the clearest lessons that anthropology has drawn in its study of witchcraft in many different societies'. The lesson was

> that the circumstances giving rise to accusations of witchcraft are not accidental. There are specific kinds of situation that are likely to lead to such charges. Frequently it is possible to show prior animosity between the accuser and the accused - usually in the form of some specific quarrel. Most importantly, in many cases the suspected witch stands in a position of moral superiority in this quarrel, so that the accuser feels guilty and reverses his guilt by projecting it on the accused. If he has denied her the hospitality or kindness that he owes her, for example, he relieves his own feeling of guilt by asserting that she is somehow morally culpable. If appropriate circumstances arise, he will charge her specifically with bewitchment of him or a member of his family.[54] The specifics identified by Thomas and Macfarlane add that English village witch accusations typically began with the denial of a request for traditional help or charity, eliciting "moral superiority" on one side and reciprocal "guilt" on the other.

One may add that - as Brian Vickers points out - there are also peculiar subtleties implicit in "violations of any system of reciprocity".[55]

In Thomas's and Macfarlane's model the witch suspect and the accuser both are typically undergoing economic hardship. The the imploring and denied villager, is the relatively poorer, but not destitute. The somewhat better off villager refusing charity is unwilling or unable to give relief because of a recently acquired opportunist ethic, and/or increasing economic insecurity. Subsequently, an unusual illness of humans or beasts, or a sudden material misfortune in the household of the refusing villager is suspected to be *maleficium*.

Some studies of witchcraft written after the work of Thomas and Macfarlane have questioned aspects of their model, but lately its main outlines have received increasing support.[56] Broad applicability in many detailed studies of many different localities, using differing source materials and approaches, suggests that the model does present the general mode of early modern witchcraft, as viewed popularly (from below) and perceptually (from within). However, few literary interpreters have fully noted the model's potential for elucidating *Macbeth*.[57] To see how it may be best applied, we will consider not just the original model, but also some of its derivatives and variants. For alternatives and exceptions help to expose the most salient aspects of its perspective 'from-below'.

With some exaggeration, a recent comparative study concludes: "The English pattern [of witchcraft first charted] by Thomas and Macfarlane turns out to be not uniquely English at all, but the traditional pattern".[58] It is true that even in radically differing early modern European settings, the outlines of witchcraft approximately match the English model. It was generally true that witchcraft allegations originally arose out of personal disputes which alleged only *maleficium*, even in places like Scotland, France and Germany where authoritarian and ideological forces exacted confessions of conspiratorial, diabolical witchcraft involving sabbaths, diabolism, flying, etc. The effects of witch hunting being, in such places, more "centrally controlled", and of it involving a "greater intensity of religious indoctrination",[59] as compared with England, appeared only after cases reached trial. Only then was there a vastly higher likelihood than in England of forced confession, non acquittal, and execution. Thus Larner argues that the often-claimed Scottish/English disjunction concerning witchcraft is overstated.[60]

Robert Muchembled, writing on French witchcraft, unreservedly approves Thomas's and Macfarlane's reconsideration of "witchcraft at the strictly village level", and finds that "an examination of trials in the north of France demonstrates the existence in this region of an identical 'model' of rural witchcraft".[61] H. C. E. Midlefort's work on south-western German witchcraft likewise praises the results of Macfarlane's "cautious functionalism" and "cautious but sympathetic use of anthropology".[62] And Robin Briggs, in an analysis of the unusually many detailed court records preserved for witchcraft cases in Lorraine between 1580 and 1630, finds very close agreement with several central aspects of the Thomas/Macfarlane

## Social History of Witchcraft    259

model: the accusations showed a "stress on refusal of charity"; many cases involved repeated accusations between neighbours of long-term *maleficium* before the law became involved; and "confessions were based very largely on an indigenous popular tradition, with relatively little contamination from elite demonology".[63] Similarly, an emphasis on *maleficium*, among other characteristics, caused Ruth Martin to find the rural England described by Thomas and Macfarlane closer than all other non-Italian settings to intensely urban Catholic Venice "as far as witchcraft practices are concerned".[64]

While studies from abroad evince many similarities, studies from other parts of England show variations on the Thomas/Macfarlane model. These regional differences provide, in fact, useful clarifications for our purposes. Annabel Gregory's analysis explicitly extends the Thomas/Macfarlane model to include among the neighbourly difficulties leading up to witchcraft accusations more diverse matters than hard-pressed villagers' refusals to share goods or services. It argues a connection between the witchcraft accusations of 1607 and a long process of decline in communal "good neighbourhood" in the town of Rye. Conflicts had been in progress for some time among the town's higher placed merchant families (some of whom were even magistrates) on account of economic hardship, rivalry for civic offices, and vying for most "godliness". Opposed factions formed around traditionally prosperous butchers, and newly dominant brewers. The larger background, a continuing slow economic collapse of the town, was due to harbour silting and/or uncontrollable shifts in patterns of trade. These difficulties had a less severe impact on capital-intensive industries like brewing, than on butchery. A gradual desertion of old traditions of festive mutuality accompanied the economic shifts. Gregory suggests that witchcraft problems are often likely when "there are differences of opinion on [the] question [of investment in social relations], and such disagreements often occur when the introduction of new resources - whether technological or commercial - exacerbates existing inequalities or creates new ones".[65] In mercantile Rye, evil and occult powers were suspected (or projected) where there was a palpable increase in opportunism and decline in "the belief that the goodwill of others is essential to the achievement of survival or success" (p. 61).

Like Gregory in regard to Rye, J. T. Swain connects the notorious Lancashire witch trials with economic problems in the region. In opposition to the narrowly taken Thomas/Macfarlane model, Swain claims that guilt for non-charity was not a specific feature in "three quarters of the detailed allegations of witchcraft in 1612" as well as "in the main events of the 1634 trial".[66] Rather than favour-seekers in Lancashire being denied and guiltily accused, "it seems likely that some of those accused of witchcraft actively fostered their reputations as witches since it enabled them to make a living by begging and extortion" (p. 81). It is not uncommon in the background of witchcraft accusations that demands for alms were perceived as extortionate.[67] In hard times, a spectacle of callously professionalised begging may pass readily from a mild discomfort to an infuriating assault on feelings of decency and security. Importuning with menaces damages the charitable impulse, induces guilty despair, and forces cognizance of a collective predicament.

I wonder whether despairing fury at an apparently incurable economic divide formed the emotional background to the famous 1602 London case of young Mary Glover, supposedly bewitched by the old, poor and irascible Elizabeth Jackson. Elizabeth's anger at Mary was "for discovering to one of her Mistresses a certaine fashion of her [Elizabeth's] subtile and importunat begging".[68] Was this Mary's reason for being so wrought by Elizabeth's towering anger as to feign or experience demonic possession?

J. A. Sharpe's two surveys of seventeenth-century witchcraft accusations in Yorkshire find an exclusive "concern of the lower orders was with *maleficium*",[69] but that relatively fewer depositions than in Essex showed an explicit "feeling of guilt on the part of the [charity] refuser [...] perhaps indicating a regional variation".[70] Although Sharpe's later work adds that a number of such cases did exist, "they do not seem to have been so salient as in the economically advanced southern county".[71] However, among a "wider range of tensions"[72] leading to witchcraft accusations recorded by Sharpe are a denial of access to a right of way, which in its own way indicates a break with traditions of sharing. Sharpe finds, also similarly to Swain, that the Yorkshire witch was "a frightening figure, sometimes using that quality to obtain considerable power in the community" (p. 8), and the same comments as before could be made about forced charity. One interesting way in which Yorkshire witches induced fear noted by Sharpe may be seen as an aggressive pre-empting of charity. This involved "witches gaining power over their victims by giving them a gift, notably food' - in particular nuts being cited.[73] While noting variations on Macfarlane's original model, Sharpe explicitly confirms its central thesis, "that understanding witchcraft accusations in England involves appreciating the importance of interpersonal relationships" (p. 17).

Like these English studies, two excellent studies of witchcraft from further afield also introduce variations of the Thomas/Macfarlane model which bring into focus its core tendencies. John Demos finds that in stressing an "essential conflict between neighborliness and individualism" Thomas and Macfarlane provided a "compelling model" for witchcraft in late seventeenth-century New England. Yet, as opposed to Macfarlane's Essex, there was little poverty there, nor need for charity, nor likelihood that widows would remain solitary and unsupported. Still, "if dependency does not figure largely, the broader issue of 'neighborliness' versus 'individualism' seems powerfully resonant". Indeed, anxiety over this issue was present "with a vengeance" in a second generation of American settlers, who were replacing the co-operative ethic of their Pilgrim parents with a rising ethic of "self-help".[74] Demos holds that witchcraft accusations arose through mechanisms of projection: made uncomfortable by their own "assertive side" the newly prospering colonists supposed that "not they, but rather their neighbor - the 'witch' - possessed the traits they so deeply despised" (p. 210). So, Demos says, witchcraft, like other psychic disturbances, was rooted in "guilt - and ultimately in the divided values of the culture at large" (pp. 298-300).

Robert Muchembled adds to the Thomas/Macfarlane pattern a background of political, religious, and social crisis on the geographical peripheries of counter-Reformation France.[75] Interpersonal cataclysms occurred when newly imposed values and institutions forcibly displaced long-held older ones. Coerced religious and secular "acculturation" of outlying regions, together with forced economic and political transformations, were unlike the natural silting up of Rye harbour, or the evolutionary shift from the co-operation in first settlements to bolder individual pioneering in white America, for they were centrally administered and deliberately pursued policies for change. In response to these, specific interpersonal conflicts and guilt arose from causes as diverse as increases in rural inequality caused by the rise of local "notables", the "intense sense of guilt [of the more literate peasants] earned by their contact with the dominant culture", or even the guilt of rural priests confronting the elimination of their old traditions of concubinage (pp. 277, 271, 273-4).[76] Such causes of conflict were very unlike those specific to England. Yet in many of the witchcraft accusations he studied Muchembled finds characteristics "identical" with the model of Thomas and Macfarlane (pp. 2534).

6

Certain of the convergences we have seen among recent studies of early modern witchcraft are particularly useful for understanding the impact of the witches in *Macbeth*. Let us summarise them. Suspicions of witchcraft *maleficium* leading to counter-measures arose spontaneously in localities, without diabolic trappings.[77] They often followed disputes arising from changes in long-held customs of mutuality. In many parts of early modern Europe such changes were forced on villages, towns or regions by the realities of rapidly changing cultural, political or economic habitats, but these changes themselves were not attributed to witches. Witch accusations arose from unaccustomed modes of social interaction, only indirectly tracking large-scale evolutions or power-shifts, and directly experienced only as newly oppressive, rigorous, hard-headed, or uncharitable. The changes were divisive, producing feelings of bitter helplessness, temptations to callous opportunism, and/or impulses to projective scapegoating. These uncomfortable feelings caused outbreaks of intense psychosocial guilt, which were the matrix for burgeoning imaginary phenomena of malign witchcraft.

The witch scenes of *Macbeth* cunningly mix together indications of highly realistic social collisions in this pattern with other more uncanny aspects of witchcraft. The poetic specifics of these scenes are too well known for rehearsing, but we should certainly note how several of their details contain clear echoes of typical (especially English) village witchcraft phenomena. These include: a suggestion of the common vengeful *maleficium* of swine killing; an angry accusation, made by the denier of a small request for food, that the importuning party is a witch; how solitary women respond to the calls of barnyard pets (commonly called "familiars" in English witch accusations).[78] Other less homely particulars, such as the witches' claims to be able to sail in sieves and raise winds, involve fables of diabolical witchcraft which had by Shakespeare's time passed from "sophisticated" demonology to popular knowledge.[79] But, as we have said, these are not matched in *Macbeth* by any claims to un-English abilities to fly to sabbaths, meet with Satan for sexual orgies, etc.

Indeed, in the limitation of the *maleficium* that the First Witch can direct toward the master of the Tiger ("Though his bark cannot be lost,/ Yet it shall be tempest-tossed"), and in the temptations made through hollow promises to Macbeth by the second and third Apparitions (4.1.79-81 and 90-1), we may perceive effects not even necessarily supernatural. These may only be the effects of sleep-robbing melancholy or hysterical delusions, the sort of mental disorders that, even in Shakespeare's period, were sometimes called the natural causes of the symptoms generally attributed to bewitching.[80] However, to accept, even without necessary anachronism, a wholly naturalising position on the play's witchcraft phenomena would be reductive of Shakespeare's intention in *Macbeth*. Rather, the affinity of many details of the play with patterns found in 'real' witchcraft accusations introduced the sensationally clamorous yet at the same time familiar outlook in which witch beliefs expressed frustrations about seemingly uncontrollable divestings or usurpation of traditional systems of mutuality, support and security.

Although the breakdown of mutuality is considered to have been a leading factor associated with witchcraft accusations, modern authorities sometimes differ as to whether the witchcraft 'accuser' or the 'suspect' was mainly the one "whose breach of the norms triggered the dispute that preceded the accusation".[81] It seems to me false to generalise blame or exoneration for either party; some 'witches' exploited the terror they induced, and others were persecuted on account of eccentric or obstreperous behaviour,[82] while still others were merely 'passive' victims.[83] Yet it seems true that, in general, the pattern of confused anger and guilt that thrust both accuser and accused into an emotionally heedless and practically impotent confrontation was due to fears and losses not of their making.[84] The mainspring of witchcraft accusations was one of personal helplessness and perplexity.

Such an image served the artist wishing to portray the emotional impact of a society severing its connections with long-honoured, worthy, or even essential human values. The plight of the vulnerable amidst the violence and terror of a tyrant's reign is partly represented in *Macbeth* by the cries of a dying child (4.2.82), the guilt of his father (4.3.224-6), the tongue-tied fears of a Doctor of Physic (5.1.76 and 5.3.61-2) or the terror of a young Servant (5.3.11-18). But this naturalism is strongly reinforced by the appearance of the supernatural and the exaggeration of natural terrors.

In fact, by means of a radical pruning of his source materials, Shakespeare distorted the actual history of Macbeth's opportunistic and ferocious regime. According to the *Chronicles of Scotland* in Holinshed, the play's main source, for ten years after he (with some justification) seized the throne, Macbeth was an effective ruler, making new laws and suppressing the brigandage allowed by weak King Duncan. Holinshed interprets the delayed descent of Macbeth from what he calls a "counterfet zeale of equity" to a "naturall inclination" to cruelty[85] in a way that illustrates a political dichotomy, which he illustrated also in his descriptions of Macbeth's and Duncan's reciprocally unbalanced temperaments:

> Makbeth, a valiant gentleman, and one that if he had not been somewhat cruell of nature, might haue been thought most woorthie the government of a realme. On the other part, [King] Duncane was so soft and gentle of nature, that the people wished the inclinations and manners of these two cousins to haue beene [...] tempered. (p. 167)

Excluding such balance in his play, Shakespeare made Macbeth promptly tyrannous, uprooting all traditions of fealty, lawfulness, hospitality, caring for the helpless, nurturance, and so forth. For Shakespeare was not here interested in exploring the balance of temperament fit for sovereignty, as he had been in writing, say, *Measure for Measure*. Instead, he discarded Holinshed's analytic bent, to produce an incisive image of a suddenly and drastically disrupted moral realm.

Whatever motivated Shakespeare's fascination with shattered ethical situations, *Macbeth*, I think, is among the most radical of the resulting tragedies. Its dramatisation of the deep distress accompanying murderous-seeming societal transformations therefore made great use of witches. For *Macbeth* appeared at the moment when social disturbances inspired in private lives the conflicts underlying the chronological mid-point of the most intense period of European witch hunting ever. Thus I would argue that too narrow and sometimes too a-historical a focus on luridly sensational aspects of witch phenomena has obscured how recently discovered patterns in the contemporaneous phenomena of 'real' witchcraft interact with the most urgent themes of *Macbeth*.

## Notes

1. For instance, Ronald Sawyer notes, concerning his set of Buckinghamshire data, "misogyny is not completely inappropriate as an explanation of why nearly all people suspected of witchcraft were women, but it is only a bare beginning for understanding the complex problem of gender and its relationship to supernatural threat" (p. 465).

2. For the literary critical debate see Callagan, pp. 355 and 357, opposing Adelman, who is, however, the more historically informed - see especially p. 100. The historian John Demos holds that disturbances in the early object relations of "mother-raised-children" account for the "usual gender of witches" (pp. 202-6); questions of witchcraft involving "dilemmas surrounding the psychic identity of womanhood" are closely investigated by Lyndal Roper, who explains how "Sexual difference has a bodily dimension" (pp. 240 and 26).

3. See Kunze, pp. 152-3, 181-2, on babys' hands, and 470ff. on sexual mutilation.

4. These are the only proposed interpolations that have been generally acknowledged by editors – see Muir (1977), xii-xxiii and xxx-xxxiii. All textual citations of *Macbeth* will be from this Arden Shakespeare edition. Other Shakespeare references will be from William Shakespeare, *The Complete Works*, ed. Peter Alexander, London: Collins, 1975.

5. Henningsen, p. 17.

6. On general audience attitudes to spirits in contemporary drama see West (1939).

7. Sawyer, p. 461.

8. Among the most valuable are fictional/political diatribes along the lines of Arthur Miller's *The Crucible*, or the anti-patriarchal poems and fictions which are, according to McLuskie "used as myth to inform [current] political debate". As McLuskie further explains, the depictions, in several plays and poems of our time, of "feminist versions of the witchcraze are obviously and explicitly inadequate as history", and yet no less valuable in their own terms. Even to scholars such artistic and political appropriations of the historical phenomena may serve, McLuskie claims, "as an important reminder of the feminist dimension of the witchcraze which can easily disappear in the less passionate analysis of its particular manifestations". (p. 60)

9. *Lancashire Hill Country*, Leaflet, Borough of Pendle Promotions Unit, n. d. I did not visit the leaflet's recommended "Witches Galore" centre at Newchurch, to see if that was less tame.

10. On this see Jorgensen.

11. The same crux appears also in mad Tom's song, *King Lear*, 3.4.122.

12. In Muir, p. xiv.

13. Reprinted ibid., pp. 171-2.

14. More explicitly sceptical was the account in the Scottish history by the great Humanist Buchanan, perhaps read by Shakespeare, see ibid., p. xxxv. He was King James's former tutor, who, according to Norbrook (p. 105), "ever anxious to minimize the mystical and irrational [...] speaks only of "three women [...] of more than human stature".

15. Williams, p. 55.

16. This history is reviewed and discussed in Furness, pp. 7-10; Wilson, pp. xix-xxi, Jorgensen, pp. 116-22, Harris pp. 34-44, and Wenterdorf, pp. 431-2.

17. See Macfarlane, pp. 3-4.

18. With more uncertain significance, Shakespeare hardly ever allows other than negative connotations to attach to his many uses of the word 'cunning' ('cunning folk' being, like 'wise women', good village witches).

19. I discuss the complexities of this in Sokol (1994a), pp. 151-66.

20. According to James the First (p. 26), this would make him of a type even more abhorrent than a sorcerer or witch, as "their error proceeds of the greater knowledge, and so drawes nearer to the sin against the holy Ghost". (p. 26) But I argue psychologically in Sokol (1993) and structurally in Sokol (1994b), that he is a good or white magician dangerously poised on the edge of becoming a black one.

21. As in the MS of Edward Pocton (17c), discussed alongside better-known sources in Sokol (1994a), pp. 154-7. Yet some intellectuals dabbled in theurgy, and it was treated with leniency in treatises such as Guazzo's.

22. James the First. See the comment in Stuart Clark (1984), p. 373.

23. See Kittredge, pp. 267-328. Notestein (pp. 101-9) incorrectly holds James responsible for a harshened English witchcraft law of 1604, but pp. 137-45 notes a falling off of James' witch-mongering in the later part of his reign, his attacks on impostures, and claims "there was always a grain of skepticism in his nature" (p. 138). Larner (1973), pp. 81 and 88 comments on Kittredge, and relates more fully James' changing attitudes (pp. 75-6).

24. Except that in *The Winter's Tale* 2.2 an angry father alleges actual erotic bewitching by a man. (There is a metaphoric parallel at *Midsummer Night's Dream* 1.1.27); in all cases some sexual misdeed is implied.

25. Notestein, p. 138, notes political motives in actions to mitigate witch panics taken by James in Scotland in 1597, and later in England. On James's 1597 Scottish Privy Council order, see Larner (1984), pp. 24-5, and for an expansion of Notestein's theory of the Anglican Church's struggle for dominance being behind official opposition to witch persecution in England see Macdonald (1991), pp. ix-lv. But religious rivalry cannot explain humane moderation in Catholic countries where Inquisition authorities restrained excesses of persecution, as detailed in Henningsen (1980) on the Basque region; Tedeschi (1987), p. 104, on Italy; and Martin (1989): pp. 26-32 and 251, on Venice. Even in religiously torn France, where Muchembled (1985) argues witch-mongering was used to dominate recalcitrant outlying regions, expedient "politico-religious" (p. 241) motives did not prevent central legal bodies from restraining provincial persecutory zeal.

26. For sixteenth-century exceptions see: Montaigne, "Of the Lame or Cripple" (pp. 375-8); also Weyer and Scot.

27. James the First, p. xi. West (1984) analyses Scot's common-sense position, claiming that the *Daemonologie* does not address it (pp. 106-7).

28. Macdonald, pp xlvii-liv

29. Stuart Clark (1984), p. 358.

30. Applied, for instance, by King James (pp. xi-xii) to Reginald Scot and Johann Weyer.

31. *Religio Medici* (1642) in *Works,* Vol. II, pp. 293-496, and p. 366.

32. The genuine philosophical engagement of *Macbeth,* at least with constitutional questions, is well argued by Norbrook.

33. Harris, p. 36.

34. The often-discussed ambiguity of the sisters in *Macbeth* is well treated in Arthur Melville Clark, pp. 24-9, although his assumptions about Shakespeare's reading are unproven. Wenterdorf reviews the long critical controversy about their nature, but argues away its difficulties. He claims the issue is resolved by reading diverse other texts - *2 Henry VI*, James the First's *Newes from Scotland* - and somewhat simplistically concludes that the witches of *Macbeth* are only "human beings in league with Satan and functioning realistically in a world of ruthless political and social opportunists" (p. 435).

35. The legal punishment for a first offence of witchcraft not involving necromancy or bodily harming was 'only' a year's imprisonment and pillorying, and after that hanging, as seen in the 1604 statute reprinted in Rosen, pp. 57-8. In *The Merry Wives*, 4.5.109-12 we hear that Falstaff was nearly put in the stocks, when he was taken to be a village witch.

36- A wife killing her husband was also punishable by burning, because her crime constituted a "pretty treason" against her Lord. In fact, only marital disobedience in a wife constituted in theory the same crime of treason, and was punishable in the same way. I discuss this theory, and what usually happened in practice, in Sokol, 1994a, pp. 153-4 and note 40 p. 237. Burning for heresy was rare, and probably illegal in Shakespeare's England under I Edward VI. c. 12.

37. On the significance of this in the play and historical contexts see Sokol (1994a), pp. 154-5, 165 and 242, n. 101.

38. Thomas, p. 525.

39. Ibid., p. 527.

40. As suggested by Spalding (1880), cited in Furness p. 7. But, as Rosen pointed out, the unique English "Sabbaths of the Samesbury witches in 1612 and the later Lancashire witches of 1634 turned out to be pure invention by a single witness" (p. 190).

41. Typical details of the antics of a famous Scottish coven investigated by King James in connection with trials for treason are reported in the contemporary pamphlet *Newes from Scotland*, pp. 13-14. On James and these trials see C.K. Sharpe (1884), pp. 55-81, Rosen, p. 190, Stuart Clark (1977), and Larner (1973), pp. 79-85.

42. Rosen, p. 190.

43. Rowland, p. 173.

44. Macfarlane, pp. 169-77.

45. Larner (1984), p. 73.

46. Sinfield, p. 103.

47. Eagleton, p. 2.

48. See Stuart Clark (1980), especially with application to *Macbeth*, p. 126.

49. The need to distinguish inversion in witchcraft from subversion is well delineated by Muchembled, p. 272.

50. The closest well-documented analogue is in discoveries through Inquisition records of a Friulian (male) anti-witch cult in Ginzburg. But (unlike Murray's imaginary witches) these fertility-protecting *Benandanti* did not actually congregate, see p..xiii.

51. Larner, quoted in Gregory, p. 31.

52. See Larner (1984), pp. 71-2, for an estimation of the degree of this difference, Thomas (pp. 522-7) for possible reasons for it, and above on the question of humanity versus expedience.

53. Larner (1984), p. 21.

54. Kieckhefer, p. 98.

55. See the discussion of witchcraft narratives in Vickers, pp. 24-7.

56. Klaits, for instance, gives the model serious attention, but doubts Macfarlane's idea that development of "capitalistic profit making" caused the tensions resulting in witch accusations (pp. 87-91). In fact, Macfarlane himself later traced the rise of English individualism to an earlier period than the sixteenth and seventeenth centuries. The careful exposition of the model in Scarre (pp. 41-4), is generally approving. But Scarre doubts the doctrine that all social manifestations can be considered to be functional in a positive sense, and therefore questions whether Macfarlane underestimates a dysfunction of early modern society mirrored in its witchcraft fears. Also Demos suspects the Thomas/Macfarlane "homeostatic model of society" in its "functionalism", but points out that social "functions themselves are not so easily dismissed" (pp. 276-8). Quaife ridicules the model, summarising it in the rhyme, "the greedy accused the needy", but in dismissing it as having 'little merit' offers no clinching evidence or reasons (pp. 189-90). More typically, Levack approves, see esp. pp. 100, 119 and 136.

57. In relation to Jacobean witchcraft plays "a literary paradigm" of the model is explicitly confirmed in Hattaway (1985), p. 61, while the distinctions of English and Scottish witchcraft and the decline of English witchcraft belief are noted in McLuskie (1989), pp. 60-2. These do not set out to apply the model to *Macbeth*; when de Bruyn (1979), does discuss *Macbeth*, p. 122 it does not recall how it cites, pp. 115-16, George Gifford's 1593 *A Dialogue Concerning Witches and Witchcraftes* in a way which exactly supports Macfarlane's model of witchcraft. Wenterdorf (1980), p. 435, ties witchcraft in *Macbeth* to "opportunists", but is likewise silent on the social-historical model which supports this theory. Stallybrass (1982), p. 189, notes the work of Thomas and Macfarlane, but dismisses its point by insisting, p. 195, that *Macbeth* avoided "reducing the play's witches to village widows" and adopting a view of witchcraft as tyrannically imposed by oppressive forces from above. Schalkwyk (1992) writing on *The Winter's Tale* finds Jacobean witchcraft "simply the Other of patriarchal political power" (p. 267), failing to observe that by the play's 1610 date James had altered his attitude of the time of the North Berwick witchcraft/treason trials of 1590-91, or that the chief traitor of these trials was Francis Stewart, the (male) Earl of Bothwell. On these complexities see Clark, Stuart (1977), pp. 158-67.

58. Burke, p. 440.

59. Larner (1984), p. 79.

60. Ibid., pp. 73-9.

61. Muchembled, pp. 253-4.

62. Midlefort, pp. 3-4.

63. Briggs, pp. 339-42, 343, 347 He finds the per capita rate of trials similar to those in Macfarlane's Essex at their peak, but in Lorraine there were 90% convictions and many executions (p.338).

64. Martin, p. 240.

65. Gregory, p. 63. My brief summary does scant justice to this fascinating and deep investigation.

66. Swain, p. 84.

67. As in South Germany, where the streets were thronged with importuning charlatan mendicants, described as a background to a particularly hideous witch panic in Kunze, pp. 44-7, 51-3.

68. Stephen Bradwell's "Mary Glover's Late Woeful Case", B.L. MS Sloane 831, Fol. 3r, transcribed in the last section of Macdonald, p. 3.

69. J. A. Sharpe (1992), p. 10.

70. J.A. Sharpe (1991), p. 186.

71. J.A. Sharpe (1992), p. 8.

72. Ibid., pp. 8-9.

73. Inversely, p. 10, a Yorkshire woman was bewitched after giving (insufficient?) alms.

74. Demos, pp. 298-300.

75. Muchembled, esp. pp. 240-1.

76. On pre-1660 concubinage, see also Sokol (1994a), p. 124.

77. Unless they were accusations forcibly extracted from other 'witches', or provided by professional witch-finders, during large scale hunts.

78. For many instances see the Index in Macfarlane.

79. These un-English abilities were certainly well known from literature readily available in Shakespeare's England. For instance, *Newes from Scotland* reports how they were confessed, probably under torture, by Agnes Tompson (pp. 13 and 17). As Larner (1984) points out, the strict division of popular and educated witch lore must have faded "as popular beliefs became educated" (pp. 76-7).

80. See Edward Jordan's treatise *Of the Suffocation of the Mother* (1603), repr. in facsimile by Macdonald. See also Sawyer's analysis of the personal illnesses, attributed to witchcraft, of Richard Napier's Buckinghamshire patients between 1597 and 1634: "none was as common among adults as disturbances of the mind, which affected the mood, perception, and behavior of victims" (p. 468).

81. Weisman holds that it "was the accuser rather than the the suspect" (p. 89). This is in the midst of a detailed analysis of the Thomas/Macfarlane type of accusation, pp. 76-95.

82. Scot reported obstreperous and opinionated women as likely to be accused (p. 5); this is supported in Macfarlane, pp. 158-9 and Larner (1984), p. 62. Demos points to the complexities of the issue in a more sophisticated manner in stating: "The intrusive, demanding traits so widely attributed to [the female witch] are best viewed as projections. Her victims were presumably uncomfortable about similar tendencies in themselves, their own wishes to intrude, to encroach, to dominate, to attack - their whole assertive side" (p. 210).

83. Muchembled describes a type of witch who was "the passive toy of a change of which she remained unaware" (p. 264).

84. I am not suggesting that crime generally was wholly a product of society, but that witchcraft was exceptional.

85. In Muir, p. 173. A similar sequence, but also driven by guilt and fear, is alleged in Buchanan's Scottish History, see Muir, p. 184.

*Bibliography*

Adelman, Janet. "'Born of Woman': Fantasies of Maternal Power in Macbeth." In *Cannibals, Witches and Divorce: Estranging the Renaissance*. Ed. Marjorie Garber (Baltimore: Johns Hopkins UP, 1987), 90-121.

Briggs, Robin. "Witchcraft and Popular Mentality in Lorraine, 1580-1630." In *Occult and Scientific Mentalities in the Renaissance*. Ed. Brian Vickers (Cambridge: Cambridge UP, 1984), 337-49.

Browne, Sir Thomas. *Works*. Ed Simon Wilkin. 2 vols. London: George Bell & Sons, 1901.

Bruyn, Lucy de. *Women and the Devil in Sixteenth-Century Literature*. Tisbury, Wiltshire. Bear Books, 1979.

Burke, Peter. "The Comparative Approach to European Witchcraft." In *Early Modern European Witchcraft: Centers and Peripheries*. Ed. Benst Ankarloo and Guster Henningsen (Oxford: Clarendon Press, 1990), 434-41.

Callagan, Dympna. "Wicked Women in *Macbeth*: A Study of Power, Ideology, and the Production of Motherhood." In *Reconsidering the Renaissance*. Ed. Mario Di Cesare (Bingham, New York: Medieval and Renaissance Texts and Studies, 1992), 355-69.

Clark, Arthur Melville. *Murder Under Trust or The Topical 'Macbeth'*. Edinburgh: Scottish Academic Press, 1981.

Clark, Stuart. "King James's Daemonologie: Witchcraft and Kingship." In *The Damned Art*. Ed. Sidney Anglo (London: Routledge & Kegan Paul, 1977), 156-81.

----. "Inversion, Misrule and the Meaning of Witchcraft". *Past & Present* 87 (1980), 98-127.

----. "The Scientific Status of Demonology." In *Occult and Scientific Mentalities in the Renaissance*. Ed. Brian Vickers (Cambridge: Cambridge UP, 1984), 351-74.

Demos, John Putnam. *Entertaining Satan: Witchcraft and the Culture of Early New England*. New York: Oxford UP, 1982.

Eagleton, Terry. *William Shakespeare*. Oxford: Blackwell, 1986.

Furness, H. H., ed. *Macbeth*. New Variorum Shakespeare. Boston: J. B. Lipincott, 1873, repr. New York: Dover, 1963.

Ginzburg, Carlo. *The Night Battles: Witch and Agrarian Cults in the Sixteenth and Seventeenth Centuries*. Transl. John and Anne Tedeschi. London: Routledge & Kegan Paul, 1966, repr. 1983.

Gregory, Annabel. "Witchcraft, politics and good neighborhood in early 17th-century Rye." *Past & Present* 98 (1991), 31-66.

Guazzo, Francisco Maria. *Compendium Maleficarum* (Milan, 1608). Transl. E. A. Ashwin. Ed. Montague Summers. London: John Rodker, 1929.

Harris, Anthony. *Night's Black Agents: Witchcraft and Magic in Seventeenth-Century English Drama*. Manchester: Manchester UP, 1980.

Hattaway, M. "Women and Witchcraft, The Case of *The Witch of Edmonton*". *Trivium* 20 (1985), 49-68.
Henningsen, Gustav. *The Witches Advocate: Basque Witchcraft and the Spanish Inquisition 1609-1614*. Reno: Nevada UP, 1980.
James the First. *Daemomologie* (1597). Ed. G. B. Harrison. London: Bodley Head, 1924.
Jorgensen, Paul A. *Our Naked Frailties: Sensational Art and Meaning in 'Macbeth'*. Berkeley: California UP, 1971.
Kieckhefer, Richard. *European Witch Trials: Their Foundations in Popular and Learned Culture, 1300-1500*. London: Routledge & Kegan Paul, 1976.
Kittredge, George Lyman. *Witchcraft in Old and New England*. Cambridge, MA: Harvard UP, 1929. Repr. New York: Atheneum, 1972.
Klaits, Joseph. *The Age of the Witch Hunts*. Bloomington: Indiana UP, 1985.
Kunze, Michael. *Highroad to the Stake: A Tale of Witchcraft*. Chicago: Chicago UP, 1982.
Larner, Christina. "James the VI and I and Witchcraft." In *The Reign of James the VI and I*. Ed. Alan G. R. Smith (London: Macmillan, 1973), 74-90.
----. *Witchcraft and Religion: The Politics of Popular Belief*. Oxford: Blackwell, 1984.
Levack, Brian P. *The Witch-Hunt in early Modern Europe*. London: Longman, 1987.
Macdonald, Michael, ed. *Witchcraft and Hysteria in Elizabethan London: Edward Jordan and the Mary Glover Case*. London: Tavistock Routledge, 1991.
Macfarlane, Alan. *Witchcraft in Tudor and Stuart England*. London: Routledge & Kegan Paul, 1970.
Martin, Ruth. *Witchcraft and the Inquisition in Venice, 1550-1650*. Oxford: Blackwell, 1989.
McLuskie, Katherine. *Renaissance Dramatists*. London: Harvester Wheatsheaf, 1989.
Midlefort, H. C. Erik. *Witch Hunting in Southwestern Germany 1562-1684: The Social and Intellectual Foundations*. Stanford: Stanford UP, 1972.
Montaigne, Michel de. *Selected Essays*. Transl. John Florio (1603). Ed. L. G. Crocker. New York: Pocket Books, 1959.
Muchembled, Robert. *Popular Culture and Elite Culture in France, 1400-1750* (1978). Transl. Linda Cochrane. Baton Rouge: Louisiana State UP, 1985.
Muir, Kennith, ed. *Macbeth*. The Arden Shakespeare. London: Methuen, 1977.
*Newes from Scotland* (1591). Ed. G. B. Harrison. London: Bodley Head, 1924.
Norbrook, David. "Macbeth and the Politics of Historiography." In *Politics of Discourse: The Literature and History of Seventeenth-Century England*. Ed. Kevin Sharpe and Steven N. Zwicker (Berkeley: California UP, 1987), 78-116.
Notestein, Wallace. *The History of Witchcraft in England from 1558 to 1718* (1911). Repr. New York: Thomas Y. Crowell, 1968.

Pocton, Edward. "The Winnowing of White Witchcraft". British Library Sloane MS 1954: ff. 161-93.
Quaife, G. R. *Godly Zeal and Furious Rage: The Witch in Early Modern Europe*. New York: St. Martin's Press, 1987.
Roper, Lyndal. *Oedipus and the Devil*. London: Routledge, 1994.
Rosen, Barbara. *Witchcraft*. London: Edward Arnold, 1969.
Rowland, Robert. "'Fantasticall and Devilishe Persons': European Witch-beliefs in Comparative Perspective." In *Early Modern European Witchcraft: Centers and Peripheries*. Ed. Benst Ankarloo and Guster Henningsen (Oxford: Clarendon Press, 1990), 161-90.
Sawyer, Ronald C. "'Strangely Handled in All Her Lyms': Witchcraft and Healing in Jacobean England." *Journal of Social History* 22 (1989), 461-85.
Scarre, Geoffrey. *Witchcraft and Magic in Sixteenth- and Seventeenth-Century Europe*. Basingstoke and London: Macmillan, 1987.
Schalkwyk, David. "A Ladys 'Verily' Is as Potent as a Lord's - Women, Word and Witchcraft in *The Winters Tale*." *English Literary Renaissance* 22 (1992), 242-72.
Scot, Reginald. *The Discovery of Witchcraft* (1584). Ed. Brinsley Nicholson. Wakefield, Yorkshire, 1973.
Sharpe, C. K. *A Historical Account in the Belief in Witchcraft in Scotland*. Glasgow: Thomas D. Morrison, 1884.
Sharpe, J. A. "Witchcraft and Women in Seventeenth-Century England: Some Northern Evidence." *Continuity and Change* 6 (1991), 179-99.
----. *Witchcraft in Seventeenth Century Yorkshire: Accusations and Counter Measures*. York: University of York, 1992.
Sinfield, Alan. *Faultlines: Cultural Materialism and the Politics of Dissident Reading*. Oxford: Clarendon Press, 1992.
Sokol, B. J. "*The Tempest*, 'All torment trouble, wonder and amazement': a Kleinian reading." In *The Undiscover'd Country*. Ed. B. J. Sokol (London: Free Association Books, 1993), 179-216.
----. *Art and Illusion in 'The Winter's Tale'*. Manchester: Manchester UP, 1994. (1994a)
---. "Numerology in the time scheme of *The Tempest*". *Notes and Queries* 41 (1994), 53-5. (1994b)
Stallybrass, Peter. "Macbeth and Witchcraft." In *Focus on Macbeth*. Ed. John Russell Brown (London: Routledge & Kegan Paul, 1982), 189-209.
Swain, J. T. "The Lancashire Witch Trials of 1612 and 1634 and the Economics of Witchcraft." *Northern History* 30 (1994): 64-85.
Tedeschi, J. "The Question of Magic and Witchcraft in Two Unpublished Inquisitorial Manuals of the Seventeenth Century." *Proceedings of the American Philosophical Society* 131 (1987), 92-111.
Thomas, Keith. *Religion and the Decline of Magic*. London: Weidenfeld & Nicholson, 1971. Repr. Harmondsworth: Penguin, 1978.

Vickers, Brian. "Introduction". In *Occult and Scientific Mentalities in the Renaissance*. Ed. Brian Vickers (Cambridge: Cambridge UP, 1984), 337-49.

Weisman, Richard. *Witchcraft, Magic and Religion in 17th-Century Massachusetts*. Amherst: Massachusetts UP, 1984.

Wenterdorf, Karl. "Witchcraft and Politics in *Macbeth*." In *Folklore Studies in the Twentieth Century*. Ed. Venetia J. Newall (Woodbridge, Suffolk: D. S. Brewer; Totowa, NJ: Rowman & Littlefield, 1980), 431-37.

West, Robert Hunter. *The Invisible World: A Study of Pneumatology in Elizabethan Drama*. Athens: Georgia UP, 1939.

----. *Reginald Scot and Renaissance Writings on Witchcraft*. Boston: Twayne, 1984.

Weyer, Johann. *De praestigiis daemonum* (1583). Transl. John Shea. Bingham, NY: Medieval and Renaissance Texts and Studies, 1991.

Williams, Gordon. *'Macbeth': Text and Performance*. Basingstoke and London: Macmillan, 1985.

Wilson, John Dover, ed. *Macbeth*. New Cambridge Shakespeare. Cambridge: Cambridge UP, 1947, repr. 1980.

# CHANGING HISTORIES AND IDEOLOGIES OF "COLONIALIST" ENGLISH DRAMA: SHAKESPEARE'S *THE TEMPEST* AND FLETCHER AND MASSINGER'S *THE SEA-VOYAGE*[1]

Rachana Sachdev
(Susquehanna University)

The primary focus of this essay is the exploration of the changing historical positions of gender in the process of the construction of the "racial" Other in the colonialist encounter. Hendricks and Parker have pointed out that the discourse of "race" (as we understand the term) did not exist in the sixteenth century.[2] "Race" denoted primarily "common descent and origin" rather than "a group of several tribes or peoples, forming a distinct ethnical stock" (OED). But "pejorative" associations had already developed around the Irish as well as the Moors and the Amerindians in the sixteenth century, as Ann Jones and Peter Stallybrass, among others, discuss.[3] Moreover, the pamphleteers who were writing about the need to settle the New World were also actively engaged in the process of constructing discourses of difference. My purpose in this study is to examine the historical developments in this emerging discourse of "race" in the years between 1611 and 1622. I am specifically interested in exploring the connections between the emergence of this discourse and the increasing immigration of Englishwomen to the colonies in the seventeenth century. The shifting and developing histories of colonial relations between England and the American colonies in the ten or so intervening years between *The Tempest* and *The Sea-Voyage* produced significant changes in the dynamics of "race" and gender in the representation of the colonial space. Even though Fletcher took over the Miranda plot from Shakespeare as Dryden contended in the preface to his own version of *The Tempest*,[4] Fletcher's ideological position regarding the exiled female figure is very different, and is contingent on the English response to the political and social situation in the North American colonies in 1622.

Indeed, I argue that the writing of *The Sea-Voyage* was itself prompted by the increasing controversy surrounding the colonies, especially Virginia. As Carl Bridenbaugh has noted from his perusal of the Stationers' Company's Register, "1622 was a banner year for promotion literature."[5] The controversy about Sir Thomas Smythe's rule had erupted in 1621 and excited a lot of comment from both within the Virginia Company and the general public. There were also public debates about the need for the colonies in America in the same year.[6] The time was ripe for re-examining the colonial space in drama, as public interest was up and the ideological response to the colonies vastly more complicated than it was at the time Shakespeare wrote *The Tempest*. In this paper, I contend that Fletcher was consciously revising Shakespeare's colonial representations of gender and "race" in his version of the Miranda plot, and that gender was inextricably linked to the development of "race" in the 1620s after Englishwomen started immigrating to the colonies in significant numbers.

Helen Carr has argued, "Woman is the European Man's primary Other: using her as an image for the racial Other transfers the asymmetrical power relation embedded in her difference from the patriarchal dominant male."[7] To describe the natives through female or animal imagery was to envisage them as "another field for the exercise of power."[8] The Amerindians were located in a place of political powerlessness that rationalized their exploitation and suppression. In Shakespeare's *The Tempest*, the colonial enterprise can be seen to end with the male English colonizer incorporating racial difference, embodied in the male native Caliban, within pre-established structures of patriarchy in an almost nuptial arrangement: "This thing of darkness I / Acknowledge mine" (5.1.275-6).[9] Since married women could not own property or take legal action on their own after marriage, Prospero's "nuptial" speech effectively seals Caliban's status as powerless. The feminization of the native is enacted here almost fully, substantiating Carr's claim.

However, a further question relates to the status of women, both English and Amerindian, in the relations between the English and the Amerindians. Does gender difference disrupt the expression of a singular "racial" discourse by the English? The point to note here is that this hierarchy established between the English and the native races does not negate the dominance relations between the masculine and the feminine spheres, it only complicates them. The positioning of "racial" difference within gender difference by the Englishmen in the beginning of the colonialist enterprise created a hierarchy of devaluation in which Englishwomen, native men, and native women occupy different subordinate positions depending on the historical and political exigencies. Looking at Shakespeare's *The Tempest* allegorically, through the lens provided by the history of settlement patterns in North America, we notice that in the play "racial" difference supplements gender difference to exclude the non–European woman, Sycorax, most strongly. However, this paradigm established in Shakespeare's *The Tempest* is not the only model for power relations in the drama dealing with colonial relations in the Americas. Gender and "race" interact in varying ways within the colonialist paradigm.

If ideological structures are subject to disjunction from within, as Foucault has asserted, they are also subject to history. As the settlement process in Virginia proceeded and the socio–economic and political situations of the English in America changed, so did the intersections of "race" and gender. The dissemination of news and propaganda about the emigration of women and religious dissenters to the New World, along with the English political mismanagement in the colonies, provoked the production of dramatic situations and paradigms in *The Sea–Voyage* that reflect the deliberate destabilization of ideological categories from *The Tempest*. The changing history of the New World produced different needs at different moments, and these needs got inscribed especially in the English dramatic texts that were directly concerned with the dynamics of "race," gender, and sexuality in the creation of a "utopian" space.

In the patriarchally powerful world of *The Tempest*, Miranda, Ariel, and Caliban all properly occupy positions of subordination to Prospero even though the degree of their subjugation varies.[10] The degree of control exercised by Prospero varies in direct proportion to the possibility of rebellion and sexual deviancy embodied in the various characters. The need to control female power and sexuality had been repeatedly addressed in misogynistic pamphlets in the sixteenth and seventeenth centuries in England, and all Englishwomen were identified as at least potentially errant.[11] The emigration of English women to the colonies made their "excessive" sexuality even more threatening, as the Amerindians were also viewed both as politically dangerous and as "lewd" and sexually uncontained. James I instructed the royal council of Virginia in 1606 to punish adultery with death, even though such a law was not even considered seriously in England except, for a brief while, by the Puritans much later in the seventeenth century. The law to contain sexuality especially in the colonies addressed the fears that the possibility of sexual or social alliances between the natives and English women created in the minds of English men.[12] Since women could not be completely forbidden from the colonial space and were actually needed as wives for Englishmen in Virginia and New England, their social position and sexuality had to be rearticulated in the New World in accordance with the fears aroused by the possibility of their erotic and social response to native men. Making laws against adultery was just one of the ways to contain female power.

Miranda is the only female on the island in Shakespeare's *The Tempest*. I contend that the text produces Miranda in order to repress and thus purify femininity through exile. She is the representative English female figure who is isolated from the traditional social network so that she can be recuperated inside it after she has been purged of licentiousness. Miranda has no playmates except the patriarchal Prospero (the "monster" Caliban is excluded by Prospero), thus checking any tendencies she might have toward rebellion. The lack of female companionship[13] is also a major factor in the "cleansing" of Miranda, as any sexually active woman would be a source of weakness by authorizing female desire. This exclusion of the possibility of a woman's desire is what makes the exercise of patriarchal authority on Miranda totally unproblematic.

The exercise of the father's authority is accomplished with the help of the "spirit", Ariel. Ariel is the unthreatening symbol of almost ungendered and inactive native sexuality from whose portrait sexual desire is erased. The only way "he" can be gendered is if Sycorax's "earthy and abhorred commands" can be read as heterosexual demands for sexual subjugation.[14] Even if he can be imagined male, Ariel himself did not enjoy the prospect of sexual intercourse with Sycorax, the only female available, and preferred perpetual bondage to it. This should make him a safe companion for Miranda, but Miranda's sexuality, his "race" (in effect, his lineage that establishes his right to the island based on his previous occupancy of the island), and Prospero's dismissal of Sycorax as an ugly witch, disqualify him. Indeed, the rejection that could project Ariel as totally "spirit" and hence, non-sexual becomes the occasion for the savagization of the female appetite embodied in Sycorax. The "male" Ariel maintains his potential for sexual behavior and for revolt. As a non-English colonized, and as probable sexual partner, he is still subject to English fears about the disruption of their authority, despite the fact that he exhibits no desire for Miranda, and can only be imagined in bondage until the marriage and relocation of Miranda destroy all possibility of rebellion through the seduction/rape of the young English female.

Caliban, on the other hand, represents a direct threat to the virginity of the Englishwoman. The text produces Caliban not only to exoticize the expression of bestiality so that the English male can be seen as untainted, but also to outline exactly the sexual danger involved in the colonial enterprise. To prevent social or sexual alliances between English women and the Amerindians, the English patriarchy portrayed both women and the natives as sexually errant and in need of being controlled from the outside. The native male, in particular, needed to be governed strictly. The "colonization" of Caliban is specifically grounded in sexual behavior in the text as the oft-quoted lines demonstrate:

> I have us'd thee,
> Filth as thou art, with human care; and lodg'd thee
> In mine own cell, till thou didst seek to violate
> The honour of my child (1.2.247–50).[15]

Prospero uses the rationalization that later became one of the classics of the history of colonization and imperialism.[16] In a brilliant ideological move, he celebrates the beauty of the European woman, making her the object of universal male desire, while simultaneously removing her from a position of being seduced by the Other who has been demonized.[17] Caliban is bestialized and enslaved for disrupting the harmony of Miranda's sexless well-being. He is categorized as a "monster" and thenceforth denied control over his desires, sexual or otherwise.

The question that has not been asked so far relates to Miranda's status and sexual freedom as a consequence of this move on Prospero's part.[18] Is Miranda even free to recognize Caliban as a possible sexual partner, as a number of other English people in the seventeenth century did when they married the native inhabitants of America? Marriages between the Europeans and the Amerindians were not uncommon, especially amongst the French and the Spanish settlers in the Americas. The English did have a fair number of intermarriages as well. John Rolfe was not the only Englishman who proposed marriage to a native woman; Ralph Hamor, in his account of the life in Virginia published in 1614, narrates that Sir Thomas Dale, "the principal commander of the English men", wanted to marry Powhatan's youngest daughter, but was refused by Powhatan. Indeed, there was even an official policy supporting intermarriages around 1612.[19] Cunega, the Spanish ambassador at London in 1612 wrote to King Philip III about the English attempts to preserve the colony in Virginia: "Although some suppose the plantation to decrease, he is credibly informed that there is a determination to marry some of the people that go over to Virginians; forty or fifty are already so married, and English women intermingle and are received kindly by the natives; a zealous minister has been wounded for reprehending it."[20] It is noteworthy that English women were not encouraged to intermarry as the purpose was to increase the English population, and even though the law against English women's loss of status on marrying a non-white man had not been formulated in 1612, children of English women and native men would not be perceived as English, and hence, the English population would have suffered a setback had English women married the natives. The need to control English women's sexual freedom was paramount, since there were so few white women in Virginia.

In the context of the settlement of the New World, what would it mean, in any case, to imagine Miranda responding erotically to Caliban? As she herself realizes, Ferdinand is "the *third man* that e'er I saw; the first / That e'er I sighed for" (1.2..448–9). If Miranda recognizes Caliban as male, and the only male available to her sexually prior to Ferdinand's arrival, why is Caliban never an object of her desire?[21] The etymological identification between Miranda and "monster" makes this question even more urgent: "The attempted rape of Miranda by Caliban figures the translation of *Miranda* by *monster*. At their roots, before the word *monster* takes on the notion of deformity, both of these words signify something *marvelous* (OED)" (Cheyfitz 171). The semantic overlap between "Miranda" and "monster" suggests that the text is positing Miranda as at least a potential monster; more particularly, she is portrayed as the sexually uncontrollable monster, a female, about whom the misogynistic English pamphleteers were writing, a "monster" whom Prospero is trying to make into a "marvelous" object. The need to maintain Miranda's status as "marvelous" precludes the possibility of Miranda's desire for Caliban, because mating with Caliban has become synonymous with buggery[22] after Prospero's bestialization of him.[23] The play erases the process of active female sexuality from its surface and leaves in its stead only a guided response to an appropriate male desire. Caliban's wish to people the island with

"Calibans" is declared illegitimate by Prospero, and this authoritarian denial excludes Caliban as a sexual mate for Miranda. The naming of Caliban's sexual desire as rape precludes the possibility that Miranda might respond to it. This naming is particularly forceful because Miranda has not been imagined as growing up in a "normal" sexual environment. The first male response to her, the one that could determine the direction of her sexual response in future, is outlawed and made unavailable. The patriarchal world of *The Tempest* does not grant Miranda, the Englishwoman, even a remote chance at an alliance with the native Caliban.

The move that ideologically estranges Caliban also curtails Miranda's freedom, even though the directions of their superficial movements are totally different. Miranda moves up in the hierarchy from a woman to "a goddess" (1.2.424), whereas Caliban becomes identified as a "monster". Both these trajectories are restrictive. Prospero intentionally confines Miranda's sexual freedom in making her a "goddess", just as he deliberately denies Caliban political autonomy. The decision to curtail female sexual freedom was even more welcome in an immigrant situation, since the delimitation of sexual freedom was, and always has been, inseparable from the decision to deny women social or political power. The transformation from "monster" to "marvelous" is still not an enabling position for Miranda.

It is in terms of this attempted containment of women that Miranda's and Caliban's positions in *The Tempest* become clear. Miranda's efforts to "estrange" Caliban do not destroy the fact that in terms of power and position, she is closer to Caliban than to Prospero, and that is the danger that haunts Miranda in the play. Caliban's presence is a constant reminder to her of the possibility of descending from her position of relative control to the total lack of autonomy represented by him. Indeed, Miranda's own internalization, partial or whole, of the shared assumptions of the European men is what makes the hierarchies of devaluation so effective. She chastises Caliban in terms that are wholly in tune with Prospero's; she is effectively emptied of desire until the patriarchy embodied in Prospero can provide her with an appropriate desiring subject to whom she can respond; and when such a man is found, she is seen to follow Prospero's unstated dictates about her response to Ferdinand almost completely. Even her "desire" is barely threatening; it is channelled and controlled throughout from the outside. The desire begins, is controlled by, and is consummated under the direction of a patriarchal figure, Prospero: "It goes on, I see / As my soul prompts it" (1.2.422–3). This is the ideal response of chaste Englishwomen to their sexuality and their lives: they are to leave themselves to be guided and governed by patriarchal wishes. It then becomes the responsibility of the father to control his daughter, "lest too light winning / Make the prize light" (1.2.453–4).

Despite the colonists' various attempts at manipulating Englishwomen's sexual choice and desire, the possibility of sexual pleasure and female desire still remained. The Englishmen in the colonies were not able to form a perfect sexual space where female sexuality would be completely governed from the outside. Even within the colonialist paradigm, female desire and power had to be acknowledged. Indeed, just over ten years later, Fletcher introduced a "desiring" and powerful version of Miranda, Clarinda, in his revision of *The Tempest*. However, the early years of colonization were characterized by the attempts to deny women the possibility of active sexuality and power. Even though women made the same journey as the men, they were often not celebrated in the same ways; they were valued only for their ability to bear children within marriage.[24] The earliest texts about the New World are directly implicated in the desire to expurgate active English female sexuality from the "utopian" landscape they seek to create. Poverty, disease, and attacks by the Indians soon destroyed one part of the projected utopianism for most Englishmen, but the need to contain women remained.

In William Strachey's report[25] and in reports of Sir Thomas Gates's expedition, the ideal womanhood is an absent womanhood. Though women were present in Gates's expedition, they appear in the texts about the expedition largely as cries and screams that accompany storms ("The women lamented").[26] The one major exception is the recurrence in the pamphlets of the case of cannibalism in Virginia in 1609 in which a man was supposed to have killed and eaten his wife to survive the famine.[27] George Percy and Gates, both of whom were in command of Virginia at different times, gave out two versions of the story, one focusing on the poverty and misery of the times and the other on the man's hatred of his wife.[28] The introduction of easily credible wife–hatred in Gates' story adds a new dimension to the incident, and can be seen obliquely to address the male anxieties about the process of female migration from England and about the status of women both in England and in the colonies.

Despite this strong anti–feminine sentiment, Englishmen recognized the desirability and usefulness of Englishwomen in the colonial space, and a recuperative effort was necessary to establish their status as "good" mothers and wives. The end of Strachey's narrative highlights a marriage and a childbirth that are, according to Samuel Purchas, "the most holy civill and most naturall possession taken of the Bermudas by exercise of Sacraments Marriage, Childbirth, etc."[29] After being portrayed as "meat" for their husbands, women are recuperated as necessary figures who, as in Leo Marx's description of Miranda, make utopia possible. Interestingly, controlled female sexuality is imagined to be the solution to the problems caused by the eruption of illegitimate female power.

Fletcher and Massinger's *The Sea–Voyage*, written just before the time of the 1622 massacre of the English by the Amerindians in Virginia, focuses in on the problem of female sexuality in the colonial context as well. However, there the problem is presented without obvious reference to the American natives. The gap left by the fearful but exotic racial Other is filled in Fletcher's play by the two Portuguese[30] men, Sebastian and Nicusa, who "like shadows" inhabit the "desart" island, but even more so by the women under Rosella's dominion who, like the Indians in the early stages of the colonial settlement, are situated further "inside" the island both topographically and ideologically. Moreover, the women are seen to have established a commonwealth that leaves out men, an obvious aberration that needs immediate correction in the way that the inner "colonies" of the natives were to be taken over by the Europeans in the early stages of the settlement process.

However, the initial moments of the play present men as the substitutes for the missing Indians. Sebastian and Nicusa, his nephew, are the ones mistaken for "monsters" at the beginning:[31]

> *Amin.* But ha! what things are these,
> Are they humane creatures?
> *Tib.* I have heard of Sea–Calves.
> *Alb.* They are no shaddows sure, they have Leggs and Armes.
> *Tib.* They hang but lightly on though.
> *Amin.* How they looke, are they mens faces?
> *Tib.* They have Horse–Tayles growing to 'em, goodly long maines.
> *Amin.* Alas what sunk eyes they have!
> How they are crept in, as if they had been frighted!
> Sure they are wretched men! (1.4. 98–106)

Given the reverberations in this interchange with the scene when Stephano and Trinculo find Caliban in *The Tempest*,[32] it is worth examining in detail the politics of the discovery of the human behind the monster. Trinculo concludes that Caliban "is no fish, but an islander", but the text erases the memory of this discovery, and Caliban is addressed as "monster" almost throughout the play. In *The Sea–Voyage*, Caliban is embodied in an unambiguously human form: he has finally attained human status, or rather the humanity of Caliban has been ideologically established in the ten or so intervening years between *The Tempest* (1611) and *The Sea–Voyage* (1622). One part of the "humanity" of the savages could be established by educating them formally in English language and culture, as Miranda attempts to do with Caliban in *The Tempest*. Although Shakespeare's play projects the uselessness of such efforts, the English in Virginia were still involved in this project. In 1619 Sir Edwin Sandys obtained ten thousand acres of land in Henrico for the establishment of a college for the education of the native people. This was part of a larger move to Christianize and to integrate, however marginally, the natives in the social life of the colonists. Around the end of the second decade, the English opened up means of communication and encouraged even some social relations with the natives to coerce them gently to send their children to be educated by the English. The Indians, in fact, succeeded in the 1622 massacre as well as they did because they had nearly unlimited access to the English in their homes. John Smith details in *The Generall Historie* that on the morning of March 22, 1622, scores of Indians came to English households to trade or converse, "yea in some places sat downe at breakfast." The English had begun to accept the humanity of the native tribes, though still guardedly, before the massacre. As I will demonstrate later, savagery has a social and sexual rather than a racial character in *The Sea-Voyage*, and the Caliban figure gets inscribed into, and infects, almost all the major characters from *The Tempest* in Fletcher's play.

However, the "Indianization" of Sebastian and Nicusa is not complete. The parallel between the suffering Englishmen in Virginia in the second decade of the seventeenth century and the starving, desperate Sebastian and Nicusa, living on the edge of a virtual utopia though unable to realize the potential of the land, is too striking to be missed. Sebastian and Nicusa represent both the monstrous natives and the colonizing English who were fighting for survival against hunger and disease. The amalgamation of the two roles is arguably motivated by a variety of factors, one of them being the contemporary controversy regarding the corruption of the Virginia Company's officers. The Virginia Company of London presented a petition to James I in January 1622 to investigate the charges against Sir Thomas Smythe (the treasurer of the Company for the first twelve years) being circulated by the document "The Tragical Relation of the Virginia Assembly." This pamphlet had arrived in England about 1621 and listed the various horrors that the planters had to undergo in order to survive in Virginia. Smythe was supposed to be supporting legislation that punished minor offenses with "torturing and starving to death."[33] The reports of starvation of the English in Virginia, in particular, aroused doubts about the absolute "rightness" of the rule by the Virginia Company and may well have prompted the presentation of Sebastian and Nicusa as both savage and European.

The ambivalence toward the English colonial enterprise was also exacerbated by the establishment of the separatists' colony at Plymouth in 1620 which divided the public in England along the lines of religion. Michael Nerlich's analysis has highlighted the disjunctions within the English commercial and colonial enterprises even in the early phase, but these instabilities increased with the introduction of religious differences.[34] By 1622, when *The Sea-Voyage* was written, the segregationists had already moved to Plymouth from Holland. Bradford articulated the anxieties of the pilgrim fathers before their move to the New World:

> On the other hand, for Virginia, it was objected, That if they lived among the English which were there planted, or so near them as to be under their government; they should be in as great danger to be troubled and persecuted for their Cause of religion, as if they lived in England: and it might be, worse [troubled].[35]

Bradford's statements point to the fact that the establishment of the colony of the religious dissenters in New England had a significant effect on the way the New World was perceived.[36] It was no longer possible to see the English in the New World as one homogeneous ideological unit living in the midst of the homogeneous mass of the "savages." When combined with the controversy about Smythe's rule, the segregationists' migration to Plymouth created an atmosphere of uncertainty, confusion, and divided loyalties in England that informs the ideologically fractured representation of almost all the characters in the play.

The differences in the religious identities of the English in America necessitated an even sterner attempt to reformulate a vision of the sanctity of the Englishmen. To maintain colonial ambitions, it was important to preserve a notion of self that was ideologically different from the way the natives were perceived.

This difference is seen to be initially destabilized in *The Sea-Voyage*, which deals explicitly with the threat of cannibalism that erupted in the earlier moments of colonization. Lamure, an "usuring merchant", suggests that he and his fellows in hardship and starvation eat Aminta:

> *Lam.* Why should we consume thus, and starve,
> Have nothing to relieve us;
> And she live there that bred all our miseries,
> Unrosted, or unsod?
> *Mor.* I have read in stories —
> *Lam.* Of such restoring meates, we have examples;
> Thousand examples, and allow'd for excellent;
> Women that have eate their Children,
> Men their slaves, nay their brothers: but these are nothing;
> Husbands devoured their wives (they are their chattels,)
> And of a Schoolemaster that in a time of famine,
> Powdered up all his Schollers (3.1. 96–106).

The parenthetical remark in Lamure's statement serves as Lamure's rationalization of *this* version of cannibalism, which involves the eating of wives by their husbands. Interestingly, the only rationalized cannibalism presented in these lines is the one that is actually reported to have occurred contemporaneously: the devouring of a wife by a husband. Aminta, the intended victim, obviously resists such an interpretation, and calls Lamure and his followers "barbarous" and unchristian; Tibalt, the master of the ship, condemns them as "devils", but he does so based almost solely on class rank. Hence, even though Lamure's rationalization does not work for everyone, the emphasis on women's guilt remains, and is supplemented by the barbarity of the lower classes. If cannibalism had threatened to disrupt a vision of the difference between the Englishmen and the natives, the destabilization is revealed to be only temporary; order is reasserted soon by pushing the blame out on the women and the lower classes. *The Sea-Voyage* repeats the trajectory of the Gates report in finding a scapegoat in the Englishwomen.

Fletcher and Massinger attempt to justify the incident of cannibalism in Virginia and partly remove the slur from English masculinity by placing it amongst the histories of similar cases in other nations, and by making an "evil" woman the "chattel" to satisfy hungry men. As they still can not erase the incident, they insert a much more relativistic statement than Gates by putting some Europeans on the level of the so–called savages. But instead of destroying the differences between the English and the natives, the creation of a relativistic world eventually helps in the restoration of the "proper" English masculinity. The text creates a disjunction among the colonizing European community in order to show that some of its parts are also in need of being civilized, and that disjunction predictably works along class and gender lines. To exile the threat of cannibalism from within the English community, women and the lower classes had to be more restrictively governed.

Fletcher and Massinger also portray the flip side of the coin in the representation of a commonwealth of women that appears to grant them the possibility of autonomy and self–government. Rosella, the "Governess of the Amazonian Portugals", has declared herself and her women inveterate enemies to men because the French pirates killed their husbands and loved ones out of greed. These women live on a lush and beautiful island, with the proverbial natural riches of the New World. Rosella's prosperous and just kingdom keeps the women satisfied on a material level, though deprived sexually, because, as Rosella understands, sexual submission to men would translate into social and political subjugation.

However, she is not able to convince her "citizens" of the need for celibacy. Hippolita, Crocale, and Juletta, the members of this commonwealth, introduce us to their dilemma:

*Cro.* Here we live secure,
And have among our selves a Common–wealth,
Which in our selves begun, with us must end.
*Jul.* I there's the misery (2.2. 17–20).

Spoken at the very moment the audience learns about the commonwealth, these lines characterize the feminist enterprise as always already problematic. Female autonomy and female appropriation of power are represented as based on an unrealistic attempted erasure of sexuality. However, as Rosella's willing abrogation of her power on meeting her husband establishes, her exclusion of men from the commonwealth is a denial only of illegitimate sexuality, and not of all desire. As soon as desire finds an ideologically acceptable object, it can function without hindrance. Despite the portrayal of female autonomy and governance of a commonwealth, Rosella's commonwealth does not really contest the conclusion suggested by Strachey's narrative that women's place in the New World could only be established through marriage and childbirth. The corollary to the necessity of "proper" marriage and childbirth is the patriarchal control of sexual desire, and Rosella is the "patriarch" in *The Sea-Voyage* who seeks to restrain female libidinous desires.

Since *The Sea-Voyage* repeats the situation of *The Tempest* with a gender reversal in the role of the hegemonic figure, it is interesting to watch the dynamics of the control of female sexuality by a woman. Since Rosella has outlawed men and sexual desire, the women have to live their lives asexually. However, as soon as men, *any men*, appear on the scene, sexual desire takes over the scene not only for the previously married and hence, knowledgeable women, but also for the "innocent" Clarinda:

*Cro.* I see, that by instinct,
Though a young mayd hath never seen a man,
Touches have titillations, and inform her (2.2.184–86).

In showing the outbreak of "natural" female sexuality in the presence of men, the text normalizes this behavior, supporting the notion that women are naturally licentious. Moreover, this representation of female libido destabilizes Rosella's authority by showing her natural complicity with this demonstration of sexual appetite. In a problematic move, Rosella gives in to the clamorings of the other

## The Tempest and The Sea-Voyage 291

women for sexual fulfillment, although ostensibly only for procreative purposes. She attempts to be a true colonialist by seeking to extend her empire through natural birth, but the text highlights her status as a woman because she decides to accept a partner herself. This is where her authority is most seriously jeopardized. Despite her established rule and her unquestioned interjection in the male domain of colonizing, and despite the fact that she does possess real power, she cannot upset gender hierarchy in matters of sexuality. When she decides to play the sexual role, she is reduced to a "woman", and as a woman, she does not get to choose her own partner from her captives; she has to be chosen by a man who would desire her.[37] Tibalt, the captain of the ship, chooses Rosella, establishing the necessary precedence of men over women in sexual matters, and highlighting the inability of a woman to maintain a patriarchal role. Since all women are proverbially licentious, no woman can restrain other women.

    Rosella is the Prospero figure in her attempts to regulate female sexuality, though without his "magic", that is, without his masculinity, she is totally ineffective, and is finally unable to control even herself. The difference between the ideological status of her "patriarchal" wishes and Prospero's is visible in the fact that despite Rosella's approval of Albert, the text does not end with Clarinda marrying Albert. Significantly, "patriarchal" dictates when enforced only by a female figure do not have complete authority and success. Only the father can decide what is legitimate sexual desire for his daughter—at the end of the play, it does not matter whom Clarinda desires, or whom Rosella desires for her daughter. Clarinda will be given over by the father whom she has hardly even seen, to a suitor who desires her: "*Seb.* Sir, in your looks,/ I read your suite of my *Clarinda* : she is yours (5.1.)." Only male desire can be given legitimacy and thus only male desire will be successful.[38] This is particularly true as the play portrays two women vying for Albert's love, as against *The Tempest*'s model of one woman for one man (two men, if we count Caliban as a "man"). Female desire *is* excessive and dangerous in *The Sea-Voyage*.

It is particularly so in the persona of Clarinda. The exclusion of a Caliban figure who can be openly bestialized for his errant sexuality has the ideological purpose of incorporating racial denigration into sexual difference. The only person whose sexual desire is declared improper by the play is Clarinda, who loves the already affianced Albert and who, through her position, can destroy his happiness. In simultaneously portraying the woman who has never seen a man, and in unguardedly loving Albert despite external obstacles, she is both Miranda and Caliban, the one who should only be desired and the one who desires inappropriately. There is already another female figure, Aminta, who has claimed Albert's loyalty and love and who renders Clarinda's desire errant. Clarinda is presented as a "native" woman who indecorously loves the visiting European man and takes the initiative in a move similar to Caliban's when he tried to start sexual relations with Miranda, even though Clarinda's attempt obviously does not involve the threat of actual rape. This is an important ideological move in the context of the increasing emigration of single Englishwomen to the colonies as mates for the Englishmen in the second decade of the seventeenth century. The Virginia Company of London sent ninety "young maids to make wives for so many of the former tenants" in 1619 alone (Kingsbury, I, 115). The only suitable wives for the Englishmen in Virginia were the Englishwomen sent by the authoritative Virginia Company and by other Englishmen, and not the native women to be found in the New World. The text is erasing the possibility of miscegenation and misalliance by insisting on the intervention of the father in the marriage, and also by eliminating the threat of the "other" woman. The need to exclude "native" women from the sphere of legitimate sexuality was so strong that it even gave birth to illegal activities in England to provide mates for the men in Virginia. A letter from Sir Edward Hexter to the Privy Council (Oct. 19, 1618) describes the activities of one Owen Evans who "under cover of being a messenger of the Chamber" had ordered the constable to press five maidens for Virginia in the hundred of Whiteleigh, had given 5/– to another to press six maidens, 1/– to Jacob Pryste to press his own daughter and had received 10/– protection money from Ottery to keep away." Such was the terror that "40 maidens fled out of one parish."[39] The bribery and abduction of women in England in the interests of forced migration to the American colonies supports the reading that, as the colonialist project went on, it became increasingly more cautious about the position of women in the formulation of "race".

This mistrust of women and their sexuality leads to a crucial question about the amalgamation of Miranda and Caliban in Clarinda. Fletcher and Massinger are much less optimistic about the possibility of the control of female and native desire in the New World, both because the restraining authority was itself fractured and less effective, and because the colonial Englishwomen approximated savagery too closely. The colonial enterprise received further setbacks in the resistance of the native tribes to the christianizing efforts of the English, the inability of the English to force the matter due to their own dependency for food on the natives, and the attempts by the migrating Englishwomen to capitalize on their limited numbers. The reality of socio–economic struggle in the colonies in the initial years of hardship in Virginia exacerbated the need to keep the presentation of the ideological threats to the English survival to a minimum.[40] Since English male authority could not be celebrated in unproblematic ways any more, there was a greater need for the reconceptualization of the positions of Caliban and Miranda: they were assimilated into the more manageable figure of the "Creole" woman who was simultaneously other and English, and who did not inhabit a space religiously and ideologically alien to the English so that the importation of a strong patriarchal figure could control the expression of alterity effectively. The ability of the father, Sebastian, to regulate Clarinda's sexuality is what distinguishes her from the danger represented by Sycorax and Caliban in Shakespeare's play. Clarinda's savagization provides the means for the excision of the uncontrollable alterity of the non–English savage. Instead of the "savages", the Englishwomen have to be recuperated from their partial immersion in the savage mode by the assertion of rightful male authority, and the text affirms that this recuperation is a necessity.

The necessity arises out of the economic desires of the English people. Fletcher and Massinger's play reflects a growing divide between the English in England and those in the New World. In a very significant way, the English were "feminizing" and colonizing not only the native populations of America, but also their own countrymen in the colonies. The formation of the Separatists' colony at Plymouth had already deepened a divide created by the migration to the "savage" land and by the struggle over control of the financial gains.[41] Thus, both the Prospero and the Miranda figures in *The Sea-Voyage* can be seen as tainted with the Caliban deviancy. What "recovers" the "Englishness" is the hope of gain: in *The Sea-Voyage*, the land inside the outer region of desert is fertile, and there is plenty of game. The mistake the two Portuguese men make is that they attempt to leave the land before its wealth has been fully exploited. They need to move inward, to recuperate and appropriate the infinitely recuperable female space, as Albert, the "French Pirate" seeks to do, and as the English were trying to do in their efforts to stay alive in Virginia. The official reports of the Virginia Company in the 1620s reiterated that the tenants in Virginia were starving because they were lazy and unenterprising. They had to make a sterner move to appropriate the interior space. Even though *The Sea-Voyage* offers a more ambiguous message about the New World than *The Tempest*, it does move beyond the horrors of starvation and un–English cannibalism that the reports from Virginia had enumerated by reinstating patriarchy at the end, a move that ideologically restores the fertility of the land at the same time that it positions Englishmen as the just and rightful rulers over women and natives in the colonial space.

*Notes*

1. John Fletcher and Philip Massinger, "*The Sea-Voyage*" in *The Dramatic Works in the Beaumont and Fletcher Canon*, ed. Fredson Bowers (Cambridge: Cambridge UP, 1994), IX. All references to the play are to this edition.

2. Patricia Parker and Margo Hendricks, ed., *Women, 'Race', and Writing in the Early Modern Period* (New York: Routledge, 1994), 2.

3. Ann Rosalind Jones and Peter Stallybrass, "Dismantling Irena: The Sexualizing of Ireland in Early Modern England", *Nationalisms and Sexualities*, eds Andrew Parker, Mary Russo, Doris Summer, and Patricia Yaegar (New York & London: Routledge, 1992), 157–71.

4. John Dryden, "Preface", *The Tempest, or The Enchanted Island* in *The Works of John Dryden*, eds Maximillian E. Novak and George Guffey (Berkeley: California UP, 1970), X, 4.

5. Carl Bridenbaugh, *Vexed and Troubled Englishmen* (New York: Oxford UP, 1968), 405 n.

6. See Susan Myra Kingsbury, *Records of the Virginia Company* (Washington, D.C., 1906), III, 518–24, 605–7, 637–8, and 645–6, for details of the debates and the controversy surrounding Smythe and mismanagement of the Virginia company.

7. Helen Carr, "Woman/Indian: 'The American' and His Others", *Europe and Its Others* (Colchester, Essex: Essex UP, 1985), 46–60.

8. Leo Marx, *The Machine in the Garden: Technology and the Pastoral Ideal in America* (London and New York: Oxford UP, 1964), 43. Marx goes on to demonstrate how the rhetoric of the "hideousness" of the Bermudas intersected with the rhetoric of colonization in Strachey's report.

9. A number of critics have dealt with this issue, though the list is too long to be detailed here. See particularly Stephen Greenblatt, *Learning to Curse: Essays on Early Modern Culture* (New York: Routledge, 1990); Peter Hulme, *Colonial Encounters: Europe and the Native Caribbean, 1492–1797* (London & New York: Routledge, 1992); Peter Jennings, *The Invasion of America* (Chapel Hill: North Carolina UP, 1975); Leo Marx, *The Machine in the Garden* (note 8), esp. ch. 2; Eric Cheyfitz, *The Poetics of Imperialism* (New York & Oxford: Oxford UP, 1991); and Bernard Sheehan, *Savagism and Civility: Indians and Englishmen in Colonial Virginia* (Cambridge: Cambridge UP, 1980).

10. In the case of *The Tempest*, this repressiveness has been commented on by various critics who have read the imprisonment of Caliban by Prospero as a necessary ideological move for the establishment of Prospero's "golden world". For colonialist readings of *The Tempest*, see particularly Karen Flagstad, "'Making This Place Paradise': Prospero and the Problem of Caliban in The Tempest", *Shakespeare Studies* 18 (1986): 205–33; Meredith Anne Skura, "Discourse and the Individual: The Case of Colonialism in The Tempest", *Shakespeare Quarterly*, 40, 1(1989): 42–69; Paul Brown, "'This Thing of Darkness I / Acknowledge Mine': The Tempest and the Discourse of Colonialism", *Political Shakespeare*, ed. Jonathan Dollimore and Alan Sinfield (Manchester, U.K.: Manchester UP, 1985): 48–71; Thomas Cartelli, "Prospero in Africa: *The Tempest* as Colonial Text and Pretext", *Shakespeare Reproduced: The Text in History and Ideology*, eds Jean Howard and Marion O'Connor (New York & London: Methuen, 1987), 99–115; Alden Vaughan and Virginia Mason Vaughan, *Shakespeare's Caliban: A Cultural History* (Cambridge: Cambridge UP, 1991). In this paper, my attempt is to locate "The Woman's Part" in the colonialist readings of the oppression of the other.

11. See Katharine Usher Henderson and Barbara F. McManus, *Half Humankind* (Urbana: Illinois UP, 1985) and Linda Woodbridge, ed., *Women and the English Renaissance* (Urbana: Illinois UP, 1984).

12. See, for example, William Walter Hening, ed., *Statutes at Large* (13 vols; Richmond, VA, 1809–23), 1: 69.

13. For a discussion of the problematic status of Miranda's mother within the play, see Stephen Orgel, "Prospero's Wife", *Shakespeare Reproduced: The Text in History and Ideology*, eds Jean Howard and Marion O'Connor (New York: Methuen, 1987).

14. Ariel has almost always been portrayed as male in theatrical productions. Dryden and Davenant's gendering of Ariel as distinctly male probably has a great deal to do with it, as the operatic version that popularized *The Tempest* to the eighteenth century and after was based on this version of the play. Though Ariel has been recuperated, along with Caliban, in various studies as a representative of different colonized peoples, the issue of his gender has been largely ignored in recent critical studies, except by Rob Nixon in his essay, "Caribbean and African Appropriations of *The Tempest*", *Critical Inquiry* (Spring 1987): 557–78. For an unproblematic reading of Ariel as male, among others, see Jose Enrique Rodo, *Ariel*, trans. A. J. Simpson (Boston: Houghton–Mifflin, 1922). See also George Lamming, *The Pleasures of Exile* (London: Michael Joseph, 1960), esp. 95–150; and Edward Brathwaite, *Islands* (London: Oxford UP, 1969), 34– 38.

15. William Shakespeare, *The Tempest*, ed. Frank Kermode, Arden edition (1954; New York: Routledge, 1983).

16. Octave Mannoni's *Prospero and Caliban: The Psychology of Colonization*, trans. Pamela Powesland (1948; Ann Arbor: U of Michigan P, 1990) locates racism in what he calls the "Prospero complex," that is, the sexual guilt related to Prospero's desire for Miranda. But whether or not we accept Mannoni's Freudian reading, we still have to contend with the fact that nearly every imperialist and colonialist regime has provided similar paradigms in which the natives fantasize about raping the colonizing nation's women. E. M. Forster's *The Passage to India* (New York: Harcourt, Brace & Co., 1924) is only one of the numerous texts that deal with the anxieties produced by the projected superiority, sexual and otherwise, of the colonizer. See also Franz Fanon, *Black Skins, White Masks*, trans. Charles Lam Markmann (London & Sydney: Pluto Press, 1986).

17. Lorie Jerrell Leininger stresses Miranda's role as "sexual bait" in "The Miranda Trap: Sexism and Racism in Shakespeare's *Tempest*", *The Woman's Part*, eds Carol Ruth Swift Lenz, Gayle Greene and Carol Thomas Neely (Urbana & Chicago: Illinois UP, 1980), 285–94.

18. Coppelia Kahn and Mark Taylor have dealt with the question of Caliban's desire, and with Prospero's own psychological and social reasons for denying legitimacy to it, but not with Miranda's response to it. See Kahn, "The Providential Tempest and Shakespearean Family", *Representing Shakespeare*, eds Murray Schwartz and Coppelia Kahn (Baltimore: Johns Hopkins UP, 1980): 217–243; and Taylor, *Shakespeare's Darker Purpose: A Question of Incest* (New York: AMS Press, 1982), esp. chs. 5 and 6.

19. Indeed, in terms of the projected colonization of America, marriage with the native inhabitants was one possibility that Robert Beverly, writing at the end of the seventeenth century, strongly wished had been realized more forcefully:

> Intermarriage had been indeed the Method proposed very often by the Indians in the Beginning, urging it frequently as a certain Rule, that the English were not their friends, if they refused it. And I can't but

think it wou'd have been happy for that country, had they embraced this Proposal.

See Beverly, *The History and Present State of Virginia* (Chapel Hill: North Carolina UP, 1947), 38. Beverly dislocates the desire for intermarriage from the English to the Indians to mask the need of the English for such unions at the beginning of the colonialist enterprise.

20. Noel Sainsbury, ed. *Calendar of State Papers*, Colonial Series (Vaduz: Kraus Reprint Co., 1964), I, 1575–1660, 13.

21. My position here is that the uncertainty about Caliban's status as a human is deliberately constructed in the text. The ideological need to justify the Englishmen's claim to Virginia necessitates that we don't see Caliban as fully human. Of course there is no way to know what the visitors to the Americas saw when they saw the natives, given the contrary positions in the contemporary discourses and the ideological nature of the discourses themselves, but the playtext gives us enough indication of the "humanity" of Caliban.

22. *OED* defines buggery as "Unnatural intercourse of a human being with a beast, or of men with one another, sodomy"; it documents that in 1538, it was "enacted that the vice of buggorie committed with man kynd or beast be adjudged felonie."

23. For ideological purposes, both Prospero and Miranda see him as a "monster" and a "freckled whelp hag-born" (1. 2. 283) after this incident. The fact that his external appearance still proves him human is attested to in Trinculo's "discovery" speech in 2. 2.

24. William Wood and Edward Johnson both mention the ability of women to bear children on the voyage as their supreme heroic achievement. See Johnson's *Wonder Working Providence* (NY: Barnes & Noble, 1967); and William Wood, *New England's Prospect* (NY: B. Franklin, 1967).

25. William Strachey, "A True Reportory of the Wracke" (1610) in Samuel Purchas, *Purchas His Pilgrimes* (1625; Glasgow: James MacLehose & Sons, 1906), XIX, 5–72.

26. "A True Declaration of the Estate of the Colonie in Virginia", published by the Virginia Council (1610). Republished in Peter Force, *Tracts and Other Papers Relating Principally to the Origin, Settlement, and Progress of the Colonies in North America* (Washington, D.C.: Wm. Q. Force, 1846), III.

27. Even though this incident is missing from Shakespeare's play, cannibalism is directly inscribed in Fletcher's revision of the colonialist paradigm in *The Sea-Voyage*. See the discussion below.

28. George Percy, "A Trewe Relacyon of the proceedings and Occurents of moment Which have Happened in Virginia from ...1609, until ...1612", *Virginia: Four Personal Narratives* (New York: Arno, 1972). Gates's version is told in "The True Declaration" (1610).

29. Quoted in Philip Brockbank, "*The Tempest*: Conventions of Art and Empire", *The Later Shakespeare*, eds John Russell Brown and Bernard Harris (N.Y.: St. Martin's Press, 1967), 195.

30. There is a possible hint about the "savagery" of the Portuguese in the text, particularly as the men are pirates, and as England was involved in many struggles for loot with other European nations. However, as the "good" characters are French, and France was also one of the rivals for

empire in the New World, it is difficult to make clear ideological alignments between these projected nationalities and the English interest.

31. Daniel Morley McKeithan suggests that the text leads us to suppose in the beginning that Fletcher has revised Shakespeare's play by providing a male version of Miranda, but goes on to dispel that belief. See McKeithan's *The Debt to Shakespeare in the Beaumont and Fletcher Plays* (New York: AMS, 1970), 178.

32. See *The Tempest* (2.2.24–37):

> Trin. What have we here? a man or a fish? dead or alive? A fish: he smells like a fish.... Legg'd like a man! and his fins like arms! I do now loose my opinion, hold it no longer: this is no fish, but an islander that hath lately suffered by a thunderbolt.

33. Preface to "A Brief Declaration of the Plantation of Virginia" in George Bancroft, *Colonial Records of Virginia* (Richmond: R. F. Walker, 1874), 68.

34. Michael Nerlich, *The Ideology of Adventure: Studies in Modern Consciousness, 1100–1750*, trans. Ruth Crowley ( 2 vols.; Minneapolis: U of Minnesota P, 1987), I, 130. See also Julie Robin Solomon, "Going Places: Absolutism and Movement in Shakespeare's *The Tempest*", *Renaissance Drama* n.s. XII (1991): 3–45.

35. William Bradford, *Bradford Ms.*, folio 55. Quoted in Edward Arber, ed., *The Story of the Pilgrim Fathers, 1606–23 A.D.: As Told by Themselves, Their Friends, and Their Enemies* (New York: Kraus Reprints Co., 1969).

36. For a detailed examination of the movement of the pilgrim fathers from Leyden to New England, see William Bradford, *Of Plymouth Plantation, 1620–1647*, ed. Samuel Eliot Morison, (New York, 1963); and Edward Arber, ed. *The Story of the Pilgrim Fathers*.

37. Women did have the power to choose their own mates in Virginia, but the authorities soon realized the need to curtail their freedom, as men started bringing in cases of broken marriage promises. Apparently, women were attempting to cash in on the sex ratio to cancel previous engagements in favor of more financially secure mates, or to contract "themselves to two severall men at one time." See "Law Against Unlawful Implied Contracts of Marriage", *Records of the Virginia Company*, ed. Susan Myra Kingsbury, IV, 487.

38. The question still remains as to who is the legitimating authority in this play since the Prospero figure is either a woman, and thus not "patriarchal" enough, or Sebastian, whose ideological status is tainted by the memory of his Caliban–like existence on the island.

In Virginia, in the second decade, the legitimacy of desire was a class issue as well. The laws outlined in *The Proceedings of the Virginia Assembly* (1619) insist that "No maide or woman servant, either nowe resident in the Colonie or thereafter to come, shall contract herselfe in marriage without either the consente of her parents, or of her Mr or Mris, or of the magistrate and minister of the place both together" (Kingsbury, 173–4). Also reproduced in *Narratives of Early Virginia*, ed. Lyon G. Tyler, 249–78.

39. Noel Sainsbury, *Calendar of State Papers*, I, 22. For the Virginia Company's efforts to transport brides for the men, see Susan Myra Kingsbury, *Records of the Virginia Company* I, 256–7; III 115, 313, 493–4, 505, 526, 583, 640, 648–9; IV 522. The company not only tried to provide the men with brides, it also attempted to control which women came to the colonies: "We

have used extraordinary dilligence and care in the choice of them and have received none of whom we have not had good testimony of their honest life and cariadge, which together with their names we send here inclosed for the sattisfaccon of such as shall marry them" (505).

40. See George Percy, "A Trewe Relacyon of the Proceedings," for a list of the unending tribulations of the English in Virginia.

41. For negative reports of the Plymouth plantation that were circulated in England in the 1620s and that were based on religious differences, see Bradford's *Of Plymouth Plantation*. There were also a number of tracts published in the 1630s and later that documented atrocities perpetrated in New England based on religious and social differences. See Major John Childe, "New Englands Jonas Cast up at London" (1647) and "Simplicities Defence Against Seven-headed Policy" (1646). Both have been reproduced in Peter Force, *Tracts*, IV.

# SHAKESPEARE'S SECRETS: FAMILY, POLITICS, RELIGION, AND A SOURCE FOR *LOVE'S LABOURS LOST*

Margarita Stocker
(St Hilda's College, Oxford)

This paper addresses itself to what might be called the intersection between Shakespeare and history: by which I mean, first, some manifestations of the impact of contemporary Reformation politics upon Shakespeare's personal life; and second, his encrypted response to those politics, in a play which is generally acknowledged to be an enigma, and has remained mysterious even to this day. The polemical iconography deployed by religionists during the Reformation can throw light on a number of Shakespeare's secrets. One of these – why he named his daughters as he did – has not even been recognised as such. Another, the question of Shakespeare's religion, has remained highly controversial. And the third is the weird anomaly of *Love's Labours Lost*, a comedy which has appeared very opaque, and for which, near-uniquely amongst his plays, no generally agreed sources have been identified. (Whilst, like this play, both *Tempest* and *Midsummer Night's Dream* lack an identified source-plot, they do possess generally recognised sources.) It is a *roman-à-clef* which has yet to be unlocked. These three puzzles are, I suggest, in fact just one.

In an attempt to unlock the mysteries of *Love's Labours Lost*, Frances Yates sought the answer in the hermetic Renaissance ideas which were her special expertise, but her theory has not carried conviction.[1] What I propose, instead, is that in order to illuminate this curious comedy we need to look not at recondite Renaissance lore, but, on the contrary, at well-known, popular and commonly understood Reformation ideas. And these ideas were profoundly imbricated in the recent events and topicalities of Shakespeare's own time. This comedy's meaning may have been difficult of access to us, and Yates therefore sought its origins in ideas difficult of access to Renaissance spectators as well; but in so doing she failed to bridge the gap between our time and Shakespeare's. What the play drew on, I suggest, was extremely familiar to its original audiences: the biblical iconography which was common coin in the heated and protracted Reformation debate between Protestants and Catholics. Within the play, a sophisticated deployment of this iconography is combined with extensive allusion to recent events. The message which Shakespeare intended to convey in *Love's Labours Lost* was historically specific and politically daring, but not difficult for a contemporary audience to decode. Had it been, Shakespeare would, of course, have been wasting his time.

The specific historical circumstances which interlink with this play, Shakespeare's religion, and his family's own history, are illuminated by an exploration of the biblical iconographies which centred on the Old Testament heroine Judith. The long history of her representations, from ancient times to the present, I have described in a book;[2] here, however, I am concerned only with Shakespeare's Judiths, and the surprising extent to which they may help us understand both Shakespeare's history and his response to contemporary history.

*Shakespeare's Daughters*

Both of Shakespeare's daughters were given names derived from the Old Testament Apocrypha: Judith and Susannah. In the context of Reformation history – the world which Shakespeare inhabited – these were highly significant baptisms. These were not, in the contentious and often dangerous sixteenth-century ambience of religious schism, names to be chosen just because a parent liked the sound of them. The connotations of biblical names were both iconographic and denominational.

Calvin instructed Protestants to choose for their children biblical names: it was a sign that they would live in the Word.[3] Consequently, by the later sixteenth century, it had become common for Protestants to prefer biblical nomenclature for their children, two of the most popular given names being Judith and Susannah. Both Apocryphal names became personal and familial signifiers of radical Protestantism, and hence were particularly popular, in England, amongst Puritans. In other words, the historical juncture at which Shakespeare chose these names for his daughters was one in which they were highly meaningful, meaningful indeed in a way which reflected the central issue of the times.

Along with her twin brother Hamnet, Judith was named for familial friends, Hamnet and Judith Sadler. But this does not preclude the name's biblical significance. Often particular names were chosen precisely because they combined kinship sentiment – perpetuating a relative's name – and Protestant significance. Thus the American Puritan Samuel Sewall named a daughter Judith after the maternal line but also because "the Signification of it [is] very good".[4] In order to achieve this effect, indeed, it was necessary for such Protestants to make choices about which kin-names they would perpetuate, and on occasion to abandon them. In so far as they could, they subsumed familial within religious piety, the latter being the more potent. Where kin-names did not offer biblical forenames they were abandoned.

Moreover, the godmother Judith Sadler's own name was probably inspired by Protestant preferences and the royal 'second Judith', the Protestant queen. Elizabeth I had long been typed in Protestant propaganda as England's Judith. Thus in 1588, when the fashion for Hebraic names was already long-established, England's victory over Catholic Spain was celebrated in a popular ballad as "Judith's" over her enemy Holofernes, Elizabeth's over Philip II.[5] The parallel between the Queen and the Apocryphal heroine was a commonplace, and when a daughter was named Judith loyalty to the Queen, nationalism and Protestantism were mutually confirming connotations. To select this name was one way of affirming one's godly, loyal Englishness. It was a social and political as much as a familial act.

Equally, in Shakespeare's case choosing the name Judith for his younger daughter meant that his daughters' names were a brace specific to the Apocrypha. In the later sixteenth-century context this was saying something. Quite what it was saying is another matter, since the Apocrypha themselves were becoming an increasingly contentious element in Reformation propaganda, and we will return to this later.[6]

The puzzle is the more interesting in that it may be connected with a perennial query in Shakespeare's biography: to wit, what was his religion? The baptismal names of his daughters have not been adduced in reference to this problem. Whilst the plays have been examined for their ambiguous evidence of religious views, it is not in the nature of drama – especially a commercial drama designed for wide appeal and concerned to evade censorship – to offer reliable evidence for something which in the Reformation was both crucial and controversial. Thus Protestant nationalist sentiments in some plays do not necessarily reflect militancy on the author's part. Nor can we find in Shakespeare's plays the kind of full-blooded Protestant propaganda which is evident in, say, some of Dekker's. It is not possible to regard Shakespeare as a Protestant zealot. There has in any case been a tendency to resist 'categorising' Shakespeare denominationally, as if religious affiliation would compromise the much-cherished view of the universalised Bard, his human sympathies untrammelled by the particularities of Elizabethan mentality. This sentimental obstacle to exploring Shakespeare's religion may be discounted at once as a failure of historical imagination.

On the other hand, the biographical evidence has been controversial. Whilst critics have mostly preferred to assume that Shakespeare was a conforming but unenthusiastic Protestant, the view that he was a Catholic has also been vigorously reasserted.[7] Despite the Reformation, his father persisted in the 'old faith', and the authenticated evidence that he made a standard Elizabethan 'Confession' of recusancy (such as were encouraged by secret Counter-Reformation missionaries) shows that his prosecution by the Stratford authorities was indeed for known recusancy. William's daughter Susannah was also examined for recusancy when she was 23, in 1606. Shakespeare's marriage may have involved a Catholic ceremony. A later seventeenth-century source asserted that William himself "died a Papist", a statement often dismissed because this was written decades after the poet's death.[8] However, Judith Shakespeare did not die until 1662, so informed opinion from his own family was still easily accessible late in the century. Duration of time is thus not a sufficient reason to dismiss this testimony. Overall, the available evidence suggests a pattern of recusancy in Shakespeare's family which was recognised at the time. In which case it is even more curious that in the naming of his daughters he should have offered what looks like an emphatic instance of Hebraic Protestant motivation.

In the case of the first child, Susannah, the choice of name may be explained in part by the circumstances of her birth. She was born within six months of Shakespeare's marriage, and the banns were truncated in order to facilitate a hasty wedding: this was a shotgun marriage legitimating the child. As I have suggested elsewhere, it was not unusual for parents to choose the name Susannah in order to invoke the Apocryphal original's personification of Chastity.[9] (A ballad on this virtue, 'The Constancy of Susannah', is quoted by Toby Belch in Twelfth Night.) In the circumstances of Shakespeare's marriage, therefore, the child's name appears to encode an implication of chaste union, as if responding to local gossip about the match between Shakespeare and his older partner. Perhaps it does suggest that they had been troth-plighted in an informal marriage before intercourse took place (even though Shakespeare's most authoritative biographer dismisses the possibility of troth-plighting as a sentimental invention of bardolators attempting to sanitise their hero).[10] It is extremely likely, in fact, that this child's given name amounted to a social announcement: that to all intents and purposes Susannah was the product of a true marriage despite its formal solemnization at a late stage. Certainly the association of this particular name with the child of a shotgun marriage cannot be a coincidence, given a contemporary context in which baptismal biblical names were regarded as iconographically significant.

To repeat an Apocryphal preference in the second daughter's name suggests that the intended iconography was both sustained and programmatic, and that the circumstances of Susannah's birth were only part of the explanation for her name, as we might expect. It suggests that the name chosen was owing to the merger of Hebraic nomenclature with the godmother's name. And the combination of both girls' names suggests radical Protestantism on the part of the parents. Is this indeed the case? Evidently Shakespeare did possess some interest in Judith's story, but of what kind? Can the plays help us in this respect?

*Iconography in 'Love's Labours Lost'*

In a play to which Shakespeare may have contributed, and which inhabits the 'Shakespearean Apocrypha' (suitably enough) there appears an allusion to Judith and her iconography as Chastity.[11] That iconography had particularly potent currency in Elizabethan England because of its aptness to celebration of the Virgin Queen.[12] As we shall see, it plays a role also in the iconographic underplot of *Love's Labours Lost*.

Like other Elizabethan dramatists, Shakespeare obediently avoids the representation of biblical characters; some very minor characters have Hebraic names, but there is no Judith in the plays. There is, however, a Holofernes, the ludicrously pedantic and rebarbative schoolmaster in *Love's Labours Lost*. In Rabelais' Holofernes from *Gargantua and Pantagruel*, there was a secular precedent for thus naming such a type-character, which made the name usable for a stage character.[13] In assessing whether the biblical Holofernes was nevertheless a source for the character, another play can help us. In Marston's *The Dutch Courtesan*, the eponymous lady is Francesina, who plies her trade in London.[14] The significance of Marston's use of an Hebraically named character only becomes apparent if we are aware that Judith's representation of Chastity had its traditional antinomy in Holofernes' priapic character as an emblem of Lust.[15] In the plebeian subplot of *The Dutch Courtesan*, a barber's apprentice named Holifernes carries the name significant of the sexual obsession which drives Malheureux in the main plot. The priapic and castratory imagery of barbering (as in the story of Samson) is evoked when Holifernes' instruments are used by an imposter as a means to gull one Mulligrub and to place a cockscomb on his head. This sort of bawdy quibbling accounts for Holifernes' role in a play about a courtesan. Similarly in Shakespeare's romantic comedy, *Love's Labours Lost*, where sexual imagery is naturally commonplace, the schoolmaster Holofernes is a witty appropriation of a *faux intellectuel* type to the personification of Lust. He is a symptom of the subtextual plot of the play.

The overt plot is simple enough, even if it seems to be encrusted with a carapace of intriguing and mysterious significances. The King of Navarre and his gentlemen, having sworn themselves to celibacy in order to pursue the life of the mind, are rapidly and comically forsworn when a visit by the Princess of France and her ladies exposes them to feminine charms. All the resistance occurs on the ladies' side, and the gentlemen's discomfiture culminates in their final humiliation, when the ladies agree to accept their suit only after the gentlemen have proved their *bona fides*, by demonstrating constancy and patience for a year. As the disappointed Byron observes, the conventional resolution of a comedy in multiple marriages is traduced by *Love's Labours Lost*: "Our wooing doth not end like an old play:/ Jack hath not Jill." (5.2.856-7). Gender-stereotypes are also overturned, for it is the ladies who win the play's battles of wit and, indeed, its battle of the sexes. The men are exposed as hypocrites and dupes, and baulked of their end. It would not be inaccurate to describe this comedy as feminist.

The play's battle of the sexes is highlighted in several ways. It is particularly rich in imagery suggesting that love is a war, and badinage its artillery. Precisely that combination of war/amour is the basis of the Book of Judith. The theme is maintained by repeated allusions to martial heroes brought low by their lovers:

Hercules and Samson, who are comically paralleled by the play's typical *miles gloriosus*, the swaggering braggart Armado. Indeed, the gallery of strong men in formal guise is imported by the travesty pageant of the Nine Worthies, mounted by Armado and Holofernes to entertain the noble characters. It is during this show that news arrives of the King of France's death, precipitating the ladies' severe injunctions, and thus implying that Navarre and his cohort have suffered the same fate as the Worthies Hercules and Samson: domination and 'defeat' by women. The subtextual joke is that the pageant would have been more appropriate had it celebrated the female Worthies, whose forcefulness the French ladies seem to parallel. Similarly, Armado's comic desire to identify himself with the martial Worthies forms a comment upon the worsted masculine pride of the lords.

Within the pageant Holofernes takes the part of Judas Maccabeus, who had indeed sometimes been one of the biblical Worthies in such series, and was increasingly popular in Protestant iconography during the Reformation. His frequent association with Judith, his Apocryphal companion, underlined the militant characteristics of both.[16] In the alternative iconography of female Worthies, it was she who occupied his place. Thus there is here another of the play's learned allusive jokes. Not only does the foolish schoolmaster Holofernes make an unlikely warrior-hero/Maccabeus, but Judith's dupe thus masquerades as the hero of his enemies, the male counterpart of her own role. Iconographically, Holofernes masquerades as his opposite. This is, in fact, a key example of how the play's iconography functions. Like its inverted comic plot and its inverted gender hierarchy, the play's iconography constantly inverts its apparent significance.

This elaborate pattern of invoking and inverting familiar iconographies also extends to Holofernes' emblematization of Lust. The lords' elaborate ridicule of the schoolmaster's 'Judas Maccabeus' – which persists for forty lines of dialogue – exploits both religious and sexual quibbles. "Judas Maccabeus clipped is plain Judas" says Dumaine, inverting the religious hero into the worst of religious villains, whilst suggesting also Holofernes' castration. "A kissing traitor", Byron adds, which was, of course, both Judas' role in relation to Christ and Judith's role in seducing Holofernes. When the lords decide semantically to 'clip' Judas to "Jude", they are refining the Hebraizing name of Holofernes, to a sobriquet for 'Jewish'. That both Judas Maccabeus and Judith were representatives of their nation was connoted by their names, and hence the wit of reducing this pattern of allusion to the root "Jude". It was the Hebraism of biblical names which underlay their Reformation significance, because Protestants identified themselves with the Old Israel. Holofernes is being characterized as Hebraic.

Similarly, in Reformation polemic when you wished to discredit your antagonist's religion as anti-Christian you characterised him as lustful.[17] The play quibbles on the word 'Jew', which editors explain (with some puzzlement) as a term of affection. "My sweet ounce of man's flesh, my incony Jew!" (3.1.131) is surely clear enough: 'cony' is a common bawdy term, and the 'Jew' is a diminutive for 'my wee man', in the crudest sense, as the 'man's flesh' of the penis. Thus 'Jew' implies penis and lechery, and Holofernes as 'Jude' is (as so often) a personification of lust. In this way he highlights the play's themes: love, and the exposure of basic human drives beneath their sophisticated wrappings. The intellectual pretensions of the lords are, at the advent of the ladies, swiftly abandoned for fervid sexual pursuit, and a contest of wills is implemented through the medium of both parties' sophisticated eloquence. Of the comic reduction of masculine pretensions, and the simple truths underlying smart conversation, the logorrhoeic schoolmaster 'Lust' is a comic emblem.

Byron picks up the military metaphor of love's "men at arms" by a comparison which suggests that courtship is an expression of *machismo*: "For valour, is not Love a Hercules...?" (4.3. 287, 315). The irony is that Hercules the invulnerable warrior was destroyed by a lover; like Armado, who compares himself to both Hercules and Samson with a comic neglect of their amorous misfortune, these noble lovers are equally misguided in their *machismo*, and will be equally discomfited by feminine overthrow. Thus the Nine Worthies theme, seeming to celebrate masculine valour, is subversively reinterpreted by the play's events as emblematic of women's ability to dominate even the most heroic of men. It is no wonder that Boyet is moved to allude to insubordinate wives, who "strive to be/ Lords o'er their lords": to which misogynist topos the Princess crisply replies, "praise we may afford/ To any lady that subdues a lord" (4.1. 37-40). The verbally emasculated Holofernes, clipped in his jew/penis, underscores this demasculinising theme by his likeness to his Apocryphal original, whose head was cropped by a woman. The feminist significance of that event was not lost on Renaissance writers, and it underlies the play's plot of feminine victory.[18]

These examples illustrate the way in which abstracted allusions to Judith's story participate in the comedy's remarkably sophisticated linguistic play. This latter characteristic has always been recognised, but its allusions to Judith's story have not been recognised, nor have the relation of those allusions to the emphatic iconography supplied by the Nine Worthies pageant. These cut deep in a drama about love, sexuality, and intersexual warfare. But they go further than this, because of the profound implication of this iconography in Reformation polemical discourse.

First, discourse itself and dissimulation (visual and verbal) are highlighted in the play's witty exchanges. The use of iconography and the comic pageant provide an emblematic parallel to the play's 'masking' theme. The lords' disguises as foreigners, which do not fool the ladies they have come to woo in this manner, are an instance of the play's exposure of affectation and pretension. The Princess rejects the concept of "painted [...] Beauty" and Byron depreciates "painted rhetoric", other forms of disguise, dissimulation, and ulterior motives. When he addresses the other lords as "affection's men-at-arms" he plays upon both meanings of affection, as both love and affectation, for, in their perception of how courtship should be conducted,[19] the lords are unable to extricate the one from the other. Whether at linguistic, visual, or theatrical levels, the play's high artifice is devoted to rejecting artifical behaviour. This, too, is an inversion. And the play is devoted to that stratagem because it centres on the idea of conversion, and hence of reformation and Reformation.

*The French Wars*

The concept of conversion links the play's courtly romance to its topical allusions, for the theme of the battle of the sexes is grounded in historical circumstance. Again, whilst apparently the most artificial of plays, this has close affiliations with contemporary realities. Whereas the play's editors have accepted that in some way the troubled marriage of Henry and Marguerite of Navarre is pertinent to the play's King of Navarre, why and how it is pertinent has remained obscure.[20] We can resolve the relationship between France's royals and the play's, I suggest, if we realise that it is implicated in contemporary iconography.

Behind the play's king of Navarre is Henry of Navarre, by the date of the play (1594-5) Henry IV of France. Like the Princess, queen of France by the end of the play, Henry's first wife was Princess of France, Marguerite de Valois. Marguerite was acutely aware of Henry's fickle and promiscuous character, and she had refused to accept his behaviour. Although the play is more respectful of its Navarre than of his lords, the implication of his real counterpart's amorousness underlies the Princess's strictness with her royal lover. Like the play's king, Henry had been notoriously forsworn, for in 1593 he converted to Catholicism in order to achieve the throne of France: an action which shocked and infuriated English Protestants. The most significant of the French lords in the play, Byron was also a famous protagonist of the French wars. The play's "civil war of wits" reflects the civil wars of religion there (2.1.224). Whilst the play's deliberate evocations of French politics have long been recognised, their embedding in its iconography has not been understood.

For this play as for the English generally, the French wars are the cynosure of the Reformation conflict.[21] It was in France that the contest between religions was at its bitterest and bloodiest, and events there were followed with the closest interest by the English. Attributed to Marlowe, *The Massacre at Paris* (c.1593) graphically portrayed recent events of the French religious wars, feeding popular interest.[22] One of its apparently least active characters, Du Bartas, was depicted in the play so perfunctorily because his significance lay merely in his presence. As Europe's leading Protestant poet as well as a member of Henry's military entourage, Du Bartas was a living Protestant icon of his times.

He also made a decisive contribution to its polemical iconography, as the author of the celebrated, widely read epic poem *The History of Judith*, based on the Apocrypha. Dedicated initially to Henry's mother and then to his wife Marguerite, it was, in fact, a close commentary on the French religious wars. As Du Bartas averred, Henry's queen was a Judith. Celebrated throughout Europe, this poem and its Reformation significance were equally well known in England.[23] Its translation was published in 1584, the year preceding Judith Shakespeare's birth.

The plot of *Love's Labours Lost* may be the only one which Shakespeare himself invented. Its template, I suggest, was the work of which Holofernes' role is a symptomatic consequence: the Book of Judith. Shakespeare's play, like Marlowe's, is familiar with the literature in English generated by current French events. It is familiar with Judith's role in French as well as English Reformation iconography. It is inspired by Du Bartas' prominent example, and ultimately derived from the Book of Judith in the Apocrypha. Already familiar with both, Shakespeare probably took the hint for a drama spun off the Reformation Judith from an admired and oft-reprinted play by Cornelius Schonaeus, of which an edition had recently been published in England.[24] Thus it is in the context of Judith's Reformation iconography and that of the French wars, that the underplot of *Love's Labours Lost* becomes comprehensible.

The most important instance of this is, in fact, the recurrent allusion to Hercules, for in French propaganda this was the common parallel for Henry IV.[25] Characterising his military prowess during the years of Huguenot resistance, the parallel is teased by the play. By linking Hercules' status as martial Worthy to the gallery of heroes undone by their susceptibility to women, the play associates Henry's fickleness in love with his cynical tergiversation in religion, suggesting a consistent inconstancy which subverts the heroic ideal. By insisting that he reform himself before she will consider his suit, the Princess in effect attaches the power of love to the dynamic of reformation. If the king of Navarre can manage to acquire constancy he will at once live up to the Herculean personification (for Hercules himself chose virtue rather than dissipation), and in metaphoric terms become religious, in love. The identification of love with religion is emphatic in the play, which exploits the common employment of devotional language in courtship. When Byron speciously suggests concerning their vow of celibacy that "It is religion to be thus forsworn" Henry IV's abjuration of Protestantism springs to mind, and it is, of course, the king who immediately responds to the idea: "Saint Cupid, then! And, soldiers, to the field!" (4.3.338-41).

Such contemporary satiric resonance is what contextualises the play's deployment of Holofernes' significance. Just as Armado personifies the Spanish enemy as a ridiculous braggart, playing on the word 'Armada', so Holofernes' name is associated with its background in polemic, and not least in the French pamphlets familiar to English readers. But just as Henry/Navarre is a lost leader of Protestantism, so Holofernes' significance is not simple either. His role here is the one that he plays in *Catholic* propaganda, as the Reforming 'heretic' vanquished by Judithic Catholicism.[26] Emphatically rejecting the ideas of the Church Fathers, Holofernes is explicitly represented as a Protestant of the firm variety: but he is also a pretentious fool, for which we may read (in the context of Elizabethan satire) 'canting Puritan'. His Hebraic name signifies their predilection for precisely that.[27] That is, if Armado comically personifies the foreign enemy, so a Puritan Holofernes represents the 'fanatic' domestic enemy. As the weighting of their names suggests, Armado's is specific to a clash of nation with nation, his significance nationalist. Holofernes' Hebraism is denominational. Together, they signify the enemies of Englishness and of Anglo-Catholicism.

To English moderates, such 'Brownists' as this Holofernes represented just as pronounced a danger as 'Popery' itself. As is usual in Reformation propaganda, the opposing side is represented as characterised by both subversive indoctrination and lubricity. Holofernes' character as Lust is the usual pejorative sexual innuendo applied to supposedly hypocrite Puritans. He boasts that "if their sons be ingenious, they shall want no instruction; if their daughters be capable, I will put it to them" (4.2.76-8). The initial sentence suggests that this schoolmaster aspires to the perversion of young minds by heresy. The second parallels this intellectual subversion with the seduction of young girls ("I will put it [the penis] to them"). Thus Holofernes' characterization as priapic is analogized to his heretic Puritanism, and he is the paradigm of unacceptable extremism. Above all, his subsequent boast that "A soul feminine saluteth us" (ll.78-9), maintaining the bawdy motif, also maintains the parallel between the seduction of women and the seductions perpetrated by false religion, between his activities with boy's minds and with girls' hearts.

Within the larger imagistic patterns of the play, this mimes the king's double character as forsworn Protestant hero and incorrigible seducer. The play carefully avoids attributing this combination to Navarre, displacing it onto the humbler caricature character. Whereas Holofernes fondly imagines the obeisance of the "soul feminine" (a quibble on the supposed gender of souls) to his phallic instruction, Navarre's instruction and humiliation by his female royal counterpart reverses this stereotype of masculine domination. His domination by the Princess's chastity, and her 'reformation' of his ways, is the mainplot event shadowed by Holofernes' clipping from would-be Protestant Maccabeus to unreformed Jude or Jew. His figuration draws out the bigoted religious contemporary meaning of Jewishness for the polemicists who wished to emphasize that Jews and heretics were equally insensible of 'true' Christian religion.

The play's complex negotiations of complementary religious, political and amatory motifs are what situates its emblematic manipulations of the Nine Worthies and of Holofernes' significance. This structure can throw some light on the play's plot. As in the Apocryphal book and the French wars, the play's scenario offers a 'war' between two antagonistic camps: literally topographized as the ladies' "tents" (4.3.348) and Navarre's enclosed estate. The Princess's unexpected arrival at his enclave is like Judith's at the Assyrian camp, and similarly finds him unsuspecting its catastrophic effect on his settled course. His implied satyriasis and 'apostasy' make him a *Doppelgänger* of Holofernes (both schoolmaster and original), who was both lustful and infidel: and this bathetic comparison with one of the play's butts itself cuts a "displaced" Navarre down to size. Just as the emblematic Holofernes inhabits the besieged masculine enclave, so the besieged Bethulia has been inverted in significance into the spiritually 'Assyrian' place. Similarly, the feminine antagonist, the ladies' camp, inverts the previously Assyrian significance of the besiegers. As the play inverts everything it touches, so it inverts the *mise-en-scène* of the Book of Judith. Above all others, the inversion of masculine into feminine domination retains the central reversal in the Book of Judith.[28] And the plot's ending, with its breathtaking reversal of comic convention, aesthetically underwrites the reversal of masculine by feminine power.

The presence of Holofernes and Armado in the male enclave types it as apostate in love and religion; therefore implicitly the ladies' leader, the victorious Princess, is functionally a Judith. Thus Holofernes is typed invertedly as 'Jewish/phallic', and his ridiculed masquerade as the Jewish warrior-hero, Judas Maccabeus, is by the feminine subtexts of the play implicitly contrasted with the Princess's function as Maccabeus' female counterpart. Queen of France by the end of the play, she is Judith in the same way as Marguerite de Navarre, Queen of France, was saluted as Judith by Du Bartas. Ironically, it is to the throne of France that Navarre (before his own accession to it) owed allegiance: in the play he is *literally* as well as metaphorically the Princess's vassal.

Thus both Holofernes' inverted ethnicity and Navarre's subjugation are witty constituents in the play's satire on the failed 'Hebraism' of apostate 'heretical' Protestantism, whether of French Huguenots such as Henry had been, or of English Puritans. The submerged parallel with English Reformation history which this suggests turns on the fulcrum of Elizabeth I's own role as a Reformation Judith. The play's Queen of France shadows Elizabeth's own diplomatic relationship with Henry, and the tensions and courtships of the political relationship between England and France.

When the Princess rejects Navarre's proposal of marriage the play's allusions to the Duc d'Alençon fall into place.[29] To the seriously projected marriage between the Catholic Alençon and Elizabeth of England the Protestant political faction had been bitterly opposed, and the resulting controversy was the most significant of her reign. By rejecting the 'heretical' Navarre the play's Judithic Queen imitates Elizabeth/Judith's own eventual rejection of Alençon's suit. The glancing allusions to Alençon, justified by the French setting, allow the play to make a submerged comparison which, if more explicit, would have been frowned upon: but the point that marriages have their place in the defence of true religion (whether of love or of denomination) is effectively encoded in the submerged Judithic plot. Artificial and highly abstracted the play may be (as critics have often stressed). But its character as a *roman-à-clef* is perceptible in the context of contemporary propaganda, both English and French.

Finally, the most striking element in the anti-comic ending is not that marriages are rejected – this is the generic reversal – but that the catastrophe which causes the play's 'resolution' is a death, that of the Princess's father. Death (tragic *dénouement*) emphatically contradicts comic resolution (marriage). But more importantly, it also brings the catastrophe of the play into line with the catastrophe of the Book of Judith. There, too, where the consummation of love was expected, death was substituted. And the irony enacted by that reversal in the Apocrypha matches the play's, that feminine intransigence overcomes masculine

'Valour', frustrates masculine seductions, and defeats the heretic. There is a rooted synonymity between the word 'infidel' and the word 'unfaithful' which underlies the play's parallel between love and religion, and finds its subject in the king of Navarre. Fitly it must be a Judith/Elizabeth who 'reforms' him, to a moderate Anglo-Catholic 'religion' of love. This shimmering, emblematic courtship between Judithic Queen and Herculean King is, in effect, Shakespeare's portrayal of how Anglo-Catholic Elizabeth and once-Protestant-now-Catholic Henry can, so to speak, work it out.

If in the play Love's Labours are indeed Lost, that is a wry comment upon Navarre's role in propaganda as a Hercules. The recurrent allusions to Hercules specify examples of his famed twelve 'labours'; and these are ironized, as in Byron's adducing the Hesperidean labour as type of the lords' own 'Valour' in love. But the central irony addresses the effort of Navarre/'Hercules' in his labour of love, to court the Princess. Just as Judith was a female Worthy in the sequence complementing the male Worthies, so Navarre/'Hercules' is the play's masculine counterpart to the Princess/Judith. Just as the biblical Judith was the sacred alternative to classical Hercules in the female Worthies, so the Princess is intellectually, spiritually, and personally the true companion of Navarre in his best incarnation. Reformed under her auspices, Navarre would live up to his prototype.

And the use of the Worthies' theme explains the title itself. It has proved difficult for editors to decide on bibliographic evidence whether it should read 'Love's Labours Lost' or 'Love's Labour's Lost'.[30] This is, however, another instance of the fact that an iconographic comprehension of the play can resolve what seems to be a technical bibliographical problem. Editors are trained to reject interpretative evidence, as if it were possible truly to extricate textual technicalities from textual components: an illogical assumption. But the play's animadversions to Hercules' Labours reveal that the title's ironic freight depends upon its summation of the plot as love's Labours lost: the failure of Herculean masculininity at Navarre's court.

Again, at this level, too, Holofernes is a bathetic *Doppelgänger* of Navarre, the unconvincing 'Judas Maccabeus' to his aspirant 'Hercules'. As the archetypes of masculine idealization, the Worthies like Navarre are compromised in favour of the feminizing trend. Particularly striking in this imagistic strand is the way in which Shakespeare diverts a standard misogynist topos – the ruin of heroes by female traducers – to the support of a feminist theme. But we should understand the historically specific character of this feminist topos. It is devised in the service of complimenting Elizabeth, before whom this play was presented at court.[31] She is to supervise the King of France – and hence dominate Reformation politics.

Equally, though, the play's politics are irenic, for it converts the wars of religion into a love story, ending on the possibility of harmony. At this level, it is a vision of the Reformation schism as healed by a centrist tendency.

If irenic, the play is nevertheless irreverent even in its deferences. It was no longer permitted to represent any biblical story on the English stage, but Shakespeare's play can do so by evoking and manipulating its derivatives, whether historical or iconographic. Whereas Du Bartas' poem treated the Book of Judith as a *roman à clef* for the French wars, Shakespeare treats the French wars as a *roman-a-clef* for Judith. In doing so, he produces a play at once timely, witty, and audacious, not least in its inferences about the Alençon marriage. Nor is the way less ingenious in which Shakespeare uses a forbidden method – biblical dramatization – to achieve the play's royal compliment: using authority against authority in order to extol authority. Ironic inversion is not merely the play's mode, but its motivating principle.

*Shakespeare's Religion*

From *Love's Labours Lost* we can deduce that Shakespeare was not merely interested in the Book of Judith, but that he used it with the fullest consciousness of its Reformation significance. We may infer, therefore, that something similar was at work in his christening of his second daughter. In *Love's Labours Lost*

Judithic iconography encrypts a loyalist Anglo-Catholicism, in a way which leans towards Catholicism by envisioning it as reformed, and hence surviving schism. Shakespeare's father's 'Confession of Faith' affirmed the Old Religion. Precisely the same sense of 'Confession' was signified by the given name Judith, as tradition (reiterated by the Elizabethan Camden's Remaines) attested.[32] Equally precisely, then, the naming of his daughter was Shakespeare's own confession of faith.

Does this mean that Shakespeare was a militant Protestant? It might. But there are several reasons which count against this apparently simple solution. Susannah was baptized in 1583 and Judith in 1585. By this date the fashion for Protestant Hebraic names in England was receding. Moreover, it was from 1584 that Judith's Catholic iconography was revived in England. The crucial reinvigoration of Judith's Protestant icon did not occur until 1588, Armada year. When Judith Shakespeare was born, the name's equally strong Catholic associations had become commonly known.[33] This was a name which could signify either side of the conflict, even though the English preferred to regard her as Protestant property.

And maybe this was precisely its appeal for her father: that because Hebraic, the name might appear fashionably Protestant, but be, in fact, accommodating to a politically loyal Catholic's convictions. Shakespeare's family were locally regarded as recusants. A sensible man wishing to counter this reputation, and thus to avoid the usual disadvantages inflicted upon Catholics, might well have bethought himself of the advantages of using a marker of Protestantism (and one of no *doctrinal* difficulty for Catholics) as a symbolic gesture suggesting sound Protestant principles on his part. To name his second daughter Judith in 1585 was to make his daughters' names sound programmatically Hebraic, to make what appeared to be a choice with denominational implications. Judith's naming was a 'confession of faith' like his recusant father's, a gesture of familial piety as well as religious significance. To remember these ambiguities, whilst solemnly enacting an apparently Protestant social gesture, would be a particularly apposite way of remaining Catholic in intention whilst outwardly conforming.

That combination of inward conviction with outward conformity was in fact the best *modus vivendi* for secret recusancy, as propounded by the pragmatists amongst Jesuit missionaries in England.[34] It was what an intellectual recusant would have done, with satisfaction in his irony. What it suggests is that those who have thought Shakespeare a Catholic were correct, and that they should have taken a close look at his naming of his daughters. They should also have closely examined Love's Labours Lost.

Whilst by this date in the 1590s Shakespeare seems to have become reconciled to Protestantism, the play shows signs of being a *roman-à-clef* about Catholic loyalism to Elizabeth. Loyal English Catholics were burdened with the facile equation of 'Popery' with 'treason', an equation which the witty, secretly Catholicized imagery of the play rebuts. *Love's Labours Lost* offers precisely the same species of ironic indirection and inversion as is represented by a recusant Hebraic baptism.

Its Holofernes is typed not as a Catholic but as an extreme Protestant. This in itself does not exclude Protestant-inspired satire, since moderate Anglicans often prided themselves on despising Brownists and other nonconformists, as Nashe did. Commentators on the play have often thought Nashe's controversies relevant to it in some way, though there is no consensus on precisely which way.[35] If we recall Nashe's rebuke in 1593 to radical Protestants who rejected the Apocrypha, accusing them of slandering the bible as "Jewish fable", this seems apt to the way in which the Apocryphal Holofernes, the canting Puritan, is typed as Hebraic/phallic. He is, as it were, the heretic Jew/Protestant, and even his 'fabling' cant is encoded as his mounting a pageant and masquerading as a Jewish hero. He caricatures at once the Hebraizing impulses of radical Protestantism, and its demotion of biblical story to "Jewish [...] legend".[36] (As Maccabees also was if the Apocrypha were rejected.) Holofernes' embodiment of this compound hereticism, Jew-Puritan, is emphasized by his abbreviated designation as 'Jude'. The Book of Jude in the New Testament is a denunciation of heresy, of 'false teachers' (such as Shakespeare's schoolmaster Holofernes) and sectarian libertines (here, Holofernes as 'Lust').[37] This Holofernes is heresy writ large as well as writ ridiculous.

That Reformation caricature can throw light on another crux in the play, the connection of Holofernes with Judas Iscariot in V.ii. 590ff., which has puzzled some editors.[38] They have confused the traitor apostle with Judas Maccabeus but then, so does the play. Byron's allusion to Judas Iscariot (and hence Holofernes) as a 'kissing traitor' is one of the play's typically dense jokes. At one level, it abuses this embodiment of Puritan heresy as emblem of a politically subversive movement; this the obverse of the charge so often made against Elizabethan recusants. That is, it is not recusancy but radical religion which threatens political upheaval.

This encoding of loyalist Catholic propaganda is facilitated by iconographic connections between Judas Iscariot's betrayal of Christ and Judithic iconography. A curious connection between these two 'kissing traitors', Judith and Judas, had been exploited in medieval literature, as I have suggested elsewhere.[39] Here, in a play which customarily inverts traditional iconographies, that parallel with Judas Iscariot becomes another stick to beat Holofernes (in the Book of Judith the betrayed, now the traitor) with.

Of course, the wildly elaborated caricature of this hapless lower-class character is a way of displacing the venomous taunts which Shakespeare will not aim too closely at Holofernes' royal double, Navarre. Nevertheless, if his status protects him from direct defamation, contemporary polemicists did vilify him as a traitor, heretic and lecher. Navarre was a forsworn former radical Protestant, generally regarded as cynically atheist because he thought Paris 'worth a Mass'. And the Princess, their Judithic antagonist, should in the historical context evoked by the play be understood as Catholic, not only because she is Queen of France but because both of Henry's wives were. Over them is superimposed the native queen Elizabeth, an Anglo-Catholic with no brief for the zealous (and certainly a chaster woman than Marguerite). The only 'Catholic' caricature in the play, Armado, is satirized not as Popish but as Spanish. All the play's satiric emphases are directed at the radical version of Protestantism.

If the overall effect of Judith's feminist iconography is to invert also the usual power-relations between the sexes which prevailed at the time, it is unlikely that Shakespeare's motivation was feminist. The gender of the ruler dictated the victor in the battle of the sexes; a victory for nationalism, in fine, just as the original Judith's had been.

Similarly, the compliment to Elizabeth is deliberately unorthodox, which is to say as 'heretical' in kind as the play's other inversions of received formulae. That is, what we are looking at is a recusant compliment to the Queen. Like Shakespeare's naming of his daughters, the play's deployment of Judith's model is a subtle indirection such as Jesuits commended. Contemporary anti-Jesuit propaganda frequently decried their proponence of 'equivocation' (and of course it is in the context of the recusant Guy Fawkes plot that this word takes on such profound significance in Macbeth). By contrast, Judith herself had been traditionally celebrated in pious commentary as an exponent of righteous equivocation.[40] Implicit in a Judithic plot, then, is a riposte to the charge most often levelled against Jesuits when excoriated as politically subversive. To this loyalist Catholic strategy is superadded the play's own role as the dramatic equivalent of an equivocating Judith, offering a recusant compliment to the Queen.

To combine loyal compliment with uncompromised recusancy in the same ingenious drama was something of a feat; one with serious value for an essentially recusant playwright, equally inclined to honour his own original affiliation and to test the limits of his professional skills. It brought his familial piety and his talent into fruitful relation. It was one of those secret victories and ingenious liberations

## Love's Labours Lost

that the Counter-Reformation fostered in its Jesuitical programme. It was this comedy's grandest joke.

And finally, Shakespeare's literary heirs have intuited that in some sense his second daughter signifies something fundamental about her parent, even if they did not know what precisely it was. David Garrick mounted an oratorio of *Judith* at his Shakespeare Festival, Virginia Woolf christened Shakespeare's fictional sister Judith, and the troubled family rebel in Edward Bond's *Bingo* is Shakespeare's second daughter. Judith continues to signify in the history of Shakespeare's literary history, too. But that is another story.[41]

### Notes

I am grateful to Emrys Jones and Rowland Wymer for helpful comments on the text.

1. See F.A. Yates, *A Study of 'Love's Labours Lost'* (1936); E.A. Strathmann, "The Textual Evidence for 'The School of Night'", *Modern Language Notes* 56 (1941), 176-86. John Kerrigan's edition of the play (New Penguin Shakespeare, 1982) is hostile to any kind of contextual interpretation.

2. M. Stocker, *Judith* (forthcoming).

3. See e.g. W. Camden, *Remains Concerning Britain* (repr. 1870), 56; C.W. Bardsley, *Curiosities of Puritan Nomenclature* (1880), 38-116; E.W.Monter, "Historical Demography and Religious History in Sixteenth-Century Geneva", *Journal of Interdisciplinary History* IX (1979), 413, and D.S.Smith, "Child-Naming Practices as Cultural and Familial Indicators", *Local Population Studies* 32 (1984), esp. 18. For Judith and Susannah, see my *Judith*, ch. 3.

4. Quoted in D.S. Smith, "Child-Naming Practices, Kinship Ties, and Change in Family Attitudes in Hingham, Mass., 1641 to 1880", *Journal of Social History* 18 (1985), 544.

5. Thomas Deloney, *Judith and Holofernes* (1588), repr. in Works.

6. For Reformation disputes over the relative status of the Apocrypha in hermeneutics, see my *Judith*, ch. 3. One effect of these was the excision of the Apocrypha from later editions of the King James Bible.

7. By E.A.J. Honigmann, *Shakespeare: The 'Lost Years'* (1985), esp. 114-125.

8. Richard Davies, quoted by Schoenbaum, p.122. For suggestions of recusancy in Shakespeare's family see S.Schoenbaum, *Shakespeare's Lives* (rev.edn. 1991), 23, 26; and on *The Last Will and Testament of John Shakespeare* see J.H. de Groot, *The Shakespeares and the "Old Faith"* (1946); J.G. McManaway, "John Shakespeare's "Spiritual Testament"", *Shakespeare Quarterly* XVIII (1967).

9. For explication of this use of the given name in the Renaissance see my *Judith*, ch. 3. Susannah Shakespeare was born six months after the marriage on 27 Nov. 1582, her baptism occurring on 26 May 1583.

10. Schoenbaum, p.25.

11. *The Raigne of King Edward the Third*, reprinted in *The Shakespeare Apocrypa: Being a collection of fourteen plays which have been ascribed to Shakespeare*, ed. C.F. Tucker Brooke (1908). The allusion to Judith is in II.i. 169ff.

12. See e.g. Richard Barnefield's *Cynthia* (1595), where Elizabeth is a 'second Judith'. For full explication of Judith's highly significant role in Elizabeth's iconography see my *Judith*, ch. 4.

13. Rabelais, *Gargantua*, Book I, ch.xiii.

14. John Marston, *The Dutch Courtesan*, ed. M.L.Wine (1965) 2.1, 2.3.

15. For this iconographic tradition see my *Judith*, ch.1. Rabelais' Holofernes reflects similar abstracted allusion and subtextual joking: he makes Gargantua read the work of Theodulus, who had cited Judith as an archetype for womankind.

16. For the relation of Judith to Judas Maccabeus in Nine Worthies iconography see my *Judith*, ch.2.

17. 5.2.581-621 (quotations from G.R. Hibbard's Oxford edition, 1990). This includes, of course, a quibble on the Jewish rite of circumcision. See also e.g. *Haec Vir* (1620), and Marston's *Holifernes Reinscure*, whose surname means *reins* (loins) cured (shaved, cut).

18. For Renaissance feminist uses of *Judith* see my Judith, ch. 3.

19. 1.2.14-15, 4.3.236, 287.

20. See e.g. R.W. David's Arden edition (1968), p. xxv, on allusions to Navarre. For sources see G. Bullough, *Narrative and Dramatic Sources of Shakespeare*, (1957), vol. I.

21. For an excellent study of the impact of the French Wars on Reformation polemic see J.H.M. Salmon, *The French Religious Wars in English Political Thought* (1959). For Henry's conversion see Lord Russell of Liverpool, *Henry of Navarre* (1969), 110-11.

22. For French pamphlet sources of *Massacre At Paris* see P.H. Kocher, "Contemporary Pamphlet Backgrounds for Marlowe's Massacre at Paris", *Modern Language Quarterly* 8 (1947), pp.151-73, 309-18; and J. Briggs, "Marlowe's Massacre at Paris: A Reconsideration", *Review of English Studies* n.s. 34 (1983), pp.257-78.

23. For Judith's important role in French Wars polemic, and for the popularity and influence of Du Bartas' *Judit* (1574), see my *Judith*, ch. 4. The 1584 translation, by Thomas Hudson, is also discussed there.

24. Cornelius Schonaeus, *Terentius Christianus sive comoediae duae* (1592).

25. E.g. *A Tocsin* (1611), sig. B. See also C. Vivanti, "Henry IV, the Gallic Hercules", *JWCI* 30 (1967). For relations between the two monarchs see J.B. Black, *Elizabeth I and Henry IV* (1914).

26. For discussion of Catholic propaganda deploying Judithic iconography, see my *Judith*, chs. 4 and 5.

27. In Catholic polemic Holofernes was 'Puritan' or Huguenot, and similarly *Massacre at Paris* designates Huguenots as Puritan in English terms (xiv. 55). Thus I think that it is correct to regard LLL 4.2. 146-7 as Holofernes' rejection of the Fathers and of the 'colours' of soi-disant idolatry. Such Reformation references litter the play: cf. Byron's animadversion to 'pure idolatry' in the next scene, 4.3.73. For the identification of Puritans with Jews see e.g. *Massacre at Paris*, xi. 21. That Shakespeare was hostile to Puritans in e.g. *Winter's Tale* is suggested by P. Milward, *Shakespeare's Religious Background* (1973), 152.

28. For the reversal in the Book of Judith, see my *Judith*, ch.1.

29. E.g. 2.1.61, 193. For a Protestant attack on the projected marriage see John Stubbs, *The Discovery of a Gaping Gulf* (1579); for diplomacy, W.T. MacCaffrey in P. Clark, A.G.R. Smith & N. Tyacke, *The English Commonwealth* (1979).

30. Thus both Hibbard's and David's editions opt for "Love's Labour's Lost".

31. The Quarto title-page (1598) refers to a recent performance, the preceding Christmas, before the Queen. It seems likely that court performance(s) also occurred before 1597-8; the play was also performed on the public stage.

32. Camden, *Remains*, 103.

33. For the name's Catholic associations see my *Judith*, ch 4.

34. For Jesuit propaganda in England see T. Clancy, *Papist Pamphleteers: The Allen-Persons Party and the Political Thought of the Counter-Reformation in England* (1964).

35. See R.W. David's discussion of the Nashe theories in his edition, pp.xxxiv-v.

36. Thomas Nashe, *Works*, III. 115-16. On the 'papist' heresy of belief in the Apocrypha's 'fables' see e.g. W. Whitaker, *A Disputation on Holy Scripture, Against the Papists* (repr. 1849), 82-5; the Catholic Douai Bible in English (1609-10) defends the Book of Judith against such Protestant attacks, 1011.

37. Jude, verses 3, 18-19.

38. R.W. David questions these lines, xxxiii.

39. For the association between Judith and Judas see my *Judith*, ch.2.

40. Judith was herself a model of righteous equivocation: marginal note to Book of Judith, ch. xi. On the Jesuits' mode of 'equivocation' see e.g. *An Exact Discovery* (1605), 41; and E. Rose, *Cases of Conscience: Alternatives open to Recusants and Puritans under Elizabeth I and James I* (1975), 88-9.

41. Garrick's, Woolf's and Bond's works are discussed in context in my *Judith*.

# 'PLAYING THE COOK':
# NURTURING MEN IN *TITUS ANDRONICUS*

### Ann Christensen
### (University of Houston)

In pre-industrial England, a crucial if mundane source of women's social and economic power resided in their capacities to produce, prepare, and provide food for their families. Whether in the supervision of servants in noble households, or in the performance of these duties themselves in houses of the middling sort, Renaissance housewives made important contributions to their domestic economies. Treatises on "domesticall duties", which proliferated in this period, "emphasized the wife's role in provisioning the household", often urging husbands not to meddle in (for example) the dairy and wash-house.[1] Yet the evaluation, if not the precise delineation, of domestic labor was beset by internal contradictions, as post-reformation England advanced toward capitalist configurations of home and work, altering the dynamic of domestic authority like other social hierarchies. As Mary Beth Rose reminds us in her study of motherhood in early modern England, during and after the Reformation, this culture "was in the throes of reconceptualizing issues of family and gender, and of redefining the significance of public and private life."[2] Domestic government was an urgent concern: the subject of scores of conduct books, sermons, and advice manuals written throughout the sixteenth and seventeenth centuries, household order needed, in the eyes of many authors and preachers, intervention and definition. The impetus and effect of this literature is to assign to "private life" – marriage and domesticity – "a new centrality and significance."[3]

Protestant marriage ideology presented women with a paradox of authority: just as marriage and the home received "new cultural importance [...] as the chief seat of patriarchal authority", so a wife's status was elevated as "keeper of that home and as the spiritual equal of her husband."[4] Social and cultural historians document that the individual household was seen at once as 'a man's castle' and 'a woman's place', observing that, despite the extensive hortatory literature about domestic conduct, in practice, labor and authority were imperfectly divided between spouses.[5] Nevertheless, the chores related to food provision were almost universally allotted to housewives. For example, Dod and Cleaver grant to the wife the responsibility "'to rule and govern her maidens; to see those things that belong unto the kitchen, and to huswifery, and to their household stuff'," and Whatley abjures husbands to avoid "'brewing, baking, washing, and the particulars of these and the like business'" (qtd. in Orlin 102). Struggles over the power to feed, and about the stewardship of 'household stuff', including the dispensing of hospitality on the Renaissance stage register broader social concerns about the hierarchical arrangements within and the meanings of the domestic sphere as it was slowly emerging in contradistinction to the "public" domain of men and work. When Shakespeare dramatizes men's infringement into this domain, his plays reflect experiences of dislocation in the "gender system".[6]

The present study considers the consequences of male characters taking over the role of food-provider on the Shakespearean stage in the context of the shifting location of domestic authority in early modern English society. Whereas psychoanalytic readings traditionally locate nurturance within Shakespeare's problematic "relationship to the feminine – most deeply, naturally to the maternal",[7] I consider the problem as a cultural construct, with the "politics of feeding" grounded not (only) in "the maternal", but in the domestic sphere itself. Placing the matrix of gender, nurture, family, and power in the historically specific category of household government may solve some of the problems feminist critics find in the use of "sentimental stereotypes of the mother as the natural source of nourishment and nurture."[8] The fact is, women's work in food production in early modern European households required great skill and was vital to the material sustenance of the family; there is nothing sentimental about this. In short, when feeding is contested on stage, household government is implicated. For the purposes of this discussion, I intend "feeding" and "nurture" to apply to both the instances of the literal service and consumption of food, as in the staged meal scenes in *Titus Andronicus* (3.2 and 5.3), and to the verbal and metaphoric representations of "nurture" in terms of domestic care and comfort, as in the cases of the professional nurse (4.2) and Lavinia, who acts a kind of nurse to her nephew. Because both literal and metaphoric forms of nurture are traditionally associated with women, Shakespeare signals deviation from the cultural norm when he places male characters in nurturing positions, relfecting the ambivalent roles of women and men within the 'private' household, and dramatizing the home as a contested space.

Certain patterns emerge when Shakespearean men assume nurturing roles. One such pattern is self-conscious role-playing: men often characterize themselves meta-theatrically, acknowledging that they are only "playing" a part which serves a specific political purpose.[9] For example, the feast that Titus serves at the end of the play is both elaborately staged by him and designed for revenge rather than the reconciliation he promises. In addition to donning a type of costume and performing the actions of cook/host: "*enter Titus like a cook, placing the dishes*" (s.d. 5.3.25), he has veiled Lavinia in readiness for her sacrifice to come; finally, he reads a kind of induction in the form of the Virginius story.[10] When Prince Hal and Poins dress up as drawers to "wait upon" Falstaff at table in order to entrap him and exact revenge for his fraud, they too stage a "scene" for political ends. The prince describes his "service", however amusing, as "[a] heavy descension [...] a low transformation" (*2 Henry IV* 2.2.162-4). Hal's sense of debasement, "from prince to prentice", reveals his awareness of the social inferiority of his adopted role, an awareness shared by other food-providing men, who "play" the cook or housewife in order to wrest power from or exert power over, women, their rivals, and their subordinates. Such men recognize that they are engaged in an alien enterprise and one of lesser value when they provide (or seem to provide) food to others. Foregoing their usual place at the head of the table, men who feed others self-consciously invert gender roles.[11] For example, Titus announces: "I will *play the cook*" (5.2.204, italics added); his cook's costume is an ironic inversion of the robes of state he had refused in the opening scene, symbolizing his descent into private life. As I will argue, the decision to refuse political power places Titus lopsidedly into the domestic sphere.[12]

The darker purpose of theatricality is deception – another common trait among male food-providers. Timon of Athens best illustrates this kind of culinary trickery when he invites his former friends to a dinner of lavish dishes filled only with water and stones (3.6.83, s.d.). Similarly, Prospero tempts his ship-wrecked captives with a meal, which he quickly orders spoiled and vanished (*The Tempest* 3.3.52, s.d.). In a comic vein, Petruchio promotes himself as a diligent husband, who has taken care "to dress [Kate's] meat [him]self and bring it [her]", but snatches it away as part of his project to tame her (*Shrew* 4.3.40). None of these meals actually feeds its participants.[13]

From the patterns of theatricality, "descension" or role-playing down, and the political deployment of meals (without the intention to feed), I infer among male hosts[14] a common recognition of the social power residing in the traditionally female occupations of food-provision and -service. These strategies also locate anxiety in men concerning their own shifting political positions within family, market, and state. As Jean-Christophe Agnew argues, new conceptions of production and exchange exacerbated a crisis in social identity for proto-capitalist Britons: "The social and political crisis of representation that agricultural and commercial capitalism introduced into England's semifeudal society raised the issue of personal intentions in new and disturbing ways."[15] The household became for early modern men a laboratory for testing out new configurations of social authority and identity. Together, the recognition of women's domestic power and men's anxiety about it in drama suggest the destabilized and destabilizing nature of domestic authority in this transitional period. Male characters' assumption of the duties of food provision and nursery comes inevitably at a cost to their female counterparts.

This leads to a fourth characteristic of Shakespearean nurturing men: that their assumption of the feeding role responds to the real or perceived vulnerability of their political power. Men's roles in local and national economies were not secure, as the crown increasingly consolidated power, and the ideological (if not the spatial) conception of the 'separation of the spheres' jostled domestic jurisdiction – these conditions are registered in the plays through what I call "the politics of feeding". Each man appears at a transitional moment; each is in danger of gaining power he may not maintain or of losing power he does not deserve. For example, Hal's drawer impersonation will be his last civilian act, the "scene", his last visit to the Boar's Head tavern before doffing all disguises to become soldier-king. Timon serves his mock-feast when his social standing has slipped, the ironic result of his excessive largesse; Prospero orchestrates his chimerical banquet as a way to regain his dukedom from the Milanese faction. Capulet and Macbeth, both threatened by insurrection from within their "kingdoms", assume their cook and host roles, respectively, in hopes of resecuring patriarchal authority. On the eve of his daughter's marriage to the man he has chosen against her will, Old Capulet insists on preparing the nuptial dinner: "I'll *play* the housewife for this once" (4.2.43, italics added). After Juliet defies her father by feigning death, he must admit the failure of his culinary labor: "Our wedding cheer [changed] to a sad burial feast" (4.5.86). In his way, Macbeth "play[s] the humble host" (3.3.5) at his inagaural (and final) state dinner, spoiled by his own guilty vision of Banquo's ghost. Each 'player-cook' clutches his role as nervously and jealously as old Capulet grasps his rusty sword – either as protection from or rehearsal for his investment in the public sphere.

Shakespeare's first tragedy, *Titus Andronicus* introduces to his stage many elements of the nurturing problematic I have been discussing. Titus, the military hero and noble father, deploys theatricality and deception in a banquet of revenge;

he offers meals not intended to nourish; and he takes on this nurturing role in response to his weakened political power. Indeed, as Naomi Liebler has recently argued, "headless Rome" (1.1.186) itself is in political crisis; from the battle for the empery to the "contesting claims for 'piety', [Rome ...] has already been fractured beyond any unified set of values."[16] Titus' retreat into a wholly domestic identity comes at the expense of women, who are literally or figuratively ousted from positions of authority in the household. Aaron, the villain and double of Titus, poses other problems as a male-feeder, to be discussed below. Most germane to my discussion, *Titus* represents acts of nurturance always by supplanting women with men as providers of nurture, and shows this replacement to be disastrous. Titus Andronicus is the patriarchal avenger, whose nurturance resembles that of Aaron, the Moor and lover of Tamora, the conquered queen of Goths: both "feed" at the expense of the maternal figures in the play, Tamora, Lavinia, and the Nurse, as well as other, marginally invoked mothers, the legendary Cornelia Gracchus and Lucius's deceased wife. As Barber and Wheeler note, "Aaron represents a vilified but actively potent version of Titus as parent" (155). Both hero and anti-hero kill in the name of feeding, as the whole play repeatedly pairs piety – civic and family honor – with butchery.[17]

The situation in Shakespeare's Rome speaks to what was happening in middle- and upper-class households in early modern English society: women were at once being relegated to the domestic sphere, increasingly excluded from public speech and action; and yet they were encountering a strengthened patriarchy at home. Women's domestic authority, with all its attendant duties and privileges, was challenged from within the household by fathers and husbands, who were themselves "retreating" from the vicissitudes of uncertain identities outside. The distinctions between private and public life were blurred.

2. "I am glad you did not nurse him"
When Tamora refuses to nurse her illigitimate child, whose birth she must hide from her husband, Saturninus, the newly crowned emperor of Rome, it is the father, Aaron, who takes up the infant to nourish (3.2). This gender role reversal typifies all acts of nurturance present in the play, which "substitutes paternal for maternal parenting" (Barber and Wheeler, 157). Placed alongside the two meals at Titus' table, Aaron's approach to nursing demonstrates how the masculine mode of nurturance implicitly challenges that nurturing power early modern culture ascribed to women. In this tragedy, however, nurturance is not only taken up by men, but it is altogether inverted, making "that strumpet, your unhallowed dam, / Like to the earth swallow her own increase" (5.2.190-1). Paradoxically, women are not only forbidden to feed others, they are also forced to consume what Titus feeds them. The perversion or deprivation of women's nurturing ability structures the play.

Consumption or swallowing, associated with "the feminine", appears in the play's rhetoric of feminized Nature, some of which accrues to women characters.[18] The "green world" dramatized in *Titus* notoriously takes the form of the "subtile hole", "loathsome", "detested, dark blood-drinking pit", "this fell devouring receptacle", "the swallowing womb" where the wedding party hunts, where illicit lovers meet, Bassianus is killed, Lavinia is raped and mutilated, and where Quintus and Martius are framed for murder (2.3.198, 193, 176, 224, 235, 239). Indeed, it even seems to Titus that "nature made [the pit] for murders and for rapes" (4.1.57).[19] The engulfing pit/womb/tomb metonymy provides evidence enough of Shakespeare's conflation of swallowing and consuming with feminine sexuality and motherhood.[20] But this imagery, in constituting female sexuality as negative (a hole, a void), also transposes female nurturance into a consuming rather than a productive force.

David Willbern's compendious study of "oral vengeance" in the play charts the equations between mouths and genitals, speech, sex and eating, and notes the elision of vaginal and oral symbolism.[21] The present study sees feeding (in the transitive sense) more materially – as an expression and a constitution of power, family position, and gender identity by the person who supplies nurture. The "pit" in *Titus* counters the image of abundant and feminine nature of Renaissance pastoral – and, by extension, replaces women's role as providers of food – with an image of feminine consumption and destruction. This imagery underlines the action of the play, which converts both Lavinia and Tamora from potential providers of nurture into "receptacles".

Against this picture of maternal consumption, Aaron projects a different, more pastoral[22] landscape in which to raise his son. After having saved it from slaughter, he promises the baby:

> I'll make you feed on berries and on roots,
> And feed on curds and whey and suck the goat,
> And cabin in a cave, and bring you up
> To be a warrior, and command a camp. (4.2.177-80)

This fantasy reconstitutes on his terms that feminine nurture increasingly absent from the world of the play: here, a goat replaces the human source of milk, a cave replaces the household, the father replaces the mother. As an "outsider",[23] the black Moor must place his son outside of Rome (he plans to exchange the dark-skinned infant for one of lighter hue, the son of a nearby countryman [4.2.153-61]). Yet Aaron's invention "of nurturance without women" (Barber and Wheeler, 155) actually corresponds to the Roman way. As any baby book would testify, neither Aaron's menu, nor his potential force-feeding tactics ("I'll make you feed . . . ") suits a new-born's needs. But this Spartan diet, Aaron presumes will "make a man" of the infant. Like Leontes, the jealous husband of *The Winter's Tale,* Aaron seems glad his lover "did not nurse" their son, for Aaron recognizes the powerful bond formed between mother and child – a bond he wants to forge himself. To this end, he must appropriate the mother's erotic bond with himself: the cave where he imagines a future with his son displaces the "counsel-keeping cave" that Tamora had described earlier for their amorous retreat (2.3.24). The cave, though, retains its evocation of the pit and, hence, female sexuality, associating the black man with women in the play.

Aaron so wholly assumes "the woman's part" in nurturance that he must literally kill the nurse and midwife in order to discharge his office. Although he does engineer Bassianus' death and boasts of killing many more, we see Aaron only in the act of murdering women whose business is giving birth to and feeding babies.[24] Threats to his power do come from women – from Tamora, with her new and rising position as Empress; from the (briefly) saucy Lavinia, who threatens along with her husband to reveal to Saturnius Aaron's affair with Tamora (2.3.72-87); and in Act 4, scene 2. from the lower-class waiting women who have witnessed the birth and had power to publish the news at court.

Aaron reveals his hatred yet envy of women, as he undermines their gossip, while expropriating their nurturing authority. When Chiron and Demetrius, the two grown sons of Tamora, with Aaron's encouragement, fantasize aloud about raping and mutilating a thousand, then "twenty thousand more" "Roman dames", Tamora's nurse enters "with a blackamoor Child" (4.2.41, 45, 51, s.d.). The juxtaposition of bawdy, braggadocio, and bastardy vilifies the act of procreation, and draws Aaron to it, since, like Tamora, his sexuality is forced into subversion and subjugation.[25] As captive, Aaron is forbidden the publicly ritualized forms of expression like marriage, which punctuate the life of Rome.[26] His sexuality is absorbed into the Black African stereotypes reinforced by such cultural texts as George Best's travel *Discourse* (1578, rpt. in Hakluyt, 1600), which include "the link between blackness and the devil, the myth of black sexuality, the problem of black subjection to authority ..."[27] Aaron exemplifies all of these. His baby is a "devil"; his sexuality is monstrous; his values are repudiations of Rome's. That he may possess a living tribute to this subversion strengthens Aaron's identification with the babe. Nearly all of his endearments concern racial identity (4.2.99-103, 119-21, 127, 176).

Because the child's blackness advertises its illegitimacy, Tamora bids the father to "christen it with thy dagger's point" (4.2.70). This play perverts both nurturance and ritual; here, it presents an anti-christening – a parody of both. In taking over the means of nurturance in defiance of the mother and usual female source of nourishment, Aaron inserts himself into a traditionally female position – one, as I have argued, accompanied with certain if localized power. Anxious to preserve his child just freed from "that womb where [he] imprisoned [was]", and because only women were privy to the occasion of even royal births, Aaron must discover how many women were present at the delivery and "ma[k]e away" with them (lines 124, 167). This project shows explicitly the displacement of women by men.

Here, at the moment when Aaron assumes the mantle of fatherhood, Shakespeare presents a muted tableau of women who in various ways represent the potential for maternal nursing – the nurse, the midwife, the Roman matriarch, Cornelia Gracchus, and Lavinia. Present only verbally (except for the nurse), these maternal figures nonetheless oppose the perverse nurture of Aaron. When the nurse informs Aaron that only "Cornelia the midwife and myself" assisted the Empress in childbirth (4.2.141), Shakespeare deliberately invokes the famous matriarch, Cornelia of the Gracchi, whose maternalism had been compared[28] to Lavinia's care of her nephew in the preceding scene (4.1.12-14). Aaron is no Cornelia. In fact, he will at the end of the scene order this Cornelia killed. Futher accentuating the aborted potential of motherhood is Lavinia. The traditional association of Lavinia with the mother of Rome (as the wife of Aeneus [*Aeneid*, VII]) is significant in its insignificance or inapplicability, since this Lavinia has consummated her marriage and has been raped, yet is apparently barren. Thus are the ritual and material functions of mothers, wives, nurses, and midwives displaced by male forms of feeding and violence; the potential for nurturing motherhood is aborted.

Aaron's flat betrayal of Tamora posits that his mode of nursery perverts the ideal of nurture located within a family setting, and spells out the necessary displacement of women by men. His statement valorizes his fatherhood over his bond with the mother:

> My mistress is my mistress, this myself,
> The vigour and the picture of my youth:
> This before all the world do I prefer;
> This maugre all the world will I keep safe, ... (4.2.107-110)

His commitment to the child forges for him a new black male identity, independent of Tamora; this identity is founded on the obliteration of the female's role if not in the production of the foetus (he admits that the baby was "sensibly fed / Of that self blood" that begot Chiron and Demetrius [4.2.122-3]), then as the usual source of nurture for the child.

Although Tamora has herself renounced the child, sharing with the likes of Lady Macbeth and Volumnia the curse of malevolent mother, the play nonetheless doggedly underscores her motherhood: first, in her ineffective yet powerful "mother's tears in passion for her son" that Titus spare her first-born in Act 1, scene 1 (line 109); second, in the repeated terms, such as "dam", which stress her maternal relation to Lavinia's rapists. For example, Titus, Marcus, and the young Lucius repeatedly refer to the brothers, not by name, as Lavinia[29] does (albeit in Latin), but only in relation to the mother – as "the lustful sons of Tamora", "the Empress' sons" (4.1.78, 114; also 5.2.144). Even the boy Lucius purchases his manhood via imagined sexual violence against this token mother: "... if I were a man / Their mother's bedchamber should not be safe" (4.1.106-7).[30] Finally her own discourse identifies her, at least rhetorically, with nursing: when she promises to be "a loving nurse, the mother to [Saturnius'] youth" (1.1.332); and when she invites Aaron to a tryst in the woods whose sounds she likens to "a nurse's song" (2.3.28).

Thus, despite Tamora's forsaking the bastard (though significantly, she does not kill him herself), and because the dramatic and rhetorical positions she occupies stress her role as mother-nurse, Aaron implicitly usurps her authority when he assumes custody of the child. His care of the child gives him new political capital. When confronted by Lucius and his Gothic army, Aaron promises, anticipating Milton's serpent, to "show [Lucius] wondrous things" on the assurance that Lucius agree "[t]o save my boy, to nourish and bring him up" (5.1.55, 84). Aaron here arranges for another male nurse, Lucius, to succeed him in the series of surrogate nurses through whose hands the new-born has already passed: from Gothic mother to professional Roman nurse, from Moorish father to Roman patriarch.[31] We shall see below that Lucius proves no Cornelia either.

The discursive replacement of maternal nursery with its paternal form is literalized in the circumstances surrounding the nurse's death. In a bit of seemingly gratuitous stage villainy, Aaron taunts the nurse to her death: "Weeke, weeke! – So cries the pig prepared to the spit" (4.2.146). While stock villainous, his mockery bears specific import in this play. First, his taunt appropriates and literalizes "This Little Pig Went to Market", a traditional nursery rhyme likely within the repertoires of sixteenth-century wet-nurses. His quotation of the rhyme denigrates the nurse's vital role in feeding by transmuting her from food-provider to food-signifier. Second, as the precursor to Titus' own butchery in Act V, this scene allows Aaron his turn to "play the cook", slaughtering a woman as a cook would kill a sow. Finally, Aaron defends his "deed of policy" in the interest of keeping the secret, which "a long-tongu'd babbling gossip" would betray (148, 150). His telling word-choice, "gossip", connotes both the guest at a christening or "churching" party and a slanderer – both female types.[32] He concludes his justification for her murder when he boasts: "The midwife and the nurse well made away, / Then let the ladies tattle what they please" (4.2.168-9). With the actual nurses out of the picture, Aaron is free to construct his ideal nursery in the wild and without women.

3. *A banquet. Enter Titus Andronicus ...*

Like Aaron, the Andronici possess strong paternalism with which to justify their usurpation of women's nurturing power. The same paternal motive that makes Aaron choose the life of his child above that of his mistress marks Titus' possession of Lavinia, and the same abstemious feeding which Aaron advocates characterizes both Titus and his son Lucius, who succeeds Saturninus as Emperor. Titus could as well have said of his debilitated daughter what Aaron says of the new-born: "Then let no man but I / Do execution on my flesh and blood" (4.2.84). Indeed, Titus alone "executes" Lavinia's revenge; he executes the care of his child; and finally he executes her death, following a long line of proud Roman patriarchs.[33]

Titus Andronicus presents himself first a patriarch of Rome, burying twenty-one sons in its name, and then as a kind of mother to the people, whom he must "wean" from their high opinion of him (1.1.211). It is the mother's part he chooses to play when the war is over: refusing the palliament and "scepter to control the world" (1.1.202) for the life of a civilian results in an "Abortive Domestic Tragedy", for all his troubles begin at this moment.[34] Soon after backing away from politics himself and casting his vote "by the book" for the eldest son, Titus must ask himself: "Titus, when wert thou wont to walk alone, / Dishonoured thus and challenged of wrongs?" (1.1.339-40). The answer is: since he abdicated his legitimate political power both as a military leader and as potential emperor. Transfering his identity wholly to the domestic sphere, Titus ushers in tragedy.

Titus' nurturance of his family both fuels and is fueled by his desire for revenge. The Andronici family meal of Act 3, scene 2 follows the long street scene charting Titus' accumulating woes (his vain plea to the judges, his discovery of Lavinia, his entrapment by Aaron's cruel trick, Lucius' departure) and precedes the other domestic scene in which Lavinia names her rapists. Added only in the Folio,[35] Act 3, scene 2 troubles critics for its stylistic and emotional ruggedness most evident in Titus' "handle not the theme, to talk of hands" pun (l. 29) and in the odd interposing of the fly at which Marcus and Titus variously stab and on which they allegorize (ll. 52-78). (Jane Howell's video production for the BBC nicely captures the oddity of the moment through the Boy Lucius' bewildered, darting eyes while the older men enact their parodic butchery.)

Despite critical disfavor, though, Act 3, scene 2 is crucial, for it sets the pattern of male-sponsored nurture. Here, Titus directs the action (as he will in the "kitchen scene" [5.2], where he kills and cooks Chiron and Demetrius, and also in the feeding of Tamora in 5.3). He "plays the housewife", performing the duties and rituals normally allotted to women in early modern English households. Titus commands his brother and his grandson to sit and eat (lines 1-3), to "fall to" or consume the food (34); and he orders servants to get drinks (35), and then to clear the table (80). The scene is framed by his direction: first, he instructs the family, "So, so, now sit ..." (1). His exit line shows him firmly in domestic space – as loving parent, and aging grandsire, ushering Lavinia and Lucius to private recreation:

... Lavinia, go with me;
I'll to thy closet, and go read with thee
Sad stories chanced in the times of old.
Come, boy, and go with me; thy sight is young,
And thou shalt read when mine begn to dazzle.  (3.2.80-4)

This domestic moment sentimentalizes Titus in his nurse-role. Yet, it is important to note that his ministry of nursing means taking over a function formerly Lavinia's own: the reading of bedtime stories to the child. Titus later reminds the boy, "Ah, boy, Cornelia never with more care / Read to her sons than she hath read to thee . . . " (4.1.12-3). Further displacing Lavinia from an active position within the household, the Boy is instructed to take over when Titus' eyes fail. Rape and mutilation, critics have shown, destroy Lavinia's powers of speech and communication; yet, equally significant is her inability to read because it prevents her from providing "kind nursery" to her nephew. In fact, the following scene shows how Lavinia's condition has alienated her from routine domestic functions. The Boy runs onto the stage, crying: "Help, grandsire, help! My aunt Lavinia / Follows me everywhere, [...] / Alas, sweet aunt, I know not what you mean" (4.1.1-2, 4). That the sight of her causes the Boy to drop his books (s.d. 4.1.4) dramatizes Lavinia's being wrested from the means of tale-telling, an important part of nursery.

Titus' parsimony at table – "eat no more / Than will preserve just so much strength in us / As will revenge these bitter woes of ours" (3.2.1-3) – prefigures Aaron's address to his son. Neither regimen offers adequate nourishment and both serve the fathers' revenge schemes, while effectively superseding their female counterparts.[36] In addition to sharpening his kinsmen's hunger for revenge, Titus in a sense fattens Lavinia for slaughter: "Come, let's fall to; and, gentle girl, eat this" (34). Like Aaron who defies the mother's will: "Tell the Empress from me, I am of age / To keep mine own" (4.2.104-5), Titus volunteers to spoonfeed his "baby", an infantalized and motherless daughter, who can neither speak nor feed herself. And like Aaron, he nourishes and "keep[s] his own" only for "his own" ends. Later, his words speak of daughter and father at once, conflating her rape with his shame: "Die, die, Lavinia, and thy shame with thee, / And with thy shame thy father's sorrow die!" (5.3.46-7). His death cry ironically inverts the phrase with which he had greeted his daughter in Act 1: "Lavinia, live, outlive thy father's days, / And fame's eternal date, for virtue's praise" (1.1.167-8).[37] Whatever their paternal feelings, both fathers use nurture as a means to incorporate the child and to serve a political aim.

Throughout Lavinia's ordeal, Titus desires so strongly to take up her part, to speak and act for her, that he inserts himself into traditionally female subject positions: in doffing political power (1.1); in replicating her mutilation (3.1); and in speaking for her: "I can interpret all her martyred signs", "I [...] will wrest an alphabet" (3.2.36, 44). Yet, in this play in which maternal nurturing is so vexed and vulnerable, we must see Titus' appropriations in the context of the pattern of women's nurturing roles taken up by men. Titus as male nurse marginalizes both the archetypal female story-teller, Cornelia, and the on-stage mother surrogate, Lavinia in Act 3, scene 2. In his gruesome revenge against Chiron and Demetrius and their "dam", Titus displaces again an on-stage mother and textual woman, as he claims to out-Procne Procne, while upstaging Tamora in the process: "I [. . . ] / will o'erreach them in their own devices, / A pair of cursed hellhounds and their dame"; "For worse than Philomel you us'd my daughter, / And worse than Progne I will be reveng'd" (5.2.129-30, 194-5). Titus usurps the woman's part in the myth, reinscribing Philomel and Procne's ritual power and justified anger as wronged women into his own patriarchal discourse. The Ovidian supper for Tereus, the rapist of Philomel and husband of Procne, is firmly centered in private domestic space.[38] This meal becomes in *Titus* a feast of state, a highly theatrical event, typical of Shakespearean nurturing men. Again, Titus orchestrates the action: "I would be sure to have all well, / To entertain your Highness and your empress" (5.3.31-2). As Eugene Waith states, "The contrast between these ceremonial gestures and the ensuing carnage fits perfectly in a play where every ceremony is in some way at odds with the situation which it solemnizes."[39] In his insistence to "play the cook", then, Titus parallels Aaron who plays the nurse: both roles parody women's power to feed and obliterate women's places in symbolic and material reproduction; both exploit the politics of nurture.

The play displaces feminine nurture with its parody by marginalizing women textually as well as theatrically. For example, though Titus takes up the Ovidian allusion, it was Lavinia who had herself literally pointed to the text of her nephew's *Metamorphoses* – significantly, a gift from his mother – another absent-present maternal force in the play (4.1.43). As Marjorie Garber argues, Lavinia's mutilation has turned her into a "ghost writer", "under erasure [...] marginalized by [...] gender."[40] And so it is Titus who must "read" in her allusion, "the tragic tale of Philomel" (4.1.46-7). Now her father revises the myth to suit his situation, rendering more horrific (because public) Ovid's sufficiently gory tale of Philomel, and co-opting the motive for revenge. Whereas Ovid recounts the "revenge of two women against the ruthless *male* violation of femininity" (Barber and Wheeler, 136, original italics), Titus enacts his own "violation[s] of femininity" by forcing her to eat Chiron and Demetrius, and by killing his own daughter.

Shakespeare preserves the conventions of revenge tragedy in designating the avenger as male, but in doing so he must revise a well-known classical source, and thwart the revenge plot of his female anti-heroine, Tamora.[41] Interestingly, as in the case of Aaron, the only casualties to fall to the hero are women and children. Placing *Titus* in the context of Renaissance revenge tragedies, Marion Wynne-Davies argues that Lavinia's role in the destruction of her assailants is uniquely active (in 5.2). Unique insofar as stage-revengers were typically male, and active because, "while her father cuts the throats of Demetrius and Chiron, [Lavinia] "'tween her stumps doth hold / The basin that receives [their] guilty blood' (5.2.182-3)."[42] From Lavinia's access to the convention of revenge tragedy, Wynne-Davies infers that she – at least momentarily – "evades containment", concluding that the play "briefly offers up this subversive possibility as an acceptable, indeed desirable, alternative" (133).

Although Lavinia actively participates in the revenge on stage, her position and privilege as housewife are greatly impaired. It is important to place the scene in another context alongside dramatic convention – that of an ordinary Renaissance kitchen, where the lady of the house directed the activity. Without placing naturalistic demands on this particularly stylized play, we may yet observe in its frequent deployment of household stuff, certain reference to the literal domestic sphere: virtually all of the scenes at Titus' house are cluttered with objects – tables, plates, books, basins, cleavers, etc., indicated by the infamous stage directions: "*Enter Titus Andronicus with a knife, and Lavinia with a basin*" (5.2.165); "*A table brought in*" (5.3.25). This visual language is not the realistic property of some twentieth-century drama, but purposeful and symbolic: in this case, the domestic tools, tables, and vessels point us to the material world of the household, while the language and action of these moments transcend the ordinary.[43] Indeed, the horror of Titus' revenge is signalled in part by the anomaly of his occupation of the kitchen, normally the domain of housewives and servants. The "subversive" potential Wynne-Davies observes is further undercut by the fact that Lavinia enacts the symbolically feminine role of *receptacle*: she bears the basin that "receives" the blood – reminding viewers at once of the "fell devouring receptacle", and of Lavinia's previous receptive roles: when she is raped (2.3); when she carries Titus's hand in her mouth (3.1); when Titus suggests that she "... get some little knife between thy teeth, / And just against thy heart make thou a hole, / That all the tears that thy poor eyes let fall / May run into that sink" (3.2.16-19); and when, with her mouth, she grasps Marcus's staff to write her accusation (4.1). Hole, victim, mouth, sink – these are not active images. Furthermore, the image prefigures Tamora's imminent consumption of that blood which Lavinia's basin had "receive[d]." So although Lavinia is present and active in the scene, it is Titus who "play[s] the housewife", who directs the action, even repeating the recipe for the pie twice.[44]

4. Ravenous Tigers

Domestic authority in early modern England carried ideological weight, as wives influenced the operation of households – figured as "little commonwealths", spiritual centers, and seminaries of good subjects. In its habitual displacement of nurturing female figures, *Titus* imagines not only a domestic sphere without women, but also a national narrative unmarked by signification by women. Women's speech, like their nurturing potential, appears only as an absence. While Titus nominally exults nurses (remembered in in the play through national myths and moral exempla), the play displaces women's discourse as it literally destroys all nurturing women – aunts, mothers, nurses, midwives. We have noted Lavinia's emptied-out significance as Rome's mother; she is early refered to as "Rome's rich ornament" and "Rome's royal mistress" (1.1.52, 241), but she is both childless and prevented from executing her household duties as aunt, wife, and daughter. Only with the intervention of father and uncle can she attend on her young nephew, who must be reminded by them that she "[l]oves me as dear as e'er my mother did" (4.1.23). The only fertile woman on stage is Tamora, whose offspring are systematically slaughtered, effectively "unmothering" her.

Against these forms of thwarted nursing adminstered by women, Titus and Aaron assume parthenogenic parenthood, achieved by destroying women's nurturing and signifying power. In order to praise his daughter's past deeds, Titus invokes Cornelia of the Gracchi, the mother of the political reformers, and one whom Plutarch praises for the exemplary education of her sons (4.1.12-14).[45] Lavinia, like this Roman mother, nursed her ward on good books, "read to thee [young Lucius] / Sweet poetry and Tully's Orator." But as noted above, Lavinia is no longer able to recite poems or Cicero and instead frightens her nephew. It is rather Titus who displaces both Cornelia and Lavinia, telling tales to the boy, offering to share them with his daughter (3.2.80 ff.), and he who is eulogized not for his former military might, but rather for his "kind nursery".[46] In a type of eulogy, Lucius reminds his son of Titus' authorizing tales and of the enduring currency of their precepts:

> Many a time he danc'd thee on his knee,
> Sung thee asleep, his loving breast thy pillow;
> Many a story hath he told to thee,
> And bid thee bear his pretty tales in mind,
> And talk of them when he was dead and gone.   (5.3.161-5)

Lucius' memory – of peaceful slumber, lullabies, and stories in the home – replaces the present, public scene of slaughter that Titus had wrought, with a safer, domestic portrait of his father. The language further contrasts with Lucius' ensuing commandments against the interlopers, Aaron and Tamora, as well as the possible destruction of the interracial baby.

In this ritualized moment, in which all the surviving notables are present, both Lavinia and Cornelia are forgotten and the grandfatherly nurse takes up the foreground. As Green observes, "almost every spectacle, deed, and character is absorbed into the titanic presence of the protagonist [...] Shakespeare's notable and notorious female characters are here made to serve the construction of Titus – patriarch, tragic hero, and, from our vantage point, central consciousness" (319). Storytelling, like its material counterpoint, nurturing, is removed from the province of women into that of the father.

The related powers of nurture and signification denied women collapse in Tamora's thwarted revenge. That Titus' ploy of the feast aborts Tamora's own Revenge banquet lends poignancy to the irony of her cannibalism, which most critics miss.[47] It was she who had suggested a feast in the first place; first, metaphorically in talk of fish bait and excessively rich food (4.4.87-92), then literally. Impersonating "Revenge", she plots to lure Lucius home, "[a]nd whilst I at a banket hold him sure, / I'll find some cunning practice out of hand" (5.2.76-7).[48] But before she can execute whatever plan she had had to drive enmity between her former compatriots and the Romans, Titus intervenes to invite them all – Lucius, and the "chiefest princes of the Goths" (among whom Tamora had once been Queen),[49] "the Emperor and the Empress too [... to] Feast at my house" (5.2.125, 127-8). Tamora's own scheme is used against her, as Ronald Broude notes: "The ingenious disguise upon which she pins her hopes backfires, [...] and, in a grimly ironic reversal, the Empress finds herself both the agent and the victim of the Revenge she has undertaken to impersonate."[50]

This "reversal" marks the action of the play with respect to its women characters. Just as Aaron had overridden Tamora's command to "christen" the child, so Titus takes over this ritual meal. As she had bidden Chiron and Demetrius to follow her ruse of the Masque, so Titus orders his own crew, "Come, come, be every one officious / To make this banquet" (5.2.201-2). Titus' feast "unmetaphors" Tamora's imagery of "animals rotted with delicious feed" (IV.iv.92) as he disengenuously invites, "Will't please you eat? Will't please your highness feed?" (5.3.53), and then reveals that the Empress's sons are "both baked in this pie, / Whereof their mother daintily hath fed, / Eating the flesh that she herself had bred" (59-61). In this inevitable rhyme merge the two lost powers of women – feeding and breeding, nurture and signification. In each case, a woman's social, rhetorical or dramatic capital is appropriated by a man, climaxing in Titus' banquet.

Shakespeare carries this masculine mode of nurturance into the next generation, although some critics ascribe to Lucius the end of "the hideous feeding."[51] In a literal sense this seems true, since Lucius's new Roman order swings dialectically to end feeding altogether. Lucius circumvents the domestic and female locus of food-provision by carrying the prerogative of feeding into the political realm. He, like his father,[52] orders his captive's mouth stopped (5.1.151) primarily to stifle Aaron's bravado, but Lucius' subsequent prevention of feeding lends a more literal cast to stopped-up mouths. When he brings Aaron inside the house, where all believe a conciliatory meal awaits, his first injunction prohibits the feeding of "[t]his ravenous tiger": "Let him receive no sust'nance" (5.3.5, 6). Having "stopped" his mouth figuratively and excluded Aaron from the ritual meal, Lucius in his final order against the Moor merely extends his tendency to withhold nurture:

Set him breast-deep in earth and famish him;
There let him stand and rave and cry for food.
If anyone relieves or pities him,
For the offence he dies; this is our doom.     (5.3.178-81)

State-sponsored starvation presents a fitting cap to this banquet which has served vengeance rather than nutriment in defiance of the terms of its invitation. "ordained to an honorable end / For peace, for love, for league, and good to Rome" (5.3.22-3).

The sense of a better world succeeding the carnage is further undermined by the silence and absence of women at the end of the play. The reconstitution of patriarchy under Lucius "exacts [a steep price] from women (and younger sons, and those without power, or those who are otherwise peripheral): they, their pain, and all their experiences are consigned to silence and illegibility" (Green, 323). Additionally, Marcus' optimistic belief in the knitting of "This scattered corn into one mutual sheaf, / These broken limbs again into one body" (5.3.70-2) sounds "a little too reminiscent of the fare of Titus' feast to be a palliative."[53] Lucius' judgment falls to a second "ravenous tiger", who receives the opposite treatment; rather than starve like her paramour, Tamora's corpse will "feed". Like the nurse-turned-sow in Aaron's mockery, Tamora's potential for nurturing motherhood is transmuted into literal food:

> As for that ravenous tiger Tamora,
> No funeral rite, nor man in mourning weed, [...]
> But throw her forth to beasts and birds to prey.   (5.3.195-6, 198)

Clearly, the application of "ravenous" to both outsiders indicates that Tamora and Aaron are punished for an appetite that Rome wants to deny in itself.

In the otherwise highly ritualized Rome, here again ritual is aborted as Lucius forbids the empress' burial, and appropriates the means of nurturance in condemning the mother who once fed children now to "feed" carrion.[54] Like the anti-christening of Act 4, scene 2, this anti-burial forbids signification by women. In light of these prohibitions against feeding, Lucius' repeated promises to "see it [Aaron and Tamora's child] nourished" offers little hope for its survival (5.1.60, 69, 84). The BBC production implies Lucius' broken promise: in the final scene Marcus presents as trophy a tiny black coffin containing the baby, whom Lucius earlier wanted to see hanged (5.1.51). In this concluding scenario, nurturance without women is institutionalized: the same situation which, for Aaron, had been renegade fantasy, now appears in the Emperor's final command, and shows the significant cultural investment in the power to provide or withhold nurture.

*Titus* presents family units – the one enduring from ancient Roman stock and the other sprung from illicit miscegenation – from which mothers, wives, and daughters are either literally absent: Titus' wife, Lucius' wife; or otherwise debilitated: Lavinia and Tamora, and hence, eliminated from the workings of household government, most notably in the production and service of food. This theatrical (in both senses of the word) expropriation by patriarchs of women's nurturing and domestic labor seems blatantly to contradict the historical situation in England where women performed most or all of the work inside their homes. But, as Raymond Williams explains of ideology, these imaginary forms bring to expression and to consciousness cultural and economic transformations.[55] In this case, the drama reflects the ironies inherent in the changing cultural evaluation of women's work – seen at once to be powerful and devalued (perhaps for that reason) – and the changes in the economy which destabilized the aristocracy and the lower classes alike. With an uncertain political fate outside, Titus crosses the threshold into domestic space where he seeks sovereignty by taking over material and symbolic feeding functions. Aaron, politically disenfranchised and culturally powerless, finds identity and power in nourishing his son, and realizes the necessity of denying or destroying maternal figures in the process. We may imagine early modern merchants and noblemen, for example, finding in domestic space opportunities to secure authority and identity – and meeting more resistance than Tamora and Lavinia can muster. The tensions, then, between performed and lived social life, enacted specifically around feeding and nursery, identify nurturance and domestic government as vital concerns in the society and culture of Elizabethan England.[56]

*Notes*

1. For example, William Gouge, *Of Domesticall Duties, Eight Treatises* (London, 1612). Gervase Markham's *The English House-wife* (1615) delineates the work of the eponymic woman: "physic, cookery, banquetting-stuff, distillation, perfumes, wool, hemp, flax, dairies, brewing, baking, and the other things belonging to a household." This list appears on the title page of the original edition of the text, "Containing the inward and outward virtues which ought to be in a complete woman." Susan Amussen, *The Ordered Society: Gender and Class in Early Modern England*. (New York: Basil Blackwell, 1988) 41.

2. "Where are the Mothers in Shakespeare? Options for Gender Representation in the English Renaissance" *SQ* 41 (1991) 3: 295.

3. Rose, p. 297.

4.  Jean E. Howard, *The Stage and Social Struggle in Early Modern England.* (New York: Routledge, 1994), p. 104.

5.  Lena Cowen Orlin, *Private Matters and Public Culture in Post-Reformation England.* (Ithaca: Cornell UP, 1994), p. 102.

6.  Catherine Belsey, *The Subject of Tragedy: Identity and Difference in Renaissance Drama.* (New York: Methuen, 1985), p. 129-221; Karen Newman, *Fashioning Femininity and English Renaissance Drama.* (Chicago: Chicago UP, 1991), p. 40-1.

7.  Richard Wheeler and C.L. Barber, *The Whole Journey: Shakespeare's Power of Development.* (Berkeley: California UP, 1986), p. 3.

8.  Jean Brink, "Domesticating the Dark Lady" in *Privileging Gender in Early Modern England.* Jean Brink, ed. (Kirksville, MO: Sixteenth Century Journal Publishers, 1993), p. 106.

9.  Paula Berggren contrasts the purposes and effects of male and female disguise in Shakespeare; her conclusions are similar to my own observations of the 'player-cooks': for male characters, she says, "disguise is no spontaneous self-extension but a shrewd political tactic ... " "The Woman's Part: Female Sexuality as Power in Shakespeare's Plays." in *The Woman's Part: Feminist Criticism of Shakespeare*, ed. Carolyn Ruth Swift Lenz, Gayle Green, and Carol Thomas Neely (Urbana: Illinois UP, 1980), p. 32, n. 6.

10.  Quotations from *Titus Andronicus* come from Eugene M. Waith, ed. Oxford: Clarendon Press, 1984.

11.  Menenius, the Roman patrician, is a notable exception: "a perfecter giber for the table than a necessary bencher in the Capitol," he invites Volumnia to "sup with [him]," and she, "Juno-like," refuses (*Coriolanus* II.i.47, 82-3, IV.ii.49, 54). He places great transformative ability on feeding, as he imagines that eating well will give Coriolanus a "suppler soul." Quotations from all Shakespearean plays apart from *Titus* come from *The Complete Pelican Shakespeare.* Alfred Harbage, ed. New York: Viking, 1969.

12.  My argument is anticipated by Barber and Wheeler, who observe that the play offers no "larger social world [... and] no ongoing business of state and private life within which the isolation and impotence of the injured hero can be presented ...", p. 125.

13.  For a discussion of the comic and tragic deployment of meals on the Shakespearean stage, see Frances Teague, *Shakespeare's Speaking Properties* (Lewisburg: Bucknell UP, 1991), p. 65-7.

14.  The complicated cultural phenomenon of hospitality in the period is beyond the scope of this paper. I have addressed it in *Private Supper/ Public Feast: Gender, Power and Nurture in Early Modern England* (*DAI*, University of Illinois, 1991). See also Felicity Heal, *Hospitality in Early Modern England.* Oxford: Clarendon Press, 1990, and Daryl Palmer, *Hospitable Performances. Dramatic Genre and Cultural Practices in Early Modern England.* West Lafayette, In.: Purdue UP, 1992.

15.  *Worlds Apart: The Market and the Theatre in Anglo-American Thought 1550-1750.* (New York: Cambridge UP, 1986), p. 60.

16. Naomi Conn Liebler, "Getting It All Right: *Titus Andronicus* and Roman History" *SQ* 45.3 (1994), p. 275. Liebler's lucid explication of "cultural disintegration" is welcome, especially when critics – however willing to discuss racial and gender otherness in the play – continue to identify political structures as monoliths. Compare Brink: "Tamora [is ...] not only alienated from, but in oppostion to *the dominant patriarchal culture*," p. 97 (italics added).

17. For fuller discussions of Roman 'pietas' see Robert Miola, "*Titus Andronicus* and the Mythos of Shakespeare's Rome." *Sh. Studies* XIV (1981), p. 92-3; and Alan Sommers, "'Wilderness of Tigers': Structure and Symbolism in *Titus Andronicus*." *Essays in Criticism*. X (1960), p. 277 ff. A family relationship is rarely invoked in the play without the simultaneous assertion of some kind of violence. See, for example:1.1., where Titus kills his son Mutius and the Andronici kill Tamora's son, Alarbus – all in the name of family honor; 2.1, where Chiron and Demetrius draw swords to execute their sibling rivalry; 3.1., where uncle, brother, and son fight over whose hand to send to the Emperor – again, this blood is thought to spare other sons' blood; and 4.2., when Aaron threatens to kill his son's half-brothers who had threatened to kill his son. For an interesting discussion of dismemberment, see Katherine A. Rowe, "Dismembering and Forgetting in *Titus Andronicus*" *SQ* 45.3 (1994), p. 279-303. On the problems with staging the violence, see Alan Dessen, *Titus Andronicus* . Manchester and New York, 1989.

18. Many studies consider the woman-as-nature analogy the play deploys, and explicate the on-stage pit as 'feminine.' See, for example, Marion Wynne-Davies, "'The swallowing Womb': Consumed and Consuming Women in *Titus Andronicus*" in *The Matter of Difference: Materialist Feminist Criticism of Shakespeare*. Valerie Wayne, ed. (Ithaca, NY: Cornell UP, 1991), pp. 129-52; and David Willbern, "Rape and Revenge in *Titus Andronicus*" *ELR* 8 (1978), p. 159-82. While I find this line of argument extremely useful, the present study focuses on the social function of nurture rather than on the symbolic feminine.

19. Whereas Shakespeare attributes the pit to nature, the prose narrative *The Tragical History of Titus Andronicus,* which may be a source for or an analogue to Shakespeare's play, specifies that the Empress, the Moor, and her sons "digged a very deep pit in a pathway." Repr. in Waith, *Titus*, p. 200. For the most recent discussion of "source study", see Liebler.

20. For a discussion of the play's shifting hole and devouring images, see D.J. Palmer, "The Unspeakable in Pursuit of the Uneatable: Language and Action in *Titus Andronicus*." *Critical Quarterly*. 14 (1972) 4, pp. 239, 330, and 333. Gillian Murray Kendall surveys the differing descriptions of "that wood", to argue that characters conceive of it "according to their ideas about what genre of play they think they find themselves in." "'Lend me thy hand': Metaphor and Mayhem in *Titus Andronicus*." *SQ* 40 (1989), p. 310.

21. "Rape and Revenge in *Titus Andronicus*" *ELR* 8 (1978), pp. 159-82.

22. Sommers accepts at face value the racist discourse of the Romans and attributes Aaron's pastoral fantasy to the fact that he "is a creature of wild nature, so conceived in many descriptive similes, and particularly in his words to his child", p. 285.

23. Emily C. Bartels argues that while Shakespeare emphasizes Aaron's otherness in *Titus*, in *Othello* he stresses "the Moor's status as an 'insider', not his difference as an 'outsider'." See "Making More of the Moor: Aaron, Othello, and Renaissance Refashionings of Race." *SQ* 41 (1990), p. 435. Martin Orkin defends Shakespeare against charges of racism by arguing that he works against "color prejudice" through his reversal of black and white associations: "It is Iago,

the white man, who is portrayed amoral and anti-Christian, essentially savage towards that which he envies and resents ..." "*Othello* and the 'plain face' of Racism" *SQ* 38 (1987), p. 170.

24. Leslie Fiedler makes the same observation, and argues further: "Aaron [...] commits no crime which equals in horror Titus' own final atrocity of feeding to a mother pasties made of the blood and bones of her two sons, who had earlier raped his daughter. And yet Titus is portrayed finally not as a villain, but as an equivocal figure, essentially noble, though excessive in his rage [...]. Aaron, however, remains a villain unqualified, since his evil is established more in speech than action, by the role he plays rather than the atrocities he commits." *The Stranger in Shakespeare.* (New York: Stein and Day, 1972), p. 180.

25. Bartels, p. 445.

26. Waith's studies of ceremony in the play remain essential; see his Introduction to *Titus* and "Ceremonies in *Titus*" in *Mirror Up to Shakespeare: Essays in Honour of G.R. Hibbard,* ed. J.C. Gray (Buffalo: Toronto UP, 1984), pp. 159-70.

27. Karen Newman, "And wash the Ethiop white: Femininity and the Monstrous in *Othello*" in *Shakespeare Reproduced: The Text in History and Ideology.* Eds. Jean Howard and Marion O'Connor. (New York: Methuen, 1987), p. 147.

28. Based on Q1, Kittredge ascribes the lines to Titus: "Ah, boy, Cornelia never with more care / Read to her sons than she had to thee / Sweet poetry and Tully's Orator" (4.1.11-13). But *The Riverside*, using F1, gives them to Marcus. In either case, one of the Andronicus patriarchs invokes Cornelia in connection with Lavinia.

29. It is important to remember that only Lavinia knows of the part Tamora had played in goading the men on and in refusing her mercy.

30. See also 2.3.142-6. Willbern identifies another implicit sexual assault: when Titus directs his grandson to shoot an arrow "in Virgo's lap" (6.3.64), he conflates his plea for justice with "the hostile and erotic (matricidinal and incestuous) impulses underlying the play", p. 170.

31. The fate of the child remains ambiguous in the text: he is carried onto the stage in 5.3. "in the arms of an Attendant" (s.d.), and Marcus later announces, "Behold the child: / Of this was Tamora delivered" (ll. 119-20), yet no subsequent direction for it is given. For the BBC production Jane Howell solved the problem by presenting a small black coffin on stage in Act 5 containing the remains of the babe and fascinating the boy Lucius. This dramatic solution jibes with my reading of the play, for the Emperor Lucius seems to me an unreliable nurse.

32. *OED*

33. See 4.1. where he and Marcus invoke Lord Junius Brutus, Lucrece's father; they quote Seneca in Latin; clap a patriotic title onto little Lucius: "Roman Hector's hope"; and endure each other's "good man's groans", while plotting revenge for "old Andronicus". Meanwhile Lavinia sits apparently unattended. Titus later acknowledges also Virginius, as a model for his narrative.

34. This is Barber and Wheeler's chapter title, carrying the thesis for their discussion of the play, p. 125. Most interpretations of the opening scene identify Titus' selection of Saturnius over the better choice of Bassanius as his "fundamental error". According to Sommers, "This failure [to choose rightly] initiates his tragedy", p. 280.

35. In his introduction to the play, Waith discusses problems with dating and authorship of the added scene, pp. 17-18; he further notes that Act 3, scene 2 is often cut or reassembled in productions, p. 54.

36. Barber and Wheeler characterize Titus' feeding habits thus: "Titus the dutiful warrior is the nurturing male parent whose curious nurture is, for him and his family, all there is: he leads male children out to death and back into the family tomb; he cherishes a daughter made sexually safe yet suggestive by disfigurement, only finally to destroy her", p. 155.

37. Miola explains how the play invites us to see Lavinia's rape as an affront to the family name, justifying Titus' "sympathy of woe": "Since Lavinia is portrayed more as the daughter of Titus and the sister of Lucius than as the wife of Bassanius, the rape is a direct assault on the Andronici family and the Roman virtue which it represents", p. 88. Douglas E. Green similarly notes that Lavinia "mirrors" Titus: "her mutilated body 'articulates' Titus' own suffering and victimization [...] Their 'sympathy of woe [...]' transforms her irremediable condition into the emblem of his." "Interpreting 'her martyr'd signs': Gender and Tragedy in *Titus Andronicus*". *SQ* 40 (1989), p. 322.

38. In Ovid's *Metamorphosis*, Procne does everything she can to keep the meal private: "And feyning a solemnitie according to the guise / Of *Athens*, at the which there might be none in any wise / Besides hir husband and hir selfe, she banisht from the same / Hir household folke and sojourners, and such as guestwise came" (Book 6, ll. 820-3). Transl. Arthur Golding (London, 1567). Repr. in Geoffrey Bullough, *Narrative and Dramatic Sources of Shakespeare* Vol. VI (New York: Columbia Univ. Press, 1966), p. 57.

39. "Ceremonies", p. 169.

40. *Shakespeare's Ghost Writers: Literature as Uncanny Causality*. (New York: Methuen, 1987), p. 25.

41. Tamora's sense of revenge is also conveyed through food imagery; see 4.4.88-92.

42. Wynne-Davies, pp. 132-3.

43. On the topic of production values in renaissance theaters, see Alexander Leggatt's recent book, *Jacobean Public Theatre*. (New York: Routledge, 1992), pp. 49-66. Leggatt contends that props "do not just help create an ambience [...] but help to point the direction of the story", p. 57.

44. See 5.2.186-9, 197-200.

45. Plutarch, "Tiberius, and Caius Gracchi" in *Lives of the Noble Grecians and Romanes*, transl. Thomas North, vol. VI. (repr. Oxford: Blackwell, 1928).

46. Barber and Wheeler similarly observe that Titus' family remembers him "not as a stern figure of authority, but as a tender, cherishing parent and grandparent", while, at the same time, Tamora is figured as devouring, p. 155.

47. Most critics see a perfect poetic justice meted out by Titus, who feeds Appetite, which Tamora is seen to allegorize, along with her sons, Lust and Murder. See Maurice Hunt, "Compelling Art in *Titus Andronicus*". *SEL*. 28 (1988), p. 210; and Sommers, pp. 283, 289.

48. She repeats the specific detail of the feast again later (lines 114-15).

49. In failing to provide a Gothic King, Shakespeare departs from the source (see "The Prose History of Titus Andronicus" repr. in Waith's edition, Appendix A, pp. 195-203). Willbern notes Tamora's paradoxical condition – absence of a spouse yet sexually active – in light of Lavinia's opposite state: married yet virginal, p. 164, n. 11.

50. "Four Forms of Vengeance in *Titus Andronicus.*" *JEGP* LXXVIII (1979), p. 502.

51. Miola, p. 94.

52. See 5.2.161, 164, 167.

53. Kendall, p. 315

54. There is a possible pun on "pray," which would make sense in terms of the anti-ritual sentiment of the ending.

55. *Keywords: A vocabulary of Culture and Society.* Revised edition. (New York: Oxford UP, 1983), p. 156.

56. I wish to thank Richard Wheeler, Carol Thomas Neely and Naomi Liebler for their generous responses to earlier drafts of this essay.

# TRIALS OF MARRIAGE IN *MEASURE FOR MEASURE*

Cindy Carlson
(Metropolitan State College, Denver)

While many earlier readers of *Measure for Measure* have discussed the play's treatment of the tension between mercy and justice and the tension between men and women, discussions of the marriages in the play have been few. An article from the early sixties and the introduction to the Arden edition take up the notion of the marriage contracts between Claudio and Juliet and between Angelo and Mariana, but later works have not found that legal material to be very suggestive or helpful.[1] More recent articles discuss the variously peculiar sexual proclivities evidenced by the play's characters, but do not treat the proposed or imposed marriages as part of those sexualities.[2] None of the treatments that I have looked at has examined the connections between good government and good marriages. Victoria Hayne surveys English marriage practices in the sixteenth and seventeenth century, along with Puritan efforts to reform the civil law to include harsh penalties for fornication, and concludes that *Measure for Measure* dramatizes the popular acceptance of sexuality prior to marriage.[3] Even so, this play makes the connection between erratic government and imprisoning marriages because the marriages permitted and promoted at the play's end do not disguise their irregularity, just as the presence of marriage and the presence of the prison do not disguise the continuing disorder they are meant to regulate and punish. Indeed, if this play provides punishment anywhere, it is in its marriages.

Tudor writers on justice and governance agree that the good ruler must use both rigor and mercy in order to promote justice. In *Measure for Measure*, Angelo rules too harshly because he apparently considers that all sexual liaisons that have not been formally entered into through a regular marriage ceremony involve their partners in fornication, a capital crime under a newly revived law. At the play's end, Vincentio chooses to regard all sexual liaisons as marriages; even partners in commercial sex end up married. Both are able to justify their governance because marriages could be created openly or clandestinely, with the result that a legal finding that a valid marriage existed, or not, might turn on the words and understandings of the couple involved. From the uncertainties of marriage creation come the play's concerns for legitimate offspring and containment of sexual slander. Vincentio's universal panacea – or punishment of – marriage will make all offspring legitimate, will perhaps control some forms of slander, and will certainly make consent to marriage, long thought to be the essence of marriage formation, irrelevant. Thus far is Vincentio willing to go in order to re-establish his rule in Vienna.

From the beginning of the play, Shakespeare has entwined the passions of unfettered rule and of unfettered sexual expression, and has set both against the rule of law in public government and the rule of marriage in domestic government. No realm or prince can do without rule and self-rule. The realm and the prince must cleave to the law, both in its rigor and its mercy, as a guard against the license of lacking rule and the oppression of overweening rule. No human being lives with congealed blood, but no human society can endure excessively liberated, even libertine, sexual activity. As society would suffer from an unruled sexuality, so would the person. Talk of marriage can be a seducer's ploy, a customer's sop to his conscience, or a wooer's sincere proposal; marriage can be oppressive or loving. At any given moment, the talk or the marriage can slide from one mode to the other. Yet marriage, the domestic arrangement of everyday, holds up the mysterious promise of chaste sexuality, of liberty and rule. No human being or human society achieves that conjunction of contraries, yet every human individual and human society negotiates between those irreconcilable impulses toward the strict and the lax, toward the libertine and the chaste.

Marriage creation is the province of all four of the main male characters. Both Claudio and Angelo have made verbal marriage contracts with their respective partners. Claudio considers that Juliet is "fast my wife," made so "upon a true contract" (1.2.136, 134).[4] Vincentio reassures Mariana (and Isabella) that the bedtrick involves no dishonor for Mariana because she has "title" to Angelo from her "pre-contract" of marriage with him (4.1.74, cf. 72). These words indicate that Claudio deems himself legally married to Juliet because of a private contract between the two of them. Even without a formal wedding ceremony, a promise of marriage expressed in the present tense and thereby supposed to take place at the time the words are said creates a valid marriage at the moment of the making the promise. Angelo and Mariana also apparently entered into a contract of marriage, an agreement that Angelo can no longer deny once he has consummated the agreement.

The play does not supply sufficient evidence to allow the audience to decide that Angelo must have entered into a marriage contract *de futuro*, with words of the future tense, while Claudio entered into a contract *de presenti*.[5] But the play's language does indicate marriages can be clandestinely entered into and that consummation supplies the evidence against the party who would seek to deny a contract that had previously consisted of words alone. Even Lucio appears to have involved himself in talk of marriage: Mistress Overdone complains that Lucio has maliciously turned her over to the law when he himself "promised [...] marriage" to Kate Keep-down, presumably as part of the seduction or business negotiations that led to Kate's pregnancy (3.2.194). Of course, Lucio's son is over a year old and his remonstrances with the Duke indicate that he is now far from wanting a marriage with the "punk" he was willing to sleep with (5.1.520). Yet he talked of marriage to his punk and will enter that state after the play. At the play's end, the Duke is proposing to propose to Isabella and does not appear to require a dowry from her, that property settlement that so unsettled Juliet's and Mariana's nuptials, before going through with the ceremony. Of the four brides, only Isabella will go through the church ceremony as a virgin. Only Isabella will marry without having expressed in act or in language love or desire for her future husband.

While legal practice off stage can not determine an interpretation of the drama on the stage, the rather tortured state of the law concerning marriage may bear on tortured administration of the law in *Measure for Measure*. The variations in forming a marriage in *Measure for Measure* follow the variations available to couples in real life. During the Middle Ages, the Church had never indicated or laid down a single way to form a valid marriage. The consent of the parties was crucial, but the form of that consent and the necessity of witnesses never became settled in law. Failure to consummate a marriage could be grounds for annulment, but would serve as grounds only if one of the parties brought suit; by itself, it did not invalidate a marriage.[6] However, marriages formed with far less evidentiary certainty than the ideal of a wedding before the officiant and witnesses followed by consummation could be and were held valid. Not until 1563 at the Council of Trent did the Catholic Church restrict the ways in which marriages could be formed. The decree *Tametsi* "reiterated the long-standing teaching that the essence of marriage consisted in the free exchange of marital consent between parties competent to marry one another" but went on to require that the "consent must take place in the presence of witnesses and that these witnesses must include the pastor of the parish where the parties made their promises" (Brundage 564). The Church in England made no such formal change, so clandestine marriages continued to be made, questioned, and enforced.

But by the end of the sixteenth century, church courts in England were withdrawing their support of such clandestine unions, refusing to declare them valid and prosecuting those witnesses who participated in the irregular ceremonies.[7] Martin Ingram sees this gradual change in the enforcibility of clandestine marriage contracts as the result of the "long-term success of the English church in fostering widespread acceptance of church weddings as the recognized mode of entry into the married state" (209). His own analysis of the cases also shows that many of the claimed contracts have very little evidentiary support. Some plaintiffs, perhaps as many as one in five, had no shadow of a real case. It is fairly clear from the surviving evidence that no contract had ever been made and, in most instances, that there had never been any serious prospect of marriage. Such litigants were naively persistent, scheming or (especially in the case of women made pregnant by their lovers) desperate (198). Bridal pregnancy in clandestine marriages appeared to run at about 20%, about the same as bridal pregnancy in more regularly solemnized unions (214). As fewer of these cases were brought by the "denied" spouse, probably because the plaintiff had smaller expectations of success in court, the later cases show that the contracts claimed "appear in actuality to have been mere engagements, legally formless promises to marry which were simply preliminary to marriage in church" (206).

During this same period, church courts were attempting more stringent prosecutions in cases of fornication. Claire Cross has documented that in the north of England, the High Commission, in its hearings of cases involving the gentry, had a case load that consisted of one fourth of marriage validity, one fourth of marriage breakdown, and nearly all the rest of fornication or adultery.[8] Ingram argues that the church courts did not impose a draconian morals code on local villages. Since "ecclesiastical justice depended so heavily on local cooperation for detection and prosecution of offenders", it was possible that villages might "construct their own disciplinary agendas" (366). That church courts gradually enforced somewhat more rigorously the long-standing rules against fornication, even against the gentry, that indicates society was growing more conservative and promoting greater conformity with its institutions' ideals. And at the same time, there would be good reason for a subject of the time to be confused or scheming in the face of this change.

While some reformers called for harsher punishments for sexual offenses, and for those offenses to be punishable by the secular courts, and though there were acts of parliament during the reigns of Elizabeth and James I concerning adultery, fornication, and bastardy, they "all foundered on legal difficulties, jurisdictional issues and reservations expressed by the mass of members of parliament" (Ingram 152). Not until the Rump Parliament did the Commons enact a measure whereby incest and adultery became felonies punishable by death, while fornicators were liable to three months' imprisonment. But the more drastic provisions of this act proved largely a dead letter, and the whole measure was allowed to lapse in 1660...." (153) Though reformers might express horror at the perceived wave of immorality about to engulf England, members of parliament were slower to involve themselves in legislating on such matters, perhaps from a reluctance to see criminal penalties visited on those like themselves (152). It is important to note that, no matter what the more righteous might propose, fornication, even in an unenforced act of parliament, never became a capital crime.

While this legal background cannot "explain" the use of law in *Measure for Measure*, it can illustrate the unreliability of the expectations that the law can create. Laws change; they are enforced or not; they bear on exactly those matters that people are accustomed to regard as private. In the process of changing the law or its enforcement, the ruler undercuts his people's sense of stable expectations, which remains one of the great benefits of living in a society ordered by law. During such a change, the person who is surprised to find himself punished or constrained could quite reasonably complain of inequity.

The Duke of Vienna, though, is not a proponent of legal innovation; he is intent on reviving existing, though long ignored, laws. Claudio complains to Lucio that Angelo intends to make his "name" by awaking a "drowsy and neglected act" from a sleep of nineteen years (1.2.157-9). Vincentio tells the Friar that the laws' enforcement has been "let slip" for fourteen years (1.3.21). Lucio claims that Angelo has "pick'd out an act/ Under whose heavy sense your brother's life/ Falls into forfeit" (1.4.64-6). Angelo himself acknowledges that the law "hath slept" so that many people have offended because they did not receive a salutary warning by the early punishment of wrong-doers (2.2.91). Now that the law is awake, it may "end" crimes now "in progress to be hatch'd and born" even before they see light (2.2.99, 97).[9] Angelo seems to propose a law so wide awake that it might discourage fornicators from continuing their crimes, and so punish the would-be perpetrators, even before they had been committed.

By a tardy arousal of the law's force, even if put into the hands of a deputy, Vincentio risks creating a name for himself, too: the name of a tyrant (but see below). At the beginning of the century, Thomas More's Utopian character Hythloday had warned that kings interested in good government and secure rule should first awake to their own duties:

> Yea, the king had better amend his own indolence or arrogance, for these two vices generally cause his people either to despise him or to hate him. [...] Let him check mischief and crime, and, by training his subjects rightly, let him prevent rather than allow the spread of activities which he will have to punish afterwards. Let him not be hasty in enforcing laws fallen into disuse, especially those which, long given up, have never been missed.[10]

Behind Hythloday's speech is Edmund Dudley's *The Tree of Commonwealth,* in which he recommends other rulers not to seek to make money out of reviving old laws.[11] Presumably he had found his own fall, the result of making old laws and their renewed enforcement provide for Henry VII's financial needs, as educational as any Angelo might wish.

At the end of the century, Edward Hake, writing on legal and equitable matters during Elizabeth's reign, deplores the weakness of the church courts to punish sin:

> For silence, O who imbraceth it not? who will not bee milde? where is hee that will punishe? In whome doeth not partiall pitye abounde? Or at the least wise, who is not afraid and loath to displease? yea, and (that worse is) who dareth to speake out and is not punished? who sinneth and is not pardoned? (18-19)[12]

At the same time, he praises Elizabeth for not being arbitrary with the laws' administration. She shows

No Force, where love may winne.
First friendly warnings sendes shee forth
Eare smarting Lawes beginns.
Her Subiectes bloud shee seekes to save
as Apple of her eye:
They live and shall, save such as law
and Justice bids to dye.[13]

While Hake occasionally writes as a reformer of morals and as one who would awaken the church courts and the Christians who use them to a greater sense of duty in seeking out and punishing sin, he also writes in praise of legal restraint and order. After all, his great work, *Epieikiea*, is a treatise on equity as an integral part of English law. Hake never loses sight of the legal necessity for both mercy and rigor, though he requires both only within the context of a predictable legal order.

That predictability allows Elizabeth's subjects political and economic security – and it is the hallmark of good legal institutions. It is missing in *Measure for Measure*, a dramatic world where people have different opinions about whether they are married or likely to be so, where an act deplored suddenly becomes a capital offense, where the law is perhaps as disguised as the Duke. Claudio wonders whether Angelo's new "tyranny be in his place,/ Or in his eminence that fills it up" (1.2.152-3). When the Duke handed over the rule to Angelo, he commanded that "Mortality and mercy in Vienna/ Live in thy tongue, and heart" (1.1.44-5). Angelo is to have the Duke's own power to "enforce or qualify the laws/ As to your soul seems good" (1.1.64-5). Angelo does not have a mere deputy's power to follow orders without question; he has all the residual power of a ruler to act where the laws are silent or inequitable, a power noted in Hake's *Epieikiea*.[14] Performing this balancing act requires that the ruler be stable enough to find the right proportions of rigor and mercy in creating justice, which indicates, in turn, that weak rule might vacillate from one extreme to the other with disastrous effect on the governed. The Duke confesses to the friar that he has not shown enough rigor in enforcing the laws, only to receive the friar's rebuke that the

Duke himself had the responsibility to rehabilitate the law's force (1.3.31-3). But the Duke has "impos'd" on Angelo the duties of a ruler's office and so may hope to have avoided the imputation of "tyranny" attendant on one who awakes the dormant law (1.3.36, 40).

In the same speech, the Duke says that he intends to see whether ruling will change Angelo from one who will "scarce confess/ That his blood flows" into a man of more open fallibility (1.3.51-2). While the Duke avoids the "ambush of [his] name" and "slander" for the abuse of a ruler's power (41, 43), he wants to see what that exercise of power will do to Angelo. As we have already seen, Claudio considers that Angelo is out to make a "name" for himself as a strict ruler by acting with an arbitrariness that marks him as a tyrant. Further, this flirtation with a tyrannous reviving of long dormant laws concerning fornication and marriage formation may force Angelo to reveal a human nature as much driven by passions as any other person's. Perhaps the Duke, with a potential abuse of power being carried on vicariously for him, also puts himself in the way of discovering whether the "dribbling dart of love/ Can pierce a complete bosom" (2-3). And he may discover that no bosom is complete enough to be proof against the piercings of love because it penetrates where it will, regardless of the law's strictures. In fact, the law itself is penetrable because of its dual nature, made up as it is of mercy and rigor. Because the ruler must interpret and apply it, it depends on the humanity and reason of the ruler.

The pervasive language of pregnancy and abortion, coining and counterfeiting in the play springs from this pervasive entwining of the governmental and the sexual. In this regard, it is important to remember that, the more prominent kinds of treason that culminate in compassing the king's death, include counterfeiting his coinage, normally stamped with his image. Legitimate children increase the productivity of the commonwealth - men and women through their private and domesticated love raise up children both for themselves and for the good of their society. Legitimate coins celebrate the legitimacy of the king's rule and increase the productivity of society. Bastards spring from an uncontrolled sexuality and are perceived as burdens to society; false coinage produces a false prosperity and undermines the rule of the king whose image has been usurped by the counterfeiter - as if the counterfeiter were a kind of adulterer with the body politic.

When Lucio informs Isabella of Claudio's arrest, he says that Juliet's "plenteous womb/ Expresseth his full tilth and husbandry" (1.4.43-4). Isabella's response, "let him marry her!" is not that of a repressed prude, but indicates her brother should become a husband in the social, as well as in the sexual, sense (49). Claudio is doing the right thing in raising children for that good, but only if his marriage is public and recognized as valid. Otherwise, his children are mere social burdens, bastards and despoilers of the common good. The whorehouses may be pulled down in the suburbs, but Lucio says that those in town will "stand for seed" because a "wise burgher" saw them as a good investment (1.2.92-3). As the editor of the Arden edition points out, Lucio's remarks are "equivocal", but they also establish the connection between breeding or husbandry and commercial profit. The profit from the whorehouse might even be for the common good if only the "law would allow it" (2.1.224). Claudio and Juliet delayed their public wedding ceremony for the "propagation" of her dowry, though her pregnancy did not await the same ceremony (1.2.139). If the law does not allow that Claudio is married, then the child is a burden to society; if the law allows or understands that Claudio is married, that same child is a profit to the commonwealth. Both prosperity and the common good depend on legitimacy.

This same language of pregnancy can be applied in cases of civic virtue when the act or the person is legitimately praiseworthy. Vincentio praises Escalus when he says that his counselor is as "pregnant" in knowledge of government as any other man that he can remember (1.1.11). The Duke's reminder that the torch of virtue that must "go forth" to light other torches is itself an image of fertility or fruitfulness (33-4). When Escalus says that many uncaught malefactors go unpunished Angelo acknowledges his pleading for Claudio by saying that Escalus' objection is "very pregnant" (2.1.23).

Yet not all acts are legitimately pregnant; some are merely obvious, such as the "too gross" character of Juliet's pregnancy (1.2.144). In this instance, Angelo means only that what Escalus says is clear or obvious, but he goes on to say that the

> ... jewel that we find, we stoop and take't
> Because we see it; but what we do not see,
> We tread upon, and never think of it. (2.1.24-6)

The obviousness of Escalus' observations on opportunity are like the law's taking advantage of what it can easily discover, like the person who finds a jewel in his path. In fact, our discovery of sexual desire is just as opportunistic as the discovery of the jewel or the enforcement of the law. So we can also read this passage forward to Angelo's observation of Isabella, the jewel who comes in his path at the moment that he has taken on power, and, as she observes, "potency" (2.2.67), and his denial of, or obliviousness to, Mariana immured in the moated grange. But the inclination to take the jewel is universal. As the Provost observes, "All sects, all ages smack of this vice" and yet only Claudio is to die of it and for it (2.1.5).

The smack or taste of sexuality implanted in our natures is universal, but yet distinctions can be drawn. Claudio considers Juliet his wife - he is, as even Lucio observes, "precise in promise-keeping" (1.2.69-70) - while to Angelo Juliet is merely a "fornicatress" who must await her child's birth in order for the law to deal with her because the law will not hang a pregnant woman.[15] As we are a community because we share the same sexual passions, so we are a community because our shared nature should make us merciful to each other. Angelo is constantly addressed in terms of trading places. He has traded places with the Duke, but he is continually invited to trade places in his imagination with those who have fallen foul of the law against fornication, even as Isabella invites him to change places, in his imagination, with her. If Angelo were to be like Claudio, he might have embraced Juliet and, in Angelo's place, Claudio would have shown mercy (2.2.64-6). If Isabella could put on the "potency" of a male judge and put off the power of a feminine suitor, she would explain to Angelo what a real judge and a real prisoner would look like (69-70).

Isabella accuses Angelo of imagining himself to be like Jove and using Jove's power in a most ungod-like way in preferring to blast the "soft myrtle", the plant sacred to Venus rather than show mercy (2.2.117). Finally, Isabella demands that Angelo go to his (I suppose complete) "bosom/ Knock there, and ask your heart what it doth know/ That's like my brother's fault" (2.2.137-9). Deep within the upright, precise Angelo, he will have to acknowledge community with his fellow human beings and "confess/ A natural guiltiness" (140) that all human beings share simply through being human. Perhaps deep within Vincentio's "complete bosom" rests the same nature that would be forced into confession and action if the Duke ever took seriously his responsibility to govern the marriages, the fertility, and the license in his realm. When Angelo acknowledges the common embrace of humanity that Isabella's presence makes him feel, that awareness makes him pregnant: "She speaks and 'tis such sense/ That my sense breeds with it" (2.2.142-3). The punning language propagates meanings, so that Angelo recognizes the rationality of Isabella's speech and responds reasonably to it even as his physical senses awake to his increasing desires for Isabella's person. The simultaneity of these responses makes Angelo into another Juliet, so that he is pregnant with desire and reason, yet outside of a legitimate, or publicly acknowledgeable, relationship with his entreating subject.

Angelo being what he is, that pregnancy soon turns rotten. A violet grows under the fructifying rays of the hot sun, but Angelo does "as the carrion does, not as the flower,/ Corrupt with virtuous season" (167-8). Angelo has had a fire lit in him by Isabella's virtue, but not quite in the way Vincentio had imagined. Angelo wants to assess fault in both the "tempter" and the "tempted" (165), but recognizes that a pure virtue would have bred in itself only virtue. Like every other human being, Angelo is not purely virtuous, and he shares with other humans the temptation to take the jewel in the path whether or not it rightfully belongs to him. But Angelo's inability to make proper distinctions has led him astray. He desires Isabella carnally and turns that carnal desire into carrion discomfort by feeling that desire as foul (174). Angelo has promised marriage to Mariana, but at the time that he is thunderstruck with desire for Isabella, he considers that he has never been "fond" before and even "wonder'd how" other men could be so (187). Indeed, he has assumed that carnal desires could only be aroused by women fallen or light and could only result in fornication. If he feels desire now, then he must feel it foully. Angelo's distinctions are precise and extreme - rule must be rigid or there is license; people must be pure or they are sinful. As Elizabethan tracts urge that justice is composed of rigor and mercy, so Angelo in his private life must come to see that desire may "smack" of vice, but chastity may combine with sensuality in the mutuality of marriage, as it has with Claudio and Juliet.

Once Isabella understands the nature of the bargain that Angelo has offered her, she compares woman's virginity to a brittle glass, as easily broken by men as they "make forms" (2.4.125). In Medieval and Renaissance medicine, one theory of pregnancy held that woman supplied the matter for the infant, men the form, the impress - woman supplied the metal, men the image on it.[16] Women are soft and "credulous to false prints", to legitimate and to bastardized coining (129). Angelo threatens a kind of treason to his society even as he threatens Isabella with a kind of rape. Just before Vincentio hands over the government to Angelo, he wonders "what figure of us [...] he will bear" (1.1.16), the first instance of the drama's play on coinage and seals. Will Angelo be a true coin or a counterfeit? Is Vincentio a strong enough father to stamp his replacement with his own image? Angelo's condemnation of Claudio equates the committing of murder to the creating of illegitimate children; such men "coin heaven's image/ In stamps that are forbid" (2.4.45-6). Such a bastard enjoys a "false" life coined from forbidden metal (49).

From these wrong pregnancies, by the end of the play, Angelo fears a detection of his guilt that will make him "unpregnant" even though his authority "bears so credant bulk" that a mere breath of scandal should not reduce its impressive mass (4.4.18, 24). As Isabella's pleas awoke in Angelo nature's law of desire, so he now fears that her accusations will awake the civil law's punishments against him. In the extraordinary final act of *Measure for Measure*, Vincentio calls for, and represses, speech so that a judgment may be given that will restore good sexual order to Vienna, a place so ripe with disorderly life that even its condemned criminals refuse to let themselves be executed.

At the end of the play, Isabella kneels to the Duke and his attendant lords and four times calls for justice (5.1.26). Speaking out about sexual crime opens up the difference between legitimate accusation and sexual slander, the most commonly complained of form of slander in English courts (Ingram, 165-6). Her accusations appear to prompt the Duke to reject her for speaking "in th'infirmity of sense" (50), irrationally and weakly.[17] When Isabella can continue to speak in sentences that one can understand syntactically, even if their meaning seems improbable, Vincentio appears on the verge of being persuaded because "Many that are not mad have, sure, more lack of reason" (70-1). Isabella speaks more sensibly than many who have been accepted as sane, even though the substance of her accusations seems mad. While the Duke, as play director, elicits these paradoxes that will serve to reveal the truth, he is also busy hushing up Lucio, ever-present with the unwanted interruption.

Lucio's tale might be "right" but he is "i'the wrong" to tell it out of turn (90). Lucio's tale-telling always has to do with the sexual improprieties of the absent Vincentio, whether in his role as Duke or his role as Friar. In this final act, he finds time to make unwanted, accusations of Mariana, Angelo, Escalus, and even Isabella. Lucio wants to tell the secret that everybody knows and is finally punished for his desire to tell by being forced to marry an incontinent woman who is already a mother through Lucio's own incontinence. Lucio's loose tongue when he promised marriage to a punk and spread scandal about the nobility has punished him with a marriage he emphatically does not want and compares to judicial murder: "Marrying a punk, my lord, is pressing to death, whipping, and hanging" (533-4).

When Vincentio invites Angelo to speak in his own defense after all opportunities for lying have been taken away, he asks if the defendant has "word, or wit, or impudence" (371). Angelo's stratagems are at an end and he confesses that he was "contracted" to Mariana (383). He will be married by the friar in a ceremony that is spoken of as a consummation (386) and will then apparently receive the death he has asked for (381). He wants to speak and then hold his peace forever in his "sentence and sequent death" (381). When the Duke extends mercy to him as a result of the pleading of the two women, Angelo says that he "crave[s] death more willingly than mercy" because Angelo has never desired Mariana though he once proposed marriage to her (487). And the consummation of that marriage contract proceeded under the mistake of taking Mariana for the desired Isabella. When Vincentio tells Mariana's woes to Isabella, her first reaction is to wish that Mariana might find release in death (3.2.233). The disguised Duke must explain that Mariana still loves Angelo, in spite of "his unjust unkindness, that in all reason should have quenched her love" (3.2.242-3). In fact, his refusal of her has made Mariana's love for her faithless suitor "violent and unruly" (244). So abject is Mariana that she says that she hopes her husband will come to be a good man because of his faults, which, as Isabella claims, were mostly faults of intent. No man's thoughts are subjects to the law because they are "merely" thoughts, and on that sighing adverb, Mariana falls silent and silently listens to her husband prefering death to the mercy of marriage (462).

Desire appears to know neither reason nor law. The Duke appears to know nothing of the nature of marriage as he forgives offenses and awards the wrongdoers the "mercy" of marriage as quickly as Angelo would have meeted out punishment to these same wrongdoers. In awarding marriage or the gallows, neither inquires too deeply about the origin of the marriage promises or the intent of their makers. Neither distinguishes between Claudio and Lucio and the circumstances surrounding their liaisons with their prospective brides. In this failure to inquire and to make distinctions, both gloss over the issue of consent in marriage formation, which is crucial, whether the marriage has been openly and formally celebrated or entered into clandestinely. Both appear to be ignorant of, or indifferent to, the nature of marriage, that state created by legal institutions but lived so intimately by the married couple.

The audience is left to presume the happiness of the silent Juliet and Claudio as the Duke warns the errant husband to right his wronged wife and adjures the reluctant Angelo to love his wronged wife. In this mixture of confession, accusation, and silence, nearly everything has been told, with the significant exception of the Duke's own proposal to Isabella. He coyly says that he has a "motion" that will mean "good" for Isabella, if only she will a "willing ear incline" (546-7). All the rest will be told, at least as much as should seem suitable, after the characters have left the stage.

Whether or not the audience at a performance of *Measure for Measure* approves the prospect of a marriage between the Duke and Isabella, they have seen enacted a thorough separation of law and desire. Just as Barnardine's desire to drink and reluctance to be executed foil the law's legitimate demands, so sexual desire in this play expresses itself entirely outside the bounds of publicly conducted weddings and marriages. Vincentio appears to be the only exception to this rule, for he notices Isabella and immediately moves toward proposing marriage. And these extra-legal yearnings and illegal actions appear more vigorous than offensive to the Viennese. How could the inhabitants of the city be offended? After all, virtually everyone seems implicated in the universality of desire and the desire to act without being too heavily burdened by the law's demands. Yet, Vienna forbids sexual activity outside of marriage and punishes speech outside the bounds of civility. In his work on the interactions of sexuality and the law, Richard Posner remarks that the laws

> inspired by Christian doctrine were on the whole stricter than the population [...] believed reasonable. This was especially so with regard to fornication, and the result was that the law against it was only laxly enforced. This has been a characteristic of sex law throughout history. Most sexual behavior takes place in private and is consensual rather than coercive, and therefore "victimless", and laws punishing private conduct are difficult to enforce in the best of circumstances and doubly so if there is no complaining witness. Especially if the will to enforce is weak because the conduct is not regarded as deeply threatening, laws punishing victimless crimes committed in private are unlikely to be enforced effectively unless the forbidden conduct is flaunted....[18]

One could say much the same thing about speech that is too free. Lucio flaunts his scandal-mongering tongue even after admonishment and chooses too mighty a person to defame. The disguised Duke captures him in the act even more effectively than the disguised Mariana captured the lustful Angelo. The bed trick and the speech trick capture the wrongdoer flaunting his wickedness before the offended party and result in the same punishment: marriage.

The Duke, meting out punishments, finally turns to Isabella and makes an offer that she does not appear able to refuse, even though everything we know about her indicates that she is serious in her desire to leave the disorderly secular world behind in favor of the strictness of the convent. The proposal will do her good, the Duke assures her, but the audience has room to wonder. Neither Isabella nor the Duke appears to experience desire, other than a desire for more order than is available in unruly Vienna. As Mariana is silent before the husband who does not want to marry her, so Isabella is silent before the suitor who seeks marriage from the seat of justice and punishment. Barnardine evades the gallows and continues his drinking in prison, but no one escapes marriage, the institution that will confine all the husbands and wives on the stage, even if it cannot create, or put an end to, their desires.

## Notes

1. See Ernest Schanzer, "The Marriage Contracts in *Measure for Measure*", *Shakespeare Survey* 13 (1960), pp. 81-9, and the introduction in the Arden *Measure for Measure*, ed. J.W. Lever (London: Methuen, 1967), pp. xi-xciii. Margaret Scott, in "'Our City's Institutions': Some Further Reflections on the Marriage Contracts in *Measure for Measure*", *ELH* 4 (1982), pp. 790-804, argues against a simple application of English Renaissance marriage law to the marriages of *Measure for Measure* because, in the first place, the law in question is made and applied in a created, "self-enclosed" world (792).

2. Eileen Z. Cohen argues that the bed-trick in *Measure for Measure* shows a rather complex Isabella willing to aid Mariana in a virtuous bedding of her own husband in "'Virtue is Bold': The Bed-trick and Characterization in *All's Well that Ends Well* and *Measure for Measure*, *Philological Quarterly* 2(1986), pp. 171-86. But Mariana's marriage and desire for her own husband do not bear in any clear way on Isabella's choices for her own celibate or married life. The bed-trick allows her to escape judicial rape without hurting the honor of another woman. In his book, *"Measure for Measure": Casuistry and Artistry* (Washington: Catholic UP, 1990), Melvin Seiden makes a convincing case that those who criticise Isabella for a cold denial of her own sexual nature are using a point of view already used by Angelo against the celibate novice (p. 53). Jacqueline Rose is very persuasive in her linking of reading and psycholoanalytical strategies that locate in characterizations of female sexuality the anxieties the reader feels in negotiating the Shakespearean text, see "Sexuality in the Reading of Shakespeare: *Hamlet* and *Measure for Measure*", in *Alternative Shakespeares*, ed. John Drakakis (London: Methuen, 1985), pp. 95-118.

3. "Performing Social Practice: The Example of *Measure for Measure*," *Shakespeare Quarterly* 44 (1993), pp. 1-29. This perceptive article includes a brief survey of English marriage law and fornication law as preparation for the central argument concerning the drama's implication of the audience in the acceptance of popular standards of sexual behavior against the rigor of the puritan reformers. As I read Haynes' essay, she takes a rather sanguine view of the marriages arranged by the Duke as appropriate resolutions to relations opened by the couples involved: "The typicality of the social practices the play performs suggests that most members of the audience would recognize that the Duke's orders complete what the couples themselves began; that, Lucio's protests notwithstanding, no one is forced to marry as punishment for crime; that the resolutions, however extraordinary the Duke's methods of achieving them, were the resolutions communities would have expected and the ecclesiastical courts did require of similar relationships in the world outside the play" (28).

4. William Shakespeare, *Measure for Measure*, ed. J.W. Lever, The Arden Shakespeare (London: Methuen, 1965, repr. 1980). All further references to this work will appear in parentheses in the main text.

5. A contract *de futuro* did not create a marriage at the time that the parties spoke the words; some other act is necessary to make the marriage valid. Often that act would be the formal marriage ceremony, but the act could be the sexual consummation of the relationship. See Richard Helmholz's *Marriage Litigation in Medieval England*, (Cambridge: Cambridge UP, 1987).

6. See James A. Brundage, *Law, Sex, and Christian Society in Medieval Europe* (Chicago: Chicago UP, 1987), pp. 496-501. Brundage treats clandestine marriage several times in his thorough book, but these pages cover the topic during the late Medieval and early Renaissance period and might be most helpful here. See also Richard H. Helmholz's *Marriage Litigation in*

*Medieval England*, (Cambridge: Cambridge UP, 1974), pp. 38-47 and passim, is also helpful. For Renaissance English practices, see Martin Ingram, *Church Courts, Sex and Marriage in England, 1570-1640*, (Cambridge: Cambridge UP, 1987), pp. 212-18 and passim. During class discussions in his Columbia University course on medieval canon law, Robert Somerville indicated that while there were no clear limits as to what practices did or did not make a marriage, canonists did agree that the legal "safe harbor" in marriage formation would require consent before two competent witnesses, neither of which need be a priest. Consummation should follow. Further references to these works will appear in parenthetical citation.

7. See Ingram, *Church Courts*, ... (note 6 above), pp. 189-237, on the formation of marriages and prenuptial fornication. Further references to this work will appear in parenthetical citation.

8. "Sin and Socity: the Northern High Commission and the Northern Gentry in the Reign of Elizabeth I", *Law and Government under the Tudors*, ed. Claire Cross, David Loades, and J.J. Scarisbrick (Cambridge: Cambridge UP, 1988) p. 197.

9. In a play ripe with the language of pregnancy and conception, it is perhaps to be expected that Angelo should speak of the law's vigilance resulting in the abortion of crimes conceived, but not yet committed.

10. Sir Tomas More, *Utopia*, ed. Edward Surtz, S.J. and J.H. Hexter, The Yale Edition of the Complete Works of St. Thomas More, Vol. 4 (New Haven: Yale UP, 1965) p. 97.

11. Edmund Dudley, *The Tree of Commonwealth*, ed. D.M. Brody (Cambridge: Cambridge UP, 1948).

12. Edward Hake, *A touchstone for this time present* (1574), pp. 18-9.

13. Edward Hake, *A commendation...Elizabeth* (1575) ff. [Aviii v]-B.

14. Edward Hake, *Epieikiea: A Dialogue on Equity in Three Parts*, ed. D.E.C. Yale (New Haven: Yale UP, 1953). This dialogue was written during Elizabeth's reign and presented to James I. Hake discusses equity as a residual power of the ruler that the judge may exercise in order to fill the inevitable gaps that the law will leave, and to avoid the injustices that might result from a literalist application of the law in a particular case. Among many amplifications of this point, I would refer the reader to Hake's discussion of the possibility of giving the monarch's ambassadors full power to speak for the ruler or a more circumscribed, limited power (26). Vincentio has left Angelo with the equitable powers, including the power to show mercy, that the Duke himself would have in Vienna.

15. See Darryl J. Gless, *"Measure for Measure," the Law and the Convent* (Princeton: Princeton UP, 1979). However, Gless is most concerned with God's law and mercy and with the issues of fornication rather than with marriage formation.

16. See Danielle Jacquart and Claude Thomasset, *Sexuality and Medicine in the Middle Ages*, transl. Matthew Adamson (Princeton: Princeton UP, 1988) p.65.

17. Here we might recall Angelo's own sense that in his confrontation with Isabella in Act II both his reason and body were tottering.

18. Richard Posner, *Sex and Reason* (Cambridge: Harvard UP, 1992) p. 73.

# A NOTE ON SHAKESPEARE'S *TEMPEST* AND IRIS MURDOCH'S *THE SEA, THE SEA*

Sabine Coelsch-Foisner
(University of Salzburg)

Murdoch's novels have always prompted critics to comment on their Shakespearian plots,[1] and she herself has related the abdication of magic in *The Sea, The Sea* to *The Tempest*.[2] Quite obviously, Prospero provides a model for both Charles Arrowby, the stage director and renowned "Shakespeare man", who intends to abjure the magic of the theatre,[3] and James, the religious mystic, who decides to renounce the spiritual tricks acquired from Tibetan Buddhists. In consciously moulding after *The Tempest* her tale of the two cousins who get divided as one strives for worldly fame and the other for mystic power, Iris Murdoch seems to have relied more on its metadramatic elements than on its plot. On the one hand, the binary organization of characters is suggestive of the novel's eclectic nature: Charles and James represent "parallel cases of magic,"[4] but the former's diary also suggests that they are antagonists, enacting the enmity between Prospero and Antonio ("he [James] could spoil anything for me by touching it with his little finger";[5] cf. Prospero: "he was / The ivy which hid my princely trunk," 1.2.86);[6] and Charles's illusions, which blind him to reality, are also reminiscent of Shakespeare's sleepwalking usurper (cf. Antonio, 2.1.218-23). On the other hand, the device provides the structural groundwork for her own aesthetic views. The relation is ambivalent, because in the light of Murdoch's professed 'anti-Existentialism',[7] Prospero would seem to provide a foil to James's death and Charles's unresolved proneness to demonic imagining, but it is precisely by this dual interpretation of Prospero's words "lie there, my art" (1.2.25) in *The Sea, The Sea* that one is led away from such facile moral idealism when comparing the two works.

On the story-level, James appears to be much closer to Prospero than Charles, since his magic is directed towards the domination of nature. He calls himself a "mountain man", lives in mysterious union with the sea (his last visit is announced by a roaring sea that enters Charles's body, "like a strong beating heart, like the strong beating of my own heart", 440) and vanquishes gravity (like a bat he *lifts* - not *drags* - Charles out of the water). Magic, in his case, springs from a pragmatic attitude and is employed as a remedy against wrongs inflicted in the past (to send Titus to Shruff End and save Charles, whom Peregrine had sought to kill; cf. Prospero's plan to avenge Antonio's usurpation of power, to secure his own return to Milan, to restore his reign and marry his daughter to the King of Naples' son). Both Prospero and James know and experience that wizardry is power and that "the exercise of power is a dangerous delight" (445), as it entails an interference with the lives of others. James, however, falls short of being a real Prospero. For one thing, he is less versed in the art of magic - Charles is rescued from drowning through a trick, but the sherpa in the Tibetan mountains died, and Titus, though figthing against the waves like Ferdinand in the *Tempest*, is killed, too (cf. Caliban of Prospero: "his art is of such power / It would control my dam's god, Setebos, / And make a vassal of him", 1.2.372-4) - secondly, the ultimate conclusion to James's creed is hostile to life, as Charles recognizes: "All this giving up of attachments doesn't sound to me like salvation and freedom, it sounds like death" (445). Oriental readings have seen in James an enlightened Buddha,[8] but in the context of his western environment James appears to be an ineffectual martyr and exiled self, very much in line with the Existentialist hero conceived in Camus' *Etranger*. Indeed, James's 'smile' is reminiscent of the latter's final feeling of a 'tender indifference' to the world.

Charles, on the other hand, is the ruthless tyrant, attracted partly out of escapist motives to the "magical delusions" (35) and "technical trickery of the theatre" (29), but mainly because, in a truly Machiavellian spirit, he recognizes that magic is power, which proves the central formula of his past career - "a theatre director is a dictator" (37) - and of his retired life. Charles's use of magic resembles Prospero's initial selfish interest in his secret books and, like Prospero, he has saved those to his marine retreat. As he leaves London (3) in order to "repent of egoism" (in both works, abdicating magic involves geographical dislocation), he is soon haunted by his art: "Have I abjured that magic, drowned my book? Forgiven my enemies? The surrender of power, the final change of magic into spirit?" (39) Both Charles and Prospero mistake their narcissist infatuation with magic for the road of goodness (Prospero: "I, thus neglecting worldy ends, all dedicated / To closeness and the bettering of my mind ...", 1.2.89-90; and Charles considers the freeing of his former mistress a redemptive act), whilst it only begets alienation and evil, enforced either by themselves (Charles's abduction and imprisonment of Hartley) or others (Antonio's usurpation of power). Prospero's potential complicity in his own downfall, which Magnusson has traced to participial constructions in his speech,[9] is reflected in the "wheel of spirituality" explored in the novel, i.e. in the nexus between Charles's literal fall into Minn's Cauldron and his ruthless meddling with other people's lives ("You don't respect people as people, you don't *see* them [...] you're a sort of rapacious magician" (Lizzie's letter to Charles, 45).

In both Charles's and James's lives there are brief moments of insight, in which they approximate Prospero's (implicitly) humanitarian message. When James rescues his cousin from drowning, he acts against his conviction that man's supreme spiritual achievement lies in detachment; and Charles, when pushed to extreme chaos by his own scheming (very much like Jake Donaghue in *Under the Net* or Mischa Fox in *The Flight from the Enchanter*), recognizes, albeit too late, the need for such unselfish love as he might have developed for his would-be son Titus. He, too, briefly understands that an imperfect meddling "in the spiritual world can breed monsters for other people," those attendant rather than attending demons, which he, like an unskilled apprentice, conjured up but failed to master. Yet, unlike Prospero, who eventually faces the prospect of being re-integrated into the society of real men (with all its threats and hazards) and implicitly affirms the need for personal commitment, neither of the two cousins draws the requisite conclusion so as to emerge as the "moral person",[10] the sage that Prospero appears to be in the end.[11] James wills himself to die, and Charles will never become *real* to his environment, as the demon's final escape from the casket suggests.

Murdoch's comment on Sartre's universe - "rational awareness is in inverse ratio to social integration"[12] might therefore be aptly applied to her solipsistic protagonists, except for their lack of virtually any capacity for rational awareness. James is "a lost soul really and [...] too mystical", Murdoch herself explains,[13] and Charles's self-delusions verge on the pathological. In either case, reflection, which seems inseparable from magic, causes estrangement. Contrary to her characters' frenzied preoccupations, the incompatibility of power and love adumbrated in Shakespeare is quite clearly what Iris Murdoch, as a moralist and philosopher, advocates against the Sartrean notion of self-invented values (cf. her interview with Bigsby, 222) and of man's final isolation (*Sartre*, 25), which has also brought her work in line with Karl Jaspers' theory of community.[14] Sartre is morally wrong, she argues, because "it is on the lonely awareness of the individual and not on the individual's integration with his society that his attention centres" (*Sartre*, 25). Depicting a moral vacuum that follows precisely from this Existentialist "irresponsible self-centred kind of luciferian attitude to the world"[15] as embodied by Charles, and a perfect reluctance to participate in life, as exemplified in James's alienating mysticism, Iris Murdoch implicitly emphasizes the need for moral values.

Any idealist reading of *The Tempest* will, therefore, regard Prospero as an immanent, but unheeded or unrivalled moral authority in *The Sea, The Sea*, in that he resigns control over his ghostly actors. Given his metadramatic function, however, which has variously been pointed out by critics and related to the play's interruptive character,[16] Prospero's moral authority has an innate aesthetic dimension, which makes it possible to see Charles and James not so much as morally flawed would-be-Prosperos, but as the two extreme poles between which Prospero hovers: resumed magic and death.

To Charles, Prospero's renunciation of magic is a self-explanatory act of what he considers the quintessence of Shakespeare's dramatic art - and so it is to critics like Cantor (75). Charles's infatuation with the theatre was nourished by the belief that "Shakespeare was *quite different* from the others" (36), in fact the "only one" amongst dramatists. His words recall Murdoch's own pronouncements in "Against Dryness": Shakespeare creates "real independent people" and abstains from magic, i.e. from creating a false impression of order,[17] whereas the rest of the theatre, as Charles and Peregrine suggest in retrospect, is "complacent vulgarity" (165-6), "the most outrageously factitious of all the arts", because more than any other art it "disfigures life, misrepresents it", and "dramatists are disgraceful liars unless they are very good" (33).

Charles's perceptiveness as a dramatist is wanting in his own life, as is shown by his overt reference to "*Tempest* scene two" (34) in his early reminiscences. The distinction between "the fine dramatic silences of the theatre" and the "deep undynamic stillness" of Shruff End proves flawed. Like Prospero, who puts off his "magic garment" in Act 1, Scene 2 and continues to behave like a dramatist until the Epilogue, Charles withdraws from active life only to become another "surrogate playwright" and again manipulate others, as many of Shakespeare's characters do.[18] In the light of this connection between the power-figure and the artist, suggested by Prospero's speech, with which he interrupts the masque in Act 4, Charles complies with a central Shakespearian paradigm. His self-conscious attempts to structure his "Prehistory", which he constantly experiences as intractable to a truthful artistic presentation, correspond to the syntactic disorderliness of Prospero's account of his past, which Magnusson has persuasively interpreted as mirroring "the unaccentuated aspect of life, not the focused significance one is accustomed in art" (57). If his mind is the shaping, plot-making instance in the play, Prospero's final act also represents defeat, which is suggested by his bitterness and "troubled brain", for he must recognize that art is a fleeting show: "Every third thought shall be my grave." (5.1.311). Thus James enacts what Prospero only alludes to: the link between the abdication of magic and death.

Charles, the fiction-maker, is also defeated. Where Prospero tries to raise life to the level of art, Charles, wary of the order art imposes, seeks to reduce it to the level of life, only to learn in the end that he is a continual victim of magic, which, in the Murdochian credo, makes him incapable of altruistic love. Although all his friends are gone and he means to start a new life in London, the final symbolic release of the demon from the casket is an inversion of Prospero's words, "These our actors, / As I foretold you, were all spirits and / Are melted into air, into thin air" (4.1.148-59), for in no time, he will weave another "insubstantial pageant" with those ghostly actors, who will return with new names in a new guise. Once more he will resemble Sartre's Roquentin rather than follow Shakespeare's Prospero.

*Notes*

1. Cf. Richard Todd, *The Shakespearian Interest* (London: Vision, 1979), 97-119; Malcolm Bradbury, *Possibilities* (London, 1973), 232; Harold Bloom, ed., *Iris Murdoch* (New York et al.: Chelsea House Publishers, 1986), 1; A.S. Byatt's analysis of *The Nice and the Good, A Fairly Honourable Defeat, The Black Prince*: "Shakespearian Plot in the Novels of Iris Murdoch", in Bloom, 87-94.

2. Cf. Murdoch's own comment: "In the *The Sea* it [the theatre] is perhaps more important because that is about *The Tempest* in a way, it is about Prospero and theatre is a great magical thing which you then have to give up and it is about giving up magic." Heide Ziegler and Christopher Bigsby, ed., *The Radical Imagination and the Liberal Tradition* (Basingstoke and London: Macmillan, 1990), 218.

3. Cf. Todd's suggestion, p. 119, that Prospero's irritability compares with that of Charles Arrowby.

4. Murdoch in Bigsby, 218.

5. Penguin, 1978, 452. All further references to *The Sea, The Sea* are to this edition.

6. W.J. Craig, ed., *The Complete Works*, London: Pordes, 1977.

7. "I'm very anti-existentialist", she told Michael O. Bellamy, "Interview with Iris Murdoch", *Contemporary Literature* 18:2 (1977), 131.

8. Cf. Suguna Ramanathan, *Iris Murdoch: Figures of Good* (London: Macmillan, 1990), 67-96.

9. A. Lynne Magnusson, "Interruption in *The Tempest*", *Shakespeare Quarterly* 37:1 (Spring 1986), 56-7.

10. The evolution of the moral person is a familiar concept in Murdoch's philosophical ideas. Cf. her interview with Bigsby, 222.

11. Thus e.g. Paul A. Cantor has discussed Prospero's outstanding role among Shakespeare's protagonists by emphasizing his wisdom, philosophical calm and detachment. "Shakespeare's *The Tempest*: The Wise Man as Hero", *Shakespeare Quarterly* 30 (1980), 64-75.

12. *Sartre: Romantic to Rationalist* (London: Bowes, 1953), 25.

13. Bigsby, 213.

14. Cf. Peter Wolfe, *The Disciplined Heart: Iris Murdoch and Her Novels* (Columbia: Missouri UP, 1966); Zohreh T. Sullivan, "The Contracting Universe of Iris Murdoch's Gothic Novels", *Modern Fiction Studies* 23:4 (Winter 1977-78), 557-69.

15. Bigsby, 213.

16. E.g. Norman Rabkin, *Shakespeare and the Common Understanding* (New York: The Free Press, 1967), 224; Todd, 118; Magnusson, 52, 55; Cantor, 75.

17. "Perhaps only Shakespeare manages to create at the highest level both images and people [...] Only the very greatest art invigorates without consoling, and defeats our attempts, in W.H. Auden's words, to use it as magic." 1961; rpt. in Bloom, op. cit, 16; cf. also an interview with Malcolm Bradbury, 27 Feb. 1976, British Council Tape, 2001 in Todd, 119.

18. A resemblance between Prospero and Antonio, the merchant of Venice is suggested by Meredith Anne Skura, "Discourse and the Individual:The Case of Colonialism in *The Tempest*," *Shakespeare Quarterly* 40 (1989), 61: "... a repressed self-assertion is hinted at in the passive/aggressive claims he makes on Bassanio and comes out clearly when he lashes out at the greedy and self-assertive Shylock with a viciousness like Prospero's towards Caliban, ...". Skura here refers to Marianne Novy, *Love's Argument: Gender Relations in Shakespeare* (Chapel Hill and London: North Carolina UP, 1984), 63-82. Oberon and the Duke's actions in *Measure for Measure* are equally seen as "figuring those of the stagemanager or even playwright", see Todd, 99.

# *M. ARDEN OF FEVERSHAM* AS A MYSTERY PLAY

### Robert F. Fleissner
### (Central State University)

In a distinguished essay published for the English Association in their journal *English,* Raymond Chapman has called *M. Arden of Feversham* "the first piece of detective work in English literature."[1] As such, it is also reminiscent of *Hamlet,* where the most obvious problem is the extensive delay in effecting justifiable regicide, if indeed revenge as such is totally defensible. In miniature, the same sort of issue arises in the Feversham play, yet in reverse fashion. There the rogues Black Will and Shakebag contrive to kill Master Arden but only after numerous unsuccessful attempts, owing to their ineptitude, achieve their dastardly goal. If this connection is considered at all *thematic,* it would be a point against Sir Edmund Chambers' notion (reiterated by Kenneth Muir)[2] that although *Arden* is clearly the pinnacle of the Shakespeare Apocrypha, it simply does not resemble the work of Shakespeare in theme.

Muir likewise says that it does not relate to Shakespeare's output in terms of *style*, though he hastens to add that the author could have modified his style to suit the theme. What exactly does he mean here by style? Various critics have remarked that the general style of the drama is actually more like that of Shakespeare than anyone else's. The most noted editor who has come forth with this bald claim is M. L. Wine in his Revels edition.[3] It is agreed, on the whole, that the best piece of scholarship pointing in this direction is an Oxford dissertation by the noted Shakespearean bibliographer MacDonald P. Jackson.[4] A number of other editors and commentators (notably Keith Sturgess and M. L. Wine) have stressed one scene in particular as most likely having been the prime contribution of Shakespeare (the only known writer with talent enough), namely scene viii containing the intense quarrel between Alice Arden and Mosby. Max Bluestone has reported that "at least thirteen English, German, French, and Dutch scholars, editors, and translators agreed that in whole or in part the play is Shakespeare's."[5] That is quite a record.

Because of fairly recent performances of this drama (such as Terry Hands's for the Royal Shakespeare Company in 1982 and that directed by John Russell Brown in Seattle, cited in the *Shakespeare Newsletter* in 1991), and because of a flurry of interest in seeing the supposed hand of the Stratford genius in other anonymous or Apocryphal plays (such as *The Birth of Hercules, The Birth of Merlin, Edmund Ironside*, and, most recently once again, *A Yorkshire Tragedy*), re-examination of Shakespeare's possible involvement in this notable work is imperative. Yet, at the start, it is well to admit that other claimants for similar authorship have not fared so well of late. For example, the basic argument for *Edmund Ironside*'s being an early, precocious work of Shakespeare's may well have foundered when Richard Proudfoot showed that the history play was, in all probability, indebted to the author's having read *The Faerie Queene* (hence must have been written later than had been claimed).[6] The argument for the dating in this case is very important. The contention, moreover, that annotations in a Folger Library law book with Shakespeare's purported signature therein provide remarkable parallels hardly buttresses the argument that this actor from Stratford had worked for a while also as a clerk in a lawyer's office,[7] the surname *Shakespeare* actually not having been that uncommon in London and the shires. (I happened to run across an example of a Shakespeare in the early 1500's in London totally unconnected with the family at Stratford.)[8] In parallel fashion, the notion that Shakespeare and Rowley were co-authors of *The Birth of Merlin*[9] has neglected the verdict that Shakespeare's name was ingeniously appended to the title-page probably following up the whim that the title had been predicted in *King Lear*; that is, the Fool there states, "This prophecy Merlin shall make, for I live before his time" (3.2.95).[10] After that only the veritable birth of Merlin could result. Q. E. D. But such an oddity would hardly prove that the Merlin play amounted to an authorial sequel. Finally, the question of Shakespeare's possible authorship of *A Yorkshire Tragedy* need not be given much treatment here, especially because of R. V. Holdsworth's recent article,[11] but because this play owes much to the historical account of the retributive Arden tragedy, as is generally acknowledged, it provides yet another way of focusing once more on the latter domestic drama.

In our dealing now with *Arden*, it helps to bear in mind some of the more important recent scholarship, such as Alexander Leggatt's helpful account,[12] various new editions (along with Martin Wine's, Martin White's in the New Mermaids, as well as the Scolar Press version), several articles, and an unpublished paper by C. H. Hobday, drama critic of the London *Sunday Times* (one which he has graciously shared with me) because it provides statistical, stylometric analysis. Still, the text of the play, as Wine indicates,[13] may be some sort of memorial reconstruction, and so computerized findings would have limited value. Hobday does find a place for Shakespearean authorship, though.[14]

The question that inevitably arises at this juncture is what constitutes a valid, as opposed to an unjustified, conjecture – historical scholarship perforce being based so often largely on the laws of probability. So let us begin with Robert Greene's *Groatsworth of Wit*, registered in September of 1592. Just five months before, a work had appeared in the Stationers' Register to which Greene may have possibly alluded: the anonymous *M. Arden of Feversham*. Is there any hint that he had in mind the character Shakebag and his accomplice Black Will when he made his now famous reference to an upstart playwright who considered himself the only "Shake-scene" but robbed from others in the process? Will and George Shakebag (we recall that Shakespeare was born on St. *George*'s day according to most interpretations of baptismal records) were both called that way because of being thieves, cutpurses to be exact. Evidently Greene had a certain precedent here for punning on Shakespeare's name – a plot then duly appropriated later by Jonson when he used the imperatives "shake a Stage" and "shake a Lance" in his well-known eulogy. The name-play by Greene relates also to Kemp's familiar "My notable Shake*rags*" in his *Nine Daies Wonder* (1600) but that throwaway phrase appeared only a number of years later. (Still, because *Arden* was republished in 1599, this could well have prompted Kemp's allusion in 1600.)[15]

So what happens if we consider that Greene associated the Shakespeare name with that of Shake*bag* in the Arden drama? Was the latter name purely accidental or at all historical? To begin, the name of Shakebag had no strict historical basis, because although the tragedy was based on an actual murder case, the prototype there was called *Loosebag*, the shift to *Shakebag* appearing as a misprint (if only once) in Holinshed's *Chronicles*. But at least Shakespeare or those who knew him and acted with him could have become *attracted* to this form of the name for obvious enough reasons, especially when other such resonant names in the play (*Greene, Gadshill*, for example) enter the picture too. Why else would they have built upon a mere misprint? It is one not found in the historical *Wardmote Book of Faversham* at all.

The psychological poser that is bound to arise is as follows: Would Shakespeare himself have been intrigued by the career of a highwayman, cutpurse, and finally murderer – attracted, that is, to the extent that he would have allowed for or endorsed any such deliberate, personal onomastic association? But, in answer, why not? We have a clear-cut precedent with Falstaff, whose own made-up name links with his creator's in terms of another portmanteau pun: if the spear will shake, then the staff falls. (This witty comparison, sometimes found silly, even pretentiously phallic, has been made by Harry Levin, for one, in his post-quatercentenary study of Shakespearean nomenclature;[16] Falstaff's staff figuratively falls not only when he plays possum on the battlefield because of his age, but when he fails to consummate love with two women in *The Merry Wives of Windsor*.) At any rate, Shakespeare's brandished lance loses the posture of assault.

True, although the rotund rascal is a highwayman, braggart (in this respect like Black Will), and former soldier, he luckily stops short of being an assassin; he would thus prefer the "hot" to the "cold" sins. Most provocative of all, though, both Sir John Falstaff and George Shakebag are, most of the time, hilariously incompetent in accomplishing the evil they try to effect. Finally, as if to clinch such matters, Black Will informs Shakebag, "I robbed him and his man once at Gadshill" (xvii.13),[17] clearly thereby anticipating the Gadshill robbery that turns out to be a non-robbery in *1 Henry IV*. Such close familiarity insinuates that Shakespeare did more than merely see the play performed or simply talked about it with fellow players. Agreed, Leggatt thinks that *Arden* also anticipates plays by Middleton – though he declines to think of him as a possible early author.

Yet, it might be countered, what use would the son of Mary Arden have had for Mistress Alice Arden in the tragedy, the lady mainly responsible for the death of her husband brought on by her adultery with the *parvenu* Mosby? Would not a playwright from another Arden family, one originally at least devoutly Roman Catholic, have been grossly offended by this Lady-Macbeth-like murderess? Possibly so. But then she does strikingly recant at the end and in strongly religious terms.

This problem is more complex, all things considered, but perhaps also not insoluble. First of all, some of the finest lines in the play stem from her, notably in scene viii, as has been pointed out often enough.[18] She definitely prefigures Lady Macbeth, even in the sense of being a strong personality, especially in terms of finding blood stains that cannot be removed.[19] The very title of the drama, *M. Arden of Feversham*, contrasts almost as if in deliberate fashion with M. Arden *of* Wilmecote (later *of* Stratford), and because the son Will liked to use the word *of* in his titles so much, this prepositional linkage should not be shunted aside as overly hypothetical (though, granted, some other playwrights used the identifying preposition from time to time also).

Basically, however, the proposition that the native *of* Stratford would have been unattracted to this story because of some vile characters therein, vile at least in behavior, if not in terms of artistic execution, is aesthetically wrongheaded; it implies that a creative writer does not have the objectivity to distinguish very strictly between his life and his work. On the practical level, it could suggest that he would have gone in for such mannerisms as type-casting, surely a relatively amateurish preoccupation even then. In any case, evident autobiographical associations *of some sort* can be deduced between an artist and whatever he creates; to deny such an affinity is, in effect, to deny the basic empirical epistemology to which most of mankind in some measure (that is, at least scientifically) subscribes; yet some cynics would still deem it irrelevant here. For instance, the former director of the Royal Shakespeare Company, Frank O'Connor, would even relate the fat rascal Falstaff to Shakespeare's own father,[20] the surnames having a similar ring to them – a position that may not seem flattering for most lay readers. Comparable enough is Keats's later esteemed conception of Negative Capability.

When Jonson borrowed Greene's "Shake-scene" allusion in his eulogy, in the same context he wrote:

> ... how farre thou didst our Lily out-shine,
> Or sporting Kid, or Marlowes mighty line.[21]

The curious point here is that these very three: Lyly, Kyd, Marlowe, have also been, however tentatively, linked with authorship of the Arden play, and Jonson could not implausibly have been cognizant of such affiliation and for that reason have connected Shakespeare's name with them, if only because of what the latter did with (or to) them in this context. In other words, Shakespeare might easily enough have collaborated with them in some form, even in the role of actor, or he could have then resorted to borrowing from them, resulting in Greene's indictment that the "upstart Crow" was beautifying himself with their feathers, though admittedly the only play explicitly alluded to in this context in the *Groatsworth* is *3 Henry VI*. (Only in 1594 did he write of the "first heir" of his "invention.") True, although Jonson had a prodigious memory, it may be deemed unlikely that he thought of Shakespeare's involvement in the *Arden* play when he composed these lines, for Lyly, Kyd, and Marlowe just happen to be some of Shakespeare's most illustrious contemporaries and predecessors.

Still, let us consider the candidacy of Lyly first of all. In an extravagant image in *Arden* (xiv. 148-53), Alice compares Mosby to Endymion, the most beautiful of men and so loved by Diana; the imagery, being in terms of the moon, relates to Lyly's *Endymion, the Man in the Moon* written only some three years earlier and appearing in print about the time *Arden* was composed (1591). Next, consider both Kyd and Marlowe, who of course were said by Kyd to have shared chambers in 1591, and so could at the same time have presumably collaborated enough from that convenient vantage point. Clearly Shakespeare borrowed from them in later plays. Hence it is by no means irresponsible to intimate a plausible correlation of some sort between all four authors in the Arden tragedy.

Whether Kyd had any hand in this play is itself an extremely complicated and controversial question. In the past, his name was indelibly linked with it, for example by T. S. Eliot, as is widely recognized,[22] but recent editors and historians, not only writers on *Arden* but Kyd specialists, have strongly brought into question such an ascription.[23] Confusion has further reigned over whether certain works (containing numerous verbal parallels with *Arden*) can definitely be linked with Kyd's authorship. One leading Kyd authority, Frederick Boas, even had gone so far as to state that a passage in the Arden play is so strongly based on another in *The Spanish Tragedy* that Kyd himself would scarcely have been the blatant imitator.[24] That assumption is itself open to question, though it is admittedly difficult to imagine that he would have copied from himself in such an obvious manner. (Boas's own preference for Marlowe as the author is another story.) Most Ardenists still argue that if Kyd did not have a direct hand in the composition of the play, he must at any rate have memorably influenced the way it was put together.

The case for Marlowe's hand is also still argued, particularly because of the play's debt to *Edward II* and owing especially to Marlowe's own Kentish background; but it made its *début* probably only by way of Kyd, and one of the leading pieces of Kentish evidence, the final disposal of Master Arden's body in the cellar, is *not* a clue recounted in the drama, showing that whoever wrote it was most probably not that familiar with the finer points of what happened in Feversham. Still, the Marlovian connection has some modish appeal, even today. For instance, the compiler of the Shakespeare Apocrypha concordance, Louis Ule, favored it in a paper presented at the second international Marlowe conference.[25] My visits to the Feversham cottage and other points of tourist interest in the town have shown me the interest in Marlowe's candidacy – always because of the Kentish connection. In any case, Lyly also came from Kent, for what that coincidence may be worth here (in offsetting Kyd's purported candidacy).

Arguing for Shakespeare's possible involvement, in any event, necessitates our reconsidering the status of acting companies. Was the tragedy tangibly linked with Pembroke's Men, as has been inferred?[26] If so, could the master dramatist have been involved? Possibly not, it is said, because modern research, as confirmed by Samuel Schoenbaum, opts for Shakespeare's being rather with the Queen's Men. Yet this dilemma is resolvable if we agree with Sir Edmund Chambers that the Stratford newcomer was in his early career not definitely linked with any single acting group, that he could have appropriated material associated with the so-called "Pembroke group" of plays and transferred it to the Queen's Men, thereby plausibly giving it the Master's touch in the process.[27] If it helps at all, Kyd for a time also wrote directly for the Queen's Men. In any case, G. M. Pinciss has argued that the Queen's Men were simply a division of Pembroke's Men.[28] In this connection, it is perhaps worth noting that the phrase "Shake thy speres in honour of his name" occurs in *Edward I*, which is generally assigned either to the Queen's or Pembroke's, and seems to reconnect with the "Shakebag" / "Shakescene" *Arden* matter.

Nonetheless, Shakespeare need not have written all of the Arden play, if any of it, because of a few rather obvious stylistic discrepancies with his work in general, such as the anti-Catholic effect of a poisoned crucifix, sometimes considered Marlovian, though Michael Marsden claims that it simply stems from folklore,[29] whereby it would be misleading to assert that this horror play deserves to be on any strong par with the canonical writing as such. Furthermore, the surprising use of high-flown language by low-class denizens like Shakebag and Black Will has suggested multiple authorship because of the inconsistency involved, though that may also be ascribed simply to relative immaturity on an author's part. A mixture of comic and serious or tragic elements is hardly what Jonson would have applauded, but *at the same time* reminds us also of the lack of classical form he criticized in Shakespeare. Circumstantial and much internal evidence, at any rate, point to another Will's plausible involvement in some form – as actor, final contributing or revising collaborator or even both together. The play presumably would not have been considered for the First Folio, in any case, for various reasons, doubtless one of them being that Heminge and Condell had no association with the Queen's Men, and *Pericles* and *The Two Noble Kinsmen* were also excluded on the grounds of their simply being obvious collaborations. *Henry VIII* did not have that reputation then and so was included.

In any event, to round this account up on a popular-culture note: it really would be going a bit far afield to accept the verdict of S. F. X. Dean, in his recent mystery novel *It Can't Be My Grave*, and announce that the bona fide author of the Arden tragedy was none other than a hitherto unknown feminist called Lucy Goodman[30], entertaining perhaps though that might be.

## Notes

1. "*Arden of Feversham*: Its Interest Today", *English*, 11 (1956), 17. The original title was *M. Arden of Feversham* in short.

2. *The Elizabethan Stage*, 4 Vols. (Oxford: Clarendon, 1923), IV, 3; see also Kenneth Muir, *Shakespeare as Collaborator* (London: Methuen, 1960), p. 3.

3. *The Tragedy of Master Arden of Feversham* (London: Methuen, 1973).

4. "Material for an Edition of *Arden of Faversham*" (Oxford, B Litt thesis, 1963); see also his "Shakespearean Features of the Poetic Style of *Arden of Faversham*", *Archiv für das Studium der neueren Sprachen und Literaturen*, 145 (1993), 279-304.

5. "The Imagery of Tragic Melodrama in *Arden of Faversham*", *Drama Survey*, 5 (1966), 171-81; rpt. in his *Shakespeare's Contemporaries: Modern Studies in English Renaissance Drama*, ed. Max Bluestone and Norman Rabkin (Englewood Cliffs: Prentice-Hall, 1970), pp. 173-83 (quotation p. 174).

6. "*Edmund Ironside*", *TLS*, 8 Oct. 1982, p. 1102. For the passage in *The Faerie Queene*, see Eric Sams, *Shakespeare's Lost Play: "Edmund Ironside"* (New York: St. Martin's, 1985), p. 12.

7. On this thesis, see especially W. Nicholas Knight, *Shakespeare's Hidden Life: Shakespeare at the Law 1585-1595* (New York: Mason & Lipscomb, 1973).

8. See Edward J. L. Scott, "The Family of Shakespeare in London", *Athenaeum*, no. 3773 (17 Feb. 1900), pp. 219-20.

9. Mark Dominik, "The Authorship of *The Birth of Merlin*", *Shakespeare Quarterly*, 42 (1992), 53; see also his edition, *William Shakespeare and "The Birth of Merlin"* (New York: Philosophical Library, 1985; 2nd ed., Beaverton, Oregon: Alioth P, 1991).

10. See my article attempting to refute Shakespearean authorship, "The Misattribution of *The Birth of Merlin* to Shakespeare", *PBSA*, 73 (1979), 248-52. The most recent edition of the play frowns on the plausibility of Shakespearean authorship (misreading my article in the process), namely Joanna Udall, *A Critical, Old-Spelling Edition of "The Birth of Merlin" (Q 1662)* (London: MHRA, 1991). (The explicit reference to my article is not in her edition itself, but in the University of London doctoral diss. upon which her work is based. Although I have examined the thesis in the Senate House Library, I do not have permission to quote therefrom.)

11. "Middleton's Authorship of *A Yorkshire Tragedy*", *Review of English Studies*, 45 (1994), 1-25. (I am indebted to Dimiter Daphinoff for calling this article to my attention.)

12. "*Arden of Faversham*", *Shakespeare Survey*, 36 (1983), 121-33. MacDonald P. Jackson, in his long article in *Archiv*, also praises this article (p. 279n).

13. Wine, pp. xxvi-xxx, xlv, 142.

14. "*Arden of Feversham*: A Case Reopened". Regrettably I do not have his permission to cite details from these unpublished findings here.

15. On the etymological relationship of *Shakebag* and *Shakerags*, see *Slang and Its Analogues Past and Present*, ed. John S. Farmer and W. E. Henley (London: Routledge, 1965).

16. "Shakespeare's Nomenclature" in *Essays on Shakespeare*, ed. Gerald W. Chapman (Princeton: Princeton UP, 1965), pp. 59-90. See especially p. 87.

17. References to *Arden* in this paper are to the Wine ed.

18. E.g., by Wine, p. lxxii.

19. The most noted critic who discerned this was Swinburne. For more details on the parallel, see *Minor Elizabethan Tragedies*, ed. T. W. Craik (London: Dent, 1974), pp. 81-2; *Arden of Feversham*, ed. Martin White (London: Ernest Benn, 1982), p. xvi (citing Jackson). Also see my *Shakespeare and the Matter of the Crux: Textual, Topical, Onomastic, and Other Puzzlements* (Lewiston, NY: Edwin Mellen Press, 1991), p. 220. (I do not deal with numerous aspects of the authorship crux in the book, although this article represents an updating and reworking of some of my findings.)

20. *William Shakespeare: A Life* (London: Hodder and Stroughton, 1991), p. 19.

21. The citations from Jonson's "To the memory of my beloved, The Author Mr William Shakespeare and what he hath left us" are from *The First Folio of Shakespeare*, prepared by Charlton Hinman (New York: Norton, 1968). Line references to Shakespeare are to the Pelican ed., *William Shakespeare: The Complete Works*, rev. ed., gen. ed. Alfred Harbage (Baltimore: Penguin, 1969); citations are to Hinman's ed.

22. See his *Selected Essays 1917-1932* (New York: Harcourt, 1932), p. 122.

23. See Wine, pp. lxxxi-ii, lxxxvii.

24. See *Three Elizabethan Domestic Tragedies*, ed. Keith Sturgess (New York: Penguin, 1969), p. 20.

25. "Marlowe's Claims to the Shakespeare Apocrypha". The paper was delivered for a session which I was honored to chair (Oxford Polytechnic, 1988). Ule claimed that Marlowe was influenced by his father, who lived in Kent. I do not have his permission to cite this unpublished paper in detail.

26. Wine, pp. xlv-xlvi.

27. See also his *The Elizabethan Stage*, 4 Vols. (Oxford: Clarendon Press, 1923), IV, 3-4. Even Chambers is not adamant about Kyd as author.

28. "Shakespeare, Her Majesty's Players, and Pembroke's Men", *Shakespeare Survey*, 27 (1974), 129-42.

29. "The Otherworld of *Arden of Feversham*", *Southern Folklore Quarterly*, 36 (1972), 36-42.

30. (New York: Walker, 1983). The author's real name is Francis Smith. The main point is that the argument favoring Shakespeare's partial or full authorship is based largely on circumstantial evidence, yet Smith fails to take into account that accrediting such a fine play to an unknown dramatist strains credulity. The argument is that no one else who is known was capable of composing such a play at that time. (This does not mean that the drama has no weaknesses as

well.) This paper was initially presented for a special session on *Arden of Feversham* at the Ohio Shakespeare Conference (Bowling Green), at which scenes from the play were also suitably enacted. That year happened to be the 500th anniversary of its publication. After this paper was composed, a textual study of mine, "On Retaining *M. Arden of Feversham*: The Question of Titular Resonance," belately appeared in *Analytical & Enumerative Bibliography*, NS 6 (1992), 208-15 (Northern Illinois University). That paper argues for the play's title, notably in that "M." happened to be also the initial of Shakespeare's mother (Mary Arden); wordplay on *fever* and *(s)ham* becomes also germane. Insofar as *ham* was short for *hamlet*, meaning a small village (hence here a village susceptible to fevers because of the marshy land), the phonological tie-in with Shakespeare's Danish tragedy provides yet another link with that later drama.

# REVIEWS

*Shakespeare's Christian Dimension: An Anthology of Commentary.* Ed. by Roy Battenhouse. Bloomington: Indiana University Press, 1994, pp. xii + 520. ISBN 0-253-31122-5.

After a weary decade of ideological discourse on the plays of Shakespeare, characterized by a bewildering succession of -isms, one breathes a sigh of relief on opening this impressive anthology of commentary, mostly by modern scholars, on "Shakespeare's Christian dimension." In what has come to seem the prevailing 'orthodoxy' in Shakespearean scholarship the Christian approach to the plays is regarded as but one, and one of the less respectable, among many possible approaches, such as the Marxist, the Nietzschean, the Freudian, the structuralist, the deconstructionist, the cultural relativist, the new historicist, the feminist and the homosexual. But now this welcome anthology furnishes overwhelming evidence as to how central and solid is the Christian approach in contrast to those other merely tangential or circumferential approaches.

In today's concern to present Shakespeare as "our contemporary", belonging no less to our time than to his own Elizabethan age, all too many scholars have come to forget, or to overlook, the obvious fact that Christianity was central to the mind of the dramatist and his age; and in their concentration on the secular or this-worldly dimension of his plays they quietly gloss over the recurring religious references in them. For the most part they are content to remain on the literal level or plane of meaning in their discussion of plot and character, while overlaying it with the subsequent ideology of Marx and Hegel, Nietzsche and Freud, Derrida and Lacan, and a consequent jargon that Shakespeare himself – with not a few modern readers – would have found incomprehensible. This volume, however, under the inspiring editorship of the late Roy Battenhouse, aptly serves to roll away all that unnecessary ideology and to disclose the deeper levels of meaning in the plays, in view of the Christian context of their age.

This context is revealed in the course of the various commentaries – no fewer than 92 by different authors, in a book of more than 500 pages – as not only Elizabethan (in the narrow sense) but also Medieval, not only Renaissance and Reformation but also including the theology and liturgy, the poetry and drama of the Middle Ages. The meaning of plays involved in this larger context may have become hidden in the post-Christian modern age – when not a few scholars have ventured to doubt if there is any such "meaning" in them – but it was not hidden from most of Shakespeare's contemporaries, even the less well educated, for whom it was (as we say) part of the air they breathed.

With the publication of R. M. Frye's *Shakespeare and Christian Doctrine* in 1963 an existing tendency among Shakespeare scholars to find religious meanings in the plays came to be rejected as an unjustifiable "allegorizing", "theologizing" or "reductionism"; and renewed emphasis was laid on the secular meaning and purpose of the dramatist. But now with the publication of this anthology "the wheel has come full circle" and the secularist emphasis is discredited. Ironically enough, Frye himself has contributed one of the more notable essays in this book, on the deep significance of the religious and biblical echoes in *Macbeth*.

There is no space here to give even a glimpse of the riches of religious meaning and implication, not willfully read into, but aptly discerned in the, text of Shakespeare in the course of the many essays gathered within this volume. What is particularly impressive is not so much their quantity – and frequent reminders are given of the many more essays that might have been included in the form of "supplementary bibliography" for each play – as their almost uniform level of excellence, even or especially when they have had to be abbreviated in view of the whole. Here is indeed what the French call an *embarras de richesses* that will have to be taken into account by all future commentators on Shakespeare's plays.

For a reviewer it is a hard but rewarding task to read through the whole volume; but for most students of Shakespeare it will serve as a mine of reference for Christian interpretations on individual plays. These are presented – after ten "key assessments" – according to the traditional division of comedies, histories and tragedies, though under the first and last of these headings the chronological order of composition has been followed instead of the chaotic arrangement in the First Folio. On this point, however, one might well fault the editor for clinging to this division instead of observing the more natural order of Shakespeare's dramatic development – at least, beginning with the romantic plays (including *Romeo and Juliet*), continuing with the plays of English history (from *Richard III* to *Henry V*), followed by the great tragedies and the Roman plays, and culminating in the comedies of forgiveness (from *Measure for Measure* to *The Tempest*). The editor feels the need of apologizing for the omission of *King John* and *Henry VIII*; but the more glaring omission of *A Midsummer Night's Dream* and *Julius Caesar* is unexplained.

For all the many merits of this anthology, certain defects inevitably remain, given the number and variety of authors chosen for inclusion. There are occasional forced interpretations, as when the structure of *Pericles* is explained by the Augustinian theory of Seven Ages of History, and attributions of a "biblical paradigm", without textual proof of authorial intention. There are several instances of super-subtle punning, as when the "sycamore" in *Romeo and Juliet* is explained as "sick-amour", in contrast to the comparative crudeness of most of Shakespeare's puns. There is an annoying tendency to speak of "Renaissance theology," meaning "Reformation theology" – if anything, the Reformation was basically anti-Renaissance – when the theology in question reaches back through the medieval theologians to St. Augustine. There is an almost complete disregard of the religious context of Catholic v. Protestant and Anglican v. Puritan in which the plays were composed, though much work has been done on this disputed topic. There is, in general, a harshness in judging the tragic heroes, from Romeo to

Othello, especially poor Hamlet, which seems far from the Augustinian ideal of *caritas* and forgetful of the warning uttered by Henry VI (himself a victim to such harshness), "Forbear to judge, for we are sinners all" (*2Henry VI*, 3.3.31).

But now it is time for me to refrain from further judgment of faults, when the merits of this volume are so much more impressive. This is, in conclusion, a book not only for every university and college library but also for every Shakespeare scholar who is at all interested in maintaining a sane balance in his approach to the plays – especially after the balance has been so violently upset during the past decade of ideological aberration.

Sophia University, Tokyo                                                             Peter Milward


Debora Kuller Shuger. *The Renaissance Bible: Scholarship, Sacrifice, and Subjectivity*. (The New Historicism: Studies in Cultural Poetics, Number 29). Berkeley: University of California Press, 1994. pp. 196. ISBN 0-520-08480-2.

Debora Kuller Shuger's third book on spiritual culture in the English Renaissance, and her second published in the "New Historicism" series from the University of California Press, explores a wide range of neo-Latin and vernacular texts written for and about the Renaissance Bible. Shuger focuses primarily on the texts related to Christ's Passion: the Last Supper, the crucifixion, Mary Magdalene at the tomb, and earlier types of Christ's death in the Hebrew Bible. Her goal is to connect biblical scholarship to this period's concept of sacrifice in order to articulate more clearly what subjectivity meant for Europeans in the sixteenth and seventeenth centuries.

In her first chapter, "After Allegory", Shuger explores the currently unknown work of what she calls Renaissance biblical scholars, a group of intellectuals in England and Europe in the seventeenth century addressing the philological, historical and cultural questions arising from biblical translation and exegesis. She distinguishes these thinkers from Christian humanists and from polemicists and theologians, characterizing them by what she sees as an almost modern interest in "thick description" and the cultural contingencies of the societies out of which the biblical texts arose. Shuger examines in particular their willingness to treat seriously the minutiae of Hebrew and Roman culture and, indeed, their willingness to interpret biblical texts by the principles of those cultures rather than by any transcendent or allegorical code.

Chapter 2, "The Key to all Mythologies", particularizes this analysis by examining Grotius's *Defensio fidei catholicae de satisfactione Christi adversus Faustum Socinum* (1617) and exposing its willingness to argue by principles of Roman law about the corporate, rather than individualistic, nature of Christ's sacrifice on the cross. Shuger argues that this issue of sacrifice is central to the tensions between "the individual" and the "mythical solidarity of the patriarchal family and tribal community" evidenced in Grotius's work and, more widely, in his contemporaries' debates over the cannibalism of New World cultures.

Chapter 3 continues with the issue of sacrifice, studying Calvinist passion narratives as they grapple with a new sense of the individual. Shuger finds here a confluence of violence and the decentered self which, she argues, is more than accidental; she also connects this in particular to an identification with the masculine subject, one in turmoil after the demise of the central defining roles of monk and knight.

In the final two chapters Shuger pushes this question of gender further, examining George Buchanan's *Jephtha sive votum tragoedia* (c.1540-47) and its identification of Jephtha's daughter with Christ. Shuger suggests that this drama is symptomatic of a larger connection between tragedy, sacrifice, and gendered subjectivity in the period. She builds on this argument in her final chapter, which examines several literary texts' unblushingly erotic meditations on Mary Magdalene at Jesus' tomb.

Of most interest to Shakespeareans, perhaps, is her suggestion of a connection in the period between tragedy and sacrificial rites, including Christ's. Shuger tries to draw correlations between the origins of tragedy in sacrificial Dionysian rites, catharsis's etymological relationship to blood-cleansing, and Renaissance conceptions of dramatic form. Sidney, she notes, particularly praises Buchanan's *Jephtha* in his analysis of English drama. In discussing the relationships between sacrifice and subjectivity Shuger also comments suggestively on the reverse *pietàs* which close *Hamlet, King Lear,* and *Othello.*

Shuger In this study Shuger clearly provides much-needed analyses of several key issues in English religious culture. As she argues in her introduction, and as critics as diverse as Gary Taylor, William Kerrigan, and Catherine Stimpson have recently suggested, current materialist and cultural criticism of the Renaissance has been insufficiently attentive to dynamics of spiritual life and thought. Shuger's impressive analysis of a wide range of texts on Christology and subjectivity helps to correct that oversight. Her work is erudite and scholarly, spanning several languages, countries, schools of thought and academic communities, and opening up fascinating pockets of intellectual life. And she is not afraid to be theoretically eclectic, drawing on Freudian analyses of taboo, new-historicist models of anthropological investigation, and feminist studies of Petrarchism and subjectivity with refreshing flexibility.

If one were to suggest any difficulties with this study, these strengths, in fact, contribute to them; the very breadth of the book's argument sometimes leads to uneven coverage. In discussing tragedy, for instance, Shuger discusses almost exclusively Shakespearean plays, and no one work gets more than a few tantalizing sentences. She begins a discussion of Petrarchism and subjectivity three pages from the end of a chapter, which leaves us wanting a more ample analysis. She attempts to explain the origins of modern subjectivity, eroticism, historicism and anthropology – rather a large undertaking for a two-hundred-page study. In fact, the book's title is a symptom of this overreaching: Shuger herself says several times that she is really not discussing the Renaissance Bible in any comprehensive way, and one might wish that the title more accurately reflected her narrower set of concerns.

Shuger's eclectic approach also makes unity of argument a rather difficult project. As Shuger herself says in the conclusion, the chapters "deal with incommensurate materials that do not share the same discursive genealogy and hence should not be lined up as stages along a single trajectory"; the connections between "scholarship, sacrifice, and subjectivity" do become clear by the end of the book, but at times it is hard to see the logic holding together the various pieces. Shuger's own theoretical eclecticism is also sometimes disorienting; considering that the final two chapters explore issues of gender, one might wish for a clearer and more consistently explicit feminist theory or strategy. One sub-text, which seems to be that new historicism has its origins in the forward-looking historicism of Renaissance biblical scholars, has a recuperative energy which could also be more explicitly articulated.

But, as always, Shuger's unique collection of scholarly interests and areas of expertise makes for a rich mixture of characters, arguments and insights, many of them both important and new to literary critics of this period. *The Renaissance Bible* takes us several steps along the way toward a fuller understanding of the spiritual cultures in early modern England, and for this alone Shuger's work is a welcome addition.

Furman University                                          Elizabeth Hodgson

*Queering the Renaissance.* Ed. Jonathan Goldberg. Durham, NC: Duke UP, 1994. pp. 388. ISBN 0-8223-1381-2.

*Queering the Renaissance*, as the title implies, attempts the same type of pan-European and multi-critical reassessment of the Renaissance in terms of sexuality that *Re-Writing the Renaissance* attempted in terms of gender over a decade ago. The collection is framed by an interesting piece by Janet Halley, which explores the historical assumptions of *Bowers v. Hardwick*, and an afterword by Margaret Hunt, which is a lucid survey of the issues raised.

The strongest pieces in the volume will be familiar to most readers. Michael Warner's "New English Sodom", which originally appeared in 1992, Valerie Traub's "The (In)Significance of 'Lesbian' Desire in Early Modern England", which first circulated in another high-profile anthology in 1992, and Alan Bray's "Homosexuality and the Signs of Male Friendship in Elizabethan England", an essay from 1990, have been so instrumental in changing the terrain of criticism that further comment is unnecessary. Only slightly less well-known is Dorothy Stephens's examination of Amoret in *The Faerie Queene*, which appeared in *ELH* in 1991. It explores criticism's writing of Amoret as a lack and attempts to complement these approaches by examining the possibilities for active female desires such as "women's friendship" (204).

The new work in the volume, as one would expect, displays divergent tendencies. Three essays attend to periods that have been underexplored. Donald N. Mager's "John Bale and Early Tudor Sodomy Discourse" delivers a particularly shrewd historicization, discussing how Bale's *Comedy Concernynge thre lawes, of Nature, Moses, & Christ*, helps to originate a polarization of sexual categories around a division which "opposes nature to its non-procreative opposite ..." (159). At the heart of his analysis is a valuable re-examination of Tudor marriage theory and the emergence of the discourse of atheism.

Richard Rambuss's "Pleasure and Devotion: The Body of Jesus and Seventeenth-Century Religious Lyric" questions "What are we to make of a cultural formation whose investment in men's desire for the male body is pronouncedly phobic and prohibitive, yet features at its core an iconic display of an unclothed male body in a state of ecstasy, rendered as such to be looked at ["*Ecce homo*"], adored, desired?" (253). His method is to trace the image of the penetrated body of Christ through the devotional lyrics of Crashaw, Donne and Herbert, and to intermix with this a skillful assessment of the (hetero)erotic predispositions of current criticism on the metaphysical poets. Unlike many others in the volume, this essay is written in crystalline prose.

Graham Hammill's "The Epistemology of Expurgation: *Bacon and The Masculine Birth of Time*" draws a correlation between Bacon's new epistemology and a production of sexuality "in which what is *not known*, what remains *un*represented, defines what counts as sexuality" (238). This sexuality, not surprisingly, ends up being a *homo*sexuality. Much of his analysis depends on Lacanian images of repressed phallic desire; however, when he then turns his attention to Bacon's own considerable interest in anal eroticism, and especially in enemas, the theorization shifts into a historicization that seems stunningly correct.

A number of other essays explore issues of textuality and textual transmission. Jeffrey Masten's essay on Beaumont and Fletcher in collaboration argues that "in the course of the seventeenth century, there is a shift in the printed and performative apparatus of drama away from homoerotic collaboration and toward singular authorship on a patriarchal-absolutist model." As such, it places the topic of sexuality within the recent attention to authorship. Similarly, Marcie Frank's essay on Dryden's uses of Shakespeare in *All for Love* provides a corrective to Bloomian notions of literary transmission (embodied in her essay in the work of Samuel Johnson and Gary Taylor) by pointing out how the oedipalization that attends many ideas of influence obscures the play's own complicated historical, textual and sexual relations to *Antony and Cleopatra*. More idiosyncratic, but still useful, explorations of textuality can be found in Carla Frecerro's Lacanian analysis of textual variants in Marguerite de Navarre's three manuscripts of the *Heptameron*, or in Forrest Tyler Stevens's interesting discussion of Erasmus's "love" letters, or in Alan K. Smith's informative close-reading of the coded sodomy within Burchiello's "non-sense" verse (which, unfortunately, ends with an idiosyncratic foray into a violently ahistorical version of Freudianism).

The two essays that most provoked thought in me also adopt sophisticated theoretical views of textuality. Goldberg's own essay, *Romeo and Juliet's Open Rs*, covers a set of concerns which also motivate his book *Sodometries*. Beginning with unflattering words to feminists who seek to prescribe "a single heterosexual trajectory" on the play (a slightly troublesome point when a similar argument could have been made using over three hundred years of male criticism on the play), Goldberg attempts to realign conceptualizations of the play by grouping its sexual meaning around a sodomitical/non-sodomitical divide, thus enabling a by-pass of both the gender (man/woman) and sexual (hetero/homo) divisions that typify modern thinking. Thus he can conclude his discussion by pointing to the text's "recognition that anyone – man or woman – might be in the place marked by the open Rs of *Romeo and Juliet*" – that is, anyone regardless of gender or sexuality might be a sodomite. This, too, is what I take to be the primary point of his introduction to the volume: that, throughout history, "contests to control the meaning of sodomy have involved shifting, opportunistic, sometimes ontologically coherent and sometimes inchoate deployments of the relationship between act and identity" (17).

Goldberg suggests that such a reading will account for the fact that "gender and sexuality in *Romeo and Juliet* do not subscribe to the compulsions of modern critics of the play" (227), and yet it seems as if the binary of sodomitical/non-sodomitical that governs the essay must at some point acknowledge a debt to the binary of queer/non-queer that governs much of current gay, lesbian and queer social theory. The essay replaces gay, lesbian and feminist presentism with a queer presentism; and while I think this is in many ways a brilliant political strategy, it needs to be represented as such.

A related point can be made from Elizabeth Pittenger's "'To Serve the Queere': Nicholas Udall, Master of Revels", which scrupulously maps out the buggary controversy around Udall in a combination of sobriety and wit that is most refreshing. Beginning with a poem by Thomas Tusser, Pittenger draws attention to the historical image of Udall as a buggerer. The evidence, as she points out, has been convoluted by a history of textual scholarship hell-bent on replacing the word "buggary" in the Privy Council records with the word "burglary." Pittenger then maps out parallels between Udall and the character Matthew Merrygreek, the parasite in *Ralph Roister Doister*. This parasitical economy of misspending, which can be correlated with Udall's own social position, parallels postmodern ideas of the historical sign "sodomy", for it displays the types of alternative spendings and mis-alliances that have, in the wake of Foucault, become the nominal essence of sodomy. The Udall/Merrygreek conflation, in other words, erases the prohibitional power of the distinction between buggary and burglary.

Nevertheless, Pittenger's conclusion to her discussion, wherein she discusses the desire to "read" Udall as homosexual, must raise a question: "I hope that I've pointed out enough of the problems to suggest that this would not be the way to go, though I concede that it has to be acknowledged as a constant temptation, one that recognizes our position as readers with particular sets of stakes and desires. In choosing another way, I don't want to minimize the importance of what the real person Nicholas Udall did. I honestly don't think there's any way to know. But I do wonder what more it would add if we did" (183). The balance of such a statement is commendable, but I question whether anyone would even think of producing such a painstaking analysis of queer desires in Udall (or his play) if the (even misguided) prospect of homosexual desire were not already present. Pittenger's essay, then, elaborates a pattern that also seems to me to be present in other essays, for it picks something (or someone) that could, with a different eye, be read as gay or lesbian, and then says, essentially, it's not really gay at all. And here, to play true confessions, is my problem (and I admit it is *my* problem): this is the same response my parents had when I came out to them.

Yet, judging from Goldberg's introduction, it is precisely such possible questions and new discussions that motivated his compilation of the volume. It is an exciting time to be a gay, lesbian or queer scholar (or any of the various permutations thereof), and this volume provocatively maps out the enduring questions that generate this excitement.

University of California, Riverside                     Gregory W. Bredbeck


Carole Levin. *The Heart and Stomach of a King: Elizabeth I and the Politics of Sex and Power*. Philadelphia: University of Pennsylvania Press, 1994. Pp. x + 243. ISBN 0-8122-3252-6.(hb); ISBN 0-8122-1533-8.(pb). Susan Frye. *Elizabeth I: The Competition for Representation*. Oxford: Oxford University Press, 1993. pp. x + 228. ISBN 0-19-50823-8 (hb).


The most vivid image of Elizabeth I currently available to students of early modern drama can be found in Louis Montrose's retelling of Simon Forman's dream from 1597 ("'Shaping Fantasies': Figurations of Gender and Power in Elizabethan Culture", *Representations* 1 [1983], 61-94). In that dream, the Queen appears as "a little elderly woman in a coarse white petticoat" who flirts with Forman, accedes to his sexual banter, and is about to bestow on him a royal kiss when the dreamer awakes. Central to Montrose's understanding of Forman's dream is the contrast between Elizabeth's aging body and her mythological status as a timeless object of national desire. Montrose calls Elizabeth a "cultural anomaly", fascinating but dangerous. Yet he himself emphasizes the queen's potential monstrosity as a sexualized crone and her consequential vulnerability to rhetorical manipulation. Thus, his essay reconstructs a sexual economy in which "a fantasy of male dependency upon woman is contained within a fantasy of male control over woman" (65), an economy that necessarily puts Elizabeth at a disadvantage.

The two books reviewed here extend, but also correct this well-known image of Elizabeth. They examine Elizabeth's self-representations throughout her reign, so that the issues surrounding the queen's two bodies in the 1580's and 1590's are contextualized within Elizabeth's broader political biography. Both studies also emphasize that Elizabeth was actively engaged in the creation of her own myth. Carole Levin tends to focus on Elizabeth's subjectivity and Susan Frye on her strategies, but both writers depict an Elizabeth who participates vigorously in what Frye calls "the competition for representation". Together, *The Heart and Stomach of a King: Elizabeth I and the Politics of Sex and Power* and *Elizabeth I: The Competition for Representation* provide a nuanced view of Elizabeth and her relations to others, in both the public and private spheres. They accomplish this aim by examining with care Elizabeth's anomalous relationship to standard categories of gender and her manipulation of expectations about gender. What interests these women scholars is Elizabeth's negotiation of her identity as both queen and king.

Levin's *The Heart and Stomach of a King* begins with the problem of female monarchy. Since Western culture traditionally has regarded women as weak, to be successful a woman must "act as a man". To become a man, however, is to be monstrous. The first three chapters of Levin's book chronicle Elizabeth's early efforts to assert herself as both woman and king without seeming monstrous. Chapter 1 provides biographical background, depicting a young Elizabeth who learned early about the dangers of royal marriage and of her own position as daughter and sister. Chapter 2, "Elizabeth as Sacred Monarch", portrays an Elizabeth who is politically astute, but also devout. Within the context of debate over female regency, Elizabeth fashions herself as a female saint. The notion that Elizabeth appropriated to herself the Virgin's cult is certainly not new. Levin shows, however, that while Elizabeth exploited the political potential of such ceremonies as washing the feet of the poor on Maundy Thursday or touching for the King's Evil, she firmly believed that she enjoyed God's special protection. From Levin's detailed descriptions of these ceremonies, there emerges a powerful picture of Elizabeth as a "young, unmarried, Anglican woman" who takes upon herself the king's priestly function and transforms it according to traditions of female piety.

Chapter 3, "The Official Courtships of the Queen", examines Elizabeth's efforts to cope with the treacherous subjects of royal marriage and succession. While Elizabeth's contemporaries often declared her "greedy" for marriage proposals, Levin suggests that Elizabeth found marriage repugnant. She insists, however, that Elizabeth's adoption of the role of virgin queen should be seen as a political strategy rather than as a sign of sexual or psychological inadequacy. Levin develops her argument by detailing the pitfalls that threatened Elizabeth in her relationships with Robert Dudley (whose terminally-ill wife died in a suspicious manner), the Duke of Anjou (whose Catholicism proved to be an insuperable barrier for Elizabeth's subjects), and finally, the Duke of Alençon (whose presence delighted Elizabeth but whose eventual departure from England may have also relieved her). Levin shows how Elizabeth's political roles as king, as queen, and as mother to her realm frustrated her courtships, but she also shows why Elizabeth might have found marriage unacceptable. From this perspective, we see Elizabeth less as a victim than as the "master-mistress" of her political situation.

While Chapters 2 and 3 examine how Elizabeth brought her public and private lives into harmony, the next two chapters demonstrate how public perceptions about Elizabeth's private life and her public status threatened the stability of her reign. Chapter 4, "Wanton and Whore," examines public interest in Elizabeth's sexuality. On the one hand, as is well known, Elizabeth was supposed to be incapable of sexual relations; on the other, she was considered a whore who would not limit her appetite to one man. According to rumor, Elizabeth bore to

Robert Dudley as many as four illegitimate children. Other rumors accused her of giving birth to bastards during her royal progresses, and even of committing infanticide. As Levin points out, these narratives provided the people with an outlet for their ambivalence toward an unmarried female monarch, allowing them to speculate about the succession while denigrating Elizabeth herself in a "typically misogynistic way – by dismissing her as a whore" (70). Chapter 5, "The Return of the King", discusses rumors of Edward VI's survival and related acts of sedition. Although the theme of a king's survival had occurred before during times of monarchical instability, the first and last decade of Elizabeth's reign were noteworthy not only for such rumors, but for the appearance of pretenders to the throne. Through the fantasy of the king's return, Elizabeth's subjects expressed their desire for a male monarch.

The final two chapters of Levin's book deal with the gendered symbolism surrounding Elizabeth. Chapter 6, "Elizabeth as King and Queen", reminds us that, while Elizabeth may have had the heart and stomach of a male king, she had a woman's body. Thus, while Elizabeth herself exploited the theory of the king's two bodies to emphasize her special position as virgin queen, seditious subjects tended to see her natural body "as potentially corrupt in a manifestly female way" (147). Nevertheless, Elizabeth's adoption of both male and female identities could valorize, rather than denigrate, the feminine. In this penultimate chapter, the only one to address explicitly the drama from Elizabeth's reign, Levin suggests that the unstable distinction between a (male) body politic and a (female) body natural can be used to celebrate feminine power. In an analysis of *Twelfth Night* that rehearses familiar arguments about cross-dressing in Shakespeare's plays, Levin argues that Olivia retains her femininity while exercising power. She, rather than the cross-dressed Viola, is the play's proper heroine. While Levin's analysis of *Twelfth Night* may seem less than revolutionary to Shakespeareans, her insistence that Elizabeth – and by extension, Shakespeare's heroines – could wield male power without necessarily sacrificing their femininity provides an alternative to Montrose's powerful vision of Elizabeth as a sexualized crone, horrifying yet pathetic in her insistence on her eternal youth. This reading, in turn, might be interrogated from the perspective of queer theory.

Levin's final chapter, "Dreaming the Queen", reviews Essex's rebellion and its aftermath. In this version of Elizabeth in the 1590's, the 'dreams' through which her subjects and her foreign enemies come to terms with the English sovereign are more plentiful and varied than one might guess from Montrose's important essay. Levin also revisits the familiar dream of Simon Forman, which she interprets less in terms of Elizabeth's sexuality than of her power: instead of idealizing Elizabeth as a love object, Forman is attracted by her powerful position. The manifest craving for sexual intimacy in his dream therefore camouflages a latent "desire for the power that intimacy with the sovereign confers" (165). Elizabeth's body natural and body politic work together to the end, protecting the queen from derision rather than exposing her to it. In Levin's analysis of "dreaming the queen", Essex's rebellion finally shatters the old dream of a loving virgin queen. Yet even under duress Elizabeth continued to inspire loyalty among her subjects. Her myth, unlike Elizabeth's decaying body, had resilience. For, although James's accession provided the English with a male monarch, before long nostalgia for the reign of "good Queen Bess" had set in.

In *Elizabeth I: The Competition for Representation*, Susan Frye examines how Elizabeth's representation of herself as an "authoritative, unmarried woman competed with her own society's conviction that women should be chaste, silent, and obedient" (vii). She focuses on three moments in Elizabeth's reign: the coronation entry of 1559, the Kenilworth entertainments of 1575, and events and literature from the 1590's that preceded Essex's rebellion. Frye's brief introduction outlines her theoretical assumptions. To avoid reifying the queen either as the passive object of others' mythmaking or as the all-powerful producer of her own iconography, Frye alludes to Judith Butler's notion that identity is performative, and so defines Elizabeth as a discursive agent. Frye also treats allegorical productions about Elizabeth as discontinuous, marked by the split between signifier and signified. Because in Saussure's linguistics signs are unstable and open-ended, these signs "constitute a material practice through which ideas become active" (35). For this reason, textual reproductions of Elizabethan allegorical pageantry are susceptible to rhetorical analysis. Although Frye's theoretical frame might be elaborated at greater length, her critical assumptions produce solid and subtle readings of specific moments in Elizabeth's reign.

Chapter 1, "Engendered Economics: Elizabeth I's Coronation Entry (1559)", offers the most satisfying reading to date of Elizabeth's coronation procession. Analyzing the event through its representation in the pamphlet *The Queen's Majesty's Passage*, Frye shows that the London aldermen who sponsored the entry cast Elizabeth simultaneously as the city's mother and as a daughter who meekly accepts advice from the city fathers. In this way, the aldermen seek to circumscribe their sovereign's "masculine" power by assigning to her traditional domestic roles for women. For instance, in a key pageant "Truth, the daughter of Time" presents Elizabeth with the English Bible, maneuvering her into a strong allegorical alliance with Protestantism by characterizing Elizabeth herself as "Truth" and Henry VIII as "Time". Elizabeth cradles the Bible as if it were a baby, allowing herself to be cast not only as her father's daughter, but also as a nurturing mother to her Protestant subjects. But Elizabeth accepts the Bible only after she has received the gift of a purse from the aldermen; in this way, the queen controls symbolically her contract with the city of London. She is an agent rather than a mere cipher in what Gayle Rubin calls the "traffic in women."

Chapter 2, "Engendering Policy at Kenilworth (1575)", takes as its subject two published accounts of the Kenilworth entertainments produced by Robert Dudley in 1575. The context is Dudley's conflict with Elizabeth over whether the English should actively support the Dutch revolt against the Spanish. Although Dudley controlled the pageants, to a large degree Elizabeth controlled Dudley. Thus, one masque in which Diana and Iris argued about marriage and a staged skirmish in which Dudley rescued the Lady of the Lake from a rapist named "Sir Bruse sans Pitie" – two pageants that cast Elizabeth as a vulnerable woman and Dudley as her martial protector – were censored. Instead, the onlookers saw entertainments that centered on Elizabeth herself. The rewritten rescue of the Lady of the Lake, for instance, confirmed the Queen's ideology that her virginity was powerful by casting Elizabeth herself as the Lady's savior. Elizabeth emerges as active virtue and Dudley is reduced to a passive spectator. By 1575, Elizabeth was responding successfully to allegorical efforts to control her. Nevertheless, one printed account of the Kenilworth entertainments, George Gascoigne's *Princely Pleasures*, retains the canceled material and so reasserts Dudley's power for a wider audience. During this period, the Queen's control of her own iconography was at its height, but in the context of military threat even she could not exercise total power over her closest male advisors.

The final chapter, "Engendered Violence: Elizabeth, Spenser, and the Definitions of Chastity (1590)", is more wide-ranging than the previous two. Focused on the third of book of Edmund Spenser's *Faerie Queene*, this chapter demonstrates that while the aging Elizabeth continued to guard her decision-making power, her personal myth, and her aging body carefully, fictions of her vulnerability proliferated during the 1590's. Elizabeth used the rhetoric of Petrarchan love, Neoplatonism, and medieval political theology to "engender" masculine discourse, so that she could claim a subject position that breached the opposition between male and female. A text such as Spenser's *Faerie Queene*, by contrast, reinscribed virtuous virginity within conventional narratives. Elizabeth's insistence on her own divinity and eternal youth – her freedom from ordinary femininity – paradoxically licensed the poet's conservative equation of feminine virtue with fertility and violability. On the printed page, Elizabeth's fictional representatives are imprisoned in captivity narratives that confront the powerful virgin with two alternatives: marriage or rape. For ordinary women, marriage is the natural end of virginity. By implication, the virgin who has escaped marriage is subject to rape. Although this analysis of Spenser's poem is not surprising, Frye's equation between the poet and the rapist Busirane reminds us that the stakes were high in the competition to represent Elizabeth. Frye concludes by analyzing Essex's rebellion as a rape narrative, the kind of social rupture that occurs when figurative language fails.

*The Heart and Stomach of a King: Elizabeth I and the Politics of Sex and Power* and *Elizabeth I: The Competition for Representation* can be read as companion pieces. They cover similar territory from different perspectives: Levin explores Elizabeth as a person, while Frye reconstructs her as a text. Most important, they work together to correct the image of Elizabeth in the 1590's as a crone helplessly embroiled in a sexual economy that makes her an object less of awe than of derision. I have used both of these books as supplementary texts in a graduate seminar on women and politics in early modern drama. I would think that the non-theoretical diction, engaging narratives, and low price of Levin's *The Heart and Stomach of a King* would make it useful as well for undergraduate courses in Renaissance literature. Both books offer important arguments, and both deserve a wide readership.

University of Georgia                                                                                          Christy Desmet


Nigel Smith. *Literature & Revolution in England, 1640-1660*. New Haven: Yale University Press, 1994. pp. 425. ISBN 0-300-05974-4.

Based on what seem to be New Historicist assumptions, Nigel Smith argues that the period of the English Civil War and the Interregnum is an important but much over-looked period in the literary history of England. The convulsions of the

English Civil War not only brought about political and civil change but, according to Smith, substantially altered the literary world of English society as well in the period between 1640 and 1660. Literary genres underwent transformations because the changed historical circumstances rendered the previous literary forms inadequate to meet the needs of the various factions who shared the political arena during the Protectorate.

The participants included more than simply the Cavaliers and the Roundheads, and Smith amply demonstrates that the various sectarian groups – Levellers, Diggers, Ranters, etc. – also contributed to literary changes. Moreover, he also argues that it is only through literary analysis of the proliferation of texts that we can discern the novelty of many of the political and religious ideas coming to birth at this time. Since the literary text does not have an ontological independence from other forms of writing, the de-stabilization in society gave rise to instability in literary production. Political and religious polemics became co-terminus with "literature" in its more restricted meaning. People despairing of their own historical predicaments reworked events of their own time into various kinds of literary texts in order to make sense of their current historical situation.

In the first section Smith lays out the ways in which the conditions of writing changed during this twenty-year period: the erosion of traditional authorities, and with the increase in printed text, a change in the culture's understanding of authorship. While it would be anachronistic to say a pluralism of religious and political views emerged during this time, clearly there was no longer one truth. Political narratives replaced public rhetoric. Moreover, the printed pamphlet and newsbook not only reflected public opinion but also created it. Significantly, at this time, with the suppression of theaters, the news function of theaters was taken over by newsbooks and pamphlets. But the newsbook also became a place where other genres might be developed.

The second section of this book deals with the debate between parliamentarians and monarchists, particularly the ways in which this controversy led to unforeseen new theories of state, the individual, and religion. Many of these new political and religious ideas emerged from areas of discourse not always observed by political and religious theorists. New understandings of self and of religious and political discourse came to be expressed in texts not usually associated with such areas of thought. Smith demonstrates the ways in which the Puritans and the Anglicans held a similar belief in a close relationship between church and state. Both groups wanted to establish a national identity, but the realm of discourse came to involve many more voices than Anglicans and Presbyterians, such as Independents, Seekers, Quakers, and others who contributed numerous versions of self, state, and religion. Smith also observes that the interiority which so often characterizes both Puritans and dissenters can also be found after the ejection of Anglican Divines in the writings of such Anglicans as Jeremy Taylor and Sir Thomas Browne. Like Calvinists and Dissenters, who were so often preoccupied with the individual's spiritual progress, Anglicans also produced texts of private devotions which came to co-exist with Calvinist ones.

One of the most notable groups of dissenters were the Levellers, and from the various texts available, Smith presents the various individuals who contributed to their political theory. What these individuals all seemed to have had in common was a printed plea for toleration and religious freedom. Much of his focus in this chapter is upon John Lilburne and Richard Overton. Smith says that, while Leveller political theory must be gleaned from the various texts, which were printed for many *ad hoc* purposes, some consistent themes did emerge, shaped largely by Puritanism and educational ideas of the sixteenth century. Most of these ideas, however, came to be absorbed by Republicans, Millenarians, or Quakers as the Leveller identity disappeared.

In contrast to this potpourri of textual forms and ideas, the political ideas of Winstanley, Hobbes, and Harrington are each respectively embodied in a unified text that Smith thinks could best be described as an aesthetic object. Only when we consider the works of these men as literary creations do we come to understand the text's full significance as political works. The final chapter of Section II deals with the extent to which the politics of Republicanism were embodied in the political life of England at that time; it is Smith's assessment that theoretical Republicanism had a more vigorous life on the printed page than in Parliament.

The final section deals with the ways in which the various genres themselves – epic, satire, and narrative – all became "contaminated" by the political and religious conflicts going on in England at this time.

This book is clearly erudite and is thoroughly researched. One criticism, however, is that Smith's assessment of Anglicanism during the civil war period receives less attention than the various off-spring of the Puritans. Also, much of his evaluation of early seventeenth-century religious lyric seems to depend upon Barbara Lewalski's *Protestant Poetics and the Seventeenth Century Religious Lyric,* and her view concerning the persuasiveness of Calvinism in such poets as George Herbert, for example, is an arguable point. John Wall's *Transformations of the Word,* for example, offers a different interpretation, one in which Anglicanism is seen as distinct from the Calvinist tradition. These are perhaps minor points, and they do not diminish the value of Smith's book. While some may find the reading of this book a challenge, it will be of value for any one interested in any aspect of seventeenth-century England as well as those interested in literary theory, political science, and religious studies.

Greenville Technical College                                    Clark M. Brittain

Ilana Krausman Ben-Amos. *Adolescence & Youth in Early Modern England*. New Haven and London: Yale University Press, 1994. pp. viii + 335. ISBN 0-300-05597-8.

Ben-Amos, a lecturer in history at Ben-Gurion University, has produced an illuminating account of the transition between childhood and adult life in England during the sixteenth and seventeenth centuries. In opposition to sociologists and some historians who have described this transition in preindustrial societies as of short duration, lasting only three or four years, the author supports the thesis of a complex and prolonged period of growth and adjustment stretching from the early teens to the mid-twenties. For young people of the middle and lower classes in England during these centuries, the transitional process normally began with departure from the parental home for an extended period of agricultural service or apprenticeship that kept the young under the supervision of an *in loco parentis* master but that nevertheless provided opportunities for personal choice, acquisition of adult skills, and the development of independence. It is this experience, commonly described as "life-cycle service", on which the work focuses.

Prior studies, of which the author is knowledgeable and to which she makes appropriate references, have explored different dimensions of life in service. What Ben-Amos attempts – and what makes this volume a particularly valuable contribution to the literature – is to provide a holistic account of how the diverse demands and opportunities of service combined to foster the maturation of the young, both psychologically and socially. Within the inherent limitations of the data, she succeeds admirably in accomplishing this goal.

The first chapter surveys the images of youth reflected in contemporary literature, moral treatises, sermons, etc. Rather than "a single vision based on shared assumptions about young age ..." (p. 34) the author finds conflicting notions and metaphors that represented divergent judgments of the young. None of these images, she contends, bore much relation to the realities of the work experience of actual young persons. These realities are spelled out in the next four chapters which describe the experience of separation from parents (ch. 2), the terms and nature of agricultural service in rural areas (ch. 3), and urban apprenticeships (chs. 4 & 5). Chapter 6 traces the parallel yet subordinate experience of young women: a very small number of girls gained admission to formal apprenticeships, but the more common opportunities of informal training at the hands of parents, kin, and neighbors and the likely period of domestic service did provide opportunities to develop confidence, skills, and autonomy. The various social ties of youth to the nuclear family, other kin, masters, neighbors and peers are explored in chapter 7.

Of greatest interest to a general audience is chapter 8, "Spirituality, Leisure, Sexuality: Was There a Youth Culture?" Over two decades ago Natalie Zemon Davis reported that organized groups of young people, called abbeys and kingdoms, existed in early modern France, giving voice to distinctive values of the young and helping to define a special social role for youth. Ben-Amos not only notes the absence of such groups in England, she also denies that most youths held values that markedly distinguished them from adults. Despite modest generational differences in matters of religion, leisure activities, and sexual practice, she finds basic continuity between generations in these three areas of life. Young persons who embraced dissident religious sects, for example, were often following the lead of dissident adults in doing so. In similar vein, the continuing low rate of illegitimate births demonstrated that youth were not, on the whole, repudiating the sexual morality of the adult community. Among the several "rites of passage" that marked the transition to adult life (the subject of chapter 9) marriage was the culminating act. Although some undertook matrimony immediately upon completing service of apprenticeship, more chose to postpone taking a spouse, either to become better established or simply to extend the time of greater personal freedom before assuming family responsibilities.

Overall, the author concludes that during the early modern past the transition to adulthood bore strong resemblances to present experience. In both contexts the experience was an extended one, spanning twelve or thirteen years or more; both reflected "a lack of synchronization between the various processes of maturation ..." (p. 237), with the result that a youth was regarded as an adult in some ways while still being treated as a child in others. Thus an apprentice who had already become highly skilled at his craft still lacked full control over his own wages. Moreover, Ben-Amos insists, English society held two incompatible sets of norms concerning the young. One set, grounded in the patriarchal family and its attendant family morality, emphasized the need for deference and submission; the other set, rooted in the normative quality of the independent nuclear household, encouraged the development of early independence by the young. These mutually contradictory norms, she suggests, help to explain the anxiety felt by some adults concerning youthful unruliness and disorder.

There are many counts on which to commend this volume. It is based upon impressive archival research, drawing primarily upon apprenticeship materials in Bristol and London. The author has also made extensive use of some seventy printed autobiographies and diaries from the period; these are quoted frequently and to good effect throughout the account. Comparisons to different parts of the realm are invoked by judicious citations of the work of other recent scholars. The work thus synthesizes nicely the author's own investigations and the findings of current historical scholarship. Moreover, the study reflects a coherent general conception, and each segment and chapter fit together with an unfailing inner logic. The style is clear and compelling. Different reading audiences will probably use the study in different ways. Specialists in early modern England, those exploring English family history, and students of the guild system will read it cover-to-cover and pursue the extensive end notes. Literary scholars will probably find chapters 1, 8, and the Conclusion most rewarding. But in this well-told story there is profit for persons of many different interests.

Furman University                                              James H. Smart

Charles Mathews. *Othello, the Moor of Fleet Street* (1833). Ed. Manfred Draudt. Tübingen & Basel: Francke Verlag, 1993. pp. xvi + 99. ISBN 3-7720-2132-8.

The reason why parody was among the most widespread genres of the early nineteenth-century theater is not hard to fathom. Faced with the dilemma of providing audiences with a constantly changing selection of three to five entertainments a night, even the most resourceful theater manager must have welcomed the opportunity of swiftly producing a text offered by the lampooning of a well-known play. As Shakespeare was so prominent in the repertoire of the London theater, the literature is rich in parodies of his work. Not surprisingly, they have attracted little interest from Shakespeare scholars, for whom parody is at best an amusing side-show, at worst a desecration. For the historian, however, parody offers as effective access to the theatrical tastes of any given age as does the performance of more serious drama.

*Othello, the Moor of Fleet Street* did not become one of the great hits of the Adelphi theater when it was first performed in 1833. It turns out, however, to be of more than passing interest because, according to Manfred Draudt, the editor of this, the first, edition of the play, it was written not by Charles Westmacott, to whom authorship has previously been attributed, but by Charles Mathews. It provides us, therefore, with an amiable example of the genius of a man whose series of performances, *Mr. Mathews at Home*, was perhaps the most representative, certainly the most popular, manifestation of comedy in the early decades of the nineteenth century.

Mildness and pale good-humor would seem to have been the essence of that comedy. *Othello* is more open to parody than most of Shakespeare's plays. The extremity of the Moor's jealousy, the metaphorical extravagance of his utterance, and the headlong drive to vengeance can all seem a little absurd when considered n relation to the transparency of their cause and the domesticity of the circumstances within which they arise. The play provides, therefore, a fine opportunity to satirize any bombastic tendencies in Shakespeare and to diagnose incongruities between the representation of character and situation. But Mathews, a man of his time if ever there was one, did not aspire to disturb or move his audience; the censor would not have allowed him to anyway. Instead, he is content to trivialize Shakespeare's poetry, reducing it to the level of domestic farce, in which thoughts that are strange, rare, or disturbing are coyly effaced by tinkling rhyme. Hence, Desdemona, in refusing to accept the Lord Mayor's suggestion that she stay for a week with Brabantio, answers:

'I saw Othello's visage in his mind' –
So, my Lord Mayor, I'll not be left behind.

Or, Iago, musing on the possibility that Othello once "leaped into his seat", jingles

I hate the Moor. By many it is thought
My wife is not more honest than she ought,
My last child certainly was of darker hue:
With woolly hair, unlike the other two.

The plot is reduced to nothing short of banality. The whole play can have taken little more than forty minutes to perform. The first four scenes provide a rudimentary summary of the first two acts, set exclusively in the low-life of London, Othello being a crossing sweeper, unaccountably turned judge, and Iago his Deputy, while Cassio and Rodrigo are a City Marshalman and a Sergeant in the

New Police respectively. The last three scenes carry the burden of the rest of the play, which is only the most rudimentary bedroom farce, that leads to Othello's discovery of the handkerchief on Desdemona's neck while he is attempting to poison [sic] her. All is forgiven. This is parody without teeth, harmless comedy, without ambition to perturb or engage the audience. No references are made to the contemporary political situation, and the principal source of comedy lies in the constant echoes of Shakespearean language in the most commonplace situations. After the stringent ambience of the Regency, this piece, redolent of early Victorianism (the queen's succession was still four years away), seems pale. Mathew's is a theater lacking in strength. Oddly enough, the cover of the book carries an illustration of Edmund Kean in *Othello*, on the grounds that his great rendition of the role is fleetingly referred to in one of the stage directions; one cannot imagine a less apt point of reference.

This edition of *Othello, the Moor of Fleet Street* comes with a forbidding critical apparatus. The introduction is strangely disjointed, partly because the editor throws us into discussion of the piece *in*, as it were, *media res*. As a consequence, one never quite gains the clear historical perspective one expects from an introduction, while the specific context of the Adelphi theater, a pivotal institution in the development of popular theatrical entertainment in London, is never explained. The discussion of Charles Mathews' probable authorship is conducted mainly through the consideration of parallels between the play text and dialogue attributed to Mathews that appears in other books, not an infallible technique. Much is also made of borrowings from Moncrieff's *Tom and Jerry*, that dramatic adaptation of Pierce Egan's famous survey of Regency society, *Life in London*, which was the Adelphi's great hit a decade before. However, nothing is made of the difference between London life in the early 1820's and the very different world of the 1830's. The introduction also contains no discussion of Shakespearean parody in London in the early nineteenth century and, sadly, because the editor hails from Vienna, no comparison with perhaps the most famous, certainly one of the funniest, of all *Othello* parodies, Kringsteiner's *Othelleri*.

The notes are exhaustive, indeed one wonders why so slight a text needs to be dignified with such a weighty apparatus. In an appendix, the editor lists all the allusions to Shakespeare's play in Mathews' text. Interestingly, he points out that several of these do not come from the radically abbreviated and bowdlerized acting-versions that were universally at use in the theater at that time, but from a more complete text of Shakespeare, which suggests that the parody might have been as much literary as it was theatrical. He does not, however, pursue this point.

All in all, a useful edition, reminding us of the ephemera of an earlier age.

University of California, Santa Barbara  Simon Williams


*William Shakespeare. 'A Lover's Complaint': Deutsche Übersetzungen von 1787-1894. Festgabe für Dieter Mehl.* Ed. and introd. Christa Jansohn. Preface Wolfgang Weiß. Berlin: Erich Schmidt Verlag, 1993, 238 ppp. ISBN 3-503-03053-0.


This book makes a virtue of necessity. Dieter Mehl, well-known for his studies on Chaucer, Shakespeare and Lawrence, and at present president of the German Shakespeare Society, has often expressed his aversion to Festschriften. Yet on the occasion of his sixtieth birthday such an eminent critic and scholar simply had to be honoured publicly by his friends and colleagues. So it was an excellent idea on the part of Christa Jansohn to produce not a *Festschrift*, but a *Festgabe* in the form of an edition of the English original and German translations of Shakespeare's poem *A Lover's Complaint*, including a few illustrations from early editions. With its introduction, textual notes, a select bibliography, and short biographies of the translators, this is a highly interesting little volume, which, in its combination of medieval and Renaissance interests, is bound to gratify Dieter Mehl's scholarly proclivities.

The starting-point for Jansohn's collection is John Kerrigan's recent remark that "*A Lover's Complaint* is still in need of readers". Her book will definitely help to make Shakespeare's poem better known. Her introduction gives an excellent account of the textual situation and the poem's generic and interpretative problems as well as its aesthetic qualities. It is followed by a fascinating chapter on the reception of *A Lover's Complaint* in Germany, focussing on German translations of which she unearthed, in painstaking (re)search, twelve specimens, comprising Eschenburg's prose translation (1787) and verse translations ranging from Kannegießer (1803) to Alfred von Mauntz (1894). She carefully describes the cultural and economic conditions under which these translations were produced, and she makes a brief, but still illuminating comparative analysis of the individual translations, concentrating on crucial words and phrases, for instance "a fickle maid" (line 5) and "too early I attended/A youthful suit" (lines 78-9), also a line with sexual connotations: "Reserved the stalk, and gave him all my flower" (147). She shows how Eschenburg and nineteenth-century verse translators in particular misunderstood individual passages and toned down or removed what they held to be sexually offensive parts of the text.

It is a pity that Christa Jansohn could not realize her original plan to add one or two new translations to her collection, which is a little curious, since there are well-versed translators among German Shakespeareans. But nonetheless Jansohn's edition remains a very successful publication, just the sort of book Dieter Mehl, who is one of the outstanding reviewers of literature on Shakespeare, would himself review very favourably. The volume includes a tribute to Dieter Mehl by his friend and colleague Wolfgang Weiß which, among other things, points out the

Munich connection of the scholar to be honoured by this edition, a connection to which German Shakespeare studies are so much indebted.

Friedrich Schiller-Universität Jena    Wolfgang G. Müller

José Manuel González Fernández de Sevilla, *El Teatro de William Shakespeare Hoy - una interpretación radical actualizada*. (Biblioteca de Divulgación Temática, 62) Barcelona: Montesinos Editor, S.L., 1993. pp. 118. ISBN 84-7639-159-5.

Spanish scholars are taking action to rescue Shakespeare from the oblivion and cultural marginalization he has largely suffered in Spain, and to bring Spanish Shakespeare criticism into the international arena. This slim paperback volume by José Manuel González, current Professor of English Literature at the University of Alicante, gives impetus to that endeavour. The modern radical interpretation posited by the title is concisely laid out in a mere 115 pages, consisting of an Introduction, three chapters subdivided into various headings, a conclusion, chronological tables of Shakespeare's era, his life, and his dramatic works, five pages of modern bibliography and the Index. A list of abbreviations used for the plays precedes the Introduction, and the book contains five black-and-white photographs. For all quotations González uses the translation into Spanish by Luis Astrana Marín.

The aim of his book is to assess the degree to which Shakespeare can be considered as our "contemporary", to find out whether his dramatic achievements are valid and applicable in the twentieth century - "Ello exige, por nuestra parte, el acercarnos a la radicalidad existencial shakespereana, a lo que fue y supuso su devenir histórico concreto, y el reinterpretarlo, desde nuestras coordenadas espaciotemporales y con nuestros propios presupuestos críticos ..." (13). This quest must be of special interest to Spanish theatre-goers and theatrical managers, in a country which did not even have a repertory company staging classics until 1985.

The adjunct to setting Shakespeare within our present-day context is his relationship to his own time and cultural environment, and this theme is developed in Chapter 1. In "El teatro como radicalidad existencial"(15), the author suggests that theatricality and existence blend inseparably, an idea reminiscent of the late nineteenth-century critics' search for the dramatist's life in his art and also more recent investigation of biographical evidence carried out in the 1970s. Although it is no longer widely accepted that Shakespeare's life is a way into the interpretation of his plays, González stresses the vital importance of the dramatist's life and historical context, examining the background closely in "La época isabelina"(19). He describes the appearance in Elizabeth I's time of a society with new social and economic relationships. Together with new trading links and colonization, there came a growing process of education and enlightenment fostered by schools, universities, the Court and the Church. The section headed "Stratford y Londres" (26 ff.) highlights the importance not only of Shakespeare's historical, but also his geographical, contexts. It follows his personal development in Stratford and his theatrical development in London, with an emphasis on the all-encompassing nature of his participation in the theatre as actor, dramatist and producer (39).

Chapter 2 (45 ff.) aims to identify the defining aspects which make Shakespeare's theatre so distinctive. Contemporary critical emphasis on the text rather than the performance has tended to relegate the dramatic function and create a divide between "el Shakespeare literario y el Shakespeare dramático" (47) with negative consequences. González reacts against what he regards as the excessive intellectualization of the plays, resulting in a process of partialization aimed at the elite few, when they were, in fact, meant for the general public. The idea of a vital interaction between spectator, actor and dramatist (57) is a familiar one, as is the view of Shakespeare's plays as a blend of classical knowledge with his own creativity (59 ff.). The last two parts of Chapter 2 argue that language is the key factor in creating plot, action and characterization, in combination with well-timed silences and use of gesture (62 ff.), that the purpose of language is to create theatre, rather than being an end in itself.

Chapter 3, with five subsections, is extremely stimulating. In "Hacia una desmitificación radical del teatro de William Shakespeare" (71 ff.), the author attempts to demythologize Shakespeare, to remove prejudices and imposed critical viewpoints and see the plays not as museum pieces but as works which adapt to specific times and circumstances. He examines the plays as deliberate acts of historiography, which become metahistory "lo histórico, de esta forma, se transforma en metahistórico"(73). Through this we can see reflections of, or parallels with, our own time.

"Machismo o feminismo en el teatro shakespereano?" (92 ff.) affirms the proliferation of feminist studies written on the role of woman in Shakespeare's dramatic works. As the author states, the importance and transcendence of the female characters is nothing new. The hard thing lies in achieving the right interpretative balance. The conclusion here is that woman is ultimately aggrandized and dignified in Shakespeare's theatre, giving it relevance for today's women, "haciendo que la mujer de hoy encuentre en él elementos de identificación y de reivindicación, porque Shakespeare está mas allá de sexos y de géneros" (98-9).

The last section of Chapter 3 is a brief summary of Shakespeare's plays outside the theatre, in film, radio and television, underlining the importance of these media in bringing Shakespeare to the general public, and in expanding the immense artistic potential of the dramas. González cites the most salient film, radio and TV productions, although he makes no mention of the transpositions of Shakespeare's work into opera, musical comedy and dance.

The key points of the conclusion identify the variety and richness of the approaches to Shakespeare, and the growing and sustained interest in his work. The value for us now lies in the inexhaustible multitude of focuses and experiences by virtue of which a play exceeds its original sense due to its contemporary context: "... un teatro en plenitud que tiene la virtud de rehacerse y de regenerarse en contacto con la vida y la historia de ahora" (104).

Overall *El teatro de William Shakespeare hoy* is refreshing in its candidly practical approach. There are a few minor typological errors, e.g. "discreminating" in the note on page 60, or "there lives ... " instead of "the lives ..." in note 21 on page 27. The text suffers at times from overstatement, e.g. "no se puede conocer el fenómeno shakespereano en toda su radicalidad e intensidad sin tener en cuenta su contextualización espacial determinada" (26). There is also a tendency to state the obvious in such sentences as "Y es que Shakespeare antes que nada es hombre de teatro" (39), which lessen the impact of the argument. Occasionally the viewpoint is marred by remarks which initially seem obvious or even contradictory, such as "la lengua se erige en el instrumento indispensable para la creación y la realización del teatro de Shakespeare... (62). While meaning can be deduced from the overall argument, individual sentences need more cogency. This being said, the book is undoubtedly of great interest, in particular to students and to the Spanish reader. It answers questions of validity which may hopefully encourage a flowering of Shakespearean productions in that country. The book has five pages of modern bibliography. Revealingly, only two works out of the many listed are by Spaniards. More are needed, and one hopes that this volume will provide just the incentive for many more new, objective and innovative approaches from Spanish scholars and critics.

Cambridge University                                  Elizabeth MacDonald